THE OUTDOOR TRAVELER'S GUIDE
CANADA

THE OUTDOOR TRAVELER'S GUIDE
CANADA

TEXT BY
DAVID
DUNBAR

PHOTOGRAPHS FROM
FIRST LIGHT ASSOCIATED
PHOTOGRAPHERS

STEWART, TABORI & CHANG
NEW YORK

Published in 1991 by
Stewart, Tabori & Chang, Inc.
575 Broadway, New York, New York 10012

Library of Congress Cataloging-in-Publication Data

Dunbar, David.
    Canada / text by David Dunbar ; photographs by First Light
Associated Photographers.
    — (The Outdoor travelers' guide)
    Includes index.
    ISBN 1-55670-169-1
    1. National parks and reserves—Canada—Guide-books. 2. Canada—
Description and travel—1981– —Guide-books. 3. Natural history—
Canada—Guide-books.   I. Title.   II. Series.
F1011.D86   1991
917.104'647—dc20   90-48520

Distributed in the U.S. by Workman Publishing,
708 Broadway, New York, New York 10003
Distributed in Canada by Canadian Manda Group,
P.O. Box 920 Station U, Toronto, Ontario M8Z 5P9
Distributed in all other territories by
Little, Brown and Company, International Division,
34 Beacon Street, Boston, Massachusetts 02108

Maps: Guenter Vollath
Natural-history consultant: John Farrand, Jr.
Design: Paul Zakris
Captions: Bettina Drew
Index: Pat Woodruff

Printed in Japan
10 9 8 7 6 5 4 3 2 1

ACKNOWLEDGMENTS

During the course of writing this book I relied heavily on experts across Canada, all of whom gave unstintingly of their time. They include the following, as well as others too numerous to mention who also reviewed the text:

ALGONQUIN PP: Dan Strickland. AUYUITTUQ NP: Yves Bosse and Norman Keenainak. BANFF NP: Heather Dempsey. BATHURST INLET: Page Burt. BRUCE PENINSULA NP and FATHOM FIVE NMP: Mark Wiercinski. CAPE BRETON HIGHLANDS NP: James Bridgland. ELK ISLAND NP: Clifford Kaleski. ELLESMERE ISLAND NP: William E. Thorpe. FORILLON NP: Maxime Saint-Amour. FUNDY NP: Rob Walker. GARIBALDI PP: Al Midnight, Garibaldi/Sunshine Coast District. GLACIER/MT. REVELSTOKE NP: John Woods, Glacier NP. GRASSLANDS NP: W. J. Masyk. GROS MORNE NP: Michael Burzynski and David Morrow. JASPER NP: James Todgham. KEJIMKUJIK NP: Peter Hope and Rick Swain; Robert G. Grantham, Nova Scotia Museum Complex. KLUANE NP: Brent Liddle. KOOTENAY NP: Ken Fisher. LA MAURICIE NP: Jacques Pleau and Marc Ampleman. NAHANNI NP: Steve Langdon. NORTHERN YUKON NP: Bill Dolan. PACIFIC RIM NP: Barry Campbell. POINT PELEE NP: Robert A. Watt and Bob Graham. PRINCE ALBERT NP: Cathy Corrigal and Susan Carr. PRINCE EDWARD ISLAND NP: Barbara MacDonald. QUETICO PP: Shan Walshe and Shirley Pruniak; Dr. Philip Fralick, Lakehead University, Thunder Bay. RIDING MOUNTAIN NP: Celes Davar and Buzz Crowston. ST. LAWRENCE ISLANDS NP: Dave Warner and Kathleen Burtch. WATERTON LAKES NP: Duane Barrus, Keith McDougall, and Mark Tierney. WOOD BUFFALO NP: John Aldag. YOHO NP: Kevin Van Tighem.

In addition, I am indebted to Kevin J. McCormick and Jacques Sirois of the Canadian Wildlife Service for their assistance on northern bird and game sanctuaries; Alex Hall, biologist and Thelon expert; and Pat and Rosemarie Keough, for their generous advice on visiting Nahanni Country.

I want to express my appreciation to the Canadian Parks Service, which was an immediate and enthusiastic supporter of the project, in particular: Ian Rutherford, Director-General, Canadian National Parks; Gary D. Sealey, Director, Visitor Activities Branch, National Parks Directorate; Sharon Budd, former Reference Officer, and Lisette Simard-Tremblay, current Reference Officer, both of whom generously extended to me library privileges at the National Parks Documentation Centre in Hull, Quebec; and G. M. Hamre, National Parks Advisor, Northern Parks Establishment Office, Yellowknife.

For their generous assistance with travel arrangements, without obligation, I want to thank especially Lois Gerber, Commercial Officer-Tourism, Canadian Consulate General, New York; Air Canada and Stephen A. Pisni Public Relations; Ron Moore of Air BC; Kevin Shackell and J. D. Austin of Tourism Yukon; E. J. Grant and Anne McKee of Simpson Air, who introduced me to the wonders of Nahanni Country; Al Kaylo, Margaret Imre, and Cheryl Grant-Gamble of Travel-Arctic, who enabled me to explore the Northwest Territories; the Yellowknife Inn, Yellowknife, N.W.T.; and Donna Copeland of Auyuittuq Lodge, Pangnirtung, N.W.T.

I would also like to thank the dedicated professionals at Stewart, Tabori & Chang: copy editor Moira Duggan, natural-history consultant John Farrand, Jr., editor Jennie McGregor Bernard, photo editors Sarah Longacre and Jose Pouso, designer Paul Zakris, and, most important, my editor Maureen Graney.

And I would especially like to thank my wife, Barbara Peck, for her unwavering support and encouragement during a long and challenging project.

CONTENTS

INTRODUCTION

WHEN I WAS GROWING UP in Saskatchewan, my grandmother had a theory about why her grandchildren had such poor eyesight: it was eyestrain, plain and simple. "You can see too far on the prairies," Grandma would say, forgetting that she herself had been born and raised there without detriment to her vision. She and Grandpa had left the far horizons and big skies of the interior plains for retirement in Vancouver, where views circumscribed by forest and mountain were on a more human scale.

Grandma may not have known much about optometry, but she was right about geography. Our family found out just how big Canada was every summer when we went out to visit our grandparents on the coast. Our parents loaded up the '52 Ford with camping gear and we drove west. And drove and drove. It seemed to take *forever* to reach Calgary where, at long last, the prairie began to rumple promisingly. We scanned the horizon until the cry went up: the Rockies! There they were, off in the distance, slate-blue ramparts floating like a mirage above the rolling farmlands.

Then we were winding among the foothills, climbing higher and higher, until hills became mountains, great slabs of layered rock cloaked with evergreens and topped with snow. Soon we reached the gates of that wondrous mountain kingdom, Banff National Park. The name still conjures up fond memories of hikes through mountain meadows, the swift, green Bow River, the turreted grandeur of the Banff Springs Hotel, refreshing mountain air and musty canvas tents, crackling campfires, and the bold predations of squirrels.

Those annual excursions to the coast may not have improved my eyesight, but they did plant the seeds of what has become an enduring love of the outdoors. And now I'm delighted to present Banff and nearly three dozen other wild, wonderful places in *The Outdoor Traveler's Guide to Canada*. This volume is an invitation to discover the spectacular wilderness heritage of the second largest country in the world. Here are the gigantic icefields of Kluane, the wild canyons of the South Nahanni, the great herds of bison in Wood Buffalo, the coastal mountains of Garibaldi, the prairie escarpment of Riding Mountain, the watery maze of Algonquin, the tide-lashed shores of Fundy, the rugged headlands of Cape Breton, the wind-swept alpine plateau of Gros Morne.

In all, the book includes 28 national parks, three provincial parks, two bird sanctuaries, two national wildlife areas, one national marine park, and one northern region (Bathurst Inlet) protected only by its isolation and its devoted native and white inhabitants. National parks predominate because they shelter so many of Canada's finest landscapes. The rationale for selecting 28 preserves out of a total of 34 is, admittedly, highly personal. These parks, I felt, offer the most outstanding natural wonders, the finest scenery, the most interesting human and natural history, and the greatest recreational opportunities.

While there are more than 600 provincial parks in Canada, the choice of Garibaldi in British Columbia and Algonquin and Quetico in Ontario was easy to make. These provincial parks, to me, are elevated out of the ordinary by virtue of their beauty, interpretive programs, and recreational facilities, although I'm sure outdoor enthusiasts could quickly name half a dozen other parks equally qualified for inclusion. The wildlife sanctuaries were chosen for their national or international significance and their relative accessibility.

Canada's national parks system, among the largest in the world, is a wonder in itself. Its dual role is preservation and recreation, "To protect for all time representative natural areas of Canadian significance . . . and to encourage public understanding, appreciation, and enjoyment of this natural heritage so as to leave it unimpaired for future generations." Eight national parks in this book have been designated United Nations World Heritage sites for their outstanding scenic wonders. Waterways in five parks have been selected as Canadian Heritage Rivers.

More than 13 million people visit Canada's national parks each year, with most activity centering around campgrounds and points of interest accessible by car. The backcountry in most parks, national and provincial, is virtually empty. Each year some 60,000 people drop by the Reception Centre of Kluane National Park in the Yukon, but most are soon back on the Alaska Highway, which skirts the park's eastern boundary. When I traveled into Kluane, I shared a wilderness half the size of Switzerland with a few dozen people. At the height of summer on the park's most popular backcountry trail, I saw one group of hikers in four days. Even in parks closer to major urban areas, a few hours of hiking or a couple of portages lead into wilderness where peace, solitude, and renewal can still be found.

The Outdoor Traveler's Guide to Canada is organized from west to east: the West, the Prairies, Central Canada, and Atlantic Canada. A special

ARCTIC   OCEAN

QUEEN

ELLESMERE ISLAND N

ELIZABETH   AXEL HEIBERG

ELLEF RINGNES I

ISLANDS

PRINCE PATRICK I

BEAUFORT

SEA

MELVILLE I

BATHURST I

BANKS I

M'Clure Strait

Viscount Melville Sound

POLAR BEAR PASS
NATIONAL WILDLIFE AR

Yukon R

ARCTIC CIRCLE

ALASKA

NORTHERN
YUKON NPR
MACKENZIE
BAY

BANKS ISLAND
BIRD SANCTUARIES

AMUNDSEN
GULF

PRINCE
OF
WALES I

M'Clintock
Channel

SOM
I

BOOTHI
PENINSU

GULF

OF

ALASKA

KLUANE
NP

YUKON

TERRITORY

R   O   C   K   Y

MACKENZIE   MTS

Mackenzie R

Whitehorse

Great Bear L.

VICTORIA I

BATHURST
INLET

NORTHWES

NAHANNI
NP

Yellowknife

THELON GAME

SANCTUARY

TERRITORIE

PACIFIC

QUEEN
CHARLOTTE
IS

Great Slave L.

OCEAN

Wollaston L.

WOOD   BUFFALO
NP

Peace R

M   T   S

ALBERTA

Lake
Athabasca

Athabasca R

SASKATCHEWAN

Reindeer L.

Churchill R

Nelson R

MANITOBA

BRITISH
COLUMBIA

Fraser R

Edmonton

ELK ISLAND
NP

JASPER NP

Saskatchewan R

PRINCE
ALBERT NP

Lake
Winnipeg

VANCOUVER I

GARIBALDI
PP

YOHO
NP

GLACIER
NP

BANFF NP

PACIFIC RIM NP

Vancouver

MOUNT
REVELSTOKE
NP

Victoria

KOOTENAY
NP

Calgary

Saskatoon

RIDING MOUNTAIN
NP

WATERTON
LAKES NP

Regina

Columbia R

GRASSLANDS NPR

Winnipeg

1 (TRANS-CANADA HWY)

QUETICO PP

CANADA

0   600 Mi

0   600 Km

UNITED

STATES

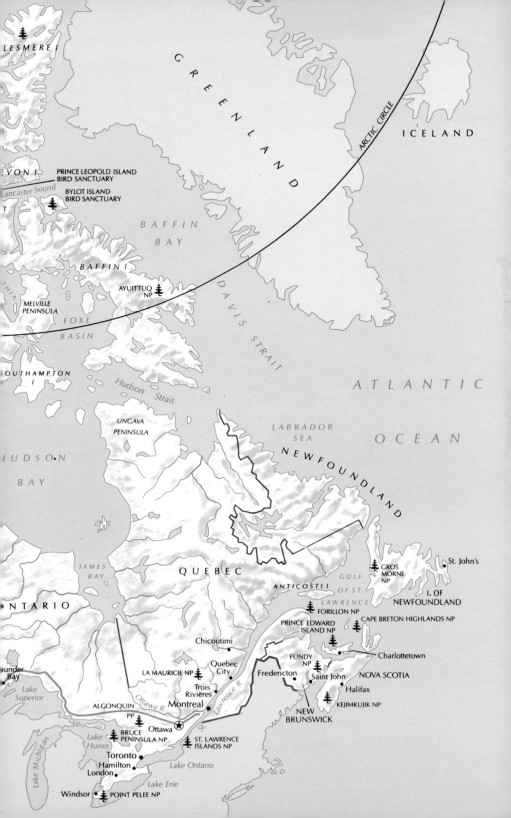

LESMERE I

GREENLAND

ICELAND

Arctic Circle

EVON I

PRINCE LEOPOLD ISLAND
BIRD SANCTUARY

Lancaster Sound

BYLOT ISLAND
BIRD SANCTUARY

T

BAFFIN
BAY

BAFFIN I

THIA

AYUITTUQ
NP

DAVIS STRAIT

MELVILLE
PENINSULA

FOXE
BASIN

SOUTHAMPTON
I

ATLANTIC

Hudson Strait

OCEAN

HUDSON

BAY

UNGAVA
PENINSULA

LABRADOR
SEA

NEWFOUNDLAND

JAMES
BAY

QUEBEC

St. John's

GROS
MORNE
NP

ANTICOSTI I

GULF

I. OF
NEWFOUNDLAND

ONTARIO

OF ST.

LAWRENCE

FORILLON NP

PRINCE EDWARD
ISLAND NP

CAPE BRETON HIGHLANDS NP

Chicoutimi

Charlottetown

under
Bay

Lake
Superior

LA MAURICIE NP

Quebec
City

FUNDY
NP

Fredericton

Saint John

NOVA SCOTIA

Trois
Rivières

St. Lawrence R.

Montreal

Halifax

ALGONQUIN

Ottawa R.

KEJIMKUJIK NP

PP

NEW
BRUNSWICK

Ottawa

St.

BRUCE
PENINSULA NP

ST. LAWRENCE
ISLANDS NP

Lake
Huron

Toronto

Hamilton

London

Lake Ontario

Lake Michigan

Lake Erie

Windsor

POINT PELEE NP

chapter, Northern Wildlands, features a selection of parks and sanctuaries in the North. Chapters describe the human and natural history of a region, as well as its outdoor activities, including scenic drives, hiking, biking, climbing, horseback riding, canoeing, fishing, swimming, diving, skiing, and other recreational pursuits.

Hikers and other backcountry travelers in national and provincial parks must register before setting off and deregister upon completion of their trip. Although intended for the safety of park visitors, registration provides a convenient opportunity to review backcountry plans with park personnel, who can provide the latest information on trail conditions, weather forecasts, and other essentials. Except where noted, trail distances are given from trailhead to destination, not for round trips. Licenses are required to fish in Canada, and can be obtained from park offices or from sporting goods stores or other retail outlets. Hunting is not permitted in national parks or in the three provincial parks described here; it is allowed in some bird and game sanctuaries. For more information, consult the sources listed in the Exploring section at the end of each chapter.

The Exploring section also describes interpretive programs, accommodations, and nearby facilities for travelers. Certain hotels, outfitters, and other private operators are mentioned as a service to readers. Entries are not comprehensive, and listing does not imply endorsement. Most parks provide on request complete lists of accommodations and outfitters in their areas. Finally, there are suggestions for further reading.

"The fundamental question in English Canada," wrote Northrop Frye, a prominent Canadian scholar, "is not 'Who am I?' but 'Where is here?'" Whether or not you're English Canadian, the national map and the 14 park maps in this book will help you find out where "here" is and guide you in planning your trip. For information on where to obtain more detailed topographic maps suitable for hiking, canoeing, and other activities, contact the sources cited in the Exploring section of each chapter. Federal topographic maps, which cover the entire country at a scale of 1:250,000 and all but a few of the high Arctic Islands at a scale of 1:50,000, also can be ordered from the Canada Map Office, 615 Booth Street, Ottawa, Ont. K1A 0E9; 613-952-7000.

Most national parks charge an entry fee. You can buy an annual pass, which admits all occupants of a private vehicle to all national parks. Daily and four-day passes are available at any national park facility where entrance fees are charged. There is no entrance fee to the three provincial parks.

Most park campgrounds operate on a first-come, first-served basis, with limits on number of persons and length of stay (usually two weeks at national parks). Some parks charge a fee for certain campsites. Some parks, however, allow campsites to be reserved by writing or phoning. Check the information under each park.

A guidebook is not a political treatise, but it is important to acknowledge the conflicts between environmental conservation and resource exploitation that afflict Canada as surely as any other place. The classic Canadian response to conflict is compromise, a response that has held the country together politically for more than a century. It may serve Canada as well in the tangled debate over wilderness, although it may be difficult to find a satisfactory middle ground between clear-cutting a rain forest and preserving it as a sanctuary. How these kinds of controversies are resolved will profoundly affect conservation policies throughout Canada. Those policies are influenced by outdoor travelers who by their very interest in wilderness promote the value of conservation. It is my hope that *The Outdoor Traveler's Guide to Canada* will stimulate interest in discovering the wild beauty of a vast and varied land.

THE WEST

PACIFIC RIM
NATIONAL PARK 16

Surf-pummeled headlands, crescent beaches, a pine-tufted archipelago, and a wilderness trail along a treacherous shoreline known as the "graveyard of the Pacific" compose a magnificent medley on the west coast of Vancouver Island.

GARIBALDI
PROVINCIAL PARK 30

An hour's drive north of Vancouver, wildflower meadows and strange volcanic formations are preserved amid the snowy coastal mountains.

GLACIER AND
MT. REVELSTOKE
NATIONAL PARKS 44

Twin parks in eastern British Columbia's rugged Selkirks embrace wildflower meadows, a mountain plateau, and more than 400 glaciers.

ROCKY MOUNTAIN NATIONAL PARKS 62

Along the Continental Divide that separates British Columbia and Alberta, an accessible year-round mountain playground of towering peaks, icefields, hot springs, and emerald lakes lies within Canada's most beloved parks—Banff, Jasper, Kootenay, and Yoho.

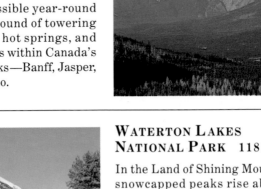

WATERTON LAKES NATIONAL PARK 118

In the Land of Shining Mountains, snowcapped peaks rise abruptly from the grasslands of southwestern Alberta, once the stronghold of the Blackfoot Indians.

PACIFIC RIM NATIONAL PARK

THE FIRST NATIONAL PARK ON CANADA'S Pacific Coast encapsulates, in three separate units, the dramatic meeting of land and sea along Vancouver Island's southwest coast. In the Long Beach Unit, wide crescents of hard-packed sand and jumbled headlands front a landscape of rain forest and are backed by snow-dusted summits. To the southeast, in the Broken Group Islands Unit of Barkley Sound, canoeists, kayakers, and other boaters explore waters sheltered by a miniature archipelago of pine-tufted islets. Farther southeast, in the West Coast Trail Unit, a shoreline path laid out at the turn of the century for the rescue of shipwrecked mariners is now one of Canada's premier wilderness hikes.

GEOLOGY

The dark lavas that form the backbone of Vancouver Island had a fiery birth nearly 200 million years ago when a chain of underwater volcanoes off Mexico or possibly South America began to spew vast quantities of magma onto the seabed. During a long period of dormancy, corals and other aquatic animals colonized these seamounts. Eventually, their remains hardened into a layer of limestone that capped much of the older volcanic material.

During this period, the archipelago was rafting northwest on a huge oceanic plate. It collided about 85 million years ago with the leading edge of the westering North American plate, an impact that thrust up Vancouver Island's central mountain range. As the oceanic plate slid beneath the continental margin, its crustal passenger—Vancouver Island—was scraped off and welded onto North America. (Almost all of the continent west of the Rocky Mountains grew by the accumulation of these drifting, fault-bounded crustal blocks, known as terranes.)

The Vancouver Island terrane, which geologists call Wrangellia, forms most of that island as well as the Queen Charlotte Islands to the north and the Wrangell Mountains of southern Alaska. The last pieces of Vancouver Island's geologic jigsaw were added 42 million years ago, when two smaller terranes, the Pacific Rim and the Crescent, brushed by Wrangellia in a slow-motion sideswipe that lasted a million years. Rocks from the Pacific Rim terrane can be seen in the headlands of Long Beach. Virtually all of the Crescent terrane, however, is buried deep beneath Vancouver Island.

HISTORY

By the time Capt. James Cook arrived on Vancouver Island's west coast in 1778 during his search for the Northwest Passage, the region's prosperous and populous Nuu-chah-nulth people had been living off the bounty of sea and forest for at least 4,000 years. These bold seafarers traded extensively with neighboring tribes. Whale products, for example, were exchanged for ceremonial canoes built by the Haida in the Queen Charlotte Islands, 350 mi/560 km to the northwest across open water.

A population of 3,000 to 5,000 inhabited the Broken Group Islands, gathering shellfish, trapping Pacific herring and northern anchovies, fishing salmon, and hunting whales, seals, and sea lions. Campgrounds on The Broken Group Islands in the park often occupy the same sites as ancient Indian encampments. Observant visitors find shellfish middens, fish traps, and the remains of other prehistoric activities. (Visitors are asked to leave the sites undisturbed.)

During the next century, American, Russian, and other European fur traders came to barter for the luxurious pelts of sea otters, which were exterminated locally by the mid-1800s. About that time, loggers arrived to hew virgin stands of spruce and cedar, and miners discovered gold in the sands of Florencia Bay near Long Beach. The rusting hulk of a dredge can still be seen on Florencia's gravelly shore. The nearby Gold Mine Trail follows a small stream that netted sourdoughs a modest $20,000 worth of gold.

Southeast of Long Beach, across Barkley Sound, reefs and rocks claimed more than 50 ships over the years, earning this treacherous shore the name "Graveyard of the Pacific." The 1906 *Valencia* disaster, in which 124 people perished, spurred construction of a reliable rescue trail between Bamfield and Port Renfrew. With improved navigation and rescue capabilities, the trail eventually fell into disuse and was virtually forgotten until the 1960s, when recreationists campaigned for its preservation and inclusion in Pacific Rim National Park as the West Coast Trail Unit.

HABITATS

Marine life on North America's northwest coast is more varied than in any other temperate waters. Along Pacific Rim's jagged shores, plants and animals of the subtidal zone remain covered by water. The most abundant plants here are the kelps, whose fronds stream back and forth with the surf.

OVERLEAF: Low tide at sunset, west coast of Vancouver Island.

Some subtidal creatures, such as sea anemones, remain anchored for most of their lives, moving only to escape danger. Chitons—sightless, primitive creatures also known as "gumboots"—leave their home base on rocks to graze but always return to the same spot. Starfish, sea urchins, and crabs leave the zone to search for food higher up on the rocks.

The intertidal zone is alternately covered and uncovered as the tides flow and ebb, and animals and plants retain enough fluid to sustain them when the tide is out. But when the tide rolls in, the key to survival is the ability to resist pounding surf. Sticky threads anchor Californian mussels, while purple starfish cling to rocks with tiny suction cups that can withstand a 100-lb/45-kg tug. Sea urchins attach themselves to rocks with hundreds of sucker-tipped feet. Acorn barnacles secrete a strong adhesive and glue themselves head down to the spot they will occupy for the rest of their lives.

Only the highest spring tides reach the splash zone above the waterline. Creatures there rely on tough coverings to withstand lengthy exposure to air and on spray to supply their seawater needs. The checkered periwinkle obtains oxygen directly from the air and eats minute blue-green algae that it scrapes from rocks with an abrasive, tongue-like radula.

The park's most abundant seabirds are glaucous-winged gulls, which nest with pelagic cormorants on White Island, the Sea Lion Rocks, and Florencia Island, all in the Long Beach Unit. Seabird Rocks, near Pachena Bay in the West Coast Trail Unit, is a nesting site for Leach's and fork-tailed storm-petrels, rhinoceros and Cassin's auklets, pigeon guillemots, and tufted puffins.

Migrants on the Pacific flyway pause to feed and rest on the park's beaches and estuaries in spring and fall. Shorebirds, including long-billed dowitchers, sandpipers, marbled godwits, and whimbrels, poke among the piles of driftwood and seaweed for food. Black oystercatchers abound, usually feeding on mussels, despite their name. Many birds winter here. From October to December thousands of Canada geese congregate on the mudflats of Grice Bay in the Long Beach Unit, along with some 16,000 dabbling and diving ducks, and as many as 75 trumpeter swans, part of Vancouver Island's wintering population of 2,000.

Ocean clouds, heavy with moisture, dump some 120 in/3,000 mm of precipitation on Vancouver Island each year in the form of mists, fogs, and rain. The forest responds with dramatic lushness. Shoreline stands are dominated by Sitka spruce, which in Canada grows only on the west coast. Near the shore, strong winds twist the branches of stunted Sitka into weird shapes, all pointed landward. In spring Indian paintbrush, yellow monkey flower, rose-colored beach pea, yarrow, and white-petaled wild strawberry bloom at the forest's edge.

Most of the area's 100 nesting pairs of bald eagles—one of the continent's highest concentrations—occupy tall Sitka spruce on Barkley Sound islets. Pacific Rim is the only park in Canada where they can be observed daily year-round, although the best viewing times are from January to May, when they fish for herring and scavenge for carrion washed ashore.

Inland from the spruce grow western hemlock, Pacific silver fir, and western redcedar, which may reach a diameter of 13 ft/4 m and live 1,200 years. Licorice ferns, mosses, and lichens festoon trees and shrubs. Deriving their moisture and nutrients from rain and fallen organic matter, these plants—called epiphytes—use other plants for support. Less than 10 percent of the sunlight may penetrate the canopy, an amount sufficient to produce nearly impenetrable thickets of salal, deer fern, huckleberry, salmonberry, and other shrubs up to 9 ft/3 m high in places. Mosses, sword ferns, false lily-of-the-valley, bunchberry, and enormous yellow skunk cabbages crowd the shaded, dank forest floor.

Visitors are not likely to see many of the park's 20 kinds of land mammals, which keep nocturnal schedules or lurk deep in the forest's depths. Red squirrels are abundant, though, along with minks and raccoons. Black-tailed deer, a race of mule deer, frequent shoreline glades and logged-over areas, where cougars stalk them. Wolves occasionally wander onto beaches. In November, black bears fish for coho salmon spawning in park rivers, including the stream alongside the Rain Forest Trail near Long Beach.

More visible are the park's marine mammals. About 17,000 gray whales swim by Long Beach each year, in greatest numbers from late February to mid-May during annual migrations from breeding grounds off Baja California to feeding grounds off Alaska. Unlike most whales in these waters, 50-ft/15-m grays may pass quite close to shore—often within 0.6 mi/1 km. About 40 grays remain near the park throughout summer, sucking up and straining the sandy sea bottom for a daily intake of 50 lbs/22 kg of tube worms, mollusks, and crustaceans. There are rare sightings of humpback, fin, sei, and minke whales.

Killer whales enter narrow inlets and bays in pursuit of sea lions, porpoises, salmon, and other prey. These toothed whales, which travel in pods of up to 50 individuals, occasionally drive seals and sea lions onto beaches. Northern sea lions congregate by the hundreds on Sea Lion Rocks just off Long Beach. (A viewing telescope is mounted on a headland below Green Point campground.) Full-grown bulls are more than 9 ft/3 m long and may weigh 2,200 lbs/1,000 kg—twice as much as the largest grizzly bear. These pinnipeds dive up to 700 ft/215 m for fish.

Elephant seals, which are larger than sea lions and have long, inflatable snouts, occasionally are seen in Barkley Sound. Major winter haulouts for

CLOCKWISE FROM LEFT: Western sandpipers, whose feathers change from rusty red in spring to gray in fall; California sea lions, the fastest aquatic carnivores; the large and common ochre sea star; a bald eagle feeding on chum salmon. OPPOSITE: Camping, hiking, birding, and whale-watching are among the attractions of Pacific Rim National Park.

smaller, darker California sea lions are Wouwer Island in the Broken Group and an islet off Half Moon Bay, southeast of Long Beach (a trail leads to a viewing area at Wya Point). Most California sea lions head south in May. Harbor seals are common in all three park units and occasionally trail in the wake of canoers and kayakers.

OUTDOOR ACTIVITIES

Long Beach attracts 80 percent of the park's 500,000 annual visitors with nature walks, surf casting, surfing, and beachcombing (Japanese glass fishing floats from fishing grounds in the North Pacific are coveted prizes). The Broken Group Islands Unit attracts anglers and boaters. Experienced backcountry hikers head for the West Coast Trail Unit.

Scenic Drives

The gateway to Long Beach is the *Pacific Rim Highway* (Highway 4). Beginning at Port Alberni, about 65 mi/105 km northeast of Long Beach, this two-lane road snakes across the island's central spine, offering views of mountain-ringed Sproat and Kennedy lakes. Clear-cut mountainsides mar a few stretches. When it reaches the park, the highway forks. A side road goes southeast to Ucluelet; Highway 4 travels the length of the Long Beach Unit, usually some distance inland. For an overview of the often misty coast, wait for sunny weather and drive to the summit of Radar Hill, a former military installation northwest of Long Beach. There, panoramas of forest-clad mountains and filigreed coast unfold.

Hiking

All 10 nature trails in the Long Beach Unit are less than 1.5 mi/2.4 km long. The *Rain Forest Trail* weaves a boardwalk through tangled thickets, past 800-year-old redcedars, and over moist ravines where luxuriant ferns and odiferous skunk cabbages grow in spongy hollows. One section spans a ravine via a walkway hewn from the wide trunk of a redcedar that toppled centuries ago. The woodland *Wickaninnish Trail,* named for a powerful Nuu-chah-nulth chief, follows part of the old Ucluelet-Tofino road, built for homesteaders about 1900. The *South Beach Trail* leads to a pretty cove where waves crash through a double sea arch and surge through channels in bluffs known locally as the "Edge of the Silver Thunder."

The park's only wilderness hike is the *West Coast Trail,* a challenging 45-mi/72-km route that takes five to eight days to walk. The trail should be attempted only by experienced backpackers who are in good physical condition. Easy stretches are literally a walk on the beach, but elsewhere, especially in the southern section, hikers wade through boggy areas, scramble over or around windfalls, and cross beaches passable only at low tide. Along the way are 160 bridges, six cable crossings, and 75 sets of ladders scaling cliffs and headlands. Near the trail's midway point, hikers cross the tidal Nitinat Narrows by motorboat. Most hikers start at Port Renfrew to get the demanding climb up Pandora Peak, the highest point on the trail (590 ft/180 m), out of the way in the first 1.8 mi/3 km.

Then the rewards roll in: streams leaping off headlands onto pebbly beaches, tunnels and sea caves carved into cliffs, misty coves where no footprint sullies the sand, quiet corridors through dripping virgin forest, seals lolling on secluded strands, tidal pools brimming with life, the battered hulks of shipwrecks, the beacons of a trio of lighthouses.

Canoeing and Kayaking

The shallow, protected waters of *Grice Bay* behind Long Beach are suitable for all paddlers, who often spot waterfowl, harbor seals, and porpoises. The put-in for the 7-mi/11-km *Kennedy River Route,* most of which is outside the park, is reached by taking Highway 4 a short distance northeast of the Ucluelet-Tofino junction, then turning left on MacMillan-Bloedel's West

Main logging road. (The road is sometimes closed to the public; it's advisable to check with the company's Ucluelet office at 604-726-7712.) A drive of 7 mi/11 km brings you to the launching site at the bridge on the Kennedy River near its egress from Kennedy Lake. There is a small lakeshore campground here and good fishing for cutthroat trout under the bridge. About 1.2 mi/2 km downstream, at a widening of the tranquil river, otters are often seen splashing among backwater lily pads. Another 3 mi/5 km downstream, a strenuous 0.6-mi/1-km portage on a logging road bypasses Kennfalls Rapids. Another 0.6 mi/1 km brings canoers to Kennedy Cove and the sea. To complete the trip, they hug the shore of Tofino Inlet down to Indian Bay, pass through a narrow channel, and cross the mouth of Grice Bay to the takeout spot at the boat ramp.

The safest approach by canoe or kayak to the *Broken Group Islands* is from Toquart Bay on the northwest side of Barkley Sound. The launching beach is accessible via a rough 10-mi/16-km MacMillan-Bloedel logging road. It's best to leave in early morning or evening when summer westerlies die down. Many paddlers head south through the bay's Stopper Islands and round Lyall Point, then—if winds are calm—they cross the 1.2 mi/2 km of open water to the campground on the nearest island, Hand Island. Some take a 1937 packet freighter, the *Lady Rose*, from Port Alberni or Ucluelet and disembark at a floating dock at Gibraltar Island, east of Hand, where there is another campground.

There are more than a hundred islands to explore. Beautiful sand beaches line the north shore of Turret Island. In summer, sea lions crowd rocks southwest of Wouwer Island, the best spot in the Broken Group to take photographs of these gregarious creatures. Clarke and Benson islands, the most westerly in the group, are perhaps the loveliest, with sand and gravel beaches, open fields, high cliffs, and sea caves. A pleasant rain-forest trail crosses Clarke Island.

Fishing

This is one of the most popular pastimes in the park. In the Long Beach Unit, anglers cast for Chinook salmon and the occasional Pacific tomcod from Wya and Portland points and other rocky headlands. Surf casters land perches and flounders. Good fishing for sea-run cutthroat trout is found near creek mouths in sheltered Tofino and Ucluelet inlets.

Barkley Sound, known as the salmon capital of Canada, has good fishing year-round for coho and Chinook salmon and excellent fishing in late summer and fall. Productive spots include Forbes Island, Lyall Point, and Toquart Bay in the western sound, Swale Rock north of Reeks Island in the

Pink fawn lilies, Erythronium revolutum, Vancouver Island.

northeastern corner of the Broken Group, and to the south, the waters off Meares Bluff, the easternmost point of Effingham Island, especially for three or four weeks starting in mid-June. Salmon show in August below the Cape Beale lighthouse in the West Coast Trail Unit, as well as at Seabird Rocks off the mouth of Pachena Bay, just to the southeast.

Whale-Watching

A dozen local companies offer expeditions to see, in particular, migrating Pacific gray whales; current names and addresses are available from the park information center and from Tourism British Columbia. Peak time is early morning from mid-March to mid-April. Favorite land-based viewing spots at Long Beach are Quisitis and Wya points and headlands near Schooner Cove.

Scuba Diving

Shipwrecks and rich marine life make this one of the finest diving areas in temperate waters. Favorite wrecks in the Broken Group of Barkley Sound include the *Thiepval*, a minesweeper that went down in 1930 in about 40 ft/12 m of water off the southwest coast of Turtle Island, and the *Vanlene*, a freighter that went down in 1972 off Austin Island (the remains are 60 to 100 ft/18 to 30 m deep).

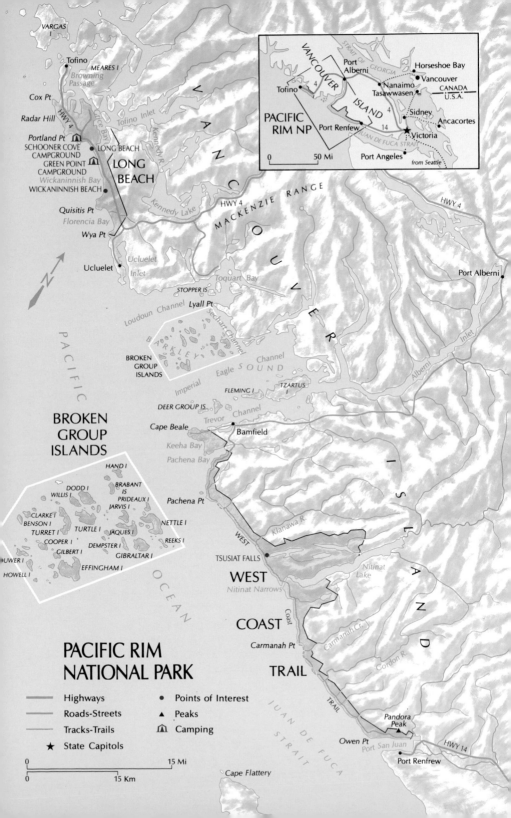

VARGAS I

Tofino
MEARES I
Browning Passage

Cox Pt

Radar Hill

Portland Pt 🏛
SCHOONER COVE
CAMPGROUND
GREEN POINT
CAMPGROUND
Wickaninnish Bay 🏛
WICKANINNISH BEACH

LONG BEACH

LONG BEACH

Quisitis Pt
Florencia Bay

Wya Pt

Ucluelet

Ucluelet Inlet

Toquart Bay

STOPPER IS

Loudoun Channel Lyall Pt

Sechart Channel

BROKEN GROUP ISLANDS

BARKLEY SOUND

Channel
Eagle

Imperial

FLEMING I

TZARTUS I

DEER GROUP IS *Channel*

Trevor Channel

Cape Beale   Bamfield

Keeha Bay
Pachena Bay

BROKEN GROUP ISLANDS

HAND I

DODD I
WILLIS I
BRABANT IS
PRIDEAUX I
JARVIS I

CLARKE I
BENSON I
TURRET I   TURTLE I

COOPER I
GILBERT I   DEMPSTER I
GIBRALTAR I
EFFINGHAM I

HOWELL I
UWER I

Pachena Pt

NETTLE I

JAQUES I

REEKS I

Klanawa R.

WEST

TSUSIAT FALLS

WEST

Nitinat Lake

Nitinat Narrows

COAST

Carmanah Pt

Carmanah Cr.

Gordon R.

TRAIL

Coast

PACIFIC OCEAN

MACKENZIE RANGE
HWY 4

V A N C O U V E R

Kennedy R.
Tofino Inlet
Grice Bay
HWY 4

Kennedy Lake

Port Alberni

Alberni Inlet

HWY 4

I S L A N D

JUAN DE FUCA STRAIT

Pandora Peak

Owen Pt
Port San Juan
HWY 14

Port Renfrew

Cape Flattery

PACIFIC RIM NATIONAL PARK

— Highways
— Roads-Streets
— Tracks-Trails
★ State Capitols

● Points of Interest
▲ Peaks
🏛 Camping

0 ——————— 15 Mi
0 ——————— 15 Km

Inset map

PACIFIC RIM NP

VANCOUVER ISLAND
STRAIT OF GEORGIA
Port Alberni
Tofino
Horseshoe Bay
Vancouver
Nanaimo
Tasawwasen
CANADA
U.S.A.
4
Port Renfrew
14
Sidney
Ancacortes
Victoria ★
Port Angeles
JUAN DE FUCA STRAIT
from Seattle

0 ——— 50 Mi

Surfing

Long Beach is the surfing capital of Canada; with no reef, 6-ft/2-m waves break close to shore. Even in August, the best month for this activity, the water is cold enough (48° to 57° F/9° to 14° C) to require wet suits.

EXPLORING THE PARK

Vancouver Island can be reached by car ferry from Seattle, Port Angeles, and Anacortes, Washington, and from Horseshoe Bay (to Nanaimo) and Tsawwassen (to Swartz Bay) from the British Columbia mainland near Vancouver. Long Beach, the destination of most visitors, is 190 mi/304 km northwest of Victoria via the Trans-Canada (Highway 1) and the Pacific Rim highways (Highway 4). Orient Stage Lines (604-723-6924) provides scheduled bus service to Port Alberni, the Long Beach Unit, and the villages of Tofino and Ucluelet at either end of Long Beach. Pacific Rim Airlines (604-724-4495) schedules flights from Vancouver to Tofino and Bamfield.

From Port Alberni, just off Highway 4 at the head of an inlet that nearly bisects Vancouver Island, the *Lady Rose* takes up to 100 passengers (not cars) to all three park units. On Tuesday, Thursday, and Saturday all year, the boat goes to Bamfield at the northwestern end of the West Coast Trail Unit. On Monday, Wednesday, and Friday from June through September, the vessel sails to Ucluelet, stopping in the Broken Group Islands at Gibraltar Island to drop off canoeists and kayakers. In summer, book at least a month in advance. Boat charters from Ucluelet, Bamfield, and Port Alberni also take passengers to the Broken Group .

Car access to Bamfield is via a 56-mi/90-km gravel road south from Port Alberni. Highway 14 links Port Renfrew at the southeastern end of the West Coast Trail Unit with Victoria, 66 mi/106 km southeast. Ferry service across the Gordon River to the trailhead and across Nitinat Narrows at the halfway point of the route operates from mid-May to the end of September, effectively cutting off the southern half of the trail for the rest of the year unless hikers make private arrangements. The trailhead south of Bamfield is accessible by car.

Park headquarters is near Wickaninnish Beach. The Park Information Centre and the Wickaninnish Centre, open from mid-March to mid-October, distribute free road maps and hiking guides, as well as tide and hydrographic charts essential for boaters. From late June to September, naturalists conduct rain-forest walks, tidal-pool talks, guided canoe trips on Grice Bay, and visits to sheltered coves where park scuba divers bring up undersea creatures for inspection. Information centers, located at both ends of the West Coast Trail, are open daily from mid-May through September.

To control the growing number of users on the West Coast Trail, park officials require hikers to obtain free permits from the West Coast Trail information centers at Port Renfrew and Pachena Bay and to register in and out. Groups are limited to 10 hikers, with starting times staggered to avoid overcrowding on the trail and at the campsites. Two kinds of fishing licenses, available from guides or tackle shops, are required: federal permits for saltwater and provincial permits for freshwater.

ACCOMMODATIONS: The park's only car-based camping is in the Long Beach Unit at Green Point (94 sites). Campers pack in gear on the 0.6-mi/1-km Schooner Trail to reach Schooner Cove campground (80 primitive sites) at the north end of Long Beach. There are no reservations and the maximum stay is seven nights. A wait-list system is in effect from late June to early September. Campers should inquire at the campground or the information center.

Primitive campsites are on eight Broken Group Islands: Gibraltar, Hand, Willis, Dodd, Turret, Clarke, Gilbert, and Benson. In summer, the sites are often crowded; the drinking water, barely potable. Equipment should include a minimum of 0.25 gal/1 liter of water per person per day. (Hand Island has no fresh water.) In summer, a park warden's float cabin is moored at Nettle Island. Ten primitive campsites run the length of the West Coast Trail.

ADDRESSES: For more information on the park, contact: The Superintendent, Pacific Rim National Park, Box 280, Ucluelet, B.C. V0R 3A0; 604-726-7721 or 604-726-4212. For information on private accommodation near the park and other outdoor recreation opportunities in the region, contact: Tourism British Columbia, 1117 Wharf Street, Victoria, B.C. V8W 2Z2; 604-387-1428.

For information on flights between Vancouver and Tofino contact: Pacific Rim Airlines Ltd., Box 1196, Port Alberni, B.C. V9Y 7M1; 604-724-4495. For information on the *Lady Rose*, a 1937 packet freighter, contact the Alberni Marine Transportation Inc., Box 188, Port Alberni, B.C. V9Y 7M7; 604-723-8313. The company also rents kayaks and canoes.

BOOKS: Bruce Obee, *The Pacific Rim Explorer: The Complete Guide.* North Vancouver: Whitecap Books, 1986. Comprehensive take-along guide.

Fred Rogers, *Shipwrecks of British Columbia.* Vancouver/Toronto: Douglas & McIntyre, 1973.

GARIBALDI PROVINCIAL PARK

THIS SANCTUARY NORTH OF VANCOUVER protects a spectacular section of the Coast Mountains. Rain forests drape valleys and lower mountain slopes, wildflowers cast vibrantly colored carpets across alpine meadows, and the turquoise waters of high-country lakes mirror vast glaciers and icefields gleaming on ridges and peaks.

Much of the park's appeal lies in its improbable combination of fire and ice. Volcanism built most of southern Garibaldi's mountains; glaciers and other agents of erosion wear away this igneous legacy, carving strange formations with evocative names—The Gargoyles, Sharkfin, and Black Tusk, a basalt wedge that once filled the vent of a volcano.

GEOLOGY

About 85 million years ago, the Coast Mountains were unimpressive hills comprising worn-down granitic and metamorphic rocks. Then the region underwent a fiery uplift triggered by geological activity on the ocean floor west of Vancouver Island. There, magma upwelled into a seabed rift, pushing the vast Pacific plate northwest toward Japan and the tiny Juan de Fuca plate eastward, causing it to slide beneath the western edge of the North American plate off Vancouver Island in a process known as subduction.

But how did this detonate volcanic eruptions on the mainland, 150 mi/240 km east of the subduction zone? At that distance, the leading edge of the Juan de Fuca plate, slanting downward, reached depths hot enough for the plate to begin to melt. Molten rock rose through fractures and built up volcanoes on the surface. Within a few million years, coastal hills had been transformed into the Coast Mountains.

More recent volcanism produced some of Garibaldi's most interesting geological features. When Mt. Price erupted some 10,000 years ago, lava flowed northwest until a glacier blocked the molten torrent with what must have been tremendous hissing and clouds of steam. The lava hardened into The Barrier, a natural dam some 1,500 ft/460 m high that converted a mountain gorge into Garibaldi Lake. No water spills over the top of the dam, but seepage along its base feeds Rubble Creek. An earthquake in 1855 sloughed off The Barrier's western side, leaving a sheer face.

A glacier-fed lake reflects brilliant blue amid the snow-covered peaks of Garibaldi Provincial Park.

South of Garibaldi Lake, lava erupted beneath a thick ice sheet, melting a circular hole. The lava continued to rise, building up a mountain like a layer cake. This steep-sided, flat-topped formation, one of only three in the world created in this way, is known as The Table. A rock arch on the southwest flank gives this strange summit the appearance of an inverted teacup.

HISTORY

One of the richest, most aristocratic aboriginal cultures north of Mexico flourished in the Pacific Northwest—a land of salmon and cedar, potlatch and totem pole. Seas teemed with fish and mammals. Shores yielded game and fruits, and beaches abounded in shellfish.

The Squamish Indians lived in villages ringing Howe Sound and up the Squamish and Cheakamus valleys adjacent to the western boundary of today's park, taking an abundant livelihood from oceans, rivers, and streams. Fish was the main article of diet, salmon the mainstay. A few weeks of feverish activity in autumn yielded enough salmon—filleted and smoke-dried—to last the winter.

In 1860, a Royal Navy squadron surveying Howe Sound received news of Giuseppe Garibaldi's successful campaign to transform Italy into a modern state. Capt. George Henry Richards fired the cannon in salute and named a snowy peak overlooking the sound in honor of the Italian patriot.

Later that decade fortune seekers struggled up the Cheakamus Valley, bound for the Cariboo goldfields in the interior of British Columbia. A few sourdoughs stayed on to farm the Lillooet Valley north of today's park, and by the 1880s the Pemberton Trail from Howe Sound linked the Garibaldi region to the outside world.

Vancouver mountaineers were scaling Garibaldi peaks by the early 1900s, and when the railway reached the area in 1914, anglers began to come for the superb trout fishing and the rustic charm of Rainbow Lodge on Alta Lake, in its day the most popular resort west of Banff. Garibaldi Park was established in 1920, and soon more lodges sprang up in the Cheakamus Valley. In the 1960s Whistler was developed as an international ski resort, bringing a highway and tourist facilities to the region.

HABITATS

The valleys and lower slopes of Garibaldi are covered with the western hemlocks, western redcedars, and Douglas-firs of the coastal rain forest—part of the greatest coniferous forest on earth. Trees here are up to 400 years old and many of them are immense—200 ft/60 m high and 30 ft/9 m around. Their age and size induce a solemnity among many visitors who walk through the shadowy aisles of these cathedral groves.

Mosses and other ground cover smother the dark forest floor with a spongy carpet that smooths out contours. Ferns are legion, especially sword and deer ferns; epiphytes drape every tree; and lichens festoon branches high up into the canopy. Wintergreen, foamflower, twin flower, queen's cup lily, and starry false Solomon's-seal fleck the overwhelmingly green landscape with tiny dabs of color.

In sharp contrast to the evergreen forests is the open, park-like subalpine zone that extends roughly from 3,200 to 5,200 ft/1,000 to 1,600 m. Here the forest is reduced to scattered stands of subalpine fir and whitebark pine with an understory of shrubs—willow, Pacific blackberry, huckleberry, and white rhododendron, which forms such dense thickets that hikers call it "mountain misery."

Two waves of color wash across subalpine meadows surrounding these isolated stands. Within a few weeks of snowmelt in July, subtle swards of white and yellow flowers appear: spring beauties, anemones, pasqueflowers, buttercups, marsh marigolds, and avalanche lilies, which often send out new shoots while still blanketed with snow. Red mountain heather and white moss heather brighten heath communities with pink and white flowers that dangle from branches like miniature bells. A second bloom in late August is more flamboyant: the red of Indian paintbrush; orange of agoseris; blue of asters and lupines; yellow of arnica; mauve of fleabane; pink of mountain daisy.

Mammals and birds react quickly to the brief mountain summer. The nutritious new shoots of sedges that fringe lakes and ponds supply voles with the first fresh food of the season. Hoary marmots, which hibernate longer than any other mammal in North America (nine months in high alpine reaches), emerge from rock-pile burrows to nibble on last year's seeds and tender wild parsnip. Mountain goats head for windward ridges blown relatively free of snow where they find the summer's first grazing. Rosy finches nest on rocky slopes overlooking meadows while late-winter storms still rage; by the time finch nestlings fly, a plentiful supply of heather buds and emerging insects is available as food.

As fall unfolds, a final spectacle closes the season of growth: the leaves of willow and mountain ash turn bright yellow and huckleberry bushes glow crimson. By this time, hoary marmots are already hibernating, but black bears are still active, gorging on blueberries and tangy, pea-sized huckleberries before denning up. Pikas—miniature cousins of rabbits that live only in loose rock piles next to mountain meadows—cut, dry, and store several bushel-size haystacks for winter food.

Price Falls, Garibaldi Provincial Park.

Throngs of thrushes, dark-eyed juncos, chestnut-backed chickadees, gray jays, and grouse also convene on subalpine slopes for a last feast. Red-tailed and sharp-shinned hawks pass through the park on their southward migration and for a few weeks join bald and golden eagles circling above the meadows, hunting for voles, chipmunks, golden-mantled ground squirrels, and small birds. By early November, winter begins to draw a thick blanket of snow over the heights. It will remain until mid-July.

OUTDOOR ACTIVITIES

Splendid in all seasons, Garibaldi attracts hikers, bikers, anglers, and climbers in summer, and skiers in winter. Mid-July to late September is the most popular time to visit the park, with late August best for wildflowers.

Five areas in the western third of the park have limited development. They are (from south to north): Diamond Head, Black Tusk–Garibaldi Lake, Cheakamus Lake, Singing Pass, and Wedgemount Lake. The eastern park is wilderness. Whistler Resort and the Cheakamus Valley west of Garibaldi are heavily developed.

Two-month-old hoary marmots greet along a rock ledge, Cascade Mountains.

Scenic Drives

North of Vancouver, the *Sea to Sky Highway* (Highway 99) weaves through some of the most spectacular coastal scenery in British Columbia. Blasted through granite on the east side of Howe Sound, the highway hugs near-vertical mountain slopes affording marvelous views. The highway heads north up the Cheakamus Valley, following much the same route as the old Pemberton Trail.

Hiking

Garibaldi's most popular day hikes start at the end of access roads from Highway 99. Trails are usually clear of snow from late June through mid-October. The 6.8-mi/11-km *Elfin Lakes Trail,* a six-hour round-trip walk in the Diamond Head area, leads to Opal Cone and weirdly shaped volcanic formations called The Gargoyles.

Farther north, the 5.6-mi/9-km *Rubble Creek Trail* switchbacks southeast through mature rain forest, passes The Barrier, and reaches emerald Garibaldi Lake with its semicircular backdrop of glaciers. From there, trails fan out to the glorious Black Tusk wildflower meadows, Black Tusk itself, and Panorama Ridge, where range upon range can be seen extending in every direction. The 1.9-mi/3-km *Cheakamus Lake Trail* is a relatively level stroll through coastal rain forest to a lovely turquoise lake framed by high ridges and peaks. The trail continues another 2.5 mi/4 km along the north shore of Cheakamus Lake to the Singing Creek outlet. More wildflower meadows and surpassing views await on the 6-mi/9.5-km *Singing Pass Trail.*

Scenic circuits can be made by linking trails. A popular 10-hour outing starts on the Rubble Creek Trail, then follows the *Helm Creek Trail* for 9 mi/14.5 km northeast to the cable-car crossing of the Cheakamus River (a highlight of the trip). From there, hikers pick up the Cheakamus Lake Trail and descend 0.9 mi/1.5 km to the access road parking lot.

Combining trails and unmarked, cross-country routes offers even greater hiking variety. On the return leg of the Singing Pass Trail, most hikers retrace their steps, but the adventurous strike off on an unmarked route along the "Musical Bumps"—the summits of Oboe, Flute, and Piccolo peaks—to the top of Whistler Mountain, then descend to Whistler Village. A challenging high-country outing suitable only for experienced mountaineer-hikers is the *Garibaldi Névé Traverse,* which crosses the vast, rolling field of badly crevassed granular ice that sprawls over the northeast flank of Mt. Garibaldi. Hikers on this three-day expedition head northeast on the Elfin Lakes and *Mamquam Lake* trails, then angle northwest at Opal Cone across the névé to Garibaldi Lake. From there, they return to an access road via the Rubble Creek Trail.

Bicycling

The *Cheakamus Lake Trail* and *Elfin Lakes Trail* are open to mountain bikes. Outside the park, mountain bikers take chairlifts and gondolas to the top of *Blackcomb and Whistler mountains,* then zoom back down on a network of trails. (To reduce erosion on Whistler, cyclists must ride with organized groups.) The *Valley Trail* consists of paved trails for cyclists and walkers connecting Whistler Village subdivisions. The network ends in the north at Lost Lake, where 9.3 mi/15 km of cycling trails loop over the Blackcomb Benchlands on the mountain's western flank.

Highway 99 north of Whistler makes a scenic day outing that is nearly all downhill with the exception of switchbacks south of Nairn Falls Provincial Park (a short trail in the park leads to the cascade). At Pemberton, 20 mi/32 km north of Whistler, a side road heads northwest in the Lillooet Valley past fields of strawberries and potatoes. Another road angles northeast to the pioneer community of D'Arcy, literally the end of the road. The D'Arcy side trip makes a memorable outing: smooth road, mountain scenery, rushing streams, and rolling terrain.

Some cyclists overnight in the Pemberton area; others return to Whistler on the south-bound train, which leaves D'Arcy at 4:30 P.M. and Pemberton at 5:20 P.M.

Climbing

The highest summits and the best weather are found in the northwest corner of the park, north of Wedge and Billygoat creeks. Peaks there tend to be rubbly but some faces are of granite. The eastern Fitzsimmons Range in the Singing Pass area is popular in summer and winter. The tight cluster of glaciated peaks and granite ridges at the southeast end of Garibaldi Lake usually are approached in spring on skis over the frozen surface of the lake. Dedicated alpinists tackle the sentinels of Mt. James Turner (8,914 ft/2,717 m) and Mt. Pitt (8,159 ft/2,487 m) near the remote eastern boundary.

Climbing areas west of the park include the north ridge of Mt. Cayley, a good spring climb on snow; granitic Mt. Ashlu; and the Tantalus Range, which offers a variety of snow and ice climbs in a compact area. The route up Mt. Tantalus itself is considered a classic three- or four-day excursion on rock, snow, and glacial ice. Rock climbing is practiced on the Smoke Bluffs in the town of Squamish and at Murrin Provincial Park south of Squamish.

Horseback Riding

Whistler Stables (604-932-6623) in the resort area and Tracker Trips (604-894-6161) in Pemberton offer hourly, daily, and overnight rides.

Boating

Electric motors are allowed on Alpha, Callaghan, Nita, Lucille, and Lost lakes in the Cheakamus Valley outside the park.

Canoeing

A few paddlers haul canoes up trails to *Garibaldi and Cheakamus lakes,* but most prefer the more accessible waters of the Cheakamus Valley. The *River of Golden Dreams,* a grandiosely named creek meandering from Alta Lake to Green Lake, is a gentle afternoon paddle. Experienced canoeists run the *Squamish and Cheakamus rivers* (Classes II and III rapids).

Kayaking

Hereabouts this sport rivals canoeing in popularity. Only experts take on the Squamish River upstream of the power house, southwest of Whistler.

A summertime spectacular of alpine flowers in Garibaldi Provincial Park.

The upper Cheakamus, south of Whistler, is good for expert white-water runners. A slalom course (Class III) is set up on the Cheakamus below the bridge in the hamlet of Garibaldi.

Rafting

Whistler River Adventures (604-932-3532) organizes short trips north of Whistler on the Green River. Sea to Sky Raft Tours (604-932-2002) has half-day floats north of Whistler on the Birkenhead River. Scenic full-day trips west of Whistler on the Elaho River, a tributary of the Squamish that flows in the lee of the Tantalus Range, involves flat water and Class III rapids.

Fishing

High-elevation lakes in Garibaldi Park are not especially productive, although hiking anglers take rainbow trout in early summer from Mamquam, Barrier, Lesser Garibaldi, Garibaldi, and Cheakamus lakes.

Whistler, however, was known for its trout fishing long before it became famous for skiing. Valley lakes and streams yield rainbow and brook trout, Dolly Varden, as well as kokanee, the freshwater species of sockeye salmon. In Alice Lake Provincial Park south of Whistler, Alice Lake is stocked with cutthroat trout; Stump Lake is stocked with splake.

From June through August, the Green River and the Cheakamus have fair to good angling for spring salmon. Angling for coho is best in October on the lower reaches of the Squamish, and in November on the Cheakamus and Ashlu Creek, a tributary of the Squamish. Late-winter runs of steelhead on the Cheakamus are also good.

Hunting

It is not allowed in the park. In tributary valleys of the Squamish River west of Whistler, hunting is good for grouse, fair for bear and black-tailed deer, and poor for goat. Nairn Falls Provincial Park, north of Whistler, is used extensively in autumn as a base for hunting parties.

Swimming

Park lakes are generally too cold for swimming, although tiny Barrier Lake west of Garibaldi Lake and Helm Lake near Black Tusk warm up enough by August for a quick dip. There are small sand beaches and swimming in the valley lakes around Whistler and at Alice Lake Provincial Park, where there are two sand beaches.

Downhill Skiing

The twin peaks towering above Whistler—Whistler Mountain (604-932-3434) and Blackcomb Mountain (604-932-3141)—draw skiers from around the world. Snowfall averages 450 in/1,143 cm, and the season lasts from November through April or early May, with skiing year-round on Black-

An inviting ground cover in moist woods, bunchberry (left) is equally attractive in flower or fruit, when its round berries form tight red clusters. The needle-like leaves and bell-shaped flowers of red mountain heather (right) are found on rocky slopes and in high mountain forests.

comb's Horstman Glacier. There is 5,020 ft/1,530 m of vertical drop on Whistler and 5,280 ft/1,609 m on Blackcomb, with a total of more than 170 ski runs. About half the runs are intermediate; the rest are evenly divided between expert and beginner.

Whistler Heli-Skiing (604-932-4105) takes advanced to expert powder skiers to the Spearhead and Fitzsimmons ranges in the park. A number of other Whistler-based companies fly skiers to pristine runs west of the park.

Cross-country Skiing

Summer hiking trails, unplowed forest roads, and alpine meadows provide outstanding *ski touring* in and around Garibaldi. The Diamond Head area, with the well-equipped Elfin Lakes Chalet, has been popular since the 1950s. The Black Tusk Meadows make a strenuous but scenically rewarding day trip via the *Rubble Creek Trail*. Some skiers get a jump on the season on the 8-mi/13-km *Microwave Road*, which ends at a ridgetop on the north side of Black Tusk. The road can usually be skied by late October, sometimes earlier. The most scenic route to the gentle alpine terrain of Singing Pass is via the Whistler Mountain ski lifts and the "Musical Bumps."

North of Whistler and the park, groomed trails circle Lost Lake. The 3.7-mi/6-km *Rainbow Lake Trail* leads to a popular day-touring area.

The southern Coast Mountains, which are more heavily glaciated than any other range in the Northern Hemisphere at a similar latitude, offer some of the continent's finest *ski mountaineering*, especially traverses of glaciers and icefields. The *Garibaldi Névé Traverse*, a three-day trip between Elfin Lakes and Garibaldi Lake, makes an exceptional spring excursion, although it is notorious for whiteouts.

The hut on Garibaldi Lake's Sphinx Bay is a fine base for exploring the dozen peaks within a day's ski. Farther north, the *Spearhead Traverse*, a challenging four-day horseshoe-shaped trip, usually starts at the Blackcomb ski area, heads southeast on the glaciers of the Spearhead Range, then loops around to return northwest via the Fitzsimmons Range, descending on the Singing Pass Trail or the Whistler Mountain lifts.

Other Activities

There is *golfing* at the Whistler Golf Club (604-932-4544) on an 18-hole course designed by Arnold Palmer; public *tennis* courts at Alpha Lake Park, Meadow Park, and Emerald Park; and *windsurfing* on Alta Lake and at Squamish Spit, where the Squamish River enters Howe Sound (steady winds blow at speeds of up to 35 knots). Local boardsailors have nicknamed the Squamish site "Gorge North," a reference to The Gorge, a renowned windsurfing area on the Columbia River in Oregon.

EXPLORING THE PARK

The Garibaldi–Whistler area is about 75 mi/125 km north of Vancouver via Highway 99. Five access roads run east toward the park boundary. There are no roads within Garibaldi and no road access to the park's eastern side. Maverick Coach Lines (604-255-1171) has bus runs several times a day to Whistler from downtown Vancouver. BC Rail (604-984-5246) offers daily train service as well as summer sightseeing excursions on the *Royal Hudson*, a restored steam locomotive.

Maps, brochures, and other information are available at Alice Lake Provincial Park, center of operations for seven parks and two recreational areas in the Squamish–Whistler–Garibaldi area. Garibaldi's summer headquarters are at the Garibaldi Lake campground, where a small library is stocked with field guides and books on natural history. Park naturalists give slide shows and nature talks at the shelters in the Taylor Creek and Garibaldi Lake campgrounds.

The park's trail network is open year-round for hiking and skiing. The ranger station at Garibaldi Lake is staffed only from early July to mid-October. The Diamond Head station usually is staffed most days in winter as well as in summer. For snow conditions, the numbers to call are: Whistler (604-932-4191 or 604-687-6761); Blackcomb (604-932-4211 or 604-687-7507); and Garibaldi Park (604-898-3024).

Whistler-based companies provide a wide range of services for outdoor adventure and organize such diverse activities as backroad biking, flight-seeing, even heli-picnicking. The companies that manage Blackcomb and Whistler mountains conduct summer nature walks, hikes, and bicycle tours.

ACCOMMODATIONS: Garibaldi's walk-in camping areas are operated on a first come, first served basis. The Diamond Head area has two campgrounds—Red Heather (20 sites) and Elfin Lakes (30 sites)—as well as the Elfin Lakes Chalet, which accommodates 30 people.

Farther north, Garibaldi Lake campground (50 sites and four shelters), with its spectacular shoreline location, usually is booked early. Sites may be easier to acquire at nearby Taylor Creek (90 sites and

two shelters), which has a wooded setting. Burton Hut accommodates 12 people on Sphinx Bay at the eastern end of Garibaldi Lake.

Two campgrounds have a total of 40 sites along the north shore of Cheakamus Lake. Two campgrounds are along the Singing Pass Trail, one in the windswept pass itself (30 sites) and another at the end of the trail, at Russet Lake (10 sites). The Himmelsbach Hut on Russet Lake accommodates eight. In the northwestern corner of the park, the trail to Wedgemount Lake ends at a campground (10 sites) and five-person Wedge Cabin on a bluff overshadowed by the cliffs of Rethel Mountain.

For winter visitors, the choice includes: Elfin Lakes Chalet, which has gas and wood-burning stoves; the six shelters in Garibaldi Lake and Taylor Creek campgrounds, which are little more than open sheds; Burton Hut; the Glaciology Hut on Garibaldi Lake's Sentinel Bay (emergencies only); Himmelsbach Hut; and Wedge Hut.

At Whistler, reservations at more than 50 hotels, condominiums, and guesthouses can be made by calling a central number, either 800-634-9622 or 604-932-4222.

ADDRESSES: For more information on Garibaldi, contact: Ministry of Parks, Alice Lake Provincial Park, Box 220, Brackendale, B.C. V0N 1H0; 604-898-3678 or 604-898-9313. For information on Whistler's visitor facilities, contact: Whistler Resort Association, Box 1400, Whistler, B.C. V0N 1B0; 800-634-9622 or 604-932-4222.

BOOKS: Bruce Fairley, *A Guide to Climbing and Hiking in Southwestern British Columbia.* West Vancouver: Gordon Soules Book Publishers Ltd., 1986. Standard reference published in conjunction with the B.C. Mountaineering Club and the Alpine Club of Canada.

Jay Page et al., *A Guide to Ski Touring in the Whistler, Garibaldi Park, Squamish, and Pemberton Areas.* Vancouver: The Varsity Outdoor Club, 1984. Distributed by Gordon Soules Book Publishers, Inc., ofest Vancouver, B.C. Includes maps and describes 43 ski-touring routes.

A volcanic landform, Black Tusk may be reached after a strenuous 6 km hike. The surrounding conservancy area affords striking examples of glacial and volcanic activity. OPPOSITE: *Pockets of lush green await discovery among the snowy mountains.*

GLACIER AND MT. REVELSTOKE NATIONAL PARKS

THESE NEIGHBORING PARKS in eastern British Columbia protect the celebrated scenery of the Selkirks, a mountain range older and more rugged
than the Rockies to the east. In aptly named Glacier National Park, there
are more than 400 glaciers and a dozen craggy spires topping 10,000 ft/3,050 m.
Glistening white even in mid-August, these mountains are smothered with a
remarkable 55 ft/17 m of snow each winter.

Mt. Revelstoke National Park, 11 mi/18 km southwest of Glacier, contains a less forbidding landscape. Flower-strewn alpine meadows and spruce
forests on a 6,000-ft/1,800-m plateau are backed to the northeast by 8,000-
ft/2,400-m peaks and the Clachnacudainn (clack-na-COO-din) Icefield. The
park is bounded on the east by Woolsey Creek, on the west by the Columbia
River, and on the south by the Illecillewaet (illy-SILLA-wat) River.

The Selkirks presented a formidable barrier to westering explorers, fur
traders, and, in the late nineteenth century, railway engineers surveying a
transcontinental route. The door through this wall of rock turned out to be
4,300-ft/1,300-m Rogers Pass in the heart of Glacier. By 1885 the rails ran
coast to coast, bringing tourists to marvel at a combination of ice, snow, and
summit rarely equaled anywhere. Some 70 years later the rail line was paralleled by the Rogers Pass section of the Trans-Canada Highway, one of the
world's most beautiful mountain roads.

GEOLOGY

Nearly 600 million years ago, rivers meandering across the coastal plain of
what was then the western shore of North America dumped silt on the continental shelf, much as today's Mississippi carries sediment into the Gulf of
Mexico. For the next 400 million years, sand, mud, and lime from coral reefs
formed tremendous beds nearly 5 mi/8 km thick in places.

About 175 million years ago, the North American plate drifted into the
Pacific plate, buckling these flat-lying sediments into a mountain range.
This compression turned mudstone to shale and slate, and sandstone to
quartzite—erosion-resistant rocks that now form the summits of mounts
Tupper, Rogers, Sir Donald, and other spectacular Selkirk peaks.

The compression also fractured the bedrock. Some fault lines eventually became river valleys. The Beaver River, near Glacier Park's eastern border, flows through the Purcell Trench, a fault line that separates the Selkirks from the Purcell Mountains to the east. The Columbia River, west of Mt. Revelstoke Park, flows in a similar fault dividing the Selkirks and the gentler Monashee Mountains to the west. The Purcells, Selkirks, and Monashees are subdivisions of the Columbia Mountains, which also include the Cariboos to the north.

One of the world's heaviest snowfalls feeds the parkland glaciers, which have carved sharp peaks, knife-edged ridges, armchair basins, and U-shaped valleys. Snowslides are powerful and spectacular forces of nature here, especially in Glacier. Each winter, thousands of avalanches thunder down Selkirk slopes at speeds of up to 200 mph/320 kmp, sweeping away trees, bridges, and railroad tracks, and occasionally burying the highway to depths of up to 30 ft/9 m. In summer, the Rogers Pass section of the Trans-Canada offers good views of active slidepaths on Mt. Macdonald's western shoulder.

HISTORY

Extensive exploration of the Selkirks did not occur until construction of the Canadian Pacific Railway. In 1881, CPR surveyor Maj. A. B. Rogers, along with his nephew and Indian porters, approached the range from the west, looking for a route through the forbidding barrier of rock and ice. The party struggled up the Illecillewaet River and discovered the pass that now bears Rogers's name. (The Avalanche Crest Trail follows part of the route.) The notch was surveyed in 1882-83; track was completed by 1885.

Glacier National Park was established in time for the commencement of regular train service in 1886. Tourists began flocking to the area to marvel at some of the world's most magnificent mountain scenery. The CPR obliged sightseers by running a connecting set of summer tracks around the line's gloomy avalanche sheds in Rogers Pass. Situated at the first crossing of the Illecillewaet, a resort hotel named Glacier House quickly became the hub of tourism in eastern British Columbia.

In 1888, the Rev. William Green of the British Alpine Club made several ascents in the Rogers Pass area. Impressed by the park's potential for mountaineering, the reverend wrote *Among the Selkirk Glaciers*. Published in 1890, this classic account inspired climbers from all over the world to scale the park's summits, considered as challenging as any in Europe. The CPR provided Swiss guides for Glacier House guests so that even

novices could climb mountains in relative safely. Many historians of mountaineering consider Glacier the birthplace of the sport in North America.

For the next three decades, mountaineering enjoyed its heyday in Glacier. Then, in 1916, the CPR opened the 5-mi/8-km Connaught Tunnel beneath Mt. Macdonald to bypass the steep grade and avalanches of Rogers Pass. What was a boon to railroaders was a bane to tourism, which soon declined when mountain scenery was replaced by a tedious—and frightening—tunnel. Passengers no longer stopped for lunch in front of Glacier House, or saw as much of the famous Selkirks. Glacier House was closed in 1925 and demolished in 1929. For nearly four decades the park had few visitors. The Rogers Pass section of the Trans-Canada Highway, which opened in 1962, introduced a new era of mountaineering and tourism.

Civic boosters helped to establish Glacier's less renowned neighbor, Mt. Revelstoke National Park. Citizens of the city of Revelstoke began promoting the wildflower meadows atop the nearby mountain through newspaper and magazine articles, photographic displays, and letters to influential politicians. In 1914, they succeeded in having Mt. Revelstoke and its surrounding drainage set aside as a national park.

HABITATS

Long, narrow valleys wrap green fingers around the parks' icy summits. Up to 4,900 ft/1,500 m, mild temperatures and abundant moisture nurture towering forests of western redcedar and western hemlock. Oak and lady ferns grow luxuriantly, and, where sunlight pierces the canopy, thickets of devil's club and Pacific yew flourish. The Giant Cedars Trail near the eastern boundary of Mt. Revelstoke Park wanders through this forest, also known as the interior rain forest, or Columbia forest. At waterlogged sites, scattered cedar, cottonwood, and alder grow above a swampy understory of yellow skunk cabbage, horsetail, and sedge. The Skunk Cabbage Trail, also in Revelstoke, passes through this type of vegetation.

Common birds of this forest include warblers, chickadees (chestnut-backed and boreal), varied thrushes, flycatchers, red-eyed vireos, Steller's jays, and rufous hummingbirds. Of the parks' 235 avian species, only about 30 winter over. Tens of thousands of "winter finches"—mainly thumb-sized pine siskins, along with larger red crossbills and white-winged crossbills—occasionally invade the mountains in late autumn to feed on abundant tree seeds. In spring, the birds disperse to breeding areas throughout the western mountains.

The rigorous hike toward the peaks of the Sir Donald Range cuts through creeks formed by glacial meltwaters.

American dippers, which live year-round near cascading creeks and rivers at all elevations, often are spotted along the Meeting of the Waters Trail in Glacier at the turbulent confluence of the Illecillewaet River and Asulkan Brook. Dippers collect food—aquatic invertebrates and small fry—by diving into the water and wading submerged along the bottom.

Deep winter snows make this forest inhospitable to many large mammals that are common in the neighboring Rocky Mountain parks. White-tailed deer, mule deer, and wapiti are sighted only occasionally in the shrubby lowlands flanking Mt. Revelstoke and in the valley of the Beaver River, which shelters a small herd of moose. Beavers and muskrats, however, are plentiful there and in wetlands bordering the Illecillewaet River in eastern Mt. Revelstoke Park.

Between 4,900 ft/1,500 m and 6,200 ft/1,900 m a closed forest of Engelmann spruce, subalpine fir, and mountain hemlock lies buried under snow for eight months of the year. Ferns, white rhododendrons and black huckleberry form a thick undergrowth. Old-man's beard, a lichen rich in carbohydrates but poor in total nutritional value, drapes tree branches, providing late-winter survival food for mountain caribou. A century ago, mountain caribou were common in the Selkirks, but for reasons still not understood, the species has greatly declined. In winter a few herds of up to 30 individuals graze near the tree line in Mt. Revelstoke Park's subalpine forests; smaller herds wander in and out of eastern Glacier Park.

At about 6,500 ft/1,980 m, forests begin to thin into scattered stands of spruce and subalpine fir. Beginning in early July, the high country explodes in a stunning display of summer color. Yellow glacier lilies bloom for two or three weeks, then yield to arnica, mountain valerian, lupine, Indian paintbrush, mountain daisies, and heather. The show is over by mid-August.

More than 20 percent of the landscape in Glacier Park is scarred by treeless swaths extending from the tree line to the valley floors—the destructive work of the area's frequent avalanches. The following spring these clear-cuts turn into favorable habitats for such sun-loving plants as the slide alder, a supple-stemmed but deep-rooted shrub that bends easily under the weight of the snowpack and usually survives the slides. Yellow avalanche lilies and white spring beauties blossom on the treeless swaths while nearby forests are still deep with snow. The early greening vegetation attracts warblers (Wilson's and MacGillivray's), southern red-backed voles, and deer mice. By mid-May mountain goats leave their winter range to graze on the shrubs. The parks' numerous grizzlies and black bears dig up the roots of slidepath plants (especially glacier lilies), feed on berries and dandelion greens, and scavenge slide-kill carcasses, often mountain goats, mountain caribou, moose, and wolverines.

Above 7,200 ft/2,200 m, isolated clumps of saxifrage and heather manage to survive, but much of the treeless alpine zone is barren rock and ice. The wildflowers that survive in this windswept terrain rarely bloom as brilliantly as relatives at lower elevations. White-tailed ptarmigan and rosy finches are at home here, as are mountain goats; with an estimated population of 300 goats in Glacier and another 50 in Revelstoke, these nimble ungulates far outnumber other large mammal species in the region. Hugging cliffsides, the goats fear only golden eagles, which occasionally carry off kids. Goats can be spotted year-round above Trans-Canada Highway snowsheds on the eastern side of Rogers Pass.

OUTDOOR ACTIVITIES IN GLACIER

The most popular pastime is hiking. The mountains attract climbers as well: each year more than 500 alpinists register for climbs. Winter brings mountain ski touring in the Asulkan Valley.

Scenic Drives

The *Rogers Pass* section of the *Trans-Canada Highway* (Highway 1) cuts through Glacier National Park, offering superlative mountain scenery at every bend. From Golden, British Columbia, the route heads north through the Columbia River valley, then follows the Beaver River up to Rogers Pass in the center of the park. The highway winds southeast through Glacier alongside the Illecillewaet River, crosses 11 mi/18 km of provincial land, then runs along the southern boundary of Mt. Revelstoke National Park. Most of the facilities, lookouts, and trailheads in Glacier are along the highway or on short branch roads.

A 15-mi/24-km stretch of road on either side of Rogers Pass in Glacier is the heart of a battle zone during "Snow War" each winter. At 17 strategic emplacements, Royal Canadian Horse Artillery teams set up 105-mm howitzers on concrete pads and lob explosive shells to bring down small, controlled slides that spill harmlessly down upper slopes and stop before they reach the highway and its protective concrete snowsheds. At Tractor Sheds Picnic Area east of Rogers Pass, a sign explains the howitzer strategy.

Hiking

Several trails, beginning at or near the Trans-Canada and its spur roads, explore life zones and lead to outstanding scenery. The trails range in diffi-

OVERLEAF: The craggy peaks of the Selkirk mountain range were formed about 175 million years ago by the collision of the North American and Pacific plates.

culty from short nature loops to strenuous day-long outings. Rugged Selkirk terrain limits backpacking opportunities to a few trails.

Many outings radiate from the Illecillewaet campground. The half-hour *Meeting of the Waters Trail* crosses the Illecillewaet River on a turn-of-the-century stone railway bridge and passes the remains of Glacier House before heading to the confluence of the Illecillewaet River and Asulkan Brook. These glacier-fed torrents are at their raging peak in late afternoon on hot August days, when maximum melting occurs. Boulders tumbled along the streambed by the rushing current shiver the timbers of a rustic bridge here; sightseers feel the vibrations.

Rated as one of Glacier's most scenic hikes, the *Avalanche Crest Trail* begins north of the campground, climbs a steep 2.6 mi/4.2 km through cedar-hemlock forest, then enters open subalpine country, and ends in an alpine basin nestled between Avalanche Crest and a ridge on Eagle Peak. From here, hikers improvise routes to the crest of the summit for panoramas of Rogers Pass, the Hermit Range, Illecillewaet Valley, Mt. Bonney, Asulkan Valley, and the glittering white of the Illecilliwaet Névé, a field of granular snow. Maj. Rogers first sighted his storied pass from this area.

South of the campground, the 3-mi/4.8-km *Glacier Crest Trail* ascends gently through dense forest, crosses Asulkan Brook, then veers east at a trail junction and begins switchbacking up a glacier-carved ridge, or arête. From the summit of this rocky spine, hikers enjoy a double Selkirk panorama—the giant Illecillewaet Glacier to the east and the smaller Asulkan Glacier to the west.

The route that continues south at the Glacier Crest Trail junction becomes the 4-mi/6.5-km *Asulkan Valley Trail*, which then angles southeast across several avalanche paths frequented by hoary marmots. Waterfalls tumble from mountain walls to the west, and as the trail twists and turns, there are views of glaciers up the valley. At Mi 2.5/Km 4, the route begins a steep climb toward Asulkan Pass, and soon the fissured tongue of Asulkan Glacier dominates the skyline. A footbridge spans the upper reaches of a brook, then the trail begins a steep ascent up the spine of another moraine. The trail-end, with Asulkan Glacier far below, is a fine lunch spot with surpassing views.

North of the campground at Rogers Pass, the 3-mi/5-km *Balu Pass Trail* (balu means "bear" in Hindi) parallels the southwestern course of gentle Connaught Creek through thick forest, then traverses the lower reaches of avalanche slopes—prime grizzly and black bear habitat—before scaling Balu Pass. The rewards include views of wildflowers in August, icefields, glaciers, and mountains.

On the other side of the Balu Pass, a trail descends steeply 2.4 mi/3.9 km south to the endpoint of the *Cougar Valley Trail.* At this junction, a short path leads to the Nakimu Caves, one of the largest systems in Canada with nearly 4 mi/6 km of passageways. The caves are closed, but old trails farther up the valley pass formations in the eroded limestone bedrock: sinkholes, disappearing streams, and collapsed gorges. From here, the descending trail crosses avalanche paths, joins up with a relatively open old roadbed, then zigzags steeply through rain forest down to the Trans-Canada Highway. Of the six bear-inflicted injuries since the park's founding, five have occurred near Balu Pass or the Nakimu Caves. Before setting out, hikers should review grizzly precautions with park naturalists.

The hour-long *Abandoned Rails Trail,* also at Rogers Pass, is well-suited to walkers of all ages who wish to learn about the park's railroading days. The route, with its gentle gradient, follows the original CPR railbed before construction of the Connaught Tunnel and passes abandoned snowsheds and the site where 62 men were killed in a 1910 avalanche.

The *Copperstain Trail* in the park's eastern extremity explores Glacier Park's narrow band of Purcell Mountains, which are lower and less rugged than the craggy Selkirks west of the Beaver Valley. From a spur road off the Trans-Canada, about 10 mi/16 km northeast of Rogers Pass, the trail heads south alongside the Beaver River through stands of Engelmann spruce and western redcedar hundreds of years old.

At Grizzly Creek, the trail angles northeast, crosses the creek, and heads up Copperstain Creek to the southeast. The fairly open forest of the Copperstain Burn, an area ravaged by fire, is prime habitat for deer and wapiti and sun-loving fireweed, Indian paintbrush, and asters. The trail ends in the alpine meadows of Bald Mountain, one of the best backpacking and wilderness camping areas in Glacier.

Climbing

Backcountry huts serve as base camps for Glacier Park's renowned climbs. The Sapphire Col hut, which sleeps six, is used by climbers in the Bonney group of peaks south of Rogers Pass; the Hermit hut houses up to eight alpinists tackling the Hermit summits north of Rogers Pass (Mt. Tupper, Hermit Mountain, and Mt. Rogers); and the eight-person Glacier Circle hut serves climbers in the Dawson summits southeast of Rogers Pass. Another popular destination is Mt. Sir Donald east of Rogers Pass, especially the northwest ridge.

The Alpine Club of Canada owns and operates the 30-bed Wheeler Hut at Illecillewaet campground. Permission to use this private facility may be

obtained in advance from the Alpine Club of Canada, (Box 1026, Banff, Alta. T0L 0C0; 403-762-4481). The club also organizes expeditions.

Fishing

Productivity is low in most Selkirk waters. Cutthroat trout and Dolly Varden (arctic char) are in the Illecillewaet River.

Winter Activities

The winter sports season lasts from December to March. Some of Canada's finest *ski mountaineering* routes are in the Asulkan Valley, with its 10 sq mi/26 sq km of deep powder and névé. Certified guides can be hired in Golden or in the city of Revelstoke for backcountry trips. *Cross-country skiing* is restricted by steep terrain and prohibited on slopes facing the Trans-Canada Highway during avalanche season from November to April. The most popular routes are the Asulkan and Balu Pass trails.

OUTDOOR ACTIVITIES IN MT. REVELSTOKE

The most popular pastimes in what is primarily a day-use park are hiking and cross-country skiing.

A world-renowned avalanche control program keeps the spectacular Trans-Canada Highway open in winter. OPPOSITE: *Stellar's jay is easy to recognize, as it is one of the few jays with a crest.*

Scenic Drive

Summit Road switchbacks 16 mi/26 km up Mt. Revelstoke, with numerous scenic views along the way of the Illecillewaet River valley to the south and the Columbia River valley and the Monashee Mountains to the west.

Hiking

Access for many of the nine trails is off Summit Road. The 6-mi/10-km *Summit Trail* matches the road's route from the base of Mt. Revelstoke to the summit, climbing more than 3,900 ft/1,200 m through redcedar-hemlock forest and into the subalpine. At the road's first switchback, the *Inspiration Woods Trail* wanders 1.2 mi/2 km through redcedar-hemlock forest and past mushroom patches that are especially impressive throughout September and October.

To enjoy the park's most spectacular display—the famous alpine flowers atop Mt. Revelstoke—hikers set out on the *Mountain Meadows Nature Trail*, which begins at the Summit Road parking lot and loops 0.5 mi/1 km with minimal elevation change. Yellow avalanche lilies and white spring beauties start the show in July, followed by an August palette of red Indian paintbrush, white mountain valerian, yellow arnica, purple lupine, and pink mountain daisies. Benches are provided at two viewpoints, and the trail passes the Icebox, a snow-filled crevice. Mountain Meadows Trail and other paths in the summit area are paved to prevent damage to the delicate high-altitude vegetation.

A trail with a gentle gradient wanders northeast from the parking lot through meadows and small stands of stunted fir, hemlock, and spruce on the rolling upland plateau to four alpine lakes, the most popular day-hike destinations in the park. About 3.4 mi/5.4 km from the parking lot, the route branches into three. The right branch leads a short distance to a glacier-carved basin now occupied by *Miller Lake*. The naturally barren lake was once stocked with cutthroat and brook trout, and some fish still are landed here.

The short left branch of the trail leads to *Eva Lake*, a spectacular lunch spot surrounded in August by asters, lupines, and avalanche lilies. Overnight camping is permitted at lakeside sites, and a primitive cabin here is open to the public. An indistinct trail around the water's edge leads to an impressive viewpoint looking north across the Coursier Creek valley.

The center fork in the trail climbs over a 900-ft/300-m ridge with commanding views, then descends to *Jade Lakes*, favorites with photographers. Overnight camping is permitted here. This difficult trek through the treeless alpine tundra should be attempted only by experienced hikers.

The *Skunk Cabbage Trail*, off the Trans-Canada 5 mi/8 km from Mt. Revelstoke's eastern boundary, is a boardwalk loop through wetlands flanking the Illecillewaet River, the best bird-watching habitat in the park. In May and June rufous hummingbirds abound, along with song sparrows, common yellowthroats, and black-headed grosbeaks (rare elsewhere in Revelstoke). Beaver and muskrat lodges are numerous in the wetlands. In spring, the green undergrowth along the boardwalk is spiked with the flowers of yellow skunk cabbage, which has gigantic leaves nearly 3 ft/1 m long.

A short distance northeast, the *Giant Cedars Trail* is a short boardwalk through a mature interior rain forest of towering western redcedars. In a flutter of wings, bats gather at dusk to drink from a rivulet trickling through the forest. These flying mammals migrate south to escape winter—but their destination remains unknown.

Climbing

The Eva Lake hut is a base camp for mountaineers tackling peaks in the Clachnacudainn Range in the center of the park.

Fishing

Cutthroat and brook trout are taken from Eva and Miller lakes and rainbow trout are landed in Upper and Lower Jade lakes. Upper Jade also has brook trout.

Winter Activities

At the base of Mt. Revelstoke is a groomed 3-mi/5-km trail for *cross-country skiing;* half the route is lighted for night skiing. Most of *Summit Road* is also open for skiing. A picnic shelter at Mi 5/Km 8 is stocked with wood and makes a pleasant lunch stop. A cabin at Mi 12/Km 19.3 and a picnic shelter at Balsam Lake near the summit are available for overnight use. The *Summit Trail* makes a steeper but more direct route to the top. *Snowshoeing* enthusiasts follow the *Inspiration Woods, Giant Cedars*, and *Skunk Cabbage trails.*

EXPLORING THE PARKS

Rogers Pass is about 220 mi/350 km west of Calgary via the Trans-Canada Highway. This road is open year-round, but it may be closed in Glacier and Mt. Revelstoke for short periods (three hours or less) during avalanche season. Snow tires or well-fitting tire chains are recommended. In Mt. Revelstoke Park, Summit Road is open in its entirety from late July to early

September; lower sections of the road open in May and June and in October and November as snow conditions permit.

Sadly, passenger trains no longer stop in Glacier and Mt. Revelstoke parks. The luxury train of Blyth & Company (68 Scollard St., Suite 300, Toronto, Ont. M5R 102; 416-964-2569) passes through the two parks on its transcontinental run, as does the two-day excursion train from Vancouver to Jasper and Banff operated by Rocky Mountaineer Railtours (625 Howe St., Suite 345, Vancouver, B.C. V6C 2T6; 800-665-RAIL in Canada and 800-627-6490 in the U.S.). Greyhound Lines operates buses in summer between the parks and Calgary and Vancouver, with scheduled stops at Glacier Park Lodge in Rogers Pass.

The parks are open year-round, although most visitors stay in the Trans-Canada corridor in winter, when heavy snows and avalanches make backcountry travel difficult and hazardous.

The interpretive program is extensive in Glacier and limited in Mt. Revelstoke. Visitors' services personnel are on hand at the Rogers Pass Information Centre in Glacier (604-837-6274) from early May to late October. Here, a cutaway model reveals the Nakimu Cave system; a film entitled

Since it opened regular service in 1886, the Canadian Pacific Railway has been continually upgraded to meet the Selkirks's challenge.

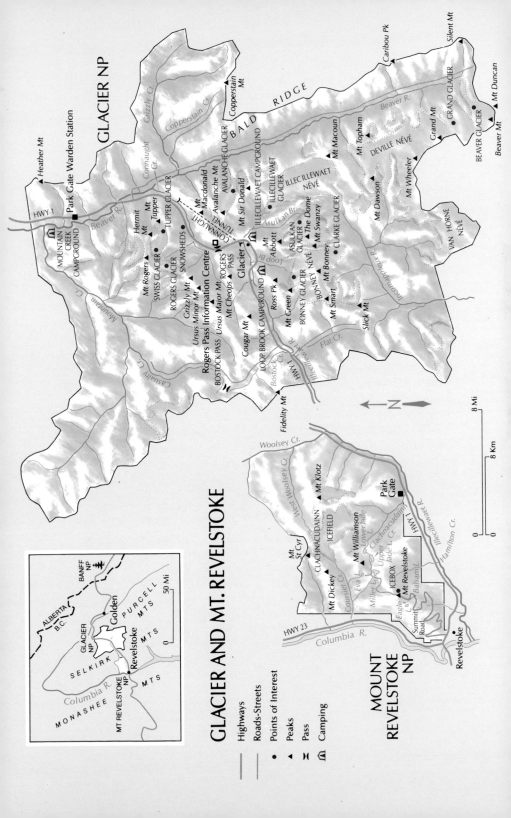

GLACIER AND MT. REVELSTOKE

GLACIER NP

Heather Mt
Park Gate Warden Station
HWY 1
MOUNTAIN CREEK CAMPGROUND
Beaver R.
Mountain Cr.
Casualty Cr.
Connaught Cr.
Grizzly Cr.
Copperstain Cr.
Copperstain Cr.
Copperstain Mt
BALD RIDGE
Caribou Pk
Silent Mt
Beaver R.
GRAND GLACIER
Grand Mt
Mt Duncan
BEAVER GLACIER
Beaver Mt
Mt Topham
DEVILLE NÉVÉ
Mt Oir
Mt Macoun
VAN HORNE NÉVÉ
Mt Wheeler
Mt Dawson
ILLECILLEWAET NÉVÉ
ILLECILLEWAET CAMPGROUND
ILLECILLEWAET GLACIER
Hermit Mt
Mt Tupper
TUPPER GLACIER
SNOWSHEDS
Mt Macdonald
Avalanche Mt
AVALANCHE GLACIER
Mt Sir Donald
CONNAUGHT TUNNEL
Mt Rogers
SWISS GLACIER
ROGERS GLACIER
Grizzly Mt
Ursus Minor Mt
Ursus Major Mt
ROGERS PASS
ROGERS PASS
Glacier
Rogers Pass Information Centre
Mt Cheops
Loop Br.
Mt Abbott
ASULKAN GLACIER
The Dome
Mt Swanzy
CLARKE GLACIER
Mt Bonney
BONNEY NÉVÉ
Asulkan Br.
Illecillewaet R.
Cougar Mt
LOOP BROOK CAMPGROUND
Ross Pk
Mt Green
BONNEY GLACIER
Mt Smart
Slick Mt
BOSTOCK PASS
Bostock Cr.
Flat Cr.
HWY 1
Fidelity Mt
Tangier R.
Incomappleux R.

N   8 Mi   8 Km

MOUNT REVELSTOKE NP

Woolsey Cr.
West Woolsey Cr.
Mt Klotz
Park Gate
HWY 1
Illecillewaet R.
Hamilton Cr.
CLACHNACUDAINN ICEFIELD
Mt St Cyr
Mt Williamson
Mt Dickey
Courser Cr.
Eva L.
Miller L.
ICEBOX L.
Eagle L.
Upper Jade L.
Lower Jade L.
Clachnacudainn Cr.
Mt Revelstoke
Balsam L.
Summit Road
HWY 23
Columbia R.
Revelstoke

Highways
Roads-Streets
Points of Interest
Peaks
Pass
Camping

ALBERTA B.C.
BANFF NP
Golden
PURCELL MTS
GLACIER NP
Revelstoke
SELKIRK MTS
MT REVELSTOKE NP
MONASHEE MTS
Columbia R.
50 Mi

Underground Rivers enables visitors to explore this closed subterranean world vicariously. The film *Snow War* contains dramatic footage of snowslides.

In July and August naturalists conduct three- to five-hour hikes on trails emanating from the Illecillewaet campground—a fascinating introduction to Glacier. Suitable for all ages, these walks lead to destinations that change daily. Interpreters also lead an annual pilgrimage the first Monday in August to wildflower meadows near Eva Lake in Mt. Revelstoke.

Fishing permits for Glacier Park are sold at the information center. The park warden's office (across the highway) dispenses registration permits for overnight backpacking, climbing, and ski-mountaineering trips and information on hiking and mountaineering, including photographs of popular mountain-climbing routes. It also has lists of commercial guides offering expeditions in the parks.

Registration for hiking in Mt. Revelstoke is done at the park administration office in the city of Revelstoke, or at the Parks and Recreation Department in City Hall. Hikers can also register during July and August at the Balsam Lake Warden Cabin near the end of Summit Road.

In both parks, dry trail conditions are from mid-July to mid-September. Hikers should be prepared for sudden changes in weather. Many trails above 6,200 ft/1,900 m are snow-free only during August and September. Trail-condition reports are posted at information outlets; there's also a 24-hour weather hotline (604-837-MTNS). In Glacier Park, hikers occasionally encounter unexploded howitzer shells fired the previous winter by avalanche-control teams. Shells should not be touched—they could detonate. Their whereabouts should be reported immediately to the nearest park office.

ACCOMMODATIONS: In Glacier Park there are camping sites at the Illecillewaet campground (58 sites), just southwest of Rogers Pass and the interpretive center; at the Loop Brook campground (19 sites) about 1 mi/1.6 km farther west of the Illecillewaet campground on the Trans-Canada Highway; and at the Mountain Creek campground (306 sites) at the northern entrance to the park. Illecillewaet and Loop are often filled by early afternoon in summer; Mountain Creek is rarely crowded. The campgrounds are open from mid-June to early September. During May, September, and October there is camping at the Beaver River picnic area.

There are no campgrounds in Mt. Revelstoke Park. Accommodation in backcountry huts is booked well in advance at park offices.

Privately owned Glacier Park Lodge at Rogers Pass is open year-round. For reservations or information, write or phone: Glacier Park Lodge, Rogers Pass, B.C. V0E 2S0; 604-837-2126. There are private and provincial campgrounds near the parks. The town of Golden, east of Glacier, and the city of Revelstoke, south of Mt. Revelstoke, have full tourist facilities.

ADDRESSES: For more information on the parks, contact: The Superintendent, Mt. Revelstoke and Glacier National Parks, Box 350, 301 Campbell Ave., Revelstoke, B.C. V0E 2S0; 604-837-5155. Golden and Revelstoke have departments that organize mountaineering activities in the parks: Town of Golden, Parks and Recreation Department, Box 350, 916 9th Ave. East, Golden, B.C. V0A 1H0; 604-344-2271, or City of Revelstoke, Parks and Recreation Department, Box 170, 600 Campbell Ave., Revelstoke, B.C. V0A 1H0; 604-837-9351.

The local park cooperative association sells a wide range of publications relating to the natural and human history of the twin sanctuaries: Friends of Mt. Revelstoke and Glacier, Box 2992, Revelstoke, B.C. V0E 2S0; 604-837-2010.

BOOKS: Pierre Berton, *The National Dream* and *The Last Spike.* Toronto: McClelland and Stewart, 1974. The story of the transcontinental Canadian Pacific Railway.

William L. Putnam, *A Climber's Guide to the Interior Ranges of British Columbia—North.* New York: American Alpine Club, 1975.

——, *The Great Glacier and Its House.* New York: American Alpine Club, 1982.

John G. Woods, *Glacier Country.* Vancouver/Toronto: Douglas & McIntyre, 1987. This comprehensive guidebook to Glacier and Mt. Revelstoke is available at the park cooperative association.

Yorke Edwards, *The Illustrated Natural History of Canada—The Mountain Barrier.* Toronto: Natural Science of Canada Limited, 1970. Entertaining introduction to Canada's cordillera.

ROCKY MOUNTAIN NATIONAL PARKS: BANFF, JASPER, KOOTENAY, AND YOHO

ICEFIELDS, GLACIER-MANTLED PEAKS, painted canyons, hot springs, waterfalls, mountain meadows spangled with wildflowers—these are just some of the natural splendors that lure more than 9 million visitors annually to the blue Canadian Rockies. Four national parks protect 7,814 sq mi/20,238 sq km of this spectacular wilderness, forming the crown jewels in Canada's park system and one of the largest areas of mountain parkland in the world.

Banff and Jasper are stacked south–north on the eastern slope of the Rockies in Alberta. Established in 1885, Banff is Canada's oldest and most popular national park. The Front Ranges rise abruptly from the foothills at the park's eastern edge and culminate in the ridges and peaks of the Continental Divide, which forms the boundary between Alberta and British Columbia. Banff's attractions abound: the translucent green waters of Lake Louise; Sunshine Meadows; Johnston Canyon; the steaming hot springs of Sulphur Mountain.

To the north, the wilder and more remote Front and Main ranges in Jasper National Park beckon backpackers and trail riders. The Columbia Icefield at the southern end of the park sprawls amid the Canadian Rockies' greatest concentration of high peaks, probing surrounding valleys with the icy fingers of glaciers. Pyramid-shaped Mt. Edith Cavell near the town of Jasper is perhaps the park's most impressive summit. Long, narrow Maligne Lake, Jasper's loveliest body of water, is set in a somberly beautiful valley with a cluster of glacier-studded peaks at one end.

Kootenay National Park, adjacent to Banff on the British Columbia side of the Rockies, protects Radium Hot Springs, the ocher-colored Paint Pots mineral deposits, narrow Sinclair Canyon, and other wonders of the Western Ranges. To the north, Yoho National Park merits its Indian name—an exclamation of awe and astonishment—with 30 peaks higher than 9,800

For several thousand years prehistoric tribes maintained a campsite on the shores of Vermilion Lakes, Banff, here shown in crisp autumnal beauty.

ft/3,000 m and Takakkaw Falls, one of Canada's highest cataracts. In southeastern Yoho lies Lake O'Hara, one of the best loved spots in the mountain parks, with its emerald waters, seven-branched falls, and backdrop of crenellated peaks. American artist John Singer Sargent, who visited the area in 1916, called it the most beautiful lake he had ever seen.

Scenic mountain drives traverse all four parks. The most spectacular, the Icefields Parkway between Banff and Jasper, commands a full range of majestic landscapes. It follows a succession of river valleys, climbs Sunwapta Pass, and skirts the Athabasca Glacier tumbling down from the Columbia Icefield. Moose, wapiti, bighorn sheep, and mountain goats frequently are seen along the way.

For outdoor travelers who seek greater solitude, more than 2,000 mi/3,200 km of trails lead to pristine wilderness never glimpsed by motorists. The Great Divide Trail, Canada's first long-distance hiking and horseback route, weaves along the backbone of the Rockies through the four parks, stitching together (with a few gaps) wilderness paths once trod by Native Americans, trappers, explorers, and surveyors. It is a Rocky Mountain sampler, traversing valleys where rivers thunder, passing glinting lakes, penetrating shaggy forests of spruce and fir, and skirting glaciers.

GEOLOGY

For more than a billion years, rivers washed tremendous volumes of sediment into shallow seas that covered much of what is now British Columbia. The seabed along the continental margin gradually sank beneath the weight of this eroded material, which accumulated in places to depths of 6,500 ft/2,000 m. Over millions of years these sands, silts, clays, and lime muds hardened into a thick sequence of sandstone, siltstone, shale, and limestone—the eventual building blocks of the Rockies.

For most of this period the land was barren. During the Cambrian, however, from about 600 to 500 million years ago, an "explosion" of marine life populated the coastal seas. The most celebrated fossil record of this period is in the Burgess Shale Beds, which outcrop on several mountains in Yoho National Park. On Mt. Wapta, a thin band of rock less than a city block long perfectly preserves the imprints of 140 marine species from some 530 million years ago. Trilobites are most abundant, but far more remarkable are fossils of soft-bodied invertebrates—rare pieces in the paleontological puzzle. Where summits now soar lived delicate jellyfish, sponges, worms, mollusks, and hitherto unknown forms of life.

The Burgess Shale Beds have yielded soft-bodied specimens so well preserved that scientists could discern the contents of their stomachs.

When the supercontinent Pangaea began to break up about 200 million years ago, North America started to drift westward. About 175 million years ago, it rammed into a group of volcanic islands rafting north on the Pacific plate. The islands were scraped off their underlying oceanic plate, crumpled together, then shoved up and over the edge of the continent as an enormous sheet of material some 8,200 ft/2,500 m thick.

The compression generated by this collision wrinkled the flat-lying sedimentary rocks, creating folded mountain ranges, including the Columbias, in the British Columbia interior. About 120 million years ago, near the end of this first phase of western mountain building, the Main Ranges of the Rockies started to rise and were gently tilted. These mountains now form the Continental Divide along the Alberta–British Columbia border.

About 85 million years ago, North America drifted into a second arc of islands that included what is now Vancouver Island and the Queen Charlotte Islands. This collision thrust up the Coast Mountains of British Columbia and rumpled the sedimentary beds even farther inland, finishing the uplift of the Main Ranges of the Rockies and creating the Front Ranges and the foothills. The rock of the Front Ranges underwent a much more tortured folding than the rock of the Main Ranges. Wherever the strain of folding proved too great, immense masses of rock fractured, or faulted; they were then thrust upward as huge blocks or were tilted on their sides like stacks of overlapping shingles, steep side facing east.

Four major glacial periods put the finishing touches on today's Rockies. About 2 million years ago, as the climate cooled, glaciers began to form on mountain slopes, spilling into valleys. Most of the glaciers east of the Continental Divide inched toward the prairies, where they joined the great continental ice sheet. West of the Divide, the rivers of ice flowed toward the Pacific. The most recent glaciation buried valleys such as the Bow in southern Banff beneath 2,600 ft/800 m of ice. Only the highest peaks would have projected above this frozen sea.

Glaciation created many of today's landmarks. Major tongues of ice ground V-shaped valleys into wide, U-shaped ones (the Bow, the Athabasca, the Kicking Horse). In places, small alpine glaciers cut high valleys, which were left "hanging" on the sides of broader, deeper valleys carved by larger glaciers. Meltwater spilling over the lip of hanging valleys forms some of the Rockies' loveliest waterfalls, such as Takakkaw Falls in Yoho.

Minor glaciers quarried into mountain flanks, forming bowl-shaped depressions called cirques. Occasionally, glaciers attacked a mountain from three or more sides to create a sharp pinnacle, or spike, called a horn. Mt. Assiniboine, a glaciered obelisk bordering Banff, is a textbook example. The glaciers' retreat left scattered moraines, great ridges of rock and gravel debris, that diverted and dammed streams to form Lake Louise and Peyto Lake in Banff, Emerald Lake in Yoho, and many other mountain lakes.

HISTORY

Prehistoric tribes inhabited the region of the mountain parks for at least 13,000 years, fishing in rivers and lakes, trapping in valley-bottom wetlands, and hunting bison, moose, wapiti, deer, and bighorn sheep. A campsite some 10,500 years old, excavated at Vermilion Lakes west of Banff townsite, contained stone tools, the bones of butchered animals, and evidence of occupation that extended over several thousand years.

Hunting and trading over vast areas, these nomadic aboriginals laced the mountains with trails. The Kootenai, who lived primarily on the west slope of the Rockies, crossed the mountains in spring and fall to hunt bison on the plains. Tribes gathered at neutral religiously significant sites throughout the parks: Radium Hot Springs in Kootenay, which was protected by a spirit named Nipika; the Kootenay Paint Pots, a source of pigment for war paint; and Banff's Bow Valley, where sundance ceremonies were held on what is now the Banff Springs golf course.

During the late eighteenth and early nineteenth centuries, David Thompson and other explorers in the employ of fur-trading companies sought ways through the mountains to the Pacific. In their wake came surveyors mapping routes for the transcontinental railways, which were to link eastern Canada with the new province of British Columbia. Work began on the Canadian Pacific Railway in 1880, with the rails heading up the Bow Valley through Banff and crossing the Main Range of the Rockies at Kicking Horse Pass in Yoho (named in the 1850s after one Dr. James Hector was walloped by his mount).

The worst engineering problem was a steep section 4 mi/6.5 km west of the pass between Wapta Lake and the town of Field. Here, the tracks climbed what was called The Big Hill by snaking back and forth across the Kicking Horse River on eight bridges at a grade that was the highest in North America. Three safety spurs enabled runaway trains to be switched uphill and quickly stopped. Some trains required four locomotives to climb the steep grade of the hill.

In 1909 the CPR halved the grade by constructing two spiral tunnels that loop through two mountains in a huge figure eight—one of the world's epic feats of railroad building. The Trans-Canada Highway follows part of the original railroad bed. Yoho's interpretive trail, Walk in the Past, passes safety spur lines and other reminders of the area's colorful railroading history.

The sawtooth peaks of the Queen Elizabeth Range near Medicine Lake, Jasper. OPPOSITE: The autumn gold of larch trees amid fir and spruce, Kootenay National Park.

In 1883, two CPR workers came upon a cave and basin containing warm, sulfurous springs on Sulphur Mountain, near what is now the town of Banff. Two years later the government designated the area as Banff Hot Spring Reserve for "the sanitary advantage of the public." The reserve around Cave and Basin Springs was soon expanded to 260 sq mi/673 sq km and named Rocky Mountains Park. Later renamed Banff, it was Canada's first national park and the world's third such preserve (after Yellowstone in the United States and Royal National in Australia).

Until the 1880s, access to the astounding scenery in the Rockies was limited to those who lived there—mountain men like Tom Wilson, Bill Peyto, and Fred Stephens—and people affluent enough to hire them as guides. But with the railroad in place, CPR president William Cornelius Van Horne prepared a publicity campaign to lure European aristocracy and wealthy Americans to "the Mountain Playground of the World." Van Horne wrote, "We can't export the scenery—we'll import the tourists."

The CPR built several mountain resorts to accommodate the flood of railroading sightseers—most notably the Scottish-baronial-French-

château-style Banff Springs Hotel, whose turreted magnificence still welcomes travelers at the confluence of the Bow and Spray rivers. In the hotel's gilded era the rich and famous arrived with steamer trunks and servants to stay the entire summer. On the shores of Lake Louise, the CPR constructed a wooden chalet where Château Lake Louise now stands, blazed trails into the surrounding valleys with shelters and teahouses at strategic intervals, and hired Swiss alpinists to guide visitors into the wilderness. It was the birth of recreational hiking in the Canadian Rockies.

Yoho, established in 1886, first gained prominence when guide Fred Stephens led Jean Habel, a professor of mathematics and alpinist from Berlin, into the previously impenetrable Yoho Valley in 1897. Habel's descriptions of such scenic wonders as Takakkaw Falls ("in beauty and grandeur hardly to be excelled by any other on our globe") attracted adventurers from around the world.

Jasper was set aside in 1907, four years before the Grand Trunk Pacific, a second transcontinental rail line, was built up the Athabasca Valley and across the Rockies at Yellowhead Pass. Kootenay was created in 1920 as a preserve flanking the first highway across the central Canadian Rockies, the Kootenay Parkway, which was completed in 1923.

HABITATS

A hike from any Rocky Mountain valley to the summit of the nearest high peak—a distance usually of less than 5 mi/8 km—passes through a variety of plant communities roughly equivalent to those found on a 1,000-mi/1,600-km trek from the prairies to the high Arctic. With each 1,000 ft/300 m of altitude, the average temperature drops 3.5° F/2° C, humidity in the air increases, and soils tend to become more acidic—changes that profoundly influence plant growth as well as the animals that depend on the vegetation for survival.

The mountain parks contain three tiers of habitat, ragged zones that rise and fall with local conditions, including topography, soil, temperature, and moisture. In sheltered valley bottoms and along watercourses of the montane zone grow willows, alders, birches, and cottonwoods. Pink pyrola, butterwort, yellow and white lady's-slippers, and other shade-tolerant plants brighten the undergrowth.

Marshy floodplains here, such as those in Banff's Bow Valley and Jasper's Athabasca Valley and Snake Indian River delta, are migratory stopovers for swans, geese, mallards, common mergansers, green-winged teal, and red-necked grebes. Red-winged blackbirds call *con-ka-ree* from marshland cattails. Delicate white water-crowfoot, buttercup-yellow bladderwort, and pink, hyacinth-like smartweed blossom in quiet coves. Valley streams and lakes attract such expert fishers as ospreys and bald eagles and support colonies of beaver and muskrat.

This habitat is frequented by moose, which feed on aquatic plants, and by wolves, which feed on moose. A wolf pack often is seen in winter near Jasper townsite. Nearly wiped out of the mountain parks by the 1950s, wolves have made a dramatic comeback and currently number about 120 in Banff and Jasper.

On lower mountain slopes up to about 4,800 ft/1,460 m, montane forests are dominated by Douglas-fir and lodgepole pine. In the days of David Thompson and other explorers, pure stands of Douglas-fir dominated the landscape. Today these evergreens, reduced by logging and fire, are found in scattered stands, usually with an understory of lodgepole pine or quaking aspen, or in open park-like stands on grassy slopes. Lodgepole pine, which grows best on upland sites, usually grows in pure stands, but occasionally in association with white spruce and quaking aspen.

Montane forests attract mountain and black-capped chickadees, mountain bluebirds, northern flickers, dark-eyed juncos, and pine siskins. Red wood lily, bluebell, wild rose, and bright yellow gaillardia flourish on semi-arid south-facing slopes. These grasslands, which are interspersed with forest throughout much of the montane, are home to Columbian ground squirrels. Golden-mantled ground squirrels and least chipmunks frequent rockslides, always on the lookout for their predators, coyotes.

Grizzlies and black bears wander through different elevations in the remote backcountry, including the montane. Black bears rely more on heavily forested areas, while grizzlies prefer open country and forest margins. In summer grizzlies range anywhere from valley bottoms to above the tree line. Both kinds of bears often are seen along the Icefields and Kootenay parkways. Wapiti and mule deer browse in lower montane valleys during much of the year, although wapiti ascend to higher elevations in midsummer. During rutting season in September, mountain valleys resound with the hoarse bugling of the bulls.

Between the montane zone and about 6,500 ft/2,000 m are dense subalpine forests of Engelmann spruce and subalpine fir, with scattered stands of whitebark pine and alpine larch. Unlike most conifers, larches turn yellow and shed their needles (but not their cones) in autumn. Montane grasses yield here to the spongy ground cover of lichens and mosses. Wildflower

OVERLEAF: *Surprise Point's alpine serenity at Amethyst Lake, Tonquin Valley, Jasper National Park.*

meadows, the summer haunts of wapiti and bighorn sheep, are the glory of this habitat, brightened throughout summer with colorful blooms.

The canopy of the subalpine forest is alive with boreal chickadees, hermit and varied thrushes, ruby-crowned kinglets, and crossbills. Along the banks of fast-moving streams, swallows and dippers occasionally are seen. The dark forest corridors are home to the spruce grouse, sometimes called a "fool hen" because of its tameness around humans. Indian hunters disdained such easy prey except in direst need. The blue grouse, unlike most mountain birds, wanders upslope to winter in the high spruce forest. Red squirrels, the most common squirrel species here, cache winter food in "midden heaps," mounds of pinecone scales on the forest floor.

In both montane and subalpine forests, lodgepole pine proliferates in the wake of forest fires. This tree's tightly packed cones require intense heat of at least 135° F/57° C to open and release seeds. Eventually, spruce and subalpine fir grow beneath the lodgepole canopy and become the dominant species. This forest succession can be seen along the Fireweed Trail at the northern end of Kootenay.

Above 7,200 ft/2,200 m, even the hardy Engelmann spruce begins to falter, twisting into gnarled, stunted forms as it approaches the upper limits of tree growth. Resembling Arctic tundra in its lower reaches, the alpine zone supports a plant cover of shrub willow, grasses, sedges, and heathers (white, yellow, and red). The growing season here seldom exceeds 60 days, and desiccating winds gust at speeds averaging three times greater than in the valleys below.

During the few short weeks of summer alpine rock gardens flourish with incredible beauty, splashing the crags and highland meadows with masses of color—moss campions, saxifrages, and mountain avens. The tiny blue flowers of the alpine forget-me-not are the midsummer beauties of the tundra. Most alpine plants develop slowly, some taking 15 years or more to mature and blossom. A fist-size clump of moss campion may be more than 50 years old.

With the notable exception of mountain goats, few animals can survive year-round above tree line. Prior to the onset of winter, bighorn sheep, mountain caribou, and other large animals migrate downslope into sheltering forests and valleys. Several distinct herds of caribou range Jasper, including one in the Maligne Valley in the southeast corner of the park.

A few small animals—mice, hoary marmots, and weasels—survive the storm-swept winter by hibernating, hunting incessantly, or by feeding on supplies stored during the summer. The pika, which lives amid boulder fields at altitudes up to 10,000 ft/3,050 m, stows the grasses it forages in large piles. This relative of the rabbit has adapted to its harsh world: its compact body conserves heat, and fur on the soles of its feet provides traction on rocks. Pikas deposit their urine in nearly crystalline form, retaining body moisture in the dry air.

American pipits, horned larks, and rosy finches breed on alpine tundra, but only one bird, the pullet-size white-tailed ptarmigan, lives at and above the tree line all year. This ptarmigan, a species of grouse, changes plumage to fit the season—mottled browns, blacks, and whites in summer and snowy white in winter.

Outdoor Activities in Banff

Canada's most popular national park welcomes nearly 4 million visitors annually. Most of those who overnight in the park stay in the Banff and Lake Louise areas, leaving a vast backcountry wilderness as the unspoiled domain of outdoor enthusiasts.

Scenic Drives

Spectacular scenery can be enjoyed along the park's three main roads. The divided *Trans-Canada Highway* (Highway 1), which angles through the southern half of the park, is often congested with through traffic. Sight-seers take the alternate route, the two-lane *Bow Valley Parkway* (Highway 1A), which parallels the Trans-Canada between Banff townsite and Lake Louise. The highlight is Johnston Canyon, where a popular hiking trail leads to two waterfalls and five cold-water springs called the Ink Pots.

The *Icefields Parkway* (Highway 93), which extends 150 mi/240 km between Lake Louise and Jasper townsite in Jasper National Park, can be covered in a day with brief stops at points of interest, or it can be traveled in several days, with time for camping and hiking on the numerous trails that cross it or start at the roadside.

The awesome power of ice is evident throughout the drive, in sculpted ice bowls, crenelated ridges, and fluted slopes. The most beautiful legacy of the Ice Age is Lake Louise, a 2-mi/3.2-km side trip west at the southern end of the parkway. This is one of the world's most celebrated mountain scenes: a blue-green tarn with glacier-hung Mt. Victoria as its snowy back-drop. Château Lake Louise, one of the CPR's mountain resorts, stands majestically at one end of the lake.

The beauty of Lake Louise is challenged by a succession of valley lakes strung like emeralds on the silver skein of the Bow River. A short side trip 25 mi/40 km north of Lake Louise leads to a viewpoint for Peyto Lake. A nature trail from the parking lot wanders through a subalpine forest to a platform with unobstructed views of Peyto, which lies 800 ft/244 m below in the Mistaya Valley.

The hoodoo formations, pillars of rock molded by erosion, grace the Bow River Valley. OPPOSITE: Bow Falls, frozen near the Icefields Parkway, Banff National Park.

Farther north 17 mi/27 km is Mistaya Canyon (*mistaya* is Cree for "grizzly bear"). Here the Mistaya River slices through limestone to create a narrow, serpentine gorge whose sheer walls have been potholed by millennia of rushing water.

At the parkway's junction with the David Thompson Highway (Highway 11), 3 mi/5 km north, the road enters the broad valley of the North Saskatchewan River, which braids in a wide gravel bed. Moose are seen occasionally hereabouts. Over the next 30 mi/50 km the road climbs to windy, cloud-blown Sunwapta Pass, an alpine plateau cloistered by 11 of the Canadian Rockies' 22 highest peaks. Just on the other side of the pass (6,673 ft/2,034 m), on the border of Banff and Jasper, sprawls the immense Columbia Icefield.

The *Vermilion Lakes Drive* west of Banff townsite winds 2.5 mi/4 km along the north shore of the vest-pocket lakes scattered on the wide floor of the Bow Valley. Wildlife seen here includes moose, white-tailed and mule deer, bighorn sheep, wolves, ospreys, and eagles. The *Lake Minnewanka Loop Drive*, a 15-mi/24-km round trip, starts at the Banff traffic circle, follows the base of Cascade Mountain, where there are excellent views of the Palliser Range to the east, and goes partway around Lake Minnewanka, a man-made reservoir created by damming the Bow River. Bighorn sheep are frequently encountered. The *Buffalo Paddock Drive* near the Minnewanka underpass at Banff townsite winds through aspen grasslands where a small herd of wood bison graze.

Hiking

Banff contains some 940 mi/1,500 km of trails, more than any other Canadian mountain park. Eleven short hikes and nature trails have a maximum length of 1.5 mi/2.4 km. The *Tunnel Mountain Trail,* one of the oldest short hikes in the park, begins on St. Julien Road at the outskirts of Banff townsite, switchbacks up the western flank of Tunnel Mountain through a thick forest of lodgepole pine and Douglas-fir, and ends on a summit ridge with fine views of the townsite, the north ridge of Mt. Rundle, and an 18-mi/30-km stretch of the Bow Valley.

The self-guiding *Fenland Nature Trail,* off Mt. Norquay Road north of town, loops through wetlands slowly evolving into a mature, valley-bottom spruce forest. Fenland and the adjacent Vermilion Lakes comprise the park's prime bird-watching area, where blue-winged teal, mallards, and mergansers may be seen, along with moose, wapiti, and deer. West of Banff townsite, the *Muleshoe Trail* ascends Mt. Cory's steep southwest flank. The route passes through montane forest and reaches a meadow spangled in summer with prairie anemone, bluebells, gaillardia, blue flax, and other dryland wildflowers.

The 4.1-mi/6.6-km *Cascade Amphitheatre Trail,* a popular day hike which begins at the Mt. Norquay ski area west of downtown Banff, gradually ascends a small tributary valley of Forty-Mile Creek, then angles up the western slope of Cascade Mountain through spruce and lodgepole pine forest to Cascade Amphitheatre, a subalpine cirque walled on three sides by rugged limestone ridges. Meadows here are carpeted with wildflowers throughout summer, starting in late June with white western anemones and yellow glacier lilies. Rockslides at the upper end of the amphitheater are home to hoary marmots, pikas, and white-tailed ptarmigans.

Sunshine Meadows, 12 mi/20 km southwest of Banff townsite, is a region unique in the Canadian Rockies. Unlike most of the Great Divide, which is composed of heavily glaciated peaks and limestone walls, this 9-mi/15-km span along the crest of the continent is a saddle of rolling meadows and alpine tundra. Moist Pacific air drops an average of 394 in/1,000 cm of precipitation here annually, nurturing lush rock gardens brimming with more than 300 species of alpine wildflowers.

The two-hour *Rock Isle Lake Trail*, the most popular of the three main trails that radiate from the resort complex of Sunshine Village, is busy with dozens of hikers on sunny summer days. The wide gravel path gently climbs south of an interpretive center past a ski chairlift and open stands of alpine fir and meadows filled with forget-me-nots, Indian paintbrush, western anemone, buttercups, and saxifrage. The trail crests the Continental Divide, then descends to a viewpoint overlooking tranquil Rock Isle Lake with the mountains of Kootenay National Park to the west and south. This alpine scene has attracted artists and photographers for decades.

Lake Louise is an equally renowned hiking area, with seven major routes and spur trails leading to three valleys set in some of the continent's most rugged alpine scenery.

The 2.1-mi/3.4-km *Lake Agnes Trail*, a classic Canadian Rockies hike, begins on the north shore of Lake Louise, west of the château, and ascends through dense subalpine forest filled in summer with jays, nutcrackers, and chickadees. After 1 mi/1.6 km, the route breaks into the open for clear views of Louise. Another 0.6 mi/1 km up the trail is Mirror Lake, a tarn backed by the dark cliffs of Big Beehive, a distinctive conical hill. Beyond, through a narrow gap in the rock wall, lies the Lake Agnes teahouse near the brink of a waterfall. The area around Agnes abounds with ground squirrels, Clark's nutcrackers, and gray jays; hoary marmots and pikas inhabit rocky slopes. The trail to the high lookout on Big Beehive starts at the far end of the lake, climbs a short, steep incline, then traverses east along the summit ridge to a gazebo with astounding views of Lake Louise 1,640 ft/500 m below.

The 15-mi/24-km *Paradise Valley Trail*, south of Lake Louise off Moraine Lake Road, angles southwest in an enclosed forest of spruce and fir, then forks south to Lake Annette, with its extraordinary backdrop of ice-clad Mt. Temple. The trail continues to climb southwest for 1.9 mi/3 km, then gradually descends to Horseshoe Meadow, which is backed by the Horseshoe Glacier headwall. Paradise Valley's only campground is in the northwest corner of the meadow. Here, the upper valley route loops back toward Lake Annette, with a brief side trip to the Giant Steps, a series of waterfalls on Paradise Creek.

The Valley of the Ten Peaks, 6.5 mi/10.5 km south of Paradise Valley, also is reached via Moraine Lake Road. The challenging 9.7-mi/15.6-km *Eiffel Lake–Wenkchemna Pass Trail* starts beyond the lodge on the west shore of Moraine Lake (which many consider more striking than Lake Louise), switchbacks west through a closed subalpine forest, then emerges onto open slopes that reveal all 10 valley summits, Wenkchemna Glacier,

Alpine wildflowers carpet the open slopes of the spectacular Valley of the Ten Peaks.

and Moraine's icy blue waters. The trail continues west through flower-filled meadows, then crosses steep scree north of Eiffel Lake, which occupies a depression left after a landslide on Neptuak Mountain to the southwest. North of the lake is Eiffel Peak, named for its likeness to the Parisian landmark. About 2.5 mi/4 km west across rolling alpine tundra, glacial moraines, and rockslides is Wenkchemna Pass, one of the highest points accessible via a hiking trail in the Canadian Rockies (8,546 ft/2,605 m). Views include the Valley of the Ten Peaks, the Eagle's Eyrie in Yoho Park to the southwest, and Prospector's Valley in Kootenay Park to the south.

Banff's most popular backcountry hiking centers are the Skoki Valley northeast of Lake Louise and the Egypt Lake area southwest of Banff townsite. Most visitors backpack in, then explore the region on day hikes that radiate from central campsites.

Bicycling

The *Icefields Parkway* is one of North America's top cycling routes, with wide, paved shoulders, spectacular scenery, and 17 campgrounds and eight hostels along the way. Among 14 shorter cycling trails are the *Fenland Trail;* the 27-mi/44-km *Spray River Fire Road,* which traverses a peaceful, forested valley southeast of Banff townsite; and the 2.3-mi/3.7-km *Sundance Trail,* which extends between the Cave and Basin Centennial Centre and Sundance Canyon.

The splendid turquoise mirror of Lake Moraine reflects the beauty of its surroundings.

Climbing

Yamnuska, just outside the park 30 mi/48 km east of Banff townsite, offers excellent climbing on a number of routes. Near the town, climbers tackle three 8,000-ft/2,440-m summits: Mt. Edith, the southwest buttress of Mt. Cory, and the precipitous limestone "Pope's hat" of Mt. Louis. South of Lake Louise, the icy 3,900-ft/1,200-m north face of Mt. Temple is one of the most difficult face climbs in the Canadian Rockies; the rugged wall was first scaled in 1966. Rock climbers tackle routes of all grades on Back of the Lake crag, a quartzite cliff rising sheer from the eastern end of Lake Louise. On the Wapta and Waputik icefields north of Lake Louise, moderate snow and ice routes head up mounts Balfour, Baker, and Collie. Still farther north, Howse Peak and Mt. Chephren have straightforward routes on their western flanks; extremely technical routes line the east and northeast faces of both mountains.

Horseback Riding

A long-established tradition in the Canadian Rockies, horseback rides are available by the hour, half-day, or day at Banff Springs Corral at the Banff Springs Hotel (403-762-2348), the Sundance Stables (403-762-2832), and Warner and Mackenzie Outfitting (403-762-4551 at the Trail Rider Store). Holiday on Horseback organizes six-day rides, including a fall foliage ride in early September (403-762-4551).

A popular ride near Banff townsite is the *Spray River Quarry Trail*, a 1-mi/1.6-km route that starts near the Banff Springs Hotel golf course and leads to a quarry that yielded stones used in the construction of the hotel and other park buildings.

The *Brewster Creek Trail* starts west of Banff townsite and angles southwest up the valley of Brewster Creek to Ten-Mile Cabin, an outfitter's camp. Beyond the cabin, the trail continues upvalley through a montane forest that opens occasionally to views of the Sundance Range to the east. A steep ascent to Allenby Pass begins immediately after reaching the outfitter's Halfway Cabin. From the summit of the pass—a spectacular defile composed of rockslides and alpine meadows—riders bound for Mt. Assiniboine contour off to the right above the valley and traverse the equally scenic Og Pass.

At Lake Louise, Deer Lodge Corral (403-522-3991) offers hourly and day rides, while overnight backcountry trips are organized by Timberline Tours (403-522-3743) and Trail Riders of the Canadian Rockies (403-287-1746), a nonprofit group formed some 60 years ago. Num-Ti-Jah Corral (403-522-2167) at Bow Lake on the Icefields Parkway has shorter rides.

Boating

Motorboats are restricted to Lake Minnewanka near Banff townsite, where there is a launching area. Sailboats and motorboats can be rented at a concession there, along with fishing tackle. Minnewanka Tours (403-762-3473) offers scenic 90-minute cruises around the lake; bears, deer, and bighorn sheep may be seen on the shore.

Canoeing

There are rental concessions at Two Jack Lake, northeast of Banff townsite, and at lakes Louise, Minnewanka, and Moraine. The two-day *Bow River Route*, suitable only for experienced paddlers, begins where the Trans-Canada crosses the fast-flowing Bow River east of Lake Louise and ends 40 mi/64 km downstream in Banff townsite, passing campgrounds at Johnston Canyon and Castle Mountain. Moose, muskrats, and beavers, as well as ospreys and eagles, often are seen along the way.

Rafting

Rocky Mountain Raft Tours (403-762-3632) conducts half-day float trips down the Bow River.

Fishing

The best angling is in Lake Minnewanka, which yields lake, rainbow, and brook trout, Dolly Varden, splake, northern pike, and lake whitefish. Two Jack and Johnson lakes yield brook and rainbow trout. Bow Lake is fished for lake trout and bull trout, a species of char.

Swimming

The Upper Hot Springs Pool (403-762-2056), south of Banff townsite at the end of Mountain Avenue, is hot enough for year-round outdoor soaking in water temperatures of 104° F/40° C. These are the highest and hottest of the five springs on Sulphur Mountain. Downslope, the Cave and Basin Centennial Centre (403-762-3324) includes a swimming pool, a reconstruction of the original 1887 bathhouse, the basin hot spring, a teahouse, and a tunnel to the cave hot spring. Outside, a boardwalk equipped with telescopes leads to a wooden blind at the bottom of the valley, where visitors can watch birds and other marsh life.

Downhill Skiing

Banff gained international renown in the 1960s as a winter sports center. Mt. Norquay, west of Banff townsite, is noted for its challenging mogul runs. The Lone Pine run, with a consistent pitch of 37 to 38 degrees, is among the steepest in the park. The season extends from mid-November to early April. Sunshine Village is in a high alpine bowl with abundant snow (up to 22 ft/6.5 m). Its season is the longest in Canada—from mid-November to mid-June; the longest run is 5 mi/8 km. Lake Louise, one of the largest ski areas in the country, has 40 runs on Mt. Whitehorn and Mt. Lipalian. There are open slopes, bowls, mogul fields, gladed timberline trails, plenty of powder, and outstanding views of the Bow Valley and the Continental Divide. The season runs from mid-November to early May.

Cross-country Skiing

Three distinct classifications based on terrain and route characteristics are used in the mountain national parks. *Nordic skiing* usually is done on relatively flat valley bottoms close to road access. More than 90 mi/150 km of groomed nordic trails include the 8-mi/12.8-km return trip on the first part of the *Cascade Fire Road* (easy); the 8-mi/12.8-km outer *Pipestone* loop near Lake Louise (easy to intermediate); and the 7.2-mi/11.5-km *Rundle Riverside Trail* from the Bow Falls parking lot southeast along the Bow River to the park boundary (easy).

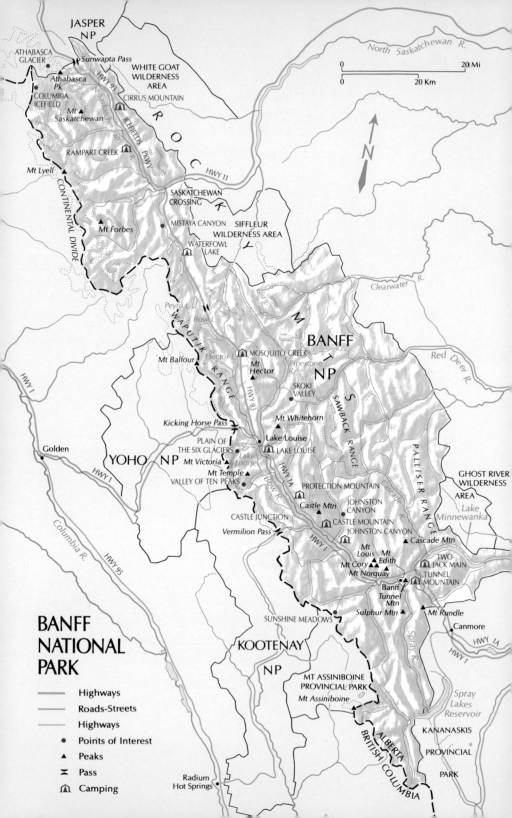

JASPER
NP

ATHABASCA
GLACIER

Sunwapta Pass

Athabasca
Pk

WHITE GOAT
WILDERNESS
AREA

COLUMBIA
ICEFIELD

CIRRUS MOUNTAIN

Mt
Saskatchewan

R O C

RAMPART CREEK

North Saskatchewan R.

0   20 Mi

0   20 Km

N

Mt Lyell

CONTINENTAL DIVIDE

HWY 11

Mt Forbes

SASKATCHEWAN
CROSSING

MISTAYA CANYON

SIFFLEUR
WILDERNESS AREA

WATERFOWL
LAKE

K

Clearwater R.

Red Deer R.

WAPUTIK RANGE

Peyto L.

Bow L.

Hector L.

Mt Balfour

MOSQUITO CREEK

Mt
Hector

Pipestone R.

BANFF

M
T

NP

SKOKI
VALLEY

SAWBACK RANGE

Golden

HWY 1

Kicking Horse Pass

PLAIN OF
THE SIX GLACIERS

Mt Whitehorn

Lake Louise

LAKE LOUISE

HWY 93

YOHO   NP

Mt Victoria

*Lake
Louise*

Mt Temple

VALLEY OF TEN PEAKS

HWY 1A

PROTECTION MOUNTAIN

Castle Mtn

JOHNSTON
CANYON

Cascade R.

PALLISER RANGE

GHOST RIVER
WILDERNESS
AREA

*Lake
Minnewanka*

CASTLE JUNCTION

Vermilion Pass

CASTLE MOUNTAIN
JOHNSTON CANYON

HWY 1

Mt
Louis   Mt
Edith

Cascade Mtn

Columbia R.

HWY 95

Bow R.

Mt Cory

Mt Norquay

TWO-
JACK MAIN
TUNNEL
MOUNTAIN

Banff
Tunnel
Mtn

SUNSHINE MEADOWS

Sulphur Mtn

Mt Rundle

Canmore

HWY 1A

BANFF
NATIONAL
PARK

KOOTENAY

NP

MT ASSINIBOINE
PROVINCIAL PARK

Mt Assiniboine

Spray R.

HWY 1

Spray
Lakes
Reservoir

KANANASKIS

━━━ Highways

─── Roads-Streets

─── Highways

●   Points of Interest

▲   Peaks

✕   Pass

⌂   Camping

ALBERTA

BRITISH COLUMBIA

PROVINCIAL

PARK

Radium
Hot Springs

Ski touring usually occurs along summer hiking trails that may cross high passes and expose skiers to hazards characteristic of mountain travel in winter. Popular areas include *Sunshine Meadows*, despite its unpredictable weather and potential avalanche conditions; the *Forty-Mile Creek Trail* to the Mystic Lake area north of Banff townsite; and *Moraine Lake Road* into Paradise Valley. This activity is pursued also in the *Skoki Valley* northeast of Lake Louise. The 9-mi/15-km route from the end of the Temple Lodge access road scales Boulder and Deception passes and winds through avalanche areas before descending into the valley, where there are two wilderness campsites and Skoki Lodge, built in the 1930s by the CPR and now commercially operated.

Ski mountaineering takes skiers into high alpine areas and often includes glacier travel. Skiers find their own routes and must be prepared for avalanches, prolonged winter storms, whiteouts, and crevasse rescue. The most popular outing is a glacier trip on the *Wapta Icefield* between Peyton Lake and Bow Lake. Four mountain huts are along the way.

Golfing

The Banff Springs Hotel's magnificent 27-hole golf course, which has outstanding scenery and no fewer than 147 sand traps, is open to the public (403-762-2962).

EXPLORING BANFF

Banff townsite, a resort community with a population of 7,000, is 80 mi/130 km west of Calgary via the Trans-Canada Highway (Highway 1) or Highway 1A. Access to the park from the north is via the Icefields Parkway. Highway 93 runs north and east from Radium, British Columbia, through Kootenay National Park and intersects with the Trans-Canada at Castle Junction in Banff. The David Thompson Highway (Highway 11) connects the city of Red Deer, Alberta, with the Icefields Parkway at Saskatchewan River Crossing.

Blyth & Company (see Addresses, below) operates a luxury transcontinental train once a week on the historic CPR tracks, with stops at Banff and Lake Louise. Rocky Mountaineer Railtours (see Addresses, below) offers more modestly priced two-day excursions from Vancouver to Banff. Greyhound Lines (403-265-9111 in Calgary; 403-421-4211 in Edmonton) offers daily bus service east and west on the Trans-Canada, with regular stops at Banff and Lake Louise and flag stops at Castle Junction. Brewster Transportation (403-762-2241 in Banff; 403-262-4222 in Calgary) and Pacific Western Transportation (403-762-4558) operate daily bus service from Calgary International Airport to Banff and Lake Louise.

Banff has one of the most extensive interpretive programs in the national parks system. Slide shows and talks are presented in six campground theaters, at the information center in Banff townsite, and at the Cave and Basin Centennial Centre on Sulphur Mountain. Campfire talks are given at Rampart Creek campground. Park interpreters conduct daily guided walks in and around Banff townsite, including the Cave and Basin Centre and the Vermilion Lakes, as well as to the Plain of the Six Glaciers near Lake Louise. Schedules of events are published in the park's newspaper, *The Mountain Guide,* broadcast on community cablevision's Channel 10, and posted at information centers, campground kiosks, and many commercial tourist facilities.

Topographic hiking maps, free backcountry permits, and information on trail conditions, trail quotas, and campsite use are available at the information center in Banff and at Lake Louise. A recorded telephone message (403-762-3600) provides a current hiking report in summer and avalanche alerts and snow-condition updates in winter. Hikers wishing to use the shelters at Bryant Creek or Egypt Lake must make reservations through the Banff information center.

An interpretive center at the upper terminal of the Sunshine Meadows gondola lift (403-762-4000) provides hiking directions and information on trail conditions in the area. The gondola usually operates from July to mid-September, and hiking prior to the seasonal opening of the lift is discouraged. After Labor Day, hikers can reach the meadows by walking a 4-mi/6.5-km access road from the gondola parking lot.

Other gondolas and chairlifts to teahouses, summit trails, and sweeping panoramas include Lake Louise (403-522-3555) and Sulphur Mountain (403-762-2523), near Banff townsite, where bighorn sheep often loiter.

ACCOMMODATIONS: Banff's campgrounds include three full-service areas. The Tunnel Mountain campground near Banff townsite is divided into three sections: the trailer court (322 sites), Village I (622 sites), and Village II (189 sites). The Lake Louise Trailer Campground has 163 sites. Nine campgrounds along park highways offer car-based travelers more limited facilities; Waterfowl Lakes (116 sites), at Mi 36/Km 58 of the Icefields Parkway, has a lovely location with a scenic backdrop of glacier-clad mountains. Three primitive campgrounds for motorists are at Mosquito Creek (32 sites), Rampart Creek (50 sites), and Cirrus Mountain (16 sites). Primitive campsites also are located along major backcountry trails.

For help in finding commercial accommodation in Banff and the other mountain parks, call Banff Central Reservations (403-762-5561), a private firm that books rooms all over western Canada. Commercial facilities in the park are concentrated in the Banff townsite and Lake Louise areas. The Banff Springs Hotel (Box 960, Banff, Alta. T0L 0C0; 403-762-2211), a 600-room complex at the foot of Sulphur Mountain, is one of Canada's best-known resorts. The 520-room Château Lake Louise (Lake Louise, Alta. T0L 1E0; 403-552-3511) benefits from a superlative location on the shores of Canada's most famous mountain lake.

Youth hostels along the Trans-Canada Highway and the Icefields Parkway are at Ribbon Creek, Banff townsite, Castle Mountain, Corral Creek, Mosquito Creek, Ramparts Creek, and Hilda Creek.

ADDRESSES: For more information, write or phone: The Superintendent, Banff National Park, Box 900, Banff, Alta. T0L 0C0; 403-762-3324. For information on activities and commercial accommodations in the park, including bicycle touring and trail ride and rafting outfitters, contact the Banff/Lake Louise Chamber of Commerce, Box 1298, Banff, Alta. T0L 0C0; 403-762-4646 or 403-762-3777. For hosteling information, contact the Canadian Hostel Association, Room 203, 1414 Kensington Rd. SW, Calgary, Alta. T2N 3P9; 403-283-5551.

For information on the gondola schedules, lodge accommodations, and downhill skiing at Sunshine Meadows, contact: Sunshine Village, Box 1510, Banff, Alta. T0L 0C0; 403-762-4000. For other downhill skiing information, contact: Mount Norquay, Box 1258, Banff, Alta. T0L 0C0; 403-762-4421, and Skiing Lake Louise Limited, Room 408, 1550 8th Street SW, Calgary, Alta. T2R 1K1; 403-256-8473.

For train fares and schedules, contact Blyth & Company, 68 Scollard St., Suite 300, Toronto, Ont. M5R 1G2; 416-964-2569, or Rocky Mountain Railtours, 625 Howe St., Suite 345, Vancouver, B.C. V6C 2T6; 800-665-RAIL in Canada and 800-627-6490 in the U.S.

BOOKS: Ben Gadd, *Handbook of the Canadian Rockies*. Jasper: Corax Press, 1986. Comprehensive field guide to the natural and human history of the mountain parks.

R. Kunelius and Dave Biederman, *Ski Trails in the Canadian Rockies*, rev. ed. Banff: Summerthought, 1981.

Brian Patton, *Parkways of the Canadian Rockies*. Banff: Summerthought, 1982. Guide to scenic drives in the four mountain parks, with excellent maps and photographs, along with natural and human history.

Brian Patton and Bart Robinson, *The Canadian Rockies Trail Guide*, rev. ed. Banff: Summerthought, 1986. The most comprehensive hiking guide to the region.

V. Spring and G. King, *95 Hikes in the Canadian Rockies*. Vancouver: Douglas & McIntyre, 1982.

OUTDOOR ACTIVITIES IN JASPER

More rugged and less developed than its neighboring preserves, Jasper is noted for wilderness backpacking, trail rides, and cross-country and downhill skiing. It is one of the few mountain parks with good fishing.

Scenic Drives

The northern half of the *Icefields Parkway* extends 67 mi/108 km between the Columbia Icefield on the Banff–Jasper boundary and Jasper townsite. The largest icefield in the Rockies at 130 sq mi/336 sq km, the Columbia Icefield feeds three major river systems—the Saskatchewan, the Athabasca, and the Columbia—and spawns eight major glaciers. Athabasca Glacier tumbles 4.5 mi/7 km from the frozen plateau, extending nearly to the parkway. This is one of the world's few glaciers accessible by car. A parking lot and ticket booth are across the highway from the glacier, adjacent to the Icefield Centre. Here, visitors board the Snocoach, a bus with oversize tires, for 90-minute tours to Athabasca's upper reaches, passing pressure ridges and crevasses to arrive at a triple icefall.

The parkway continues north 40 mi/65 km in the Sunwapta Valley to the junction with Highway 93A, a 15-mi/24-km alternate route. Here, spectacular Athabasca Falls thunders over a ragged ledge of Precambrian quartz sandstone 75 ft/23 m high, then hurtles through a narrow gorge.

About 11 mi/18 km north of the falls, a spur road switchbacks 9 mi/14.5 km southwest to the magnificent snow-covered dome of Mt. Edith Cavell, at 11,050 ft/3,368 m the highest peak in this part of the park. Named for a British nurse executed by the Germans in World War I, the mountain is set apart from all other peaks on the landscape by its pyramidal layers. Angel Glacier occupies a huge amphitheater in the great rock wall of Cavell's sheer north face and spills over a 1,000-ft/300-m cliff in spectacular icefalls. The road is open June to October.

Highway 93A rejoins the parkway 3 mi/5 km north of the Cavell turnoff. From there, it is 4.3 mi/7 km to the parkway's junction with the Yellowhead Highway (Highway 16) at Jasper townsite.

The *Maligne Lake Road*, which angles southwest from Jasper town, leads to a number of scenic highlights: Maligne Canyon; Medicine Lake, which is fed by the Maligne River but flows into the Athabasca via one of the world's largest underground rivers; and Maligne Lake, the Rockies' largest glacially fed body of water (17.2 mi/27.5 km long).

Covering 325 square kilometers, the Columbia Icefield is the Great Divide's largest chain of icefields, feeding eight glaciers.

Hiking

Jasper's trail system of more than 600 mi/1,000 km includes numerous nature walks and day hikes, especially in the vicinity of Jasper townsite and adjacent to the Icefields Parkway. A long, lone wilderness backpacking route ventures into the roadless northern half of the park. Until the 1970s, this remote country was well known only to park wardens and a handful of adventurous trail riders. Now, hundreds of hikers explore the North Boundary country each summer.

A popular short walk, the *Maligne Canyon Trail,* parallels the most spectacular limestone slit canyon in the mountain parks. Swirling, churning water has worn a twisting gorge more than 160 ft/50 m deep and only 7 ft/2 m wide in places. Most people drive up the Maligne Lake Road and start their walk from the teahouse at the head of the canyon, where there is an interpretive display. The footpath descends gradually, passing waterfalls, potholes, and unexpectedly lush plant life. Five footbridges span the gorge, which is deepest at the Second Bridge.

The *Valley of the Five Lakes Trail* makes a pleasant half-day stroll in the rolling hills southeast of Jasper townsite, where wapiti, mule deer, and coyote often are spotted. Beaver may show themselves in the slough near the trailhead off the Icefields Parkway 5.6 mi/9 km south of the Yellowhead Highway. From there, the nearly level route wanders northeast through open lodgepole pine forest, crosses a small stream, and climbs a low ridge with superb views southwest across the Athabasca Valley to Mt. Edith Cavell. From the top of the ridge the trail dips into the valley, with its five jade-colored, pond-size lakes, circles the largest lake at the north end of the valley, then loops southeast past the other four.

The *Cavell Meadows Trail,* a half-day alpine ramble, begins at the parking lot at the end of Edith Cavell Road and follows a paved path to a small lake formed by glacial meltwater. The Meadows route goes left at a fork in the trail and switchbacks up a lateral moraine, climbs through a sub-alpine forest, then emerges near the timberline to face awe-inspiring Mt. Edith Cavell and Angel Glacier. From this viewpoint, the trail loops even higher to alpine meadows ablaze with flowers from mid-July to late August, then descends to close the loop near the first viewpoint.

For a day-long outing to another exceptional panorama, head west from the parking lot at Maligne Lake on the 3.2-mi/5.2-km *Bald Hills Trail.* This former fire road climbs gradually through a fire succession forest of lodgepole pine, then scattered spruce, and finally pleasant open meadows and stands of stunted subalpine fir and Engelmann spruce. The trail ends atop the Bald Hills, a rolling ridgetop with 360-degree views. To the east are the turquoise waters of Maligne Lake, with Leah and Samson peaks looming beyond. To the northwest stand the rounded summits of the Maligne Range; to the north, the sawtooth peaks in the Elizabeth Range. To the south are wildflower meadows where mountain caribou occasionally are sighted and, beyond, glacier-clad Mounts Unwin and Charlton.

The 2.5-mi/4-km *Sulphur Skyline Trail*, a demanding but scenic half-day outing, begins at the Miette Hotsprings pool complex, then climbs steadily for 1.4 mi/2.2 km to Shuey Pass. Here the trail branches right and rises steeply to a ridge overlooking the hot-springs area. Southerly views embrace the remote, winding Fiddle River valley and pyramidal Utopia Mountain. Equally impressive views of wilderness valleys and mountains stretch to the north.

The 7-mi/11.2-km *Wilcox Pass Trail*, which epitomizes the finest in Jasper day hiking, leads to an alpine valley with spectacular views of the Columbia Icefield unavailable to car-bound travelers. From the Wilcox Creek campground just south of the Icefield Centre, the trail ascends steeply through mature alpine forest, then climbs more gradually to an open ridge overlooking the parkway. To the southwest are the scenic wonders straddling the Great Divide: mounts Athabasca, Andromeda, and Kitchener, Athabasca Glacier, the Snow Dome, and Dome Glacier. Here the trail levels, wandering north in a gradual ascent of a broad valley visited by bighorn sheep. Many hikers spend the entire day here amid mountain streams, marshes, turquoise tarns, and rolling meadows abloom in summer with fireweed and golden aster.

Among Jasper's splendid backcountry trails is the *Skyline Trail*, which rises and falls 27.5 mi/44 km along the ridges of the Maligne Range, a chain of rounded peaks southeast of Jasper townsite. The highest trail in the park, with more than half of its distance traveled above the tree line, the Skyline route wanders through wildflower meadows, past tumbling streams, and into areas abounding with alpine mammals, including mountain caribou. Because of the fragile nature of the terrain, use is controlled carefully by hiking quotas, which fill early in midsummer.

Northeast of Jasper townsite, the 108-mi/173-km *North Boundary Trail* passes through wilderness inhabited by moose, grizzly, black bear, and the largest wolf population in the mountain parks. The trail, which is usually hiked east to west, requires eight to 14 days to complete and provides the only access to Jasper's rugged northern half. From Celestine Lake, 27 mi/43 km east of Jasper townsite on the Yellowhead Highway and the Celestine Lake Road, the trail angles northeast on a fairly level fire

The most unpredictable and dangerous bear, the Grizzly puts on up to 400 pounds of fat in winter. This female is about three years old. OPPOSITE: *Morning finds a lone bull elk crossing the Athabasca River near Pyramid Lake, Jasper.*

road in the valley of the Snake Indian River. At Mi 13/Km 21, the river breaches a limestone cliff in a thundering waterfall. Beyond the falls the trail leaves the fire road and follows the valley's curve west toward the Great Divide, passing through open country dotted with stands of aspen and lodgepole pine.

One of the hike's most inspiring views occur at Mi 32/Km 52, where a small, unnamed lake reflects the jagged summit of Mt. Simla to the south. Nearby Blue Creek, which flows into the Snake from the northwest, marks the start of more serious mountain travel. At about Mi 43/Km 70, the route's first major glacier can be seen in the distance across the Snake River valley clinging to the slopes of Upright Mountain. At Mi 50/Km 80, site of the Hoodoo Warden Cabin, the climb to Snake Indian Pass begins, a moderate but steady uphill hike that breaks out of the trees in 3.7 mi/6 km for unobstructed views of the narrow pass straight ahead.

The pass (6,627 ft/2,020 m) is set in rolling alpine terrain. To the north steeply tilted slabs of limestone form the two most prominent peaks of the region—Snake Indian and Monte Cristo. From this pleasant summit the trail descends Twintree Creek, up and over the forested crest of Twintree Mountain and down into the rough and rocky Smoky River valley, where the scenery continues to improve. At Mi 87/Km 139, the trail travels beneath Mural Glacier as it begins its ascent of Robson Pass to the west. The long-awaited view of Mt. Robson, highest summit in the Canadian Rockies (12,972 ft/3,954 m), finally appears near Adolphus Lake.

At the Robson Provincial Park boundary (which is also the British Columbia boundary), hikers pass from relatively untrammeled territory to one of the busiest backcountry areas in the Rockies. The scenery is exceptional. For its final 14 mi/22 km, the North Boundary Trail follows Robson's *Berg Lake Trail,* ending at the Robson Service Center on Highway 16.

Climbing

Mt. Morro, about 12 mi/20 km northeast of Jasper townsite, is the most popular training area hereabouts. Short technical climbs on firm rock are done in the "Rock Garden" area of Maligne Canyon. More elaborate expeditions head for the Columbia Icefield region to tackle Mounts Kitchener, Athabasca, Andromeda, and Columbia, the last of which at 12,293 ft/3,747 m is the highest peak in Alberta. (Columbia was climbed first in 1902 by Swiss guide Christian Kaufmann and James Outram, an Englishman who took up mountaineering to cure what he called "brain collapse.") Ten or more routes with a full range of difficulty head up Athabasca and Andromeda, the most accessible snow and ice peaks in the icefield area. On Mt. Edith Cavell, the blocky east ridge is the highly recommended standard route. At least four routes line Cavell's extremely technical north face. In winter, ice climbers attempt the east face of the Snow Dome in the Columbia Icefield area and a 75-ft/23-m icefall in Maligne Canyon.

Horseback Riding

Jasper offers some of the most varied and interesting trail rides in western Canada. Privately operated stables include the Jasper Park Riding Academy (403-852-5794), which provides lessons and rides on the Jasper Park Lodge grounds as well as along trails surrounding the lodge, and Pyramid Riding Stables (403-852-3562) at Pyramid Lake. A number of outfitters organize extended backcountry trips. Popular outings include the *Tonquin Valley* southwest of Jasper townsite; the *Skyline Trail* in the Maligne Range between Wabasso and Maligne lakes; and the *Moosehorn Lake region* in the northeast corner of the park.

Boating

Rowboats and boats with small electric motors are allowed on most ponds and lakes. Motorboats are restricted to Pyramid Lake. Boat rentals are available at Pyramid, Patricia, Maligne, Beauvert, Edith, and Annette lakes. From June through September, Maligne Tours (403-852-3370) offers perennially popular two-hour boat cruises on Maligne Lake.

Kayaking

White water on the *Athasbasca River* from below Athabasca Falls to Old Fort Point near Jasper townsite provides an exciting two-day outing for experienced paddlers. Kayakers also tackle the *Maligne River* below Maligne Canyon.

Rafting

Jasper Raft Tours (403-852-3613) takes sightseers on half-day and full-day expeditions down the *Athabasca River*. For the more daring, White Water Rafting (403-852-7238) offers trips on the turbulent waters of the upper Athabasca River. Maligne River Adventurers (403-852-3370) organizes expeditions on the *Maligne River*.

Fishing

The park's most popular fishing spot is Maligne Lake, which yields record-size rainbow trout, as well as brook and lake trout. Amethyst and Patricia lakes and the pond-sized lakes in the Valley of the Five Lakes also contain trout. Tackle outlets are at Maligne and Pyramid lakes. Backpackers hike four hours southeast of Miette Hotsprings to trout-rich Mystery Lake just inside Jasper's eastern boundary. Several Jasper-based companies provide professional fishing guides.

Swimming

Lakes Annette, Edith, and Pyramid near Jasper townsite all have sandy beaches; Annette is the most popular, with water temperatures that may reach 68° F/20° C in July. The hottest thermal waters in the Canadian Rockies are at Miette Hotsprings, northeast of town. The sulfurous waters are cooled to 100° F/37° C and channeled into an outdoor pool, which is open in summer. Jasper townsite also has an indoor pool that operates year-round.

OVERLEAF: *Beneath Pyramid Mountain, scenic Pyramid Lake offers swimming and boating. Jasper National Park hosts one of the Rocky Mountains' last great wildlife ecosystems.*

Scuba Diving

The best diving east of the Rockies and west of the Great Lakes is in the cold-water lakes clustered in the Athabasca Valley near Jasper townsite. Lakes Annette, Edith, and Beauvert are fed by underground springs, which results in visibility of more than 65 ft/20 m. Rock gardens and lush aquatic vegetation are found in Annette. On the bottom of Patricia Lake are the remains of the *Habakkuk*, a barge built during World War II for esoteric experiments on the construction of ship hulls made of ice. There are no rental facilities in the park. Divers should come equipped, or rent equipment from sports shops in Edmonton or Calgary.

Downhill Skiing

Privately operated Marmot Basin (403-825-3816) 12 mi/19 km south of Jasper townsite has 48 runs through alpine bowls and along tree-lined trails, seven lifts, and 2,300 ft/700 m of vertical elevation. Ski season extends from early December to mid-April.

Cross-country Skiing

Four areas have groomed nordic trails. When there is adequate snowfall, moderately difficult loops are set in the *Pyramid Bench* area on the outskirts of Jasper townsite, and a single trail through *Whistlers campground* is illuminated for night skiing. Trails on the *Jasper Park Lodge* grounds are open to the public. The *Athabasca Falls–Whirlpool* area south of Jasper townsite has trails ranging from easy to moderate. The most extensive trail system is around *Maligne Lake*, where mountain goats can be seen in their winter range on Mt. Leah across the lake from the Upper Moose Lake Loop. Caribou appear in open subalpine forest along the Evelyn Creek Loop. The *Bald Hills Trail* attracts telemarking and ski-touring enthusiasts. March through May are popular months for parties to climb the Columbia Icefield's summits on telemark skis or alpine touring gear. Ski mountaineering objectives include Castleguard, Columbia, Snow Dome, Kitchener, East and West Stutfield, and North Twin.

Other Activities

The *tennis* courts and the 18-hole *golf* course at Jasper Park Lodge are open to nonguests (403-852-3301 for reservations). Golfing hazards include Canada geese, coyotes, and wapiti. (A bull moose once took over a water hazard on the tenth hole for two months.) The town of Jasper also maintains indoor and outdoor tennis courts.

EXPLORING JASPER

The town of Jasper, a resort community with a full range of visitor facilities and home of park headquarters, is 230 mi/370 km west of Edmonton, Alberta, via the Yellowhead Highway (Highway 16). Many motorists drive north into Jasper National Park from Banff National Park via the Icefields Parkway (Highway 93). The nearest airports are at Edmonton and Calgary, 256 mi/412 km southeast.

VIA Rail's transcontinental train stops three times a week in Jasper. VIA has 12 regional toll-free information lines throughout North America; check directory assistance. The *Rocky Mountaineer* also stops on its weekly run from Vancouver (604-683-5811). Greyhound Lines (403-421-4211) operates daily scheduled service from Edmonton and a number of British Columbia cities; flag stops can be arranged along the Yellowhead Highway for travelers to the park. Brewster Transportation (403-852-3332) has daily bus service between Calgary International Airport and Jasper, traveling via Banff, Lake Louise, and the Icefields Parkway. Marmot Basin (403-424-8834) offers daily summer bus service from Edmonton during ski season.

The information center at park headquarters, open year-round, is housed in a rustic fieldstone structure. Topographical hiking maps are available here. The Icefield Centre (403-762-2241), open from May to September, has exhibits and slide presentations. Jasper's interpretive program includes guidied hikes; evening slide shows at Wapiti and Whistlers campgrounds; and campfire talks at Wilcox Creek, Wabasso, Honeymoon Lake, and Pocahontas campgrounds.

Permits for backcountry travel, fishing licenses, and grazing permits for trail riders are available in summer at the Jasper and Icefield information centers. Fishing licenses can also be purchased from sports shops. Hikers are permitted to reserve up to 35 percent of the sites at wilderness campgrounds as much as 21 days in advance; bookings can be made at the trail office in Jasper town by writing the superintendent, or by phoning the trail office (403-852-6177). The rest of the sites are taken on a first come, first served basis. In winter, backcountry camping permits are distributed at the park warden headquarters along the Maligne Road and the Sunwapta warden station.

From April to October, the privately operated Jasper Tramway (403-852-3093) whisks passengers to barren alpine tundra near the top of The Whistlers (8,103 ft/2,470 m), just south of Jasper townsite. From the upper terminal, a two-hour trail leads to the summit of the peak, which is named for the distinctive call of the resident hoary marmots.

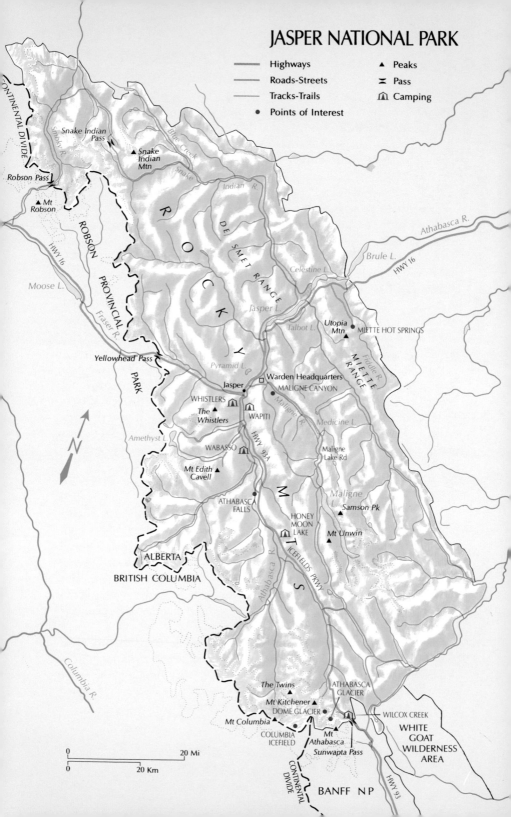

JASPER NATIONAL PARK

Highways
Roads-Streets
Tracks-Trails
● Points of Interest

▲ Peaks
✕ Pass
⌂ Camping

CONTINENTAL DIVIDE

Snake Indian Pass

Smoky R.

▲ Snake Indian Mtn

Blue Creek

Snake Indian R.

Robson Pass

▲ Mt Robson

ROBSON

HWY 16

Moose L.

Celestine L.

Brule L.

Athabasca R.

HWY 16

PROVINCIAL

Fraser R.

R
O
C
K
Y

DE SMET RANGE

Jasper L.

Talbot L.

Utopia Mtn ▲

MIETTE HOT SPRINGS

PARK

Yellowhead Pass

Pyramid L.

Jasper

Warden Headquarters

MALIGNE CANYON

MIETTE RANGE

Fiddle R.

WHISTLERS

The Whistlers ▲

WAPITI

Maligne R.

Medicine L.

Amethyst L.

WABASSO

HWY 93A

Maligne Lake Rd

Mt Edith Cavell ▲

M
T
S

ATHABASCA FALLS

Maligne L.

Samson Pk ▲

HONEY MOON LAKE

Mt Unwin ▲

ALBERTA

BRITISH COLUMBIA

Athabasca R.

ICEFIELDS PKWY

Columbia R.

The Twins ▲

ATHABASCA GLACIER

Mt Kitchener ▲

DOME GLACIER

WILCOX CREEK

Mt Columbia ▲

Mt Athabasca ▲

WHITE GOAT WILDERNESS AREA

COLUMBIA ICEFIELD

Sunwapta Pass

CONTINENTAL DIVIDE

HWY 93

BANFF N P

0   20 Mi

0   20 Km

ACCOMMODATIONS: Two full-service campgrounds are south of Jasper townsite: Whistlers (781 sites) and Wapiti (340 sites). More limited services for car-based travelers are at Pocahontas campground (140 sites) near Miette Hotsprings and Wabasso campground (238 sites), south of Jasper town on the Icefields Parkway. Nine smaller campgrounds are scattered around the park, mostly south of the townsite. Campgrounds are open from mid-May to mid-October. Some sites in Wapiti also remain open for winter camping.

The most noteworthy of the park's abundant commercial accommodations is Jasper Park Lodge (Box 40, Jasper, Alta. T0E 1E0; 403-852-3301), a rustic 400-room counterpart to the Banff Springs Hotel, now open year-round. Log chalets are set in the woods around the low-slung, glass-and-stone main lodge. Canoes, kayaks, paddleboats, and sailboats are provided free to guests and may be rented by nonguests.

ADDRESSES: For more information, write or phone: The Superintendent, Jasper National Park, Box 10, Jasper, Alta. T0E 1E0; 403-852-6161. For information on accommodations and other commercial tourist facilities, write or phone: Jasper Chamber of Commerce, Box 98, Jasper, Alta. T0E 1E0; 403-852-3858.

OUTDOOR ACTIVITIES IN KOOTENAY

This reserve extends roughly 5 mi/8 km on each side of the 65-mi/105-km Kootenay Parkway, which passes scenic and geologic points of interest along its entire length. More than 20 nature trails and hikes begin at the parkway, leading to glaciers, lakes, and alpine meadows.

Scenic Drive

The *Kootenay Parkway* (Highway 93), the first road to cross the central Rockies (1923), is one of the prettiest routes in the mountain parks. It branches off the Trans-Canada Highway at Castle Junction in Banff National Park, then heads 7 mi/11 km southwest, climbing to Vermilion Pass on the Continental Divide, where it enters British Columbia and Kootenay National Park.

At Mi 10.7/Km 17.2 is the narrow gorge of Marble Canyon, its walls of gray limestone and quartzite shot with layers of white and grayish dolomite; 1.5 mi/2.5 km beyond are the ocher beds of the Paint Pots, a series of mineral-rich cold springs. The road then angles southeast alongside the Vermilion River. To the west looms the Rockwall, a sheer limestone escarpment of the Vermilion Range on the park's western boundary. At

Mi 30.3/Km 48.6, just north of Wardle Creek, a roadside mineral lick attracts moose, wapiti, and deer at dawn and dusk in summer. Mountain goats often are seen on Mt. Wardle, 4.7 mi/7.6 km south.

At Mi 42/Km 68, the parkway enters the valley of the Kootenay River and passes through a prime wapiti grazing area, especially in early summer and autumn. South of Mi 48/Km 77 south, the typical moist Rocky Mountain subalpine forest gives way to the drier, patchy Douglas-fir forest of the British Columbia interior.

The parkway's most expansive views are at the Kootenay Valley Viewpoint (Mi 55.3/Km 88.5). Here, the parkway leaves the river and heads southwest. The 6-mi/10-km section between Sinclair Pass (Mi 57.4/Km 91.9) and the Aquacourt is especially beautiful. Sinclair Creek tumbles alongside the parkway, nurturing stands of western redcedar in moist, shady sections; fireweed brightens sunny stretches. The road passes through the Iron Gates, the first of the towering red sandstone cliffs of Sinclair Canyon, and ends at the town of Radium, just outside the park's southwestern corner on the banks of the Columbia River.

Hiking

More than 125 mi/200 km of trails include half-day and day hikes from the parkway and scenic backpacking trails in the park's northwestern corner.

The short *Marble Canyon Nature Trail* follows a fault in limestone and marble rock up to 120 ft/36 m deep. The trail bridges the narrow gorge in several places, providing dizzying views into the depths below, where Tokumm Creek froths in a cool, misty grotto. At the head of the canyon, glacier-ground rock particles suspended in the water give a 70-ft/21-m waterfall a milky color.

The nearby *Paint Pots Trail* leads to three ponds stained bright red and yellow by the iron oxide in the springs that feed them. Over the years iron deposits have built up in layered rings, creating a caldron with raised edges. Inside, green water wells up and spills down the hillside in streams of bright rust. Kootenai and Stoney Indians used the ocher muds here to make pigments for war paint, pictographs, and tepee decorations, fearing and revering a place they believed was ruled by the thunder spirit.

The most scenic of three family-oriented nature trails exploring Sinclair Canyon near the hot springs is the *Juniper Trail*, which starts just inside the Kootenay Park West Gate, descends to Sinclair Creek, then switchbacks up to the rim of Sinclair Canyon, where there are views to the west of the Columbia River Valley and the Purcell Mountains.

In the northeastern corner of the park, the *Stanley Glacier Trail* is an easy half-day hike into a lovely valley backed by the retreating ice of Stanley Glacier. In spring and early summer the trail is fringed from beginning to end with fireweed, yellow columbine, and arnica. The rocky amphitheater cradling the glacier abounds with hoary marmots, pikas, and white-tailed ptarmigans.

The 9.3-mi/15-km *Kaufmann Lake Trail*, one of Kootenay's most rewarding backpacking trips, picks up where the Marble Canyon Nature Trail leaves off. It runs northwest along an old access road, then turns into a footpath through dense subalpine forest. Just beyond Mi 1.8/Km 3, the trail reaches open meadows in Prospector's Valley alongside rushing Tokumm Creek. A steep climb at the head of the valley leads to Kaufmann Lake, a turquoise beauty cradled by the glacier-mantled Wenkchemna Peaks. Mule deer occasionally browse here in meadows of yellow columbine, red Indian paintbrush, white fringed grass-of-parnassus, and purple asters. There are two lakeside campsites.

The 33.7-mi/54-km *Rockwall Trail*, which parallels the park's northwest boundary, is one of the most popular wilderness backpacking trips in the Canadian Rockies. It rises and falls like a roller coaster, ascending three passes and plunging into three valleys as it travels beneath a massive limestone rampart of the Vermilion Range known as the Rockwall. Most hikers take at least two days to complete the route, beginning with a 6.5-mi/10.5-km hike southeast from the parkway up Floe Creek to Floe Lake, a pale blue gem fed by small glaciers. Camping is available at the lake.

Here the Rockwall Trail proper starts, angling northwest up to Numa Pass, then down into Numa Valley and its campground. (Hikers who prefer an abbreviated version of the trip return to the parkway here on a spur trail that heads northeast down the Numa Creek Valley.) The main trail continues northwest, rising to Tumbling Pass beneath Tumbling Glacier and descending to Tumbling Creek, where there is a campground. From here another spur trail angles northeast to the parkway via the Tumbling Creek and Paint Pots trails.

From Tumbling Creek, the main trail continues northwest to a campground, then up Rockwall Pass beneath Mt. Drysdale and past the vast Washmawapta Glacier on the west. The route ends at the Helmet Falls campground, where a 9.3-mi/15-km trail angles east to join *Ottertail Trail*, which leads back to the parkway.

Climbing

Popular summits in the northern third of the park include Deltaform Peak (11,233 ft/3,424 m), which is part of Banff's Valley of the Ten Peaks; Mt. Foster (10,610 ft/3,234 m); Stanley Peak (10,351 ft/3,155 m); Tumbling Peak; and Mt. Allen.

Horseback Riding

Horses are permitted on all park trails except self-guiding nature trails. Overnight camping and grazing are allowed at Helmet Falls and along the Verdant Creek Trail. No commercial outfitters operate in the park.

Canoeing

Easy access, numerous rapids, and fine scenery make the *Vermilion–Kootenay river system* excellent for experienced canoeists. The 105-mi/168-km route, which is run from late May through September, is usually divided into three sections, or reaches. The put-in for the 54-mi/87-km *Park Reach* is at Vermilion Crossing on the Kootenay Parkway. En route to the Settler's Road bridge at Kootenay's southern boundary is Hector Gorge, where a set of rapids varies in difficulty from Class IV at high water to Class III at medium water. The McLeod Meadows campground, the only place where canoe camping is permitted in the park, is at Mi 34/Km 55.

The *Canyon Reach*, which extends 30 mi/49 km from Settler's Road bridge south to the confluence of the Kootenay and White rivers, has the finest scenery along the waterway. Here the river has carved beautiful steep-walled canyons through soft shale and glacial outwash. The numerous rapids, which range from Class I to III, can be run with care in an open canoe. Since the river flows through provincial land south of the park, wilderness camping is allowed at any suitable site.

The Kootenai Indians used the Paint Pots' mineral-rich ocher beds as a source for their decorative vermilion paint.

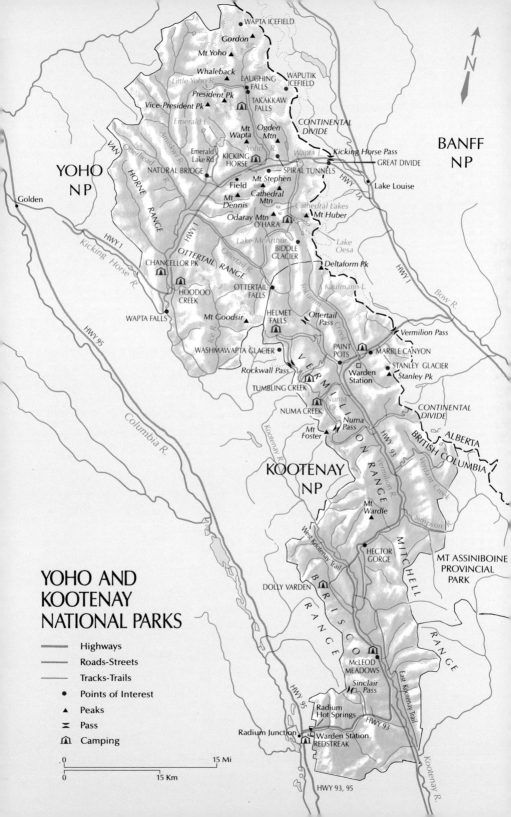

WAPTA ICEFIELD
Gordon ▲
Mt Yoho ▲
Whaleback ▲
Little Yoho R. LAUGHING FALLS
President Pk ▲
Vice-President Pk ▲ TAKAKKAW FALLS
Emerald L.
Mt Wapta ▲
Ogden Mtn ▲
WAPUTIK ICEFIELD
CONTINENTAL DIVIDE
Emerald Lake Rd
KICKING HORSE
Yoho R.
Wapta L. Kicking Horse Pass
GREAT DIVIDE
SPIRAL TUNNELS
Mt Stephen ▲
Field ●
Mt Dennis ▲ Cathedral Mtn ▲
Odaray Mtn ▲ O'HARA
Cathedral Lakes
Mt Huber ▲
HWY 1A
Lake Louise ●

BANFF NP

YOHO NP

Golden ●

Otterhead R. *Amiskwi R.*
HORNE RANGE
NATURAL BRIDGE
HWY 1
Kicking Horse R.
HWY 1
OTTERTAIL RANGE
Ottertail R.
Lake McArthur
Tokumm
BIDDLE GLACIER
Lake Oesa
Deltaform Pk ▲
Kaufmann L.
Bow R.
HWY 1

CHANCELLOR PK
HOODOO CREEK
OTTERTAIL FALLS
WAPTA FALLS
Mt Goodsir ▲
Ice R.
HELMET FALLS
WASHMAWAPTA GLACIER ●
Rockwall Pass
TUMBLING CREEK
Ottertail Pass
Ottertail Creek
PAINT POTS
Vermilion Pass
MARBLE CANYON
STANLEY GLACIER
Warden Station
Stanley Pk ▲
CONTINENTAL DIVIDE
ALBERTA
BRITISH COLUMBIA

HWY 95
Columbia R.
Kootenay R.
VERMILION RANGE
Numa Cr.
NUMA CREEK
Mt Foster ▲
Numa Pass
Vermilion R.
Verdant Creek
Simpson R.

KOOTENAY NP

Mt Wardle ▲
HWY 93
MITCHELL RANGE
MT ASSINIBOINE PROVINCIAL PARK

West Kootenay Trail
HECTOR GORGE
DOLLY VARDEN
BRISCO RANGE
RANGE
East Kootenay Trail

YOHO AND KOOTENAY NATIONAL PARKS

McLEOD MEADOWS
Sinclair Pass
Radium Hot Springs
Warden Station REDSTREAK
HWY 93
Radium Junction
Kootenay R.
HWY 93, 95

— Highways
— Roads-Streets
— Tracks-Trails
● Points of Interest
▲ Peaks
≍ Pass
⌂ Camping

0   15 Mi
0   15 Km

N

The 24-mi/38-km *White River Reach* extends from the White River bridge to Canal Flats, where the Kootenay flows into the Columbia River. The canoeing is tamer on this section of the river, but the scenery is still spectacular as the river cuts through the westernmost ranges of the Rocky Mountains and enters the Rocky Mountain Trench. One highlight is 80-ft/25-m Pedley Falls.

Rafting

Kootenay River Runners (604-347-9210) conducts excursions on the *Kootenay River* from the park's southern boundary toward the White River.

Fishing

Dolly Varden, kokanee salmon, mountain whitefish, and trout (cutthroat, rainbow, and brook) are found in the Kootenay, Vermilion, and Simpson rivers, and Cobb, Dog, Kaufmann, and Floe lakes.

Swimming

The mineral content of the water at the Radium Hot Springs Aquacourt is similar to that of thermal waters in Bath, England, and Baden-Baden, Germany. The odorless water is as radioactive as a luminous watch dial. Fed by mineral springs heated by rock deep in the earth's crust, the Aquacourt's hot pool (104° F/40° C) is excellent for soaking; a cooler pool (80° F/27° C) is more suitable for swimming. Both pools are outdoors and open year-round.

Golf

The privately owned Best Western Radium Resort has a public 18-hole course, as well as indoor swimming and racquetball, squash, and tennis courts (Box 310, Radium Hot Springs, B.C. V0A 1M0; 604-347-9311). The Springs Golf Resort, also privately owned and open to the public, is one of the most challenging 18-hole courses in Canada (604-347-6444).

Winter Activities

Conditions for *cross-country skiing* are excellent from mid-December to the end of March in the southern part of the park, especially along the *East and West Kootenay fire roads*. Two groomed trails circle the Redstreak campground, a 1.6-mi/2.6-km loop and a 1-mi/1.6-km loop. The longer loop joins up with a 3-mi/5-km trail on the Radium Resort golf course. *Snowshoeing* sport is done on backcountry trails in the northern half of the park. Snowshoers must check avalanche conditions at information offices.

ACCOMMODATIONS: There are three campgrounds: Redstreak campground in a forested setting near Radium Hot Springs (242 sites); McLeod Meadows (98 sites) along the Kootenay River 16 mi/26 km north of Radium in a good area for seeing moose, wapiti, and deer; and tranquil Marble Canyon (61 sites) near the northern park boundary. The campgrounds are open from mid-May to mid-September. In addition, there are 11 backcountry campsites scattered throughout the park; the largest and most heavily used is at Floe Lake (18 sites). Reservations for backcountry camping can be made 21 days in advance in summer by phoning the West Gate Information Centre (604-347-9505) and in other seasons by writing or phoning the Park Superintendent. Winter camping is at Dolly Varden picnic area, 23 mi/37 km north of Radium.

Private accommodation is available at Vermilion Crossing, Radium Hot Springs, and private campgrounds on Highway 95.

ADDRESSES: For more information, write or phone: The Superintendent, Kootenay National Park, Box 220, Radium Hot Springs, B.C. V0A 1M0; 604-347-9615.

For information on private facilities in and near the park, write or phone the B.C. Rocky Mountain Visitors Association, Box 10, Kimberley, B.C. V1A 2Y5; 604-427-4838.

EXPLORING KOOTENAY

Radium, British Columbia, at the southern end of Kootenay Park, is the site of park headquarters. The town has a full range of tourist facilities. Information centers are located there at the West Gate, as well as at Marble Canyon in the north end of the park.

The Kootenay Parkway (Highway 93) provides the only access by road to Kootenay. Greyhound buses stop at Radium daily (for information and schedules, phone 604-426-3331). The nearest major airports are at Calgary (160 mi/99 km east) and Cranbrook, 100 mi/160 km south of Radium.

The park's interpretive program includes talks and slide shows presented during July and August at the Redstreak, McLeod, and Marble Canyon campgrounds. Naturalists conduct five-hour field trips to Stanley Glacier, as well as other points of interest. Park staff at information centers distribute permits for backcountry camping, fishing, and horse grazing, as well as topographic trail maps, paddlers' guides, and fishing maps pinpointing prime angling spots.

Yoho's Kicking Horse River was named after an explorer's unruly mount. A few miles below Emerald Lake along its course, torrents have sculpted a flat-rock natural bridge across the river.

OUTDOOR ACTIVITIES IN YOHO

Yoho richly deserves its Cree name signifying wonder, amazement, and awe. This reaction is provoked by the rushing Kicking Horse River, the Takakkaw and Wapta falls, and the frozen beauty of the Wapta and Waputik icefields. In Yoho's eastern half, chiseled peaks of the Eastern Main Ranges of the Rockies soar upwards of 10,000 ft/3,000 m to form a section of the Continental Divide.

Scenic Drives

The westbound Yoho section of the *Trans-Canada Highway* angles through the center of the park in northeast–southwest direction. The road crests Kicking Horse Pass, then hurtles down the valley of the Kicking Horse River on part of the original CPR roadbed, dropping 1,300 ft/400 m in only 6 mi/9.6 km. In 1909, the CPR constructed two spiral tunnels on "The Big Hill" to halve this steep grade. The entrances to the Ogden Mountain tunnel can be seen from a viewpoint at Mi 5.5/Km 8.9.

At Mi 7.8/Km 12.6, the *Yoho Valley Road* leads north of the Trans-Canada to an exhibit on the Burgess Shales and the Kicking Horse River campground. From the exhibit are views to the south of the Cathedral Mountain tunnel and spectacular Mt. Stephen (10,495 ft/3,199 m), one of the most imposing peaks in the Rockies. North of the campground is an overlook above the Meeting of the Waters, where the torrential, glacier-fed Kicking Horse and Yoho rivers join in thundering union. Two tight switchbacks lift the road high above the valley floor as it heads north to Takakkaw Falls, Canada's third highest at 1,260 ft/384 m (*takakkaw* is a Cree word meaning "it is magnificent"). Here, meltwaters from Daly Glacier plunge over the lip of a hanging valley to the floor of the Yoho Valley.

Back on the Trans-Canada, just southwest of Field, the *Emerald Lake Road* heads 5 mi/8 km north past the broken arch of a natural bridge to striking blue-green Emerald Lake at the foot of the President Range.

Hiking

Yoho's 250 mi/400 km of trails extend into nearly every corner of the park. Popular nature trails are scattered along the Trans-Canada Highway. The 1.9-mi/3.1-km *Hoodoos Trail* in southwestern Yoho climbs steeply from the Hoodoo Creek campground into a narrow valley where a mountainside is covered with hoodoos—sentinel-like pillars of silt and gravel capped by erosion-resistant rock.

About 1 mi/1.6 km west on the Trans-Canada, motorists drive a short distance south of the highway on the Wapta Falls access road. From the parking lot, 45 minutes of nearly level walking on the *Wapta Falls Trail*

Wildlife commonly found in the Rockies include the willow ptarmigan (left), a member of the grouse family, and the ermine (right), a swift predator of mice and shrews.

leads to a viewpoint above a wide, 100-ft/30-m cataract on a bend in the Kicking Horse River. A side trail descends steeply to a lower viewpoint near the base of the falls.

Yoho's most popular day hikes are around Lake O'Hara at the eastern edge of the park. Within a 3-mi/5-km radius of the central campground and lodge are 25 small lakes and some of the highest and most rugged peaks in the Rockies. An extensive and well-maintained trail system built over the last half-century leads to five distinct destinations. Quotas control the number of hikers.

The most popular route, the 2-mi/3.2-km *Lake Oesa Trail*, climbs steeply above O'Hara's eastern shore, ascends a series of rock terraces occupied by three small lakes, and ends at a high, barren cirque containing Lake Oesa. Sometimes frozen year-round, the turquoise tarn has the towering spine of the Great Divide for a backdrop. Surrounding talus slopes, rockslides, and moraines abound with pikas and hoary marmots.

The *Opabin Plateau Circuit* loops 3.3 mi/5.3 km southeast of Lake O'Hara to a beautiful hanging valley with flower-filled meadows, stands of alpine larch, and numerous turquoise tarns. The *Lake McArthur Trail* winds 2.2 mi/3.5 km south to the region's largest lake. McArthur's deep blue waters contrast strikingly with the white of Biddle Glacier, the green of sparse subalpine vegetation, and the tan of surrounding rock bluffs—a juxtaposition that has made the lake a longtime favorite of artists and photographers.

The *Odaray Plateau Trail* cuts through Alpine Meadow west of Lake O'Hara, then climbs steeply through subalpine forest. At Mi 0.9/Km 1.4, the trail to Odaray Prospect branches right and angles northwest to a junction at Mi 1.4/Km 2.2. There, it turns left (southwest) and climbs another 10 minutes to the prospect. The rewards for this short but steep hike are panoramas of Morning Glory Lake and Cathedral Mountain to the north and Odaray Mountain to the northwest. The trail leads south across the flower-filled meadows of Odaray Plateau, where the turquoise waters of Lake O'Hara can be seen far below through scattered larches, then returns east to the Alpine Meadow.

The *Linda Lake–Cathedral Basin Trail*, longest and least crowded of the spokes radiating out from Lake O'Hara, usually takes a full day to complete. From the O'Hara campground, the trail heads north through forest to a junction with a trail running west from the access road. Keep left and follow this trail west to Linda Lake, and there take the lakeside trail (a right turn) to the north shore, where there are views south to Yukness Mountain and east to the Great Divide.

This outing is sufficiently diverting for many hikers. Others, however, follow a trail that angles steeply northwest through subalpine forest dotted with meadows. The route crosses a bridge between the first and second Cathedral lakes, then begins a steep northeastern ascent across a rockslide to the mouth of Cathedral Basin. Here, at the lip of a cirque high on the side of Cathedral Mountain, the area's full glory is laid at the hiker's feet—the Duchesnay Valley to the southeast and, beyond, Lake O'Hara at the foot of the Great Divide.

The exceptionally beautiful Yoho Valley, northwest of Lake O'Hara on the other side of the Trans-Canada, has attracted hikers and climbers since the 1890s. The CPR and the Alpine Club of Canada constructed the valley's extensive trail system, which connects with routes from the Emerald Lake area to the south. The most direct access is from the Takakkaw Falls parking area at the end of the Yoho Valley Road. This area has no quotas, so its trails are always available to those who can't get into Lake O'Hara.

The most frequently hiked route, to *Twin Falls*, is relatively flat throughout much of its 5.3-mi/8.5-km distance to the head of the valley. From the Takakkaw Falls parking area, this day trip heads north in a pine and spruce forest, passing three waterfalls—Angel's Staircase, Point Lace, and Laughing falls—before ending at the Twin Falls Chalet, where a double cataract plunges 262 ft/80 m.

From Twin Falls Chalet, the 4.1-mi/6.6-km *Whaleback Trail* switchbacks up the cliff over which Twin Falls leaps. At the top, the trail descends to turbulent Twin Falls Creek and Whaleback campground, which occupies a spectacular setting on a rock ledge near the brink of the falls. From the campground, the trail heads southeast near the tree line across the flank of the Whaleback—a route with breathtaking views of Yoho Glacier and Glacier des Poilus. The route reaches its highest elevation at Mi 2.8/Km 4.5, where views open up of the Yoho Valley to the east and Little Yoho Valley to the south. The route then descends to the Little Yoho River and a T-junction. A right turn takes hikers west up the Little Yoho River valley, a prime backpacking area. A left turn leads east back down to Twin Falls.

The 6.9-mi/11.1-km *Iceline Trail*, the highest and newest hike in the Yoho Valley and one of the most spectacular, replaces the environmentally damaged Highline–Skyline trail system, once one of the most popular in the park. From the Whiskey Jack Hostel near Takakkaw Falls, the Iceline Trail switchbacks southwest up open avalanche slopes, passes through mature spruce forest, then emerges high upslope on the rubbled moraines of Emerald Glacier, which looms above on the flanks of The Vice-President. From there, the route trends northwest, constantly climbing and dropping,

The massive Yoho Glacier, part of a large icefield in northern Yoho National Park. Lying on the western side of the Great Divide and receiving more snow than the other

crossing moraines and unbridged meltwater streams. Hiking on these rock piles is tiring, but superlative views provide ample rewards. Because of its high altitude, the route is more susceptible to snowfalls than other trails in the area; expect snow patches most of the summer.

At the halfway point, a connector trail heads downslope to Lake Celeste. The Iceline soon drops steeply to the Little Yoho River, which it follows upstream to a bridge. Just on the other side of the river are the Little Yoho campground and the Stanley Mitchell hut, operated by the Alpine Club of Canada. Most hikers return to the hostel and Takakkaw Falls by walking east on the *Little Yoho River Trail* and south on the Twin Falls Trail.

Mountain Biking

Routes include the following fire roads: *Amiskwi River Valley* (up to Mi 15/Km 24); the *Kicking Horse* (12 mi/20 km); the *Ottertail* up to the warden's cabin (9 mi/15 km); the *Otterhead* from its junction with the Kicking

Rocky Mountain parks, Yoho was appropriately named for a Cree word signifying amazement, wonder, and awe.

Horse fire road to the Tocher Ridge junction (5 mi/8 km); the *Ice River* to the lower warden's cabin (11 mi/18 km); and the *Tallyho Road* just west of Field to its junction with the Emerald Lake Road (2 mi/3 km).

Climbing

This is one of the most popular activities in the park. A number of challenging summits surround Lake O'Hara: Mt. Victoria (11,365 ft/3,464 m); Mt. Huber (11,050 ft/3,368 m); Mt. Lefroy (11,230 ft/3,423 m); Mt. Ringrose (10,764 ft/3,281 m); and Mt. Hungabee (11,457 ft/3,492 m).

The President Range near Emerald Lake, a group of heavily glaciated peaks, has been a popular climbing area for nearly a century. British alpinist Edward Whymper, the first to climb the Matterhorn, visited here in 1901. Access is via the Little Yoho Valley. Mt. Stephen and Mt. Wapta near Field also attract alpinists. Waterfall ice climbers head for frozen Takakkaw Falls and icefalls on the lower slopes of Mounts Stephen and Dennis.

Horseback Riding

Horses may be rented at Emerald Lake from Banff-based Holiday on Horseback (403-762-4551). A popular ride is the 4.8-mi/7.7-km *Emerald River Trail* from Emerald Lake south down to near the Amiskwi River Picnic Area about 4 mi/6.5 km west of Field.

Rafting

There is no rafting within the park, but the *Kicking Horse River* below Yoho is one of the most popular rafting rivers in British Columbia, with Class III and IV whitewater. An 18-ft/5.5-m ledge at Portage Rapids is the highlight of day-long outings between the western park boundary and Golden, offered by Glacier Raft Company (604-344-6521) and Alpine Rafting Company (604-344-5016). High season is usually mid-June to early July.

Cross-country Skiing

Conditions for *nordic skiing* are excellent from December to mid-April. Track is set on the *Emerald Lake Trail*, the *Wapta Falls Trail*, the *Kicking Horse fire road* (3.7 mi/6 km), the *Yoho Valley Road*, the *Lake O'Hara Road*, the *Tallyho Road*, and the 17-mi/27-km stretch of *Highway 1A* between Lake Louise and Lake O'Hara, which is closed to traffic in winter. Most of the skiing in the Lake O'Hara area, where avalanche conditions may exist, is in the intermediate to advanced level.

Three- to five-day *ski mountaineering* traverses of the *Wapta and Waputik* icefields usually start in Banff National Park and end in Yoho. The Alpine Club of Canada maintains several huts along the way. The *Presidential Range* is also popular for this activity.

EXPLORING YOHO

Highway access is via the Trans-Canada. The town of Field, located in the center of the park, is a flag stop for Greyhound buses and is park headquarters. Limited tourist facilities are available. More extensive travel services are in Golden, 33 mi/54 km west, and in Banff, 50 mi/80 km east.

The park's information center, beside the Trans-Canada Highway at the western entrance to Field, has interpretive exhibits, a book and map store, and a picnic area.

Hikers and mountain climbers overnighting in the backcountry must register at the information center or with wardens. Since major campgrounds have quotas, popular areas often are filled during peak season;

travelers should consider alternative campsites. Detailed hiking maps produced by the Lake O'Hara Trails Club are sold at Lake O'Hara Lodge, at the day-use shelter there, as well as at the information center.

Detailed descriptions of mountain-climbing routes are available at the information center and at the warden's office in the Boulder Creek Compound. Local guides for mountain climbing and mountain ski touring can be contacted through the Association of Canadian Mountain Guides, Box 519, Canmore, Alta. T0L 0M0; 403-678-2885.

The interpretive program consists of evening slide shows in outdoor theaters at Kicking Horse and Hoodoo Creek campgrounds; campfire talks at Chancellor Peak campground; and guided hikes to such points of interest as the Burgess Shale fossil beds. The number of participants in the fossil walk is limited to 15; reservations can be made up to three weeks in advance. Some of the finest fossils are displayed in a diorama at the information center. On the most popular interpretive program in the mountain parks—the Spiral Tunnels—visitors walk atop a re-created train trestle to a viewpoint where trains can be seen entering and exiting the tunnels.

ACCOMMODATIONS: Three campgrounds are accessible by car: busy Kicking Horse near Field (92 sites); peaceful, wooded Hoodoo Creek (106 sites); and Chancellor Peak (64 sites) alongside the Kicking Horse River (pick a site close to the river and as far away from the busy CPR tracks as possible). Takakkaw Falls (35 sites) is a short hike from the end of the Yoho Valley Road. Lake O'Hara (30 sites) is a 7-mi/11-km hike on a gravel access road or on the Cataract Brook Trail. People with reservations for Lake O'Hara Lodge, the Abbot Pass and Elizabeth Parker huts (both operated by the Alpine Club of Canada), or the O'Hara campground can ride to the lake on a private bus that runs three times daily in summer. The bus can also carry up to 26 day-trippers.

Maximum stay is four days at O'Hara and seven backcountry campsites. Reservations for Lake O'Hara as well as for backcountry campgrounds can be made up to one month in advance by calling the park office (604-343-6433). Winter camping is at the Kicking Horse campground overflow area on the Yoho Valley Road just north of the Trans-Canada.

Two huts are operated by the Alpine Club of Canada: the 24-person Elizabeth Parker hut in the Alpine Meadow west of Lake O'Hara, and the 30-person Stanley Mitchell hut near the head of the Little Yoho Valley.

Built by the CPR in the early 1920s, Lake O'Hara Lodge (from June to October—Box 55, Lake Louise, Alta. T0L 1E0; 604-343-6418; from October to June—Box 1677, Banff, Alta. T0L 0C0; 403-762-2118) is perhaps the most exclusive retreat in the Canadian Rockies. In addition to the main lodge perched on a knoll above the lake, there are one-room shoreline log cabins and cedar-log "Panaview Cabins" on a shelf of land overlooking the lake and Seven Veils Falls. The lodge is open year-round, except for brief closings in fall and early winter. Winter guests ski or snowshoe in from the access road parking lot. In summer, guests and visitors can explore the lake in rented canoes.

The West Louise Lodge (Box 9, Lake Louise, Alta. T0L 1E0; 604-343-6311 or 604-343-6486), a motel and restaurant open year-round, is located at Wapta Lake near the eastern park gate.

The 27-bed Whiskey Jack Hostel, south of Takakkaw Falls in the Yoho Valley, is open from mid-June to mid-September. For information and reservations, contact the Canadian Hostelling Association, 203 Recreation Square, 1414 Kensington Rd., Calgary NW, Alta. T2N 3P9; 403-283-5551. The Twin Falls Chalet (Suite 11, 230 21st Ave. SW, Calgary, Alta. T2S 0G6; 403-228-7079 in Calgary), a two-story lodge built by the CPR in the 1920s at the foot of Twin Falls in the Yoho Valley, offers meals and spartan accommodations for up to 14 people with three or four to a room. The chalet is open in summer; book early.

The Cathedral Mountain Chalets (Box 40, Field, B.C. V0A 1G0; 403-343-6442) near the Kicking Horse campground is open year-round. Emerald Lake Lodge (Box 10, Field, B.C. V0A 1G0; 604-343-6321), beside lovely Emerald Lake, rents canoes to guests and visitors.

ADDRESSES: For more information, write or phone: The Superintendent, Yoho National Park, Box 99, Field, B.C. V0A 1G0; 604-343-6324.

For information on the two huts operated by the Alpine Club of Canada, write to the club at Box 1026, Banff, Alta. T0L 0C0; 403-762-4481.

BOOKS: Donald Beers, *The Wonder of Yoho.* Calgary: Rocky Mountain Books, 1989. Guide to the park's geology, human and natural history, and recreational facilities.

Stephen Jay Gould, *Wonderful Life: The Burgess Shales and the Nature of History.* New York: W. W. Norton & Company, 1989. Provocative theories on what the fossils of the world's oldest soft-bodied animals say about evolution.

A rainbow softens the craggy peaks and steep rock faces surrounding one of Yoho's many glacial waterfalls.

WATERTON LAKES NATIONAL PARK

TUCKED IN THE extreme southwestern corner of Alberta, Waterton Lakes presents a dramatic and abrupt transition from prairie to mountain. Within less than half a mile, the elevation soars 4,000 ft/1,200 m, sweeping southwestward from rolling grassland to the tumultuous peaks and ridges along the eastern slope of the Rockies. A string of glittering lakes nestled at the foot of these ragged summits bisects the park. From north to south they are: Maskinonge Lake and the three Waterton lakes—Lower, Middle, and Upper—connected by narrow channels named Bosporus and Dardanelles. Waterton Park townsite, the only community in the park, is on Bosporus Narrows between Middle and Upper Waterton lakes.

The prairie in the northeast corner of the park supports luxuriant rough fescue grasslands dotted with aspen groves and carpeted with prickly rose, many-flowered aster, and geranium. The area around the three large lakes is thickly forested with Douglas-fir, white spruce, and lodgepole pine, species that also grow on lower mountain slopes. In the cold, dry air of the subalpine zone, subalpine larch and Engelmann spruce predominate. Above the tree line, where rock and ice rule, the few year-round inhabitants include American pipits, hoary marmots, white-tailed ptarmigans, and mountain goats.

Waterton Lakes National Park has one of the best trail networks in Canada's mountain parks. Scenically routed, they wander for 100 mi/160 km across the interior, providing access to painted canyons, waterfalls, alpine lakes, and ridges with spectacular mountain views.

GEOLOGY

About 1.5 billion years ago, this section of Alberta was a broad, shallow bay along the coastline of a Precambrian ocean. For millions of years, great rivers flowing from an eastern upland deposited thick beds of sediment here, which eventually hardened into rock. Beds of clay were compressed into shale, sand into sandstone, and lime from the shells of sea creatures into limestone.

Subjected to tremendous heat and pressure, some of this sedimentary rock metamorphosed. Shale was transformed into argillite, one of the most distinctive and colorful rocks in the park. (Red Rock Canyon in the northern part of Waterton is named for its thick beds of argillite, which get their carmine hues from oxidized iron particles.) Sandstone was compressed into green, gray, and white quartzite; some limestone beds became dolomite in shades of tan, brown, and gray. Cameron Falls near Waterton townsite spills over a lip of dolomite and limestone that dates back 1.5 billion years, one of the oldest formations in the Rockies.

Starting 175 million years ago, surging pressures within the earth's crust began to thrust up the sediments that had accumulated on the sea floor to a depth of more than 1 mi/1.6 km. This mountain-building, which went on for about 50 million years, caused twisting, folding, and buckling in rock that had lain flat in layers, like sheets on a bed, for more than a billion years.

Some sheets moved horizontally and overrode younger sheets, or strata, producing an overthrust. All the mountains in Waterton were created from an overriding slab known as the Lewis Overthrust. This giant arch of rock stretches 100 mi/160 km between Marias Pass in Montana's Glacier National Park and Crow's Nest Pass northwest of Waterton. Forces that geologists still don't understand lifted this billion-year-old mountain mass from the interior of present-day British Columbia and Montana, slid it eastward over the plains, and deposited it some 60 mi/100 km away atop rock 60 million years old. In sedimentary formations, older rock usually is surmounted by younger rock. In Waterton this order is reversed to produce upside-down, or rootless, mountains.

The rough touch of the glaciers shaped much of Waterton's beautiful scenery—from the sharp, chiseled ridges, or arêtes, to the steep, hollowed-out bowls called cirques. (The cirque cradling Goat Lake in the northwestern corner of the park is a textbook example.) Glaciers also widened V-shaped stream valleys into U-shaped valleys, such as the one occupied by Upper Waterton Lake, the deepest body of water in the Rockies (500 ft/150 m). A warming climate stranded small tributary glaciers high on mountain slopes, where they gouged out "hanging valleys"—depressions in the mountainsides far above the valley floor. Today, these hanging valleys often are curtained by waterfalls. One example is Cameron Falls in the Cameron Creek valley north of Waterton townsite.

HISTORY

This "land of shining mountains," as the Kootenai Indians called it, has been inhabited almost continuously for 8,500 years. Some 60 archaeological sites dot the valley of the Waterton lakes; a tributary valley, the Blakiston, contains an estimated 200. All reveal the presence of nomadic tribes, probable ancestors of the Kootenai, who hunted bison on the prairie in summer and wintered in sheltered valleys in the lee of the Rockies.

In 1858, Lt. Thomas Blakiston, a member of John Palliser's British North American Exploring Expedition, crossed South Kootenay Pass on the present-day British Columbia–Alberta border and descended east down the valley of Blakiston Creek. He was the first European to see the Waterton lakes. In 1911, as settlers became numerous, the area was preserved and protected as Canada's fourth national park. In 1932 it was linked to Glacier National Park in Montana to create Waterton–Glacier International Peace Park, the world's first such sanctuary.

HABITATS

Waterton has six major bioclimatic communities: prairie, parkland, wetland, montane, subalpine, and alpine. These communities support more than half of all the known floral species in Alberta—some 900 kinds of plants. In the northeast corner of the park along Highway 5, a tiny pocket of prairie marks the western extent of the Canadian grasslands. In spring and summer, lupines, golden asters, and pink prairie roses splash color on a tawny

Early morning and evening are good times for viewing park wildlife, such as the mountain goat. OPPOSITE: *Red Rock Canyon, a technicolor creation of argilite and other mineral deposits.*

carpet of bunchgrass, fescue, and oatgrass. Coyotes, the park's most prevalent predators, lope after ground squirrels. A herd of about 20 bison graze in a paddock just inside the park along Highway 6. In autumn great flocks of waterfowl traveling along the Pacific and Central flyways congregate on prairie ponds and on Lower Waterton and Maskinonge lakes. American coots, mallards, goldeneyes, ruddy ducks, Canada geese, and tundra swans rest and feed before skying south. It is not unusual to see 12 or 13 species sharing the waters.

In the southeast corner of the park near Belly Creek campground and, in the same area, along the first section of the Vimy Peak Trail off Chief Mountain International Highway, the prairie is dotted with groves of quaking aspens. This mixed habitat of grasses and trees is called parkland. Beneath the aspen canopy grow bluebell, prickly rose, snowberries, and Oregon grape (Waterton is the only place in Canada that this plant is found east of the Rockies). This zone is home to black-capped chickadees, ruffed grouse, snowshoe hares, and white-tailed deer. After rutting season in late fall, large herds of wapiti, or elk, migrate to the area around Lower Waterton Lake and winter in the parkland and prairie.

Around shallow Maskinonge Lake and Blakiston Creek grow aquatic plants such as pondweed, mare's tail, and duckweed, a favorite food of moose, which occasionally can be seen browsing at dawn and dusk in spring and summer. In the shallows, a tall spike of yellow flowers resembling a snapdragon identifies the bladderwort, a carnivorous plant which traps aquatic insects in tiny bladders attached to thread-like streamers. Cattails, horsetails, bulrushes, and sedges along swampy fringes protect and feed muskrats; minks also live hereabouts. Killdeers and spotted sandpipers pursue the nymphs of dragonflies and caddisflies (they can't catch the adults), while garter snakes prey on leopard frog tadpoles. Beavers emerge from the Belly River to fell aspens for food and building materials.

The mountain valleys and lower slopes are carpeted with lodgepole pine and Douglas-fir. Under this canopy mingle Rocky Mountain maple along with thimbleberry, silver buffaloberry, and other shrubs, and such flowers as clematis, cow parsnip, and queen cup. In autumn, the park's 50-odd black bears feast in the valleys on saskatoon berries and chokecherries. The mountain lion, or cougar, one of Canada's most graceful predators, tracks mule deer. The lower section of the trail encircling Bertha Lake (just southwest of Upper Waterton Lake) cuts through this zone.

Around Cameron Lake and along the steep trail up to tiny Summit Lake in the southwestern corner of the park hikers encounter the subalpine zone.

Bighorn sheep frequent the slopes above Upper Rowe Lake in this same area. Omnivorous grizzlies (an estimated 200 of the bears roam Waterton–Glacier) grub for bulbs and vetch roots, dining occasionally on marmots and golden-mantled ground squirrels, named for the tawny fur that adorns their head and shoulders. Steller's jay, Clark's nutcracker, and varied thrushes live here in forests of Engelmann spruce, subalpine larch, whitebark pine, and alpine fir (Indians used its gum as an antiseptic). Blanketing mountain slopes and open forests in this zone is beargrass, found in no other Canadian national park. In June and July, this member of the lily family produces a showy cluster of creamy white flowers that looks like cotton candy atop a tall stalk. Indians once traded beargrass leaves with West Coast tribes, who used the long blades to weave strong, watertight baskets. Wapiti munch on its blossoms, and mountain goats nibble its leaves; grizzlies use the leaves to line winter dens. Other wildflowers that bloom in beargrass season include globeflower, buttercups, and gentians.

Withering winds and biting cold stunt trees in the alpine zone, which can be viewed along the western park boundary on the Tamarack Trail. Lichens cling to rock faces, and such colorful alpine flowers as moss campion, sky pilot, and saxifrage grow where shallow mats of soil have formed in rock crevices. The delicate sky pilot and the rare alpine poppy bloom for only a few days; hardier saxifrages blossom for several weeks. Rosy finches, American pipits, and white-tailed ptarmigans thrive in this Arctic environment. Rabbit-like pikas gather grass stems and stalks on alpine scree slopes. Hoary marmots sun themselves on outcrops around Carthew Lakes in Waterton's southwest corner, easy pickings for golden eagles soaring above. Hikers often see mountain goats poised on steep headwalls overlooking Goat Lake northwest of the townsite, and around Crypt and Bertha lakes in the southern part of the park.

OUTDOOR ACTIVITIES

The park is busiest in summer when hotels, motels, restaurants, and other services in Waterton townsite are available. Most people come by car and stay in one of the three main campgrounds. They take day hikes and trail rides, boat and fish on the lakes, golf, participate in the park's interpretive programs, and cruise down Upper Waterton Lake to Montana aboard a launch called *The International.* More athletic visitors hike into Waterton backcountry. The park is open year-round but winter visitors are few.

The baronial and magnificently situated Prince of Wales Hotel is the largest wooden
structure in Alberta. In addition to huge fireplaces and an open foyer rising up six

Scenic Drives

Much of Waterton's scenery can be enjoyed from the three main roads.
Most trailheads, campgrounds, and other facilities are accessible from
these routes. *Chief Mountain International Highway* runs along the eastern boundary of Waterton to the international boundary. Its highlight is
Chief Mountain, a castellated summit known as a klippe—a peak separated
from its mountain range by erosion. From Waterton townsite, *Red Rock
Canyon Parkway* angles 9 mi/14 km northwest up Blakiston Creek to Red
Rock Canyon. *Akamina Parkway* extends from Waterton townsite 10 mi/
16 km southwest to Cameron Lake, a blue gem set in a bowl-shaped valley
at the foot of Mt. Custer in the southwestern corner of the park.

Hiking

Most of the park's 48 trails are day hikes, accessible from Waterton townsite or the parkways. Backpackers must obtain camping permits, available
in the townsite at the Information Centre, the administration building, or
the park warden's office. Groups of hikers must not exceed six. Several
trails connect with the trail network in Glacier National Park across the
U.S. boundary.

floors, the Prince of Wales has a grand formal dining room with spectacular views of Upper Lake Waterton.

Short, self-guiding interpretive trails—usually two hours (5 mi/8 km) or less—serve as scenic introductions to the park's natural and human history. *The Red Rock Canyon Trail* along Blakiston Creek follows the lip of 65-ft/20-m-high canyon walls streaked red, purple, green, and yellow by chemical changes of minerals in the rocks. Ripples in cliffs and fossils of algae are evidence that an ancient sea once covered this area. Looming above the canyon is Mt. Blakiston (9,600 ft/2,926 m), Waterton's highest. The *Bison Viewpoint Trail* ambles over fescue prairie to a paddock that encloses a small herd of the great, shaggy ruminants that once numbered 60 million in North America. The *Summit Lake Trail* begins at the Cameron Lake exhibit center and winds through a 300-year-old forest of Engelmann spruce and past beargrass meadows. The *Cameron Lakeshore Trail,* a pleasant 1-mi/1.6-km shoreline walk popular with families, leads to scenic views of Mt. Custer. Grizzly bears sometimes are spotted on the avalanche slopes beyond the end of the trail.

Longer trails range in difficulty and length. *The Tamarack Trail,* one of the finest highline treks in the Canadian Rockies, runs 22 mi/36 km between the Akamina Parkway and the Red Rock Canyon Parkway, tracing the park's western boundary. Most hikers start at the southern trailhead, off Akamina Parkway. The route skirts a series of cascades tumbling over the red argillite streambed of Rowe Creek, then climbs to the two Upper Rowe Lakes, sparkling bodies of water surrounded by stunted alpine fir and larch and backed by cliffs where bighorn sheep congregate.

About 2 mi/3.3 km and 1,600 vertical feet (500 meters) later is Lineham Ridge, highlight of the hike. The ridge is nearly as high as the surrounding peaks, yielding a magnificent panorama of mountains stretching out in all directions. On the opposite side of the ridge, the beautiful, deep-blue Lineham Lakes lie in a verdant basin of spruce and subalpine fir. The trail proceeds northwest through forest and across subalpine meadows to Lone Lake and Twin Lakes. The last 5 mi/8.2 km double as the *Snowshoe Trail* along an old fire road down Bauerman Valley to Red Rock Canyon.

The *Crypt Lake Trail* is one of the most unusual routes in the Rockies. Hikers take a water taxi from the townsite marina to a landing at a dock across Lower Waterton Lake. The trail switchbacks through a forest of white spruce, Douglas-fir, and lodgepole pine and passes Burnt Rock Falls, a beautiful 50-ft/15-m cascade of water that spills over a lip of Precambrian rock. At Mi 4.9/Km 7.9, hikers ascend a ladder to a 65-ft/20-m tunnel that cuts through a mountain spur. At the other end, a narrow ledge carved in an exposed rock face (a cable reassures the faint-of-heart) leads to Crypt Lake, a splendid example of a glacial amphitheater. Cliffs 2,000 ft/600 m high rise up on all but the north side of the cirque. Even in summer, ice bobs in the emerald waters; mountain goats often can be seen on the surrounding rock faces.

The 32-mi/20-km *Carthew–Alderson Trail* between the townsite and Cameron Lake is one of the few routes in the mountain parks that offer all the elements of "ideal" alpine travel: a spectrum of botanical zones; views of lakes and glaciers; windswept mountain passes; subalpine meadows spangled with wildflowers; and mountains brightly colored with argillites and quartzites. Particularly beautiful in midsummer is Summit Lake (2.5 mi/ 4 km east of Cameron Lake), where mule deer browse in meadows abloom with beargrass, fleabane, valerian, and arnica.

Horseback Riding

This has long been a popular pastime in Waterton. Horses can be rented by the hour or by the day at the park's licensed private stable; outfitters arrange overnight tours. The most popular trail goes to Alderson Lake, a five-hour ride southwest from Waterton townsite. The route heads through subalpine forest and ascends to the alpine zone around the lake.

Boating

On calm summer days, boats, canoes, and windsurfers dot Upper and Middle Waterton lakes. Small boats and canoes can be rented at Cameron Lake.

Waterton Shoreline Cruises (403-859-2362) schedules boat trips on Upper Waterton Lake into the heart of the mountains. The trip from the townsite to Goat Haunt Visitor Center at the southern end of the lake in Montana takes approximately 45 minutes each way. One of their boats, the diesel-powered launch *The International*, has been plying these waters since 1927.

Fishing

Although Waterton certainly is not known as a fisherman's paradise, rainbow trout are taken from Cameron and Crandell lakes. Maskinonge Lake has northern pike and mountain whitefish. Most of park's alpine lakes, including Carthew and Alderson, contain cutthroat trout. Anglers require a National Parks Fishing License, available for a fee from the Information Centre, the administration office, or a park warden. The season varies: Maskinonge Lake and the Lower Waterton River are open year-round; lakes in the lower valleys usually are open from mid-May to late September; alpine lakes generally open for fishing early in July and close early in September. Some bodies of water are off limits to anglers, so check at the Information Centre before dropping a hook.

Winter Activities

The most dependable snow for *cross-country skiing* usually is found from late December to early March at the upper end of *Cameron Lake Road* and on *Red Rock Canyon Trail*. Conditions are less reliable at lower elevations. Recommended *snowshoeing* trails are *Red Rock Canyon, Crandell Lake,* and *Blakiston Falls*. Large mammals active at this time of year include moose, wapiti, deer, and coyote.

EXPLORING THE PARK

Two highways lead to the park. Highway 6 runs south 30 mi/48 km from the town of Pincher Creek to the park's northeastern entrance; Highway 5 reaches the same juncture from the east. Chief Mountain International Highway provides the most direct route from Glacier National Park in Montana, but is open only from mid-May to mid-September.

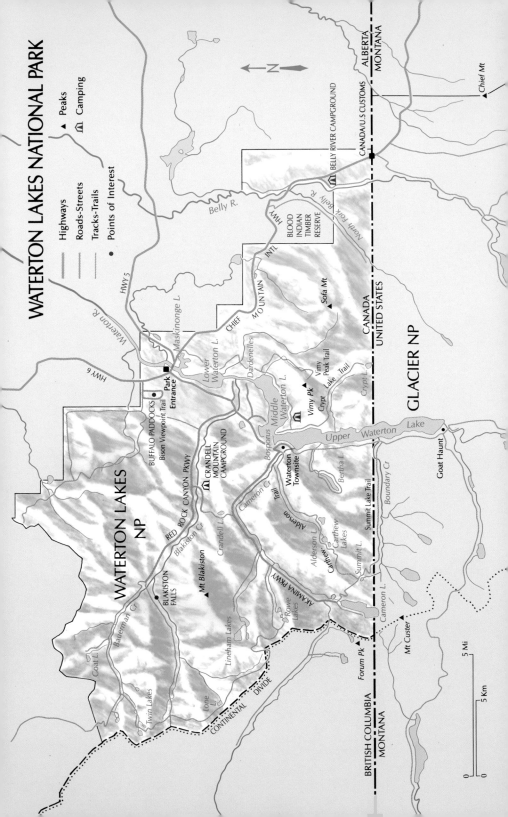

WATERTON LAKES NATIONAL PARK

Highways
Roads-Streets
Tracks-Trails
● Points of Interest
▲ Peaks
⌂ Camping

CANADA/U.S CUSTOMS
BELLY RIVER CAMPGROUND
ALBERTA
MONTANA
Chief Mt

Belly R.

North Fork Belly R.

BLOOD INDIAN TIMBER RESERVE

INTL
HWY

Sofa Mt

CANADA
UNITED STATES

MOUNTAIN

CHIEF

Dardenelles

Maskinonge L.

Lower Waterton L.

Middle Waterton L.

Vimy Pk
Vimy Peak Trail

Crypt L.
Crypt Lake Trail

GLACIER NP

HWY 5

HWY 6

Waterton R.

Park Entrance

BUFFALO PADDOCKS
Bison Viewpoint Trail

Bosporus

Upper Waterton Lake

Goat Haunt

WATERTON LAKES NP

CRANDELL MOUNTAIN CAMPGROUND

RED ROCK CANYON PKWY

Blakiston Cr

Crandell L.

Cameron Cr

Waterton Townsite

Bertha L.

Boundary Cr

Cameron Cr

Summit Lake Trail

Mt Blakiston

BLAKISTON FALLS

Alderson Trail

Alderson L.

Carthew L.
Carthew Lakes

Summit L.

Bauerman Cr

Goat L.

Lineham Lakes

Rowe Lakes

AKAMINA PKWY

Cameron L.

Mt Custer

Twin Lakes

Lone L.

CONTINENTAL DIVIDE

Forum Pk

BRITISH COLUMBIA
MONTANA

5 Mi

5 Km

0
0

The nearest airports are at Lethbridge (81 mi/130 km northeast) and Calgary (165 mi/264 km north). Greyhound Lines of Canada offers year-round bus service to Pincher Creek, where taxis can be rented to complete the trip to Waterton. (There are no car rental companies in Pincher Creek.) The nearest VIA Rail stop is in Calgary. In the United States, Amtrak trains stop in Montana at East Glacier and West Glacier (Belton) Park. A hikers' shuttle provides transportation from Waterton townsite to Cameron Lake and Red Rock Canyon by appointment (403-859-2612 in summer; 403-859-2378 in winter).

ACCOMMODATIONS: There are three campgrounds for car-based travelers. The main campground is at the south end of the townsite (230 sites). Crandell campground, sheltered in a grove of lodgepole pine along the Red Rock Canyon Parkway, has 140 sites. Belly River campground occupies a lovely riverside setting in the southeast corner of the park off the Chief Mountain International Highway (29 sites).

Hotels, motels, and lodges at the townsite are open in summer. The grandest accommodation is the chalet-style Prince of Wales Hotel, a seven-story, 81-room lodge situated on a sand-and-gravel terrace deposited by melting glaciers. The largest wooden structure in Alberta, the Prince of Wales offers impressive views of Upper Waterton Lake (403-226-5551). Only the 27-unit Kilmorey Lodge (403-859-2334) remains open in winter.

ADDRESSES: For more information, write or phone: The Superintendent, Waterton Lakes National Park, Waterton Park, Alta. T0K 2M0; 403-859-2224.

BOOKS: Annora Brown, *Old Man's Garden*. Sidney, B.C.: Gray's Publishing Ltd., 1970.

Heather Pringle, *Waterton Lakes National Park*. Vancouver/Toronto: Douglas & McIntyre, Publishers, 1986.

Andy Russell, *The Rockies*. Edmonton: Hurtig Publishers, 1975.

Richard J. Shaw and Danny On, *Plants of Waterton–Glacier National Parks and the Canadian Rockies*. Banff: Summerthought, 1979.

THE PRAIRIES

ELK ISLAND NATIONAL PARK 132

In central Alberta's Beaver Hills, abundant wildlife—bison, moose, elk, deer, and waterfowl—finds haven in a fenced sanctuary surrounded by towns and farmland.

PRINCE ALBERT NATIONAL PARK 142

Aspen parkland meets boreal forest in this central Saskatchewan park, where bear, moose, elk, deer, and rare white pelicans find refuge and conservationist-author Grey Owl found inspiration.

GRASSLANDS NATIONAL PARK 154

Spared the plow, a pocket of mixed-grass prairie thrives at the arid southern edge of Saskatchewan, where the deer and the antelope still play and Canada's only prairie dogs live in bustling "towns."

RIDING MOUNTAIN NATIONAL PARK 160

Rising out of broad plains, this prairie "mountain" forms the natural playground of Manitoba and an island of wilderness for bison, moose, and wolves.

ELK ISLAND
NATIONAL PARK

THIS SMALL RECTANGULAR PARK east of Edmonton is insular only in the sense that its rolling, forested hills are surrounded by the towns and flat farmland of central Alberta. Elk Island has been a refuge for wildlife since 1906, when an area around Astotin Lake in the northern end of the Beaver Hills was withdrawn from settlement and designated a sanctuary for wapiti, or elk, which were then close to extermination in the province.

The following year some 400 plains bison purchased from Flathead Indians in Montana arrived in the park. Most were later shipped to a now-defunct park in central Alberta, but the 50 bison that remained became the progenitors of Elk Island's current herd of 500 animals. In 1965, wood bison, a larger and darker subspecies, were introduced to the southern third of the park. These animals, which number about 400, are kept separate from the plains bison to prevent interbreeding. Canada's only fenced national park also protects moose, deer, coyotes, and a host of waterfowl.

GEOLOGY

A succession of inland seas submerged part or all of the prairies beginning 600 million years ago. The last sea retreated 65 million years ago, as the Rockies rose in the west. These warm, shallow seas left behind thick deposits of sand, mud, and lime that over time hardened into sandstone, shale, and limestone. The far older and harder rock of the Canadian Shield is unseen in the prairies, buried by this sedimentary mantle to depths of up to 10,000 ft/3,000 m.

In the park, the sedimentary rock is, in turn, covered by the Beaver Hills, which rise about 200 ft/60 m above the surrounding prairie. Some 10,000 years ago, at the end of the Pleistocene era, a chunk of ice broke off the main ice sheet retreating north. When the isolated chunk eventually melted, its load of sand, gravel, and boulders formed a "dead-ice moraine"—a hummocky upland of small rounded hills and bowl-like depressions known as "knob and kettle" terrain. Cupped in hollows between "knobs," or hills, are more than 200 shallow "kettle" ponds and lakes.

History

Paleo-Indians first came to the grasslands some 5,000 years ago, following the herds of bison and camping in or near river valleys. More recently, the Plains Cree and the Blackfoot kept the Beaver Hills as a winter hunting preserve for wapiti and deer where fighting and raiding were not allowed. Archaeologists have discovered more than 200 sites in the park, some dating back 500 years.

At the turn of the century, colorful government posters portrayed the Canadian prairies as "Canada West—The Last Best West," and told of its ranching and farming potential. A quarter-section (160 acres/64 hectares) could be bought for $10. Farmers' sons from Ontario and the Maritimes, adventuresome (but inexperienced) Britons, oppressed Mennonites, and Americans whose own West was filling up flocked here.

People of Ukrainian origin, the largest ethnic group in this region, arrived in their greatest numbers between 1892 and 1910. These hardy, self-reliant settlers cleared land and farmed, worked in lumber camps, or laid track. Their first shelters, called *boordays*, were dugouts lined with logs and roofed with aspen boughs and sod. Two dark cramped rooms often housed several families while they built sturdy log dwellings in a style that recalled the architecture of the Old Country. As soon as their homes were completed, these deeply religious people built a church—a simple log structure topped with a distinctive pear-shaped dome.

Settlement accomplished in two decades what the Cree and Blackfoot failed to do over the centuries—the local extirpation of black bear, gray wolf, cougar, river otter, marten, beaver, and trumpeter swan and the near eradication of moose, wapiti, and mule deer. Fortunately, five settlers who foresaw the inevitable outcome of excessive hunting and destruction of habitat petitioned the federal government to establish a fenced sanctuary for wapiti in the Beaver Hills. In 1906 the game preserve was created, and eventually it became Elk Island National Park.

Habitats

The park is a mélange of shallow lakes, reed- and cattail-fringed wetlands, and sluggish streams interspersed with grassy meadows and mixed forest. The Beaver Hills are a meeting ground of trees from the boreal forest, mainly white and black spruce, and deciduous trees from the surrounding

A beaver swims in Elk Island National Park, an island of nature ringed by a region of

aspen parkland—primarily balsam poplar and the Canadian prairie's signature species, quaking aspen.

Aspen parkland, which arcs from southern Manitoba to the Alberta foothills, is a transition zone between open prairie and boreal forest. Before settlement, aspens and other drought-resistant trees were kept in check by the grazing of countless bison, lightning-sparked fires, and a tough carpet of native grasses—"prairie wool" to homesteaders—that prevented saplings from taking root. The aspen parkland developed only after the eradication of the bison and the abandonment of marginal farmland.

Quaking aspen is a fast-growing, short-lived tree that forms open, domed groves. These "bluffs" shelter native animals otherwise unable to survive on today's radically altered prairie. Wapiti and deer browse on aspen saplings, as well as on beaked hazelnut, alder, red-osier dogwood, and other understory shrubs. The bark of young aspens sustains snowshoe hares in winter. This species is sometimes called the varying hare for its changeable coat: gray-brown in summer, white in winter.

Yellow warblers and least flycatchers use the gossamer fluff encasing aspen seeds as nesting material. Ruffed grouse feed on aspen buds and rose hips, which are a favorite delicacy of snowshoe hares, deer mice, and a host

industries and towns once known as Beaver Hills for its quiet lakes and beaver ponds.

of other species. Saskatoons, highbush cranberries, chokecherries, pin cherries, Canada buffaloberries, currants, and other fruit-bearing shrubs attract least chipmunks and songbirds, including American robins and waxwings. Downy, hairy, and pileated woodpeckers drill bluff softwoods to find insects and excavate nests.

Horned larks, western meadowlarks, and lesser yellowlegs inhabit park grasslands, where summer brings forth masses of blue violets, white-starred strawberry flowers, golden corydalis, and the park's most commanding wildflower, hot-pink fireweed. Red-tailed hawks and great horned owls nest in aspen bluffs and hunt over grasslands for voles, shrews, and ground squirrels. Most burrowing mammals use underground dens for nesting and refuge but leave their dens to forage aboveground. The northern pocket gopher, however, is truly subterranean; it surfaces infrequently, living off grass roots that work down through the roofs of tunnels.

Here, where big game abounds, coyotes probably form permanent packs like those of wolves, although individuals hunt alone for smaller prey—hares, mice, voles, and occasionally an unwary beaver or muskrat. In winter at dusk and occasionally at sunrise, particularly during the January and February mating season, the high-pitched yips of coyotes echo across the frozen lakes and ponds, a chorus that serves to reunite the pack and proclaim its territory.

Lakes and ponds cover almost a quarter of the park, attracting migratory and nesting waterfowl and shorebirds from late April to June and again from August to mid-September. In early summer, duckweed, pondweed, and algae spread filmy sheets over the shallow, oxygen-poor waters, which abound in sticklebacks, minnows, insect larvae, microscopic crustaceans, and other bird food. Along the shore in early summer aquatic invertebrates are so dense that the water turns soupy.

The best place for sighting water birds is at the northwest end of Astotin Lake, which is accessible by canoe, and south of Astotin along the Tawayik Lake Trail. (Astotin, the largest body of water in Elk Island, is near the northern boundary of the park.) Birders can rack up an impressive list of sightings here: the park has recorded some 230 species, including common loons, four of Alberta's five grebe species, black-crowned night-herons, and great blue herons.

Trumpeter swans, which were wiped out locally around the turn of the century, recently have been introduced to the southern part of the park. Mature pairs with young are captured during the molt from around Grande Prairie in north-central Alberta and transported to Elk Island. After wintering in Yellowstone National Park and farther south along the Central Flyway, the adult swans return in spring to Grande Prairie. Their young, however, migrate back to Elk Island, where they learned to fly.

Nearly all the species of prairie ducks—more than a dozen kinds of waterfowl—arrive in April, with blue-winged teal, mallards, lesser scaups, northern shovelers, and ring-necked ducks most abundant. Migrating ducks that will remain in the area all summer scatter almost immediately after arrival to isolated shoreline nesting and feeding sites; transients stay in close-knit feeding flocks. Astotin is one of the few breeding areas outside the western mountains for Barrow's goldeneye, a striking black-and-white diving duck with a large white crescent between eye and beak in place of the common goldeneye's circle of white. In May a few pairs of Barrow's goldeneye fly in to Astotin for a week or 10 days, then disappear.

Certainly the most impressive wild species encountered in the park are the large grazers. Moose range the woodlands and wetlands. Wapiti frequent forest-edge and open habitats. These stately creatures, which carry a magnificent rack of antlers up to 5 ft/1.5 m wide, are more often heard than seen, especially at dawn or at night during the late-summer rut. Wapiti are harem breeders, and their bugles—actually piercingly shrill three-step whistles—are designed to lure females. The strongest whistles broadcast the whereabouts of the biggest, most dominant males.

A display herd of plains bison roams a paddock just north of Highway 16, which cuts through the southern part of the park. These shaggy ruminants are seen also from the Elk Island Parkway, which extends north of Highway 16 through the center of the park; their favorite places are the open meadows along the northern section of the Hayburger Trail east of the parkway, and the sedge meadows around Tawayik Lake, where marsh grasses grow as luxuriantly as hay. Telltale signs of favored bison habitats include wallows, trees with bark rubbed off, shrubs tufted with fur, and flat cakes of dung, known on the prairies as "buffalo chips."

During summer mating season, herds of up to 70 animals gather in meadows to graze and mate. Fights between bulls for control of harems is a ground-shaking, noisy spectacle. Usually bulls first roll in wallows, posture and paw the ground, then lunge at each other from a short distance. Their head-to-head shoving matches continue until the weaker animal tires, backs up, and turns away. The bellows that accompany such jousting are heard up to 5 mi/8 km away on open prairie. During the rest of the year herds break up into smaller groups of cows, calves, and yearling bulls. Mature males often congregate, although solitary bulls occasionally establish their own ranges and may challenge encroaching hikers and skiers.

Hikers on the Wood Bison Trail south of Highway 16 may see North America's largest land mammal wallowing in clouds of dust or maneuvering its 2,000-lb/900-kg bulk through stands of aspen and spruce with the grace of a deer. The park's herd is the result of a remarkable stroke of luck farther north in Wood Buffalo National Park. Wood Buffalo was established in 1922 to protect Canada's last remaining herd of wood bison. The later introduction of plains bison into the park led to extensive interbreeding. In 1957 officials discovered an isolated herd of pure wood bison and moved 22 of the animals here to protect the strain. The rest of the herd went to a sanctuary bordering Great Slave Lake.

OUTDOOR ACTIVITIES

Elk Island is primarily a day-use park for people driving from Edmonton and smaller centers in central Alberta. They come to see bison, wapiti, and other wildlife; to boat, picnic, and golf at the Astotin Recreation Area, the only development in the park; and to hike trails that reach nearly every corner of Elk Island.

Hiking

The park's 12 trails extend for more than 60 mi/100 km. Six trails are short nature walks; the other six are longer day hikes. All are rated easy to mod-

In 1906, Elk Island National Park was set aside to preserve a herd of twenty elk roaming the area. OPPOSITE: Mixed-woods forests and meadows and wetlands form a habitat for more than 230 species of birds.

erate. Dams built by the park's numerous beavers regularly flood the trails; check with park officials before setting out.

Five trails are in the Astotin Lake area. *The Lakeview Trail*, northwest of the recreation area, is a pleasant, hour-long stroll that covers all the major park habitats: marsh, beaver pond, kettle pond, aspen and spruce forest, and lake shoreline. A pleasant picnic site, Beaver Bay, is at the halfway point of the paved *Shoreline Trail*, which follows Astotin's southern margin and provides access to two of the 17 islands in the lake. Muskrats, beavers, ruffed grouse, and tree-nesting ducks are seen from the *Amisk Wuche Trail*, which circles a kettle lake east of Astotin. (The trail's name means "beaver hills" in Cree.) Some of the park's largest and oldest spruce trees are along this route.

South of Astotin and west of the parkway, the 7.8-mi/12.6-km *Shirley Lake Trail* explores a gently rolling landscape of aspen forests and large meadows where wapiti often are sighted. The *Tawayik Lake Trail*, south of Shirley Lake, offers the park's best bird-watching. A viewing platform near the trailhead has a telescope and illustrations of waterfowl in different plumages. Boggy terrain between Tawayik and Little Tawayik lakes closes the western half of the trail in summer. Wood bison are seen year-round along the *Wood Bison Trail*, which loops 11.6 mi/18.6 km around Flying

Shot Lake south of Highway 16. An exhibit at the trailhead explains the park's role in conserving these magnificent animals and tells how to distinguish wood bison from plains bison.

Boating

Canoes, sailboards, and sailboats are allowed only on Astotin Lake. A boat launch and dock are at the north end of the recreation area.

Swimming

Although the recreation area has a beach, park officials do not recommend swimming in Astotin Lake for several compelling reasons: leeches, parasites that cause "swimmer's itch," and algae blooms that film the water.

Golfing

There is golfing (403-998-3161) at the recreation area on a nine-hole golf course laid out in the 1930s.

Winter Activities

Most of the hiking trails are groomed for *cross-country skiing*. The *Moss Lake Trail*, south of Astotin, is perhaps the park's most challenging route. It loops 8 mi/13 km over rolling terrain forested with aspen, spruce, and birch interspersed with meadows and beaver ponds. The short *Simmon's Trail*, just off the parkway in Elk Island's midsection, is a demanding but rewarding 2.8-mi/4.6-km route over aspen hills. Other park trails groomed for skiing include the *White Spruce, Beaver Pond, Shoreline, Shirley Lake, Hayburger,* and *Tawayik* (its full length, 10.5 mi/16.8 km, is open in winter).

The *Lakeview* and *Amisk Wuche* trails are designated routes for *snowshoeing*, but one can explore the entire park. A popular outing is to the islands in Astotin Lake, most of which have old-growth spruce.

EXPLORING THE PARK

Elk Island is 28 mi/45 km east of Edmonton via Highway 16. North of the park boundary, the Elk Island Parkway connects with Highway 831 and the town of Lamont. Greyhound Lines (403-421-1364) will stop on request near the south gate on Highway 16. The company also has service to Lamont.

The park information center (403-922-5790) on the parkway just north of Highway 16 is open daily from mid-May to early September. The Astotin Interpretive Centre (403-992-6392) in the recreation area is also open in summer. Field guides, trail guides, and other books on the natural and human history of the park and Alberta are sold at the interpretive and information centers through the Friends of Elk Island, a nonprofit organization. One of the most popular of numerous family-oriented activities in the interpretive program is the "Buffalo Chip Flip"—a contest to see who can fling an "organic frisbee" farthest.

A thatched-roof, whitewashed dacha in the recreation area commemorates Ukrainian immigrants and houses the Ukrainian Pioneer Home's displays of historic photos, traditional clothing, handcrafted wooden furniture, and other artifacts. The home is closed Wednesdays and Thursdays during the summer. Just east of the park along Highway 16 in the Ukrainian Cultural Heritage Village (403-662-3640) are about a dozen pioneer buildings dating from the 1890s.

ACCOMMODATIONS: Sandy Beach campground (80 sites) in the recreation area is very popular on summer weekends. Those planning to stay over-night should arrive by midafternoon on Friday to be sure of getting a site, or plan trips for midweek. The more primitive Oster Lake group tenting area is reserved for organized nonprofit or educational groups. Winter campers use an area by the boat launch in the recreation area or the group tenting site. There is no backcountry camping.

Commercial accommodation is available in Edmonton, in Fort Saskatchewan (15 mi/25 km west), and in Lamont (3 mi/5 km north of the park boundary).

ADDRESSES: For more information, contact: The Superintendent, Elk Island National Park, Site 4, R.R. #1, Fort Saskatchewan, Alta. T8L 2N7; 403-992-6380. The Friends of Elk Island Society can be reached at the same address and telephone number.

BOOKS: Jean Burgess, *A Walk on the Wild Side: An All-Season Trail Guide to Elk Island National Park.* Edmonton: The Friends of Elk Island Society, 1988.

Deirdre Griffiths, *Island Forest Year: Elk Island National Park.* Edmonton: Univ. of Alberta Press, 1979. A former park naturalist chronicles the cycle of the seasons.

PRINCE ALBERT NATIONAL PARK

LOCATED IN CENTRAL SASKATCHEWAN, Prince Albert National Park witnesses the transition from southern to northern Canada. The southernmost part of the preserve is aspen parkland, a transitional forest of quaking aspen patched with prairie. Farther north, where the climate is moister, the pockets of grassland disappear as spruce and pine join the aspen to form boreal forest, part of the great woodland that sweeps across northern Canada from the Yukon to Labrador.

Prince Albert Park contains a subdued, undramatic landscape. The central Waskesiu Hills rise a mere 400 ft/122 m above the surrounding terrain. A third of the park is covered with water. Waskesiu, Crean, and Kingsmere lakes, which account for much of that figure, attract fishermen and fishing birds such as eagles and osprey. Lavallée Lake in the northwest corner is so remote that the easily disturbed American white pelican breeds there in Canada's second largest colony (after Alberta's Primrose Lake).

GEOLOGY

Virtually every landscape feature in Prince Albert was produced by the advance and retreat of Wisconsin ice. Advancing glaciers carved the basins of the park's myriad lakes. The Hunters Lake Trail near the southern boundary of the park crosses ice-push ridges made by glaciers thrusting against a bedrock upland.

The Waskesiu Hills were formed when a lobe of retreating ice deposited glacial till in the center of the park. Meltwater channels now form outsize valleys for such modest waterways as meandering Mud Creek southwest of Waskesiu townsite. When chunks of ice buried in glacial till melted, the soils above slumped, creating features called "kettles." These depressions, usually water-filled, are found all over the park. Boundary Bog near the East Gate occupies a kettle at the bottom of a meltwater channel.

Glacial meltwater also deposited stratified drift in conical hills, called "kames" (the Waskesiu River Trail north of the townsite passes a textbook example). The Lee Ski Trail in the same vicinity crosses several eskers,

Level terrain in Prince Albert National Park provides for leisurely hikes. The woods and wildlife here inspired the famous author and woodsman Grey Owl, who once wrote, "Remember you belong to nature, not it to you."

snaking ridges of sand and gravel that were once the banks of meltwater streams flowing beneath the ice. Boulders scooped up by glaciers in the Canadian Shield were dropped in unlikely places when the ice melted. One such "erratic" adjacent to the park administration building in Waskesiu townsite weighs about 275 tons/250 metric tons, offering dramatic evidence of the power of ice.

HISTORY

An archaeological site at The Narrows on Waskesiu Lake provides evidence of seasonal occupation for some 5,000 years. People who eventually came to be called the Cree spent summers in small groups along lakes and streams, fishing, trapping, and hunting. South of the park, the Assiniboine summered on the plains, following the great bison herds. Winter brought these two culturally distinct groups together in the sheltered aspen parkland.

There is sparse evidence of recent habitation: the remains of minor fur-trading posts at The Narrows; the ruins of sawmills and fields of rotting stumps left from lumbering operations; commercial fishing camps and freight trails reclaimed by the forest; disintegrating foundations of Depression-era work camps.

During the early years of Prince Albert Park, the internationally renowned conservationist, author, and orator Grey Owl worked as a park naturalist on programs to stabilize the beaver population. In the fall of 1931, he moved to a cabin on Ajawaan Lake, where he lived with his wife, Anahareo, and Jellyroll and Rawhide, two of the orphan beavers that were immortalized in his writings.

After his death in 1938, it was revealed that Grey Owl, who wore buck-skins and braided his long black hair, was not a Canadian Indian, but an Englishman named Archibald Stansfeld Belaney. Despite posthumous stories of drinking binges and bigamy (he never divorced an earlier Indian wife), he is still honored for writing with love and sympathy about the plight of wildlife and native peoples. The remote cabin and nearby graves of Grey Owl, Anahareo, and their daughter attract hundreds of visitors each year.

HABITATS

Fescue grassland along the southwestern and southern park boundaries represents the most northerly extension of prairie in the province, the home of badgers, ground squirrels, and other typical prairie creatures.

A large colony of American white pelicans breeds in Prince Albert National Park. These graceful birds migrate in flocks, flapping their wings in unison; they often fish cooperatively, seizing prey in their large, pouched bills.

Elsewhere in the south, aspen parkland forms a distinctive transition zone between prairie and boreal forest. The aspen is a boon to wildlife: it grows back rapidly after a fire or other disturbance, it has abundant nutrients in its leaves, and it forms a canopy for other plants that are useful to animals. Wapiti, white-tailed deer, ruffed grouse, beaver, snowshoe hare, and a host of other species depend on these open forests.

A herd of 50 surplus plains bison from Elk Island National Park outside Edmonton were released in the vicinity of Prince Albert Park in 1969. The animals quickly dispersed, and now a herd of 75 has established a range in the southwest corner of the park. (Indigenous bison were eliminated hereabouts in the 1890s.) One of the original transplants, a bull, did not take up residence, however; it headed straight back to Elk Island, traveling 375 mi/600 km west across farmland, forests, and the North Saskatchewan River in one of the most impressive cases of homing instinct ever documented in a large terrestrial mammal. The bull was found in poor condition roaming the perimeter of Elk Island. The animal's hide was raw from neck to chest from knocking down barbed-wire fences that stood between it and its goal. It had also been shot several times with small-caliber rifles, possibly by farmers and ranchers trying to drive it off their land. After unsuccessful attempts to herd the bison back into the preserve, park wardens were forced to destroy it.

Throughout the rest of the park, vegetation is typical of the mixed spruce and aspen forest of the southern boreal plains. White spruce and quaking aspen grow on the well-drained uplands, while club-topped black spruce and feathery tamarack occupy poorly drained soils, and jack pine flourishes on the sandy ridges.

In this patchwork forest, understory vegetation and the wildlife it supports vary with the dominant tree species. Beneath the sun-dappled aspen canopy, red-osier dogwood and beaked hazel provide fodder for moose and deer. Wood lily, twinflower, and pink pyrola brighten the forest floor.

The floor of white spruce forest is dark and acidic, reducing heavy undergrowth. Spruce grouse survive on spruce buds and the tree's bitter-tasting needles. Territorial red squirrels maintain high populations with a diverse diet of spruce cones, mushrooms, bird's eggs, even sap. Feather moss, stair-step moss, and knight's-plume intermingle beneath the black spruce canopy to form a rich, green carpet.

Most typical boreal forest creatures range throughout the park. Beaver, once nearly exterminated in North America, are plentiful again, as are river otter and mink. Bird species most easily spotted include the gray jay, boreal chickadee, and black-backed woodpecker, and such warblers as the magnolia and Cape May.

The park's 60 to 80 wolves cover vast areas in search of moose and other game. One of the largest of the park's five or six packs dens in the Waskesiu Hills. In late June and early July, the packs move from birthing dens to rendezvous sites on sandy ridges that rim wetlands. Here, two-month-old pups scrap for food and develop hunting skills until they are seasoned enough to travel with the adults.

Black bears and red foxes also den in the easily excavated gravelly soils of the Waskesiu Hills. Fox burrows can be seen at Prospect Point just south of Waskesiu townsite and along road embankments throughout the park.

Sphagnum bogs have formed where drainage is restricted. The most extensive wetlands are in the northwest near Lavallée Lake. Floating plants such as the water lily and pondweed colonize the open water. The remains of these aquatic species form a fine, soft layer called a "false bottom," which gradually rises as sediment accumulates.

Reeds, sedges, and marsh cinquefoil grow in the shallows; buckbean sends "runners" along the surface to form a floating mat. Sphagnum, a moss that can absorb 20 times its weight in water, fills the spaces between plants. (Indians fashioned strips of dried sphagnum moss into baby diapers.) The mat thickens and may form hummocks and ridges that support shrubs such as bog birch, leatherleaf, and bog rosemary, which are less tolerant of water and have thick leaves to conserve nutrients derived from photosynthesis. Scattered clumps of black spruce and tamarack fringe the bog and extend to the edge of the surrounding forest.

Few herbivores live in bogs, and therefore there are few predators. Northern bog lemmings, voles, and mice are exceptions, feeding on herbs and sedges. These rodents, in turn, are preyed on by boreal and great gray owls. In the northern half of the park, about 25 woodland caribou in a couple of small herds winter around frozen bogs, feeding on ground lichens where snow cover is thin, and on tree lichens where snow is deep.

Three large lakes—Waskesiu, Crean, and Kingsmere—dominate the northern half of the park. Their clear, cold water supports northern pike, lake trout, and other species that attract bald eagles, ospreys, and other fishing raptors. A colony of some 7,000 American white pelicans breeds on the shores of Lavallée Lake, along with double-crested cormorants and great blue herons.

OUTDOOR ACTIVITIES

Most park visitors spend all or part of their stay in Waskesiu. Recreational facilities include commercial accommodations and services, a beach, a marina, a golf course, tennis courts, and campgrounds. Fishermen, hikers, and canoeists venture on trails and waterways into the central and southeastern parts of the park. Winter brings cross-country skiers and ice fishermen.

Scenic Drives

Follow the 15-mi/24-km *Narrows Road* along the south shore of Waskesiu Lake in early morning for the best chances of sighting wildlife. The route starts at Waskesiu's main beach and travels south to Prospect Point, a high bluff that offers an excellent view of the lake. Beyond the townsite the mixed forest of aspen and evergreens closes in as the road winds through the Waskesiu Hills. At Mi 6.2/Km 10, the road crosses Mud Creek, where herons, eagles, beavers, and otters are frequently seen.

Songbirds perch in beachside trees along Trippes Beach at Mi 7.7/Km 12.3. Lake views are to be had at Paignton Beach, where the sand is colored with brown silica, black magnetite, and purple garnet. Watch for fox dens and moose as the road tops a sandy hill west of the beach, and look for loons, grebes, mallards, ospreys, and bald eagles at The Narrows, a channel joining the two parts of the lake.

The 20-mi/32.5-km *Kingsmere Road,* which follows the north shore of Waskesiu Lake, passes picnic areas, two marinas, and trails at Waskesiu

PRINCE ALBERT
NATIONAL PARK

Highways

Roads-Streets

Tracks-Trails

● Points of Interest

⌂ Camping

Wabeno Lake

Lavallee Lake

Wassegam Lake

Maclennan R.

Wasaw Lake

Paquin Lake

GREY OWL'S CABIN AND GRAVE

Bladebone Lake

Milawanga Lake

Ajawaan Lake

Bagwa-Lily Canoe Route

Hemming L.

Mikisew Lake

Bladebone Canoe Route

Purvis Lake

Bagwa Lake

Osten Lake

Kingsmere Lake

Grey Owl Trail

Crean Lake

Waskesiu R.

Nova Lake

Lily Lake

Clare Lake

Kingsmere Road

Hanging Heart Lakes

NARROWS PENINSULA

57 Trail

NARROWS CAMPGROUND

Treebeard Trail

Narrows Road

PAIGNTON BEACH

Waskesiu Lake

Waskesiu River Trail

Mud Creek Trail

Waskesiu Townsite

Boundary Bog Trail

TRIPPES BEACH

East Gate

HWY 264

HWY 2

Sturgeon R.

Shady Lake

NAMEKUS LAKE CAMPGROUND

Namekus Lake

Trappers Lake

Moose Trail

Spruce R.

Spruce River Highlands Trail

HWY 263

TRAPPERS LAKE CAMPGROUND

Amyot Lake

SPRUCE RIVER HIGHLANDS TOWER

Sturgeon R.

Fish Lake

Sandy Lake

Anglin Lake

Elk Trail

Hunters Lake

Hunters Lake Trail

Fish Lake Trail

SANDY LAKE CAMPGROUND

Spruce R.

HWY 240

South Gate

N

0 ——— 10 Mi

0 ——— 10 Km

River, The Narrows Peninsula, and Kingsmere River. *Highway 263*, which rolls through aspen parkland along the southeastern boundary from the South Gate to Waskesiu townsite, is a more leisurely and scenic route than Highways 2 and 264 (the usual route). Highlights include the display herd of plains bison in the paddock near the park's gate and viewing towers at Spruce River and the Height-of-Land, a watershed south of the townsite.

Hiking

The park's 95 mi/150 km of hiking routes are divided into short nature trails and backcountry trails. The hour-long *Boundary Bog Trail* just inside the East Gate on Highway 264 heads through spruce and aspen forest, across a bog on a boardwalk, and up the edge of a small lake where loons glide and dive. The route then winds back up a forested ridge to a tower that provides hikers with overviews of this waterlogged landscape.

Another popular hour-long circuit, the *Mud Creek Trail*, takes walkers through aspen parkland and boreal forest, past a creekside beaver lodge, and along the shore of Waskesiu Lake, where beaver, otter, herons, and eagles are sometimes seen. The *Treebeard Trail*, a 1.8-mi/3-km loop at The Narrows, gets its name from the old man's beard, a lichen that hangs from the boughs of the huge spruce and fir trees bordering the route. Some of the park's largest trees provide excellent habitat for woodpeckers, nuthatches, and black-throated green warblers. The bridge on the 90-minute *Waskesiu River Trail*, north of town on the Kingsmere Road, is a prime spot for sighting pelicans, beaver, and, in spring, spawning northern pike.

The 12.5-mi/20-km *Grey Owl Trail* to the cabin of the famed naturalist has long been a popular backcountry route. From the trailhead at the end of the Kingsmere Road, the route follows the lake's eastern shoreline, alternating stretches of beach with paths through the mixed forest and across grassy hillsides. The trail fords three creeks; crosses a fourth on a boardwalk; skirts a mineral lick at Mi 8.1/Km 13, where there are often signs of wildlife; and passes three wilderness campgrounds.

The hilly *Spruce River Highlands Trail*, an 5.3-mi/8.5-km loop south of Waskesiu townsite on Highway 263, is perhaps the park's most scenic route, particularly enjoyable when wildflowers peak from late June to early August and in September when fall colors highlight the hillsides and wapiti begin to bugle. The Spruce River Tower, located a short distance from the trailhead, is one of the park's best bird-watching spots, and also provides sightseers with panoramic views.

Taken clockwise from the tower, the trail ascends and descends several glacier-formed morainal hills, passing meadows colorful in summer with purple spikes of giant-hyssop, scarlet Indian paintbrush, and white northern bedstraw. Where the trail loops south, it climbs a hill affording views of Anglin Lake to the southwest, then returns to the starting point back through mixed forest.

Bicycling

Two warden patrol roads double as popular cycling routes. The *57 Trail* branches off The Narrows Road west of Trippes Beach and heads west through the Waskesiu Hills. The *West Side Road* parallels the Sturgeon River in the southwest corner of the park, prime bison habitat. A network of hiking trails near the southern boundary, passing Fish, Elk, and Hunters lakes, also beckons bikers.

Horseback Riding

The Waskesiu Riding Stables (306-663-5286) conducts one- to five-hour rides on a nearby trail network.

Boating

Motorboats are allowed on Kingsmere, Waskesiu, Hanging Heart, Crean, and Sandy lakes. Launches are at The Narrows, Sandy Lake, and the Waskesiu and Hanging Heart lakes marinas. Boaters traveling between Waskesiu and Kingsmere lakes portage their vessels on a miniature-railway flatbed car that rolls on a 325-ft/100-m length of track.

Canoeing

Although the park does not offer whitewater opportunities, its extensive network of lakes and streams makes canoeing a popular activity. The 12.5-mi/20-km *Bagwa–Lily Canoe Route* is a seven-hour circuit suitable for most paddlers. It starts at the Kingsmere River landing, hugs the western shore of Kingsmere Lake, and connects with Bagwa Lake to the southwest, which in turn connects with Lily Lake. After crossing Lily, canoeists portage to Clare Lake, then portage again between Clare and Kingsmere. Both portages are less than 325 ft/100 m.

An unnamed route to Grey Owl's cabin and grave parallels the hiking trail. Canoeists depart from the dock at the end of Kingsmere Road and land at the dock, picnic site, and beach area at the north end of the lake. After a 2,300-ft/700-m portage to Ajawaan Lake, a short paddle ends at the cabin on the northwest shore. Canoeists should budget two or three days to allow for windy lake conditions. Early morning and early evening are generally the best times to travel on Kingsmere, which is often rough due to strong northwesterly winds.

Experienced paddlers and wilderness enthusiasts spend five to seven days on the remote *Bladebone Route* in the northwestern section of the park. The route starts at Bladebone Bay near the end of Kingsmere Lake, then heads northwest through a chain of rivers and lakes to Mikisew, Bladebone, then Mitawanga Lake. From there, paddlers head south through Hemming and Purvis lakes, make a clockwise loop through Axhandle and Osten lakes, then return to Kingsmere via Mitawanga, Bladebone, and Mikisew. Fifteen portages, some quite challenging, punctuate the trip. Primitive campgrounds are along the way.

Fishing

The lakes of Prince Albert Park, once renowned for trophy-sized catches, have been overfished in recent years. Park officials now emphasize sustenance fishing for backcountry canoeists and hikers. The catch includes northern pike, lake trout, walleye, whitefish, and yellow perch. The ice-fishing season extends from mid-December through March.

Swimming

The most popular of several beaches found along Waskesiu Lake is within the resort area of Waskesiu. Excellent beaches are also on Kingsmere, Crean, Namekus, and Sandy lakes.

Cross-country Skiing

More than 95 mi/150 km of trails are concentrated in the southwest corner of the park. Eight novice and intermediate trails are tracked; the *Spruce River Highlands Trail*, which loops 5.3 mi/8.5 km, is packed for advanced skiers. Prime places to see wapiti, deer, and other winter wildlife are on the *Wapiti Trail*, which follows the golf course, and on the *Fisher Trail* adjacent to the Highway 264 entrance to Waskesiu.

Other Activities

Waskesiu has *golfing* (306-663-5302) on one of the province's finest 18-hole courses (it was designed by Stanley Thompson, who was also responsible for the Banff Springs course); six courts for *tennis;* and *lawn bowling.* In summer, hour-long cruises on the paddle-wheeler *Neowatin* leave from the Waskesiu marina.

A large sandy beach, boat rentals, tennis courts, lawn bowling greens, and a golf course can be found at expansive Waskesiu Lake; beyond this hub of activity, a vast wilderness awaits exploration.

EXPLORING THE PARK

The park is 40 mi/65 km north of the city of Prince Albert. Most people arrive via Highways 2 and 264 to Waskesiu townsite. From June through September, the Saskatchewan Transportation Company (306-933-8000) has daily service to Waskesiu townsite. Service is limited in winter.

The Nature Centre in Waskesiu contains displays of the park's natural history and geologic formations, as well as a theater where audiovisual shows are regularly presented. The summer interpretive program features daily hikes, wolf howls, and star-gazing expeditions. There are slide shows nightly at the outdoor theater in the Beaver Glen campground and three nights a week at The Narrows campground theater. Winter interpretive programs are held Saturday nights from January through March in one of the Waskesiu hotels.

Backcountry permits are issued at the Nature Centre, the East and South gates, and The Narrows campground. Boats and canoes can be rented from marinas at Waskesiu townsite, Hanging Heart Lakes, and The Narrows. Park waters are cold and lakes often are subject to sudden squalls. Prudent canoeists stay close to shore.

ACCOMMODATIONS: The largest and most developed campgrounds are densely wooded Beaver Glen in Waskesiu townsite (213 sites), the nearby trailer park (153 sites), and The Narrows (87 sites), where some sites are close to the lakeshore. The Narrows marina offers canoe and boat rentals. Smaller campgrounds are at Namekus Lake (21 lakeshore sites), Sandy Lake (26 sites), and Trappers Lake (8 sites). Twelve primitive campsites service backcountry boaters, and hikers.

Winter camping is available at the Tern Street campground in Waskesiu and at the Trappers, Namekus, Crean, and Fish lakes campgrounds. Trappers is a 2.5-mi/4-km ski in from Highway 263. Crean is a 5.9-mi/9.5-km ski from the North Shore (Kingsmere) Road. Fish Lake is a 7.5-mi/12-km ski from either of its trailheads on Highway 263 or the Cookson Road. Tern and Namekus are accessible by car.

The town of Waskesiu has some 300 beds in hotels, motels, lodges, and cabins. Service stations and food stores in Waskesiu are closed in winter. The following lodgings, which all rent skis, remain open: Château Park Chalets (306-663-5556), Hawood Inn (306-663-5911), and Lakeview Hotel (306-663-5311).

ADDRESSES: For more information, contact: The Superintendent, Prince Albert National Park, Box 100, Waskesiu Lake, Sask. S0J 2Y0; 306-663-5322. Friends of Prince Albert National Park (Box 11, Waskesiu, Sask. S0J 2Y0; 306-663-5213), a nonprofit organization promoting the park, operates a bookstore in the Nature Centre with a wide range of publications on the park's natural and human history. The Waskesiu Chamber of Commerce (Box 216, Waskesiu, Sask. S0J 2Y0; 306-663-5410 in summer, 306-922-3232 in winter) has information on commercial services for visitors.

BOOKS: Grey Owl's classics, *Sajo and Her Beaver People* and *Tales of an Empty Cabin*, are available at the Friends of the Park bookstore.

Beavers (left) often build dams with underwater entrances and a dry upper living lodge carpeted with wood chips. A stand of poplars (right), a favorite beaver food and building material, testifys to their industriousness.

GRASSLANDS NATIONAL PARK

WITHIN THE LAST CENTURY, the Canadian prairies have been transformed from wilderness into one of the most altered, ecologically simplified regions in the world. Two-thirds of Canada's native grasslands have been "improved," a government classification meaning that indigenous prairie flora has been plowed under and replaced with domesticated pasture plants or the single-crop fields that form the archetypal farmland checkerboard.

In two disjunct parcels of land in south-central Saskatchewan, Grasslands National Park preserves a remnant of mixed-grass prairie, some of which has never felt the bite of the plow. It is a windswept realm of grandeur and solitude little changed since the days of the great bison herds and wandering Native American tribes. The West Block contains a classic rolling prairie landscape dissected by the broad Frenchman River valley. The East Block comprises the Killdeer Badlands, a confusion of gullies, buttes, coulees, and other bizarre landforms. A richly endowed oasis, the park protects native plants and animals threatened elsewhere by cultivation; it is a refuge for prairie smoke and beard tongue, as well as for pronghorns, golden eagles, burrowing owls, and Canada's only black-tailed prairie-dog colonies.

GEOLOGY

As in most of Canada, the landscape here bears the scars of the great ice sheets that covered the continent at least four times in the last million years. Meltwater from retreating glaciers formed such watercourses as the Frenchman River, now a small stream meandering through an outsize valley. When the glaciers retreated, large boulders embedded in the melting ice dropped onto the prairie; these so-called erratics are scattered over the East Block especially, far from their place of origin in the Canadian Shield to the northeast.

In the East Block, wind and water erosion carved the intriguing landforms of the Killdeer Badlands: buttes (flat-topped hills with nearly vertical sides); hoodoos (columns of glacial till capped with erosion-resistant rock); and coulees (stream-eroded ravines). Eroded clay hills that support no vegetation dot the area. Some of these "dobbies" are circular, up to 300 ft/90 m in diameter and 200 ft/60 m high.

HISTORY

For thousands of years, until settlement at the turn of the century, Gros Ventre and Assiniboine followed the bison herds over the grassy uplands and through the eroded gullies of the Killdeer Badlands, which they found to be good lands for hunting. Remnants of tepee rings—circles of stones that held down tepee coverings in stiff prairie winds—are scattered in the Frenchman River valley. This was also a favorite hunting ground of the Métis, people of mixed Indian and French ancestry, during the early days of Manitoba's Red River colony.

In 1874, Sir George Dawson discovered Canada's first dinosaur bones in the Killdeer Badlands while serving on an international commission surveying the U.S.–Canada boundary. Two years later, after the Battle of the Little Big Horn, 4,000 Sioux led by Sitting Bull fled across the newly demarcated border from Montana into Canada, camping at Wood Mountain north of the park's East Block. Within a few years, the bison had been slaughtered almost to extinction, primarily by whites on both sides of the border. Much of the hunting was a deliberate killing off of herds to deprive the Indians of their main source of food and starve them into submission. The desperate Sioux began to trickle back to reservations in the United States. Sitting Bull and his last 200 followers held out until 1881, then crossed the border and surrendered to the U.S. Army.

Later homesteaders found the region too marginal to farm. The area continued to be used for ranching and remained an island of virgin grassland surrounded by a sea of cultivation.

HABITATS

Stereotyped as bleak and barren, the grasslands are, in fact, a richly populated ecosystem, supporting a wide variety of plants and animals. The region is semiarid, with two-thirds of the 12–16 in/30–40 cm of annual precipitation falling from May to September. Woody plants have a hard·time in this climate, but nearly 50 species of grasses thrive, mainly blue grama, western wheatgrass, speargrass, and needle-and-thread. These drought- and fire-resistant native grasses form a tough carpet called "prairie wool" that stabilizes the soil, preventing erosion. Wildflowers enliven the subdued grays, greens, and blues of a grassland spring: brilliant golden beans, feathery avens, and starbursts of asters. Ubiquitous prickly pears unfold lovely yellow flowers and provide food for the white-tailed jackrabbit, whose powerful hind legs can propel it up to 45 mph/72 kph.

Pronghorn antelopes, once 15 to 30 million strong on the plains, still sprint across rolling prairie uplands. Pronghorns, which are not really antelope but a species of ruminant unique to North America, use exceptional eyesight (comparable to a person using eight-power binoculars) and a keen sense of smell to avoid coyotes, their main enemy. Their oversized lungs, heart, and windpipe enable pronghorns to sprint at up to 60 mph/100 kph, making them North America's swiftest mammal.

Mule deer favor sagebrush-covered hillsides and sheltered badland coulees, where some trees and shrubs manage to survive. Willows line streambeds and the meandering Frenchman River. Green ashes and boxelders (Manitoba maples) shade sheltered areas. Creeping juniper is by far the commonest evergreen, forming extensive mats on badland clays. Deep-rooted sagebrush spreads a blue-green carpet over wide areas. White-tailed deer browse in gullies clogged with saskatoon, red-osier dogwood, and buffaloberry—all important food sources for birds and other wildlife.

Sedges, bulrushes, and cattails fringe floodplain marshes on alluvial flats, oxbow lakes, and abandoned loops of the Frenchman River, where ducks, geese, herons, and American bitterns gather in spring and fall. If

Providing a brilliant grasslands display, wildflowers such as the pincushion cactus (upper left), the three-flowered prairie smoke (lower left), and the globemallow (lower right), are specialists in conserving water. OPPOSITE: *Frenchman River Valley is home to pronghorn antelope, black-tailed prairie dogs, and rare prairie falcons.*

water levels remain high, some migrants stay all summer. The long-billed curlew, North America's largest shorebird, forsakes a watery environment in summer, nesting and feeding on the open prairie.

The park's most common rodent is the Richardson's ground squirrel, known regionally as the gopher (from the French *gaufre de miel*, or "honeycomb," a word that describes the animal's tunnel system). The park's most appealing ground squirrel, however, is the larger black-tailed prairie dog, which congregates in Canada's only remaining colonies here in the Frenchman River valley. Elsewhere hunted, trapped, and poisoned nearly to extinction, this gregarious rodent is active during the day and easily observed with binoculars or a telephoto lens.

Prairie-dog colonies, or towns, support an array of squatters and predators. Abandoned burrows become nesting sites for the burrowing owl. When western rattlesnakes slither down the main entrance to a burrow, the prairie dogs exit via a back door. Badgers work the outskirts of the towns, digging out new, shallow dog burrows in an effort to catch the occupants. Golden eagles, prairie falcons, rare ferruginous hawks, bobcats, and coyotes round out the lengthy list of prairie-dog predators.

The Frenchman River valley is also prime habitat for the sage grouse, which performs an elaborate courtship dance similar to that of the sharp-tailed grouse. In spring at day's first light male sage grouse gather on open communal display areas called "leks" to strut, swell their breasts, and battle other males. Occasionally, a male draws air into two frontal sacs, causing the breast to expand until it nearly conceals the head. Then the wings droop, the neck feathers ruffle, and the tail spreads like a fan. In this puffed-chest posture, the male races forward a few steps while loudly rubbing its bristly breast feathers with the leading edge of its wings and forcing air from the sacs with a strange gurgling sound.

Other park denizens have bizarre traits. When attacked, the short-horned lizard (or horned toad) responds by shooting jets of blood out of its eye sockets. Scientists have yet to explain fully the chemical mechanism involved in such a sudden pressurization, rupture, and resealing of the circulatory system. The wind-scorpion, a little-known arthropod that runs swiftly with its large forelimbs held high like massive projecting taste buds, finds one of its few Canadian homes in the park. This voracious predator sports a formidable stabbing and shearing mouth part and will feed on virtually anything it can subdue, even lizards.

OUTDOOR ACTIVITIES

At present, the focus is on preserving and acquiring land, not on recreation. When the park is fully developed, interior traffic will likely be limited to visitors on horseback and hikers wandering over the grasslands to various points of interest.

Scenic Drives

Free maps available at the park headquarters and visitors' center in Val Marie enable motorists to follow a gravel grid road south of town into the West Block. There, typical prairie trails lead to scenic views of the Frenchman River valley, weathered landforms, and prairie-dog towns. Pronghorns usually are sighted along the way, and hawks and eagles often are seen wheeling in the wide prairie sky.

EXPLORING THE PARK

The town of Val Marie, gateway to the park, is 80 mi/128 km south of Swift Current via Highway 4. Park officials at the visitors' center in town can answer questions about the park and provide driving-tour maps. Videotapes on Grasslands National Park are presented in a viewing room. Until park boundaries are finalized, interpretive programs, campgrounds, and other facilities will remain minimal.

ACCOMMODATIONS: The Val Marie Hotel (306-298-9080) and the more rustic Alex's Cabins (306-298-2048) provide the only commercial accommodation near the park. Two private campgrounds are being developed in the Val Marie area. More extensive visitor facilities are in Swift Current and in Regina, 152 mi/240 km east of Swift Current on the Trans-Canada Highway (Highway 1).

ADDRESSES: For more information on the park, contact: The Superintendent, Grasslands National Park, Box 150, Val Marie, Sask. S0N 2T0; 306-298-2257.

BOOKS: Wallace Stegner, *Wolf Willow*. Lincoln: University of Nebraska Press, 1980. Reminiscences of the southern plains of Saskatchewan, where the author spent his boyhood.

RIDING MOUNTAIN NATIONAL PARK

RIDING MOUNTAIN is not a "mountain" but part of an escarpment jutting like a great green wedge 1,500 ft/460 m above the flat farmland of southwestern Manitoba. Those who approach the park from the south—the thin edge of the wedge—may wonder where the mountain is, so gradual is the change in elevation. The height of the plateau at the top of the escarpment can only be appreciated from the north and east, where steep slopes rise dramatically from the prairie.

The park is a wilderness meeting ground of plant and animal communities from the east, west, and north. Hardwood forests, more typical of southern Ontario than Manitoba, grow on the eastern edge of the park, sheltered in the lee of the escarpment. High above on the plateau, a patchwork of coniferous forest, lakes, and wetlands spreads across a hummocky land that still bears the scars of recent glaciation—relic beaches, meltwater channels, and morainal ridges. A windswept expanse of prairie, dotted with water-filled glacial depressions called "potholes" and groves of aspen (known regionally as bluffs), rolls across the western third of the park.

GEOLOGY

The same geologic forces that raised the Rocky Mountains, beginning some 85 million years ago, thrust up flat-lying terrain far to the east. The western edge of that elevation remains today as the Manitoba Escarpment, a discontinuous upland that arcs some 1,000 mi/1,600 km from North Dakota through Manitoba and into Saskatchewan. Rivers tumbling over the escarpment eventually sliced the ridge into isolated "mountains," including Riding Mountain.

Pleistocene glaciers bulldozed enormous quantities of shale from Riding Mountain south into North Dakota. As the ice retreated northward, meltwater pooled in Lake Agassiz, which lapped against the base of the escarpment and spread over southern Manitoba, western Ontario, and North Dakota, the largest body of fresh water ever known. About 8,000 years ago, Lake Agassiz drained northeast into Hudson Bay, leaving behind vestigial lakes (Winnipeg, Manitoba, and many others), and a flat clay bed that is now rich farmland.

Amid a field of golden flowers, a simple wooden house against a backdrop of hills creates a classic prairie landscape in Riding Mountain National Park.

True to its name, Winding Creek snakes through a section of Riding Mountain National Park.

HISTORY

The forests, prairies, and lakes of Riding Mountain were favorite hunting grounds for the Woodland Cree, who lived in the highlands, and the Assiniboine, a tribe that lived off bison herds on the surrounding prairie. Between 1731 and 1749, Pierre de la Vérendrye and his four sons explored and traded in the region. At the request of the Cree, la Vérendrye established a post in 1741 at Dauphin Lake, north of today's park. By 1800, trading posts ringed the mountain, which yielded a rich harvest of furs. The easiest way to ascend the rugged highland was by horseback, hence the mountain's name.

By the 1850s, bison, wolverine, river otter, marten, and fisher had disappeared from the mountain; beaver hovered on the brink of extermination. After the Canadian Pacific Railway reached the area in 1881, homesteaders began farming the rich plains surrounding the plateau, which they used as a source of timber and game. The upland was withdrawn from settlement at the end of the last century; it was designated a forest reserve in 1906 and a national park in 1930.

HABITATS

Riding Mountain National Park includes coniferous trees of the transcontinental boreal forest as well as hardwoods from the southeast and prairie from the southwest. The meeting of these diverse life zones produces a rich and varied assemblage of plants.

Along the park's eastern boundary at the base of the escarpment, the growing season is a month longer than atop the plateau and rainfall is greater—conditions that nurture an eastern woodland far west of its main range. Dense stands of American elm, bur oak, green ash, boxelder, and mountain maple tower over a thick undergrowth of shrubs, vines, and ferns. Golden-winged warblers, a true eastern species, nest here, along with northern orioles and rose-breasted grosbeaks.

The eastern gray squirrel and eastern chipmunk, also far west of their main Canadian range, gather the plentiful nuts and seeds scattered by the hardwoods. Black bears wander down from their usual plateau haunts to feast all summer long on fruit bushes and other nutritious food: saskatoons and pin cherry in July; nannyberry, chokecherry, and acorns in August; highbush cranberry, American plum, and hazelnut in September.

The eastern two-thirds of the upland are robed with mixed forest dominated by white and black spruce. In places, dense conifer stands sprinkle needles and debris that render the soil too acidic and nitrogen-poor for most understory plants, except moss, twinflower, and bunchberry. Birds and mammals here make efficient use of the coniferous forest's limited food supply. Six species of woodpeckers in narrow biological niches can feed on a single tree without competing directly with one another. Spruce grouse survive on a meager diet of conifer needles and buds, augmented in season with berries.

Water-tolerant black spruce and tamarack encircle eastern wetlands, along with balsam willow and other shrubs. In pools and sphagnum bogs, sundews make up for the lack of nitrogen by capturing and consuming

Commonly known as buffalos, baby bison (left) are born singly in May, standing up to nurse within thirty minutes and joining the herd in a day or two. Born in litters of two, the lynx (right) sometimes waits in forest trees to leap on passing prey. Large, thickly-furred feet allow for silent stalking and powerful swimming.

insect prey. Exquisite wildflowers—the round-leaved orchis, gaywings, and one-flowered wintergreen—seem almost too delicate to flourish near these acidic waters.

Moose forage on shrubs and aquatic plants in beaver ponds and lake shallows. These massive ungulates are shadowed by the park's 70-odd gray wolves, which prowl in 12 packs. The park is also home to North America's last pure herd of Manitoba elk. Once threatened by overhunting but now 3,500 strong, the elk graze in meadows and forest clearings on grasses and shrubs. Lynx range throughout the boreal forest preying on hares, rodents, and birds; these wild cats have wide, furry paws that act like snowshoes and make them extremely efficient predators, even in winter.

Boreal lakes are the summer breeding grounds for common loons and four of Canada's five species of grebes. Juvenile American white pelicans summer near the resort town of Wasagaming and in ponds around Lake Audy. Bald eagles, which nest in eight locations around the park, are most readily seen at Audy and Moon lakes.

Nearly exterminated when the park was established, the beaver has made such an astounding comeback that this amphibious creature can be seen in nearly every pond, lake, and stream. No other wild animal, with the exception of the elephant, modifies the landscape as much as beavers do. Ponds created behind their dams provide breeding and feeding habitats for waterfowl, fish, muskrats, and moose.

In the western third of the park, lighter rainfall, sandy soil, and frequent fires have created a mosaic of aspen parkland interspersed with grassland meadows carpeted with rough fescue, needle grass, and june grass. Pothole lakes are home to thousands of mallards, blue-winged teal, and other migratory waterfowl. Open expanses are fringed with such drought-resistant shrubs as snowberry and bearberry. An impressive wildflower palette lasts all summer: prairie buttercup (May and early June), three-flowered avens and field chickweed (June), black-eyed susan and stiff goldenrod (July and August), and smooth aster (August and early September).

Coyotes, the grassland predator most often sighted by park visitors, thrive on abundant ground squirrels, meadow voles, and northern pocket gophers. Red-tailed hawks, red foxes, and badgers also prey on gophers.

The elaborate mating rituals of the sharp-tailed grouse entertain observant hikers along the Birdtail Valley Trail. Early on spring mornings, competing cocks gather, droop their wings, erect their tails, puff themselves up, and inflate the colorful air sacs on their necks. Then they stamp, run, and leap in a frenzied group dance, competing for dominance and the attention of the hens. The winner services several females.

OUTDOOR ACTIVITIES

Open year-round, the park has long been a beloved retreat for Manitobans. Summer brings fishermen, boaters, hikers, and mountain bikers who enjoy the best backcountry cycling on the prairies. Winter attracts skiers (both downhill and cross-country) and ice fishermen.

Scenic Drives

The *Riding Mountain Parkway* (Highway 10) runs 30 mi/48 km north of Wasagaming through the heart of the preserve. The Agassiz lookout tower, 4 mi/6.5 km inside the park's northern boundary on the brow of the escarpment, provides views of a magnificent sweep of prairie. On *Highway 19*, which heads east of Wasagaming, the Norgate viewpoint on the eastern escarpment overlooks a checkerboard of fields that stretches 50 mi/80 km across the former Agassiz lakebed.

Hiking

The 32 trails that wander through Riding Mountain's three environments are divided into 17 day-use hikes and 15 overnight routes.

On the hour-long *Ominnik Marsh Trail* at the Wasagaming townsite, a floating boardwalk extends into a willow swamp where red-winged blackbirds, ducks, beavers, and muskrats can be seen. The double-looped *Burntwood Trail*, just east of Clear Lake, wanders through an area where conifers have been burned off by forest fires three times in the past 60 years, enabling an isolated pocket of fescue prairie to survive. The second loop heads through black spruce to the marshy edge of Kinosao Lake, home to several loons. Burntwood connects with the *Grey Owl Trail*, which extends north 5.5 mi/8.8 km to Beaver Lodge Lake and an abandoned cabin of Grey Owl, a conservationist and internationally known author who helped to reestablish beaver populations here in the 1930s.

The *Gorge Creek Trail* starts at the Dead Ox Creek picnic site 3.9 mi/ 6.2 km inside the East Gate on Highway 19 and descends the escarpment, providing splendid views along the way. The route drops 1,470 ft/450 m in 4 mi/6.4 km and ends at The Birches picnic site, where far-sighted hikers station vehicles to take them back up the escarpment. Bears are often seen along the nearby *Burls and Bittersweet Trail* through the eastern hardwood forest.

In the same corner of the park, the rugged overnight *South Escarpment Trail* wanders 14.5 mi/23.2 km south from the Dead Ox Creek picnic site into the lovely McFadden Valley, a broad, flat-bottomed glacial meltwater channel. Two campsites are along the way. The *Ochre River Trail* starts at a parking lot 10 mi/16 km north of Wasagaming on Highway 10, then descends 15.6 mi/25 km from plateau to prairie via one of the deep ravines that streams have cut into the escarpment. It also has two campsites.

The 45.6-mi/73-km *Central Trail* provides the main access to the western half of Riding Mountain. Five spur trails branch off the main route to seldom-visited corners of the park. The eastern trailhead is at the north gate of the Lake Audy bison enclosure. At Mi 6.5/Km 10.5, a short spur trail south leads to the Whitewater Lake campground, the site of a World War II prisoner-of-war camp and a good place to see wapiti. The main trail continues west through aspen parkland to a campsite on Gunn Lake, an easy 1.2-mi/2-km side trip over ridgetops where wapiti are seen year-round in hazelnut and hawthorn scrub.

Farther west 2.9 mi/4.6 km, the 6-mi/10-km *Baldy Lake Trail* to the south provides an excellent wilderness hike through mixed forest, then rolling grassland. At Mi 27/Km 43.5, the Central Trail enters the Birdtail Valley, the loveliest feature of the western plateau. Here, over the ages, Birdtail Creek has carved a broad channel between high, rolling hills known as the Birdtail Bench. The trail follows the south bank of the creek through mixed forests and meadows, then climbs south out of the valley, passing through spruce-fir, oak-ash, and poplar forests. Atop the bench, the landscape opens into prairie grasslands that extend as far as the eye can see.

Birdtail's undulating prairie is a magnificent feature of Riding Mountain National Park.

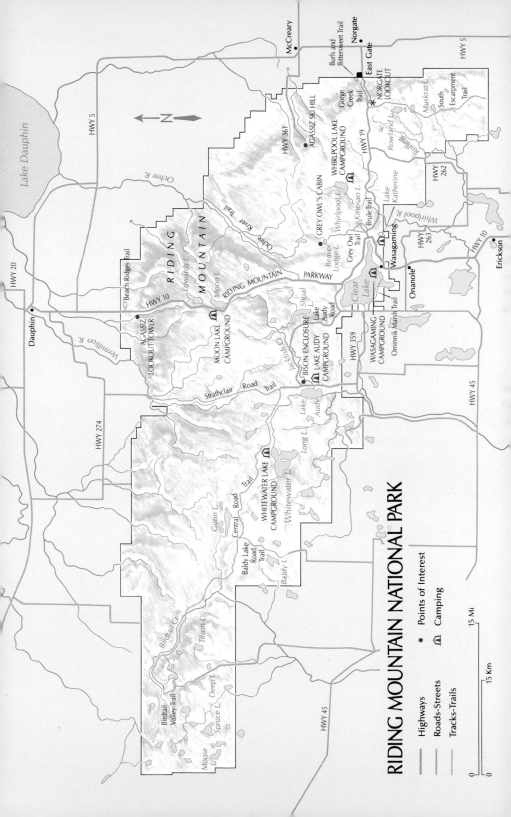

RIDING MOUNTAIN NATIONAL PARK

Points of Interest

Camping

- Highways
- Roads-Streets
- Tracks-Trails

0 — 15 Km
0 — 15 Mi

Bicycling

Riding Mountain is noted for the length and excellent condition of its trails. Cyclists have a choice of eight routes. The two most popular outings have the same starting point at the north gate to the bison paddock: the Central Trail, which heads west, and the northbound Strathclair Trail, which follows the original Indian trail north across Riding Mountain.

Horseback Riding

The means of conveyance that gave Riding Mountain its name is still popular. Horses are permitted on two day-use trails (Clear Lake and Grey Owl) and on all 15 overnight trails. There are several outfitters who organize day and overnight trips in the park.

Boating

Motorized boats are allowed on Clear, Audy, and Moon lakes (boats must be carried about 330 ft/100 m to the Moon Lake launch site). Rentals are available at the pier in Wasagaming.

Fishing

The park is well known for the number and size of its sport fish. Clear Lake yields northern pike up to 28 lbs/13 kg, as well as walleye, yellow perch, whitefish, and lake trout. Rainbow and brook trout populate Lake Katherine and Deep Lake. Moon, Whirlpool, Long, and Audy lakes also have northern pike. Ice fishing is permitted on Clear Lake from December through mid-April.

Swimming

The only supervised swimming is at Wasagaming's main beach on spring-fed Clear Lake.

Winter Activities

The *downhill skiing* season lasts from mid-December through March. The modest Agassiz Ski Hill (204-835-2246), accessible from the town of McCreary via Highway 361, has a 500-ft/152-m vertical drop on the escarpment, five lifts and tows, snow-making equipment, and a chalet.

For *cross-country skiing,* there are 106 mi/170 km of groomed trails. Favorites include Grey Owl-Burntwood, Lake Katherine, and Beach Ridges off Highway 10 just inside the northern boundary.

Other Activities

Wasagaming offers golfing on an 18-hole course built in the 1930s (204-848-7445 for reservations), tennis, and lawn bowling.

EXPLORING THE PARK

Riding Mountain is 165 mi/265 km northwest of Winnipeg via the Trans-Canada Highway (Highway 1) and Highway 10. Greyhound Lines (204-783-8840) has daily service to the park in summer.

Park headquarters and visitor facilities are at Wasagaming, a resort town on Clear Lake and the only development in Riding Mountain. Free permits required for overnight trips into the backcountry are available at the information center, open daily in summer, as well as at the north and south park gates and all warden stations.

Summer interpretive programs include: instruction in elk-bugling, wolf-howling, and moose-calling; car caravans to scenic places on the park's network of roads; and day hikes to bear dens and elk mineral licks. "Discovery kits" are popular with children and adults alike. The kits, which are borrowed from the interpretive center, consist of a magnifying glass, waterproof field guide, checklist, net, and other items essential for catching water insects from the boardwalk in Ominnik Marsh, identifying them, and returning them to the water.

ACCOMMODATIONS: The largest of four serviced campgrounds is Wasagaming (500 sites). Waterside camping is available at Lake Katherine campground (108 sites), which has a beach, and Moon Lake (29 sites). Lake Audy campground (50 sites) is south of the bison enclosure. Whirlpool Lake (14 sites) affords the peace and quiet of a hike-in, tents-only facility. Primitive campsites are found along 11 back-country trails. Winter camping occurs at Moon, Katherine, and Whirlpool lakes (ski-in only), and at the main parking lot in Wasagaming.

Privately operated lodges, cabins, and motels in Wasagaming are heavily booked in July and August.

ADDRESSES: For information on the facilities in Wasagaming, contact: The Superintendent, Riding Mountain National Park, Wasagaming, Man. R0J 2H0; 204-848-2811.

BOOKS: Donald Smith, *From the Land of Shadows: The Making of Grey Owl*. Saskatoon, Sask.: Western Producer Prairie Books, 1990. Biography of the enigmatic, controversial conservationist and author.

CENTRAL CANADA

QUETICO PROVINCIAL PARK 172

This watery maze of lakes and rivers along the Canadian-American border in western Ontario forms North America's premier canoeing country, where paddlers follow in the wake of the voyageurs.

POINT PELEE NATIONAL PARK 184

Jutting into Lake Erie at the southernmost point on the Canadian mainland, this gentle mixture of beaches, woodlands, ponds, and marshes each year attracts thousands of migratory birds and bird watchers.

BRUCE PENINSULA NATIONAL PARK AND FATHOM FIVE NATIONAL MARINE PARK 194

This finger of land separating Lake Huron and Georgian Bay is rimmed with cliffs, pocked with caves, and clothed with forests where orchids bloom; offshore, shipwrecks litter the floor of Fathom Five.

ALGONQUIN PROVINCIAL PARK   206

More than 1,500 lakes scattered across this park in southeastern Ontario beckon canoeists, who glide past smooth outcrops of Precambrian rock and hillsides covered with thick pine forests.

ST. LAWRENCE ISLANDS NATIONAL PARK   220

A small mainland area, 18 wooded islands, and 80 rocky islets are scattered among the Thousand Islands in the St. Lawrence River, a beloved vacationland in southeastern Ontario.

LA MAURICIE NATIONAL PARK   232

Swift-flowing rivers, pristine lakes, and woodlands ablaze with autumn color weave a scenic tapestry in the gently rolling Laurentians of south-central Quebec.

QUETICO PROVINCIAL PARK

QUETICO PROVINCIAL PARK in northwestern Ontario and the adjacent Boundary Waters Wilderness of Minnesota protect what is perhaps the finest canoeing area in North America. Paddlers here explore a wilderness of lakes, forests, and granite cliffs little changed since the days of the Ojibwa and the voyageurs. In this riparian jigsaw, more than 600 lakes are linked by streams flowing smoothly through bedrock channels, tumbling over rapids, and flaring out in ragged falls.

Canoeists ply river and lake from May to October, challenging rapids on the Maligne and Basswood rivers, or searching out enigmatic rock paintings still sacred to the Ojibwa. Some paddlers laze along where voyageurs raced, lingering at remote campsites, dropping a hook for walleye or trout, swimming in the surprisingly warm lake waters, or just lolling on a lichen-streaked granite outcrop, watching summer float by.

GEOLOGY

The park is on the southern edge of the Canadian Shield, an exposed segment of the earth's original crust. Quetico rocks, among the oldest anywhere, were all formed during the Precambrian era, which ended about 600 million years ago. Some of the earliest life forms on earth also are found in Quetico country: rare fossils of blue-green algae, an estimated 2.8 billion years old, were discovered in an open-pit iron mine north of the park boundary. The only life forms more ancient are from Australia and the Transvaal of southern Africa.

The oldest and least common of Quetico's three major types of bedrock, greenstone, dates back some 2.7 billion years. It is found in the southeast corner of the park near the Man Chain lake system and McKenzie and Cullen lakes. All across the Canadian Shield belts of greenstones weave between areas of granite. Greenstones are thought to be lavas formed under water, because their characteristic structure—great blobs, or pillows —are similar to those that form when magma erupts and cools on the ocean floor. These former lavas may indeed be the vestiges of ancient seabeds.

From the eastern and western boundaries of the park extend fingers of younger sedimentary rock formed on the floor of an ancient sea. Toward the end of the Precambrian era, heat and pressure generated by volcanic activity and mountain-building changed, or metamorphosed, these sediments, as it tilted and folded them. Quetico metasediments, usually gray-colored and layered, can be seen south and west of Sturgeon Lake, and around Zephira, Cache, and Lindsay lakes. Metasediments are softer than granite and erode more easily, releasing nutrients that enrich the soil. Consequently, metasedimentary basins support a larger number and a greater diversity of plants and animals than areas underlaid with more erosion-resistant granite.

The volcanism and mountain-building that rearranged the sediments raised the Algoman Mountains 2.5 billion years ago, a range long since ground down by erosion. Granite, the park's youngest and most widespread rock, was formed about this time. It began as magma oozing into cavities between buckling and folding sedimentary layers. Subsequent erosion has, in many places, removed the overlying metasediments and exposed coarse-grained, smooth-surfaced granite outcrops colored white, pink, gray, or tan.

Over the ages, massive faulting produced the park's signature feature: long cliffs that aboriginal artists used as granite canvases. These nearly vertical ramparts are along many park lakes, including south-central Agnes Lake, bordered by cliffs and ridges up to 250 ft/76 m high, and the nearby Man Chain lakes, where bluffs rise 150 ft/45 m. West of Agnes, a chain of four lakes, aligned as though with a colossal ruler, lies along a fault some 20 mi/32 km long. Spectacular cliffs are also found along Lake Kahshahpiwi.

Starting around a million years ago, the Pleistocene glaciation ravaged Quetico country. Ice sheets scraped off topsoil and pushed it southwest, exposed underlying bedrock, and scooped out basins that later filled with meltwater and became the park's myriad lakes. Throughout Quetico, smoothed and rounded boulders and striated outcrops, clawed as though by some primordial beast, mark the passing of the ice sheets, which retreated about 10,000 years ago.

HISTORY

The park's rich prehistory is represented by more than 300 archaeological sites, some dating back 9,000 years. In the late 1600s, French explorers reached Quetico country, just in time to witness the Ojibwa displacing the Sioux from the region. Like the Sioux, the Ojibwa lived a nomadic life of hunting, fishing, trapping, and gathering. In spring, they camped along the Maligne River and other waterways to fish for sturgeon, a food source as important to the Woodland Indians as bison was to the Plains Indians. In summer, wild rice was harvested from backwater bays of Lac la Croix. Moose and duck bagged during autumn hunts were smoked for winter use. A favorite wintering ground for the Ojibwa was Saganagons Lake, which abounds with fish.

The Ojibwa recorded exploits, legends, and dreams in pictographs, or rock paintings, and Quetico has the largest such collection in eastern North America, with more than 30 sites scattered throughout the park. Sitting or standing in a birchbark canoe beside a cliff, the artist finger-painted 6-in/ 15-cm figures in red, a color symbolic of life, virtue, and good fortune; the medium used was red ocher. The flow of ions from iron in the ocher penetrated the crystalline matrix of the granite, creating a bond that has withstood the elements for up to 500 years. At some sites, lime leaching out of the rock has started to shroud the rock art, making it appear faded.

The largest and best pictograph site in the park is on the west shore of Irving Island, near the Lac la Croix entry station, where aptly named Painted Rock is decorated with representations of a fox, bull moose, caribou, warrior, handprints, and abstract figures. Another outstanding site is Darky Lake, where artists drew the aquatic god Mishipizhiu, who caused storms on lakes by thrashing a dragon-like tail. (Some Ojibwa still make tobacco offerings to this spirit before venturing out on large lakes.)

By the late 1700s, the main route west of the fur-trade brigades ran through Quetico country. Tough, wiry French-Canadian voyageurs—sitting six to ten in their birchbark canoes—were the engines of a sprawling commercial enterprise. The voyageurs took a break about every hour in their sprints across the water. For ten minutes they puffed on long-stemmed pipes, then returned to the paddles, often singing to keep time to the strokes. They calculated the length of lakes in *pipes*, or the number of breaks required for a crossing.

Most of the time, voyageurs battled through rough water to avoid time-consuming portages, but disaster awaited if the *gouvernail* (sternman) and *avant* (bowman) misread rapids. In one stretch of the Basswood River rapids, archaeologists have found objects from a capsized canoe, including trade axes, beads, musket balls, and a pewter pipe with tobacco still in the bowl. Even so, the voyageurs, known for their stamina and strength, cursed the portages, the last resort around impassable water. They packed on their backs two *pièces* at a time—90-lb/40-kg bales of furs or trade goods—and trotted (they did not walk) over the rough and often tangled trail.

The traditional voyageur route through Quetico country became Canada's border after the Treaty of Paris in 1783. But to the dismay of the Montreal-based North West Company, the boundary gave the United States control of the Grand Portage, the easiest access from Lake Superior to the

Quetico Provincial Park has been home to man for almost 9,000 years. The placid waters of over 600 lakes are perfect for canoeing, and entry quotas help to avoid overcrowding.

water routes heading northwest. The Nor-Westers eventually shifted operations north and built palisaded Fort William at today's Thunder Bay, their great midcontinent entrepôt, where partners who had brought trade goods from Montreal met *hivernants* (wintering partners) laden with furs from the far Northwest, the *pays d'en haut*. They paused for boisterous bacchanalia, swapped cargoes, discussed business, and headed back where they had come from before freeze-up.

In 1857, a civil engineer named Simon Dawson surveyed an all-Canadian route from Lake Superior to the Red River settlement (now Winnipeg). The rugged Dawson Trail, which combined travel by wagon road, steamboat, and portage along the old fur-trade route, proved its worth in 1870 when Lt. Col. Garnet Wolseley and 1,400 troops followed it west to quell the Riel Rebellion in Manitoba. Later, settlers bound for prairie homesteads slogged over the trail.

By 1875, Canadian settlers could ride an American railroad in comfort from Duluth to the Red River in Minnesota, where they boarded Manitoba-bound riverboats. Thereafter, the Dawson Trail was used mainly to transport material for the construction of its successor, the Canadian Pacific Railway, completed in 1885.

HABITATS

Canoeists spend more time on the water than anywhere else in Quetico, so they see mostly plants of lake, marsh, and shore—the cupped blossoms of fragrant white water lilies floating in a sea of green pads, the rustling shoreline fringes of rushes, sedges, and reed grass.

Red and eastern white pines, characteristic of the Great Lakes–St. Lawrence forest, are usually limited to warmer, richer sites close to rivers and lakeshores. They are, therefore, frequently seen by canoeists, who may think they are more common than they really are. The most impressive stands of large red and white pines are along the Mack–Munro portage in eastern Quetico and deep in the park interior, especially in the vicinity of McNiece Lake.

The boreal component of this mixed community, mainly jack pine, black spruce, quaking aspen, and paper birch, comprises nearly 70 percent of Quetico's forests. There are widespread wetlands, including raised bogs where black spruce grow out of a thick, soft carpet of sphagnum. Northern white-cedar is abundant only in greenstone country, where a few trees that are an estimated 900 years old have such a prodigious girth that two people can barely join hands to encircle the trunk.

Portages between Quetico's lakes range from calm passages to white-water rapids. Some can be run only by experts; park rangers provide information to help visitors plan safe canoeing trips.

About 20 percent of the park is exposed granite encrusted with extensive lichen communities. To many, the patterns and colors of these primitive, durable plants—orange star, map lichen, toadskin—form as striking a visual aspect of Quetico as the jack pines struggling for a foothold on an exposed bedrock ridge.

Flower lovers who are prepared to deal with blackflies come to Quetico during the last week of May and the first two weeks of June, the brief season when forest plants bloom while there is abundant light on the forest floor. In places, almost solid yellow carpets of clintonia mix with the delicate whites of goldthread, bunchberry, star-flower, and false lily of the valley, a common forest flower.

About the third week of May, three shrubs—leatherleaf, bog laurel, and bog rosemary—along with hare's-tail cotton grass, bloom simultaneously, producing a dazzling display of pinks and whites in Quetico's bogs. Orchid lovers visit bogs in late June or early July to see rose pogonia and grass-pink, two of the loveliest of Quetico's 658 species of native flowers. In summer, snow-white meadowsweet and the gaudy yellow spikes of swamp candles form almost continuous lakeshore fringes. In August, shorelines bloom with white, blue, and purple asters intermingled with yellow goldenrod.

Marshes yield the greatest variety of water-loving plants—three-way sedges, blue flags, and hundreds of other species. The Ojibwa made flour from the dried roots and seeds of wild calla. Bur-reeds, which usually grow in clay or silt along shorelines, are an important food source for waterfowl, muskrats, and beaver, as is arrowhead, a member of the water-plantain family. Ojibwa women would feel around with their toes in the mucky lake bottom (fine lakebed silt is known locally as "loonshit"), dislodging the arrowhead's potato-like tubers, which floated to the surface. Indians also collected tubers cached by muskrats.

Most portages in Quetico are in valleys along small streams that form the drainage channels between lakes. Here, in rich, basic soils, grows a community of black ash, red maple, and American elm that has an understory of such southern species as poison ivy and Virginia creeper. This localized "portage community," as it is known to park naturalists, is virtually absent elsewhere in Quetico because of acidic, sandy, or peaty soils. For cross-pollination purposes, the carrion-flower, found along portages in the southwest corner of the park, has the odor of dead flesh, which attracts bluebottle flies. (The Ojibwa chew the plant's berries to soothe sore throats.)

Long winters with deep snow and closed coniferous forests limit the abundance and variety of parkland wildlife. The most characteristic Quetico animals are such aquatic creatures as the beaver, muskrat, and mink, and small mammals—the deer mouse, boreal red-backed vole, red squirrel, and the squirrel's primary predator, the marten. In years when mice and voles are plentiful, campers may hear the hooting of barred owls as they swoop through dark forests in search of prey.

In northeastern Quetico, the logging of jack pine and black spruce exposed the deep, rich soils of the Steep Rock Moraine to sunlight. Veritable jungles of aspen, birch, beaked hazelnut, mountain-ash, mountain maple, and willow sprang up to create abundant browse for moose. Few canoeists spend more than a week in this part of the park without sighting a moose, especially those who visit the McKenzie Lake area. Black bears, gray wolves, and red foxes are also unusually abundant in this area. Wolves are the main predators of moose, but bears occasionally take the defenseless calves.

Quetico is a major nesting ground for such birds of prey as the bald eagle and, to a lesser extent, the osprey. But it is the common loon that strikes the most resonant wilderness chord with its eerie, ululating cry echoing over granite-rimmed backcountry lakes. Sometimes a pair of loons claims an entire small lake for itself and its young, barring others from its breeding territory.

OUTDOOR ACTIVITIES

Car-based vacationers stay at the Dawson Trail campgrounds in northeast Quetico to swim, picnic, fish, and hike nature trails. Most of the park's 30,000 visitors each year are experienced canoe campers who spend considerable time and effort planning backcountry trips.

Hiking

Three self-guiding interpretive trails and two nature trails, all 1.5 mi/ 2.5 km long or less, are clustered near the Dawson Trail campgrounds at French Lake. The *French Falls Trail* starts at Highway 11, just east of the campground entrance, and heads south through piney woods. The *French Portage Trail*, which also starts on Highway 11 but just to the west, angles southwest down to French Lake, tracing the historic route of voyageurs and westering settlers. The *Pickerel Point Trail* leads to the mouth of the reedy Upper Pickerel River, then through a forest where pink lady's-slipper orchids bloom in June.

Farther south, the *Beaver Meadows Trail* begins at the Chippewa campground and circles through a soggy forest opening where wildflowers flourish. The *Whiskey Jack Trail* starts opposite the Ojibway campground and loops through a forest of black spruce and jack pine, dipping down to the banks of the French River where it empties into French Lake.

The park's longest route makes for a pleasant day-long outing from the campground. The 4-mi/6.4-km *Pickerel Lake Trail*, which initially follows the Whiskey Jack Trail, is an easy, two-hour stroll, much of it along the Pickerel River. The destination is The Pines, a lakeside site that has been occupied seasonally as far back as 9,000 years and is now a splendid wilderness campground with grand views of Pickerel Lake, an extensive sand beach, and shallow, warm water for swimming.

Canoeing

There are more than 870 mi/1,400 km of routes. Canoeing Quetico country usually amounts to long, straight-ahead hauls punctuated by numerous portages to avoid Class III and Class IV rapids run only by experts. Portages tend to be of medium length (usually about 1,300 ft/400 m) and moderate difficulty, with a few notable exceptions, one of which is known locally as the Death March. The scenery is more serene than spectacular—blue sheets of water, unbroken palisades of trees, granite-lined shores—except where tall granite cliffs border waterways.

Aloft with outstretched wings, the stately bald eagle has found a comfortable nesting place in Quetico. OPPOSITE: Near these dramatic cliffs along Lake la Croix are Ojibwa rock drawings up to 500 years old. Many such pictographs in Quetico were painted along lakeside cliffs by artists in canoes.

There are no set routes. Interconnecting waterways and lakes make for nearly endless variations. Most people plan circular trips to avoid the need for return transportation from take-out points to starting points, although Highway 11 makes this arrangement practical near the northern boundary.

Fishing

Fishing is good to excellent almost anywhere in the park. The best months are June and September. Sport species include walleye (known as pickerel in many parts of Canada), northern pike, smallmouth bass, and lake trout. Largemouth bass are fairly common in southern lakes. Lake sturgeon is still found in the Maligne River and in Sturgeon, Russell, and Wolseley lakes.

Swimming

Five gorgeous beaches are scattered around French Lake, including two at the Dawson Trail campgrounds. Another fine beach, accessible via a hiking trail, is on Pickerel Lake at The Pines.

Golfing

The Little Falls Golf Course (807-597-6886) near Atikokan has nine holes.

EXPLORING THE PARK

The road to Quetico is the Trans-Canada Highway (Highway 11), which parallels the northern park boundary. Canoeists reach the park interior via six entry stations on the north, west, and south sides of the park; the stations usually are open daily from 8:00 A.M. to 5 P.M. Rangers register canoeists, handle emergencies, issue camping permits and fishing licenses, and sell waterproof canoeing maps of the park, which pinpoint portages and points of danger. (The maps are sold also at park headquarters.)

The northeastern entry station, at the Dawson Trail campgrounds on French Lake, is about 100 mi/160 km west of Thunder Bay, Ontario. Those who register at French Lake can also take a gravel access road 6.7 mi/10.7 km west of the campgrounds to Stanton Bay on Pickerel Lake. The north-central Nym Lake entry station is near the turn-off for Atikokan, where park headquarters is located, about 30 mi/50 km west of the Dawson Trail campgrounds. The Beaverhouse Lake entry station near the western boundary is accessible via a 14-mi/22-km gravel road (parking is allowed); the turn-off for the access road is 25 mi/40 km west of Atikokan.

Three southern entry stations are accessible by water from the Boundary Waters Canoeing Area in Superior National Forest, Minnesota: Lac la Croix in southwestern Quetico; Prairie Portage on Basswood Lake near the middle of the southern boundary; and Cache Bay on Saganaga Lake in the southeastern corner of the park.

Paddlers entering Quetico (and, therefore, Canada) at these stations must report to Canada Customs officers, either at Sand Point Lake, 40 mi/65 km west of the Lac la Croix station; at the Customs office adjacent to the Prairie Portage station on Basswood Lake; or at Government Island, 7.5 mi/12 km northeast of the Cache Bay station.

To preserve the wilderness experience, entry quotas distributed among the six stations are in effect during the operating season (mid-May to early September). Reservations, which are required, can be made starting the first Monday in February by phoning or writing the park office. The small registration fee can be charged on MasterCard or Visa. Many quotas are filled by mid-May. Once inside the park, canoeists are free to paddle anywhere. Maximum size of canoe parties is nine people.

Facilities at Atikokan, the park's main service center, include four hotels, restaurants, private campgrounds, and outfitters. Float planes can be chartered to drop off canoeists at Beaverhouse Lake and Lac la Croix.

The park is open year-round but facilities and services, including campgrounds, are maintained only from mid-May to mid-October and winter visitation is virtually nil. Development in Quetico is limited to the Dawson Trail campgrounds, where the Quetico Information Pavilion and the John B.

Ridley Research Library are located. The library, which is open to the public by appointment (807-929-2571), contains monographs, articles, pamphlets, maps, slides, and oral-history tapes. Park interpreters conduct evening programs and half-day canoe outings on Pickerel Lake and along the Pickerel River, part of the historic voyageur route.

ACCOMMODATIONS: The Dawson Trail campgrounds have two subdivisions. Some of the 36 sites in the Chippewa division are beachside; others are on a small cliff overlooking French Lake. The Ojibway division (96 sites) nestles beneath a canopy of jack pines alongside the French River where it empties into French Lake. Camping reservations (807-929-2571 or 807-929-3141) are held until 5:00 P.M. on the day of arrival. More than 1,800 primitive campsites are scattered around 600 lakes in the interior.

ADDRESSES: For more information, contact: Quetico Provincial Park, Ontario Ministry of Natural Resources, 108 Saturn Ave., Atikokan, Ont. P0T 1C0; 807-597-2735.

The Quetico Foundation is a nonprofit organization dedicated to the maintenance and preservation of the park: Suite 610, 48 Yonge St., Toronto, Ont. M5E 1G6; 416-941-9388. The foundation's extensive publications, which include a brochure that describes and pinpoints park pictographs, are available at the Friends of Quetico Park sales outlet in the French Lake pavilion and at park entry stations. For lists of outfitters, resorts, and general information, contact: Atikokan Chamber of Commerce, Box 997, Atikokan, Ont. P0T 1C0. For information on guides, contact: Sunset Country Guides Associa-

tion, c/o Mike Beninger, 150 Cedar Crescent, Atikokan, Ont. P0T 1C0; 807-597-1364.

BOOKS: Robert Beymer, *A Paddler's Guide to Quetico Provincial Park.* Virginia, Minn.: W. A. Fisher Co., 1985.

Selwyn Dewdney and Kenneth Kidd, *Indian Rock Paintings of the Great Lakes.* Toronto: University of Toronto Press, 1973. A study of native rock art. Out of print; available at libraries.

Grace Lee Knute, *The Voyageurs' Highway.* St. Paul: Minnesota Historical Society, 1976.

———, *The Voyageur.* St. Paul: Minnesota Historical Society, 1972.

Eric W. Morse, *Fur Trade Routes of Canada: Then and Now.* Toronto: University of Toronto Press, 1971. Pioneering study of the voyageurs' routes. Out of print; check libraries.

Sigurd F. Olson, *The Singing Wilderness.* New York: Knopf, 1956. Lyrical evocations of the North Country.

Shan Walshe, *Plants of Quetico and the Ontario Shield.* Toronto: University of Toronto Press, 1980. Color illustrations and interesting notes on plant uses make this reference by Quetico's longtime chief naturalist an essential and interesting source for plant identification. Available from the Friends of Quetico Park.

POINT PELEE NATIONAL PARK

THIS SMALL PARK occupies the bottom half of a dagger-shaped peninsula thrust into Lake Erie, mainland Canada's southernmost point. Vine-draped hardwood forests, ponds, and cattail marshes form a lush, almost tropical landscape that brims with some 700 plant species, many usually associated more with the southern United States than with Canada.

Situated on an overlap of the Mississippi and Atlantic flyways, Pelee is internationally renowned as a stopover for migrating birds. Over the years, 350 kinds have been sighted in the park during spring and fall migra-tions—nearly 40 percent of the continent's total number of species. Each May, in a spectacular rite of spring, migrants in colorful mating plumage arrive in vast numbers. As many as 100,000 mergansers, 20,000 white-throated sparrows, 2,500 tundra swans, and 1,000 barn swallows have been sighted in a single day. Dozens of species of brightly colored warblers are the most gaudy attractions.

Spring migration is noted also for its "vagrants"—species seen outside their usual areas. Sighting one is a bird watcher's coup. In May 1981 a her-mit warbler was observed at Pelee, far from its usual range along the west coast of the United States. It may have been lost or blown off course. Other vagrants, such as the Mississippi kite, may be gradually extending their ranges into southwestern Ontario.

The autumn gathering is more subdued. Most species that stop here in spring return for fall's southbound journey, but most wear drab winter plumage. Birds of prey, especially sharp-shinned hawks, accumulate in impressive numbers, feeding and building up their strength for the long flight ahead. These skilled hunters engage in fierce aerial battles with equally numerous blue jays.

GEOLOGY

Some 10,000 years ago, retreating glaciers left a layer of sand and gravel atop a submerged limestone ridge that extends across the western end of

Winding out into a long loop among the cattails, Pelee's Marsh Boardwalk provides a mile-long vantage point for bird-watching. The peaceful pink light of dawn makes sightings especially memorable.

Lake Erie. Lake currents then deposited sediments on top of this glacial till, and eventually two sandbars rose above the waves to form a V-shaped spit of land, today's Point Pelee. The lagoon between the two arms of the V evolved into a freshwater marsh that makes up two-thirds of the park.

Some of the forces that created Pelee are still at work reshaping the peninsula. Lake currents sweep the narrow barrier beach on the eastern side of Pelee, carrying away more sand than they deposit. In addition, this side of the park bears the brunt of Erie's northeasterly storms, which also gnaw at the shoreline. At the same time, but to a lesser degree, lake currents deposit sand on Pelee's broader, forested western shore. This unequal exchange—more erosion on one side than deposition on the other—means that the peninsula is gradually becoming shorter as it shifts westward.

Another Ice Age remnant here is black magnetite, an iron ore that stripes the sands of East Beach. Glaciers scraped it from rocks in the Canadian Shield and carried it some 300 mi/480 km south to its present location. An even earlier geologic legacy are fossils of corals, crinoids, and brachiopods found along the park's gravelly East and West beaches, as well as at The Tip. These marine creatures date back to 300 million years ago when this region lay beneath a shallow sea.

HISTORY

In the days before European settlement, Algonquian-speaking tribes canoeing along the north shore of Lake Erie established a portage route across Pelee to avoid swirling currents at the treeless extremity now known as The Tip. Seventeenth-century French explorers following in their footsteps named the peninsula Pelée—"bare" or "bald." In 1799, the British declared the southern portion of the peninsula a naval reserve; its boundaries approximated today's national park. During the next century squatters hacked farms out of the forest, trappers harvested muskrats and beavers from the marshes, and fishermen established commercial operations on the lake.

The park is the legacy of farsighted naturalists who were awed by the multitudes of migrating birds that stopped on the peninsula. The Great Lakes Ornithological Club met regularly at its headquarters on the East Beach Road from 1905 to 1927 and lobbied for the protection of Pelee's bird-luring habitats. A national park was created in 1918, Canada's ninth and the first to be established on biological, rather than on scenic or recreational, merit.

HABITATS

Pelee embraces five plant communities within its 6 sq mi/15.5 sq km. The eastern two-thirds of the park is freshwater marsh, a watery jigsaw of open ponds separated by vast expanses of cattails and water lilies. The ponds are home to two introduced species of fish, carp and their close relative, the true goldfish. In the shallows, where bulrushes and purple loosestrife encroach on open water, grow the delicate pink blossoms of the swamp rose-mallow, Canada's only wild hibiscus.

This is the haunt of muskrat and mink, common moorhen and sora. Overhead northern harriers and regal great blue herons fly on 6-ft/2-m wingspans. Victorian fashion sought these birds' feathers to adorn ladies' hats. Federal law now protects the heron and a dozen other species in Pelee.

Six kinds of turtles live in the marsh, including three endangered species (Blanding's, spotted, and spiny softshell). The snapping turtle deserves its name and surly reputation: its powerful beak can inflict painful wounds and crunch fish, frogs, even baby ducks. A prime spot for sighting painted turtles, the most common hereabouts, is the big pool at the start of the Boardwalk Trail.

On the western side of the park, southern plants flourish as a result of the mild climate, moderated by the waters of Lake Erie. This dryland forest is part of the Carolinian vegetation zone; the predominant tree is hackberry. Among species rarely found elsewhere in Canada are blue ash, tuliptree, spicebush, common hoptree, and fragrant sumac. White and chestnut oak, honeylocust, shagbark hickory, and other southern species grow alongside more typical Canadian trees like eastern cottonwood, American basswood, and silver maple.

Northern cardinals and cerulean, blue-winged, and golden-winged warblers wing through the forest's thick canopy. Most warblers forage in bushes or trees, but the ovenbird, a type of warbler named for its dome-shaped nest, walks through leaf litter on the forest floor in search of insects.

Hoptree and eastern redcedar in this forest attract two beautiful southern butterfly species, the giant swallowtail and the tiny olive hairstreak, both rare in Canada. Swallowtail larvae feed on hoptree leaves; olive hairstreak caterpillars survive almost exclusively on redcedar leaves. Scientists have observed the park's rich array of insects ever since William Saunders's 1882 survey of Pelee's huge dragonfly populations. Naturalist Percy Taverner collected moths during field trips from 1909 to 1919 by painting trees with a concoction of molasses, brown sugar, and beer; the large,

Lush marshlands abundant with wildlife cover parts of Point Pelee National Park. The peninsula marks the shortest route a land bird can take across Lake Erie, and migrating birds stop to rest and feed in its woodlands before their long journeys ahead.

fast-flying species, attracted by the sweetness of the mixture, became intoxicated on the beer, which slowed their reactions and made them easier to capture. This method is still commonly used.

Among the park's most colorful transients are monarch butterflies, insects with true migratory behavior. After a summer spent flitting over fields and gardens in southwestern Ontario, up to 10,000 monarchs congregate in September on hackberry trees near The Tip, awaiting tail winds and fair weather before crossing Lake Erie en route to wintering grounds in the rugged Sierra Madre of central Mexico.

South of the visitors' center, within the hardwood forest, is cedar savanna, an open woodland where fields and apple orchards planted by early settlers are gradually reverting to their natural state. A few eastern redcedars and tangles of sumac, wild potato-vine, and flowering spurge have already erased some signs of cultivation. This is prime insect-hunting grounds for sparrows, kingbirds, and flycatchers, as well as the park's five varieties of bats. These flying mammals flit across the savanna at dusk, the hour of the whip-poor-will's melancholy song.

Climbing vines drape the wet woodlands, which are best observed in Tilden's Woods north of the visitors' center. Virginia creeper, poison ivy, fox grape, and wild potato vine entwine silver maples, American sycamores, hackberry, American basswood, and sassafras, giving the matted forest a lush, almost tropical appearance. In seventeenth-century England, sassafras tea was as popular as coffee, and sassafras ships transported the aromatic bark from North America to Europe in the lucrative trade.

In spring, the floor of these woods is dotted with trillium, sweet cicely, and mayapple. Jewelweed and fragrant Herb-Robert add blooms in June, also the season for the distinctive flower spike of jack-in-the-pulpit. This bitter plant was a test of Indian manhood: braves had to eat its raw, underground stem, the corm, without wincing. In July, goldenrods spike open fields with masses of tiny yellow flowers on 3-ft-/1-m-high stems.

The five-lined skink, whose favorite haunts are the rotting stumps and logs of this damp forest, has a detachable, electric-blue tail that breaks off near the base when the creature is threatened. Gullible predators attack the still-twitching appendage while the skink escapes. Over the next 10 months the skink grows another, shorter tail.

From the sloughs of these wet woodlands comes the curious mewing call of the wood duck, or the abrupt squawk of the green-backed heron, both of which make this their summer home. Turtles bask on the trunks of dead trees, toppled over the stagnant waters like jackstraws.

Distinguished by its delicate and dappled late spring blooms, impatiens capensis is commonly known as touch-me-not or jewelweed. Perennial wildflowers provide a continuously changing display in spring and summer.

Bracketing the marsh and forest is a sand and pebble beach, an area of constant deposition and erosion. A short distance from the shoreline, the deep-rooted grasses stabilize the soil. Along the western shoreline, this beach is backed by a large stand of hoptrees. Brewers once used this tree's fruit as a substitute for hops. An alternative name, skunkbush, derives from the pungent odor of the hoptree's twigs and leaves. The barrier beach along the eastern shore is fringed with a narrow band of cottonwoods and green ash, which yield to the vast cattail marshes and ponds of the park's interior.

At The Tip during the early hours of the spring migration, sandpipers and American pipits patrol the beach; ring-billed gulls and semipalmated plovers cluster wing to wing on the wave-soaked sands. Offshore in Lake Erie are shorebirds and waterfowl—grebes, ducks, egrets, jaegers, loons, and tundra swans.

OUTDOOR ACTIVITIES

The density of visitors to this day-use park, Canada's second smallest (after St. Lawrence Islands), is perhaps higher than in any other preserve. Spring is noted for watching northbound birds and for smelt fishing. In summer, swimming and picnicking are popular activities. Autumn is gathering time for southbound migrants. Winter activities include cross-country skiing and skating on Thiessen's Channel near the Marsh Boardwalk.

Hiking

There are five trails in Pelee; all are level, well maintained, and open year-round. The *Marsh Boardwalk*, about a third of the way down the western side of the peninsula, offers birders 1 mi/1.6 km of dry vantage points, ideal for catching glimpses of the abundant wetland wildlife. An observation tower at the start affords overviews of the sea of cattails, dotted with the open water of ponds where American coots, moorhens, and ducks are plentiful.

Halfway down the western side, the 0.9-mi/1.4-km *DeLaurier Trail* leads to a reconstruction of the 1890s dwelling inhabited by the area's first settler, then passes through abandoned asparagus fields and apple orchards before reaching a series of man-made canals dug along the western edge of the marsh in the 1940s and 1950s.

Two trails start from the visitors' center, two-thirds of the way down the peninsula. A favorite with birders, the 0.6-mi/1-km *Tilden's Woods Trail* tunnels north through a wet woodland canopy of hackberry and silver maples, busy in summer with cardinals, scarlet tanagers, and orioles. The redcedar grove north of the center's parking lot brightens in June and July with the yellow flowers of prickly pear, whose entire eastern range in Canada lies within the park.

South of the center, the three separate loops of the 1.8-mi/3-km *Woodland Trail* explore three habitats: Pelee's dry-land forest, a cedar savanna, and a wet woodland, where footbridges span water-filled ditches green with duckweed. This last loop winds along the crest of Lake Erie's ancient shoreline, a corduroy of ridges and hollows frequented by water thrushes, Kentucky warblers, great horned owls, and prothonotary warblers.

The boardwalk *Tip Trail* leads to the southernmost point of mainland Canada, an excellent bird-watching route and the best spot in the park for viewing monarch butterflies in September.

Bicycling

Bikes can be rented at a private concession at the Marsh Boardwalk and used along the *Centennial Trail,* which extends 2.5 mi/4 km between the Boardwalk and the visitors' center. (This route can also be walked.) Hackberry and hickory trees line the way, and in spring the undergrowth blooms with purple appendaged waterleaf and Dutchman's-breeches (named for pantaloon-shaped petals strung on a stem like washing on a line). At dusk the trail is also a good place to observe white-tailed deer.

Canoeing

Canoes rented from a private concession at the Marsh Boardwalk enable visitors to explore the park's wetland realm.

Fishing

Anglers 16 years and older can buy a fishing permit from the park warden at the entrance gate. There is an open season from May 15 to September 30 for all species except largemouth bass (June 30 to September 30), and a five-fish limit on bass and northern pike. The best spots for fishing in the park are at Northwest and West beaches for yellow perch, walleye, and white bass; Lake Pond yields largemouth bass and pike.

Thousands of smelt wriggle ashore in nocturnal spawning runs during the second or third week in April; special smelt fishing permits are available from local sports shops. Fishing is permitted in the park from an hour before sunrise until two hours after sunset.

Swimming

More than 12 mi/20 km of beaches and sand dunes bracket Pelee's marshes and forests. Lifeguards supervise only Northwest Beach. East Beach is the

most secluded. Swimming and wading are forbidden at The Tip, where dangerous currents break over an unstable submerged ridge. Warm water is found on the west side of Pelee Point, which divides Lake Erie's shallow western basin from the deeper, cooler eastern basin.

EXPLORING THE PARK

Point Pelee is 230 mi/370 km southwest of Toronto via Highway 401 and Highway 77, and about 60 mi/96 km southeast of Detroit and Windsor via Highway 3.

The park is open daily 6 A.M. to 10 P.M. year-round. It opens one hour earlier for bird-watching in late April, a season also noted for smelt fishing. The best times to visit are during May and September migrations. The visitors' center, 4.3 mi/7 km south of the park entrance, introduces visitors to Pelee with films, slide shows, and displays. A billboard announces the estimated arrival and departure times of various bird species and expected times of wildflower blooms along nature trails. Naturalists at the visitors' center lead birding hikes and direct beginning bird watchers to the best viewing spots.

Cars are banned beyond the visitors' center from April 1 to Labor Day and on weekends in September. The Pelee Express—a rubber-tired propane-powered tram—runs daily every 20 minutes from 9 A.M. to 9 P.M. between the interpretive center and East Point Beach near The Tip. During peak bird migration in mid-May, trips start at 6:00 A.M. A cycling path along the west shore road between Northwest Beach and West Beach also gives access to the peninsula in summer.

ACCOMMODATIONS: Point Pelee is too small to permit individual camping, although prearranged group camping is allowed at three sites —Little Raccoon, Marsh Hawk, and Black Walnut. Individual camping is available at Wheatley Provincial Park, 12 mi/19 km northeast on Highway 3. There are private campgrounds, hotels and motels in Leamington 6 mi/10km north of the park. Pelee is most popular in May; reser-

vations should be made several months in advance.

ADDRESSES: For information, write or phone: The Park Superintendent, Point Pelee National Park, R.R. 1, Leamington, Ont. N8H 3Z4; 519-322-2365. Another source of information is: Southwestern Ontario Travel Association, 186 King St., Suite 200, London, Ont. N6A 1C7; 519-649-7075.

Often called the "wild canary," the familiar American goldfinch travels in flocks, calling "per-chick-o-ree" in undulating flight.

BRUCE PENINSULA NATIONAL PARK AND FATHOM FIVE NATIONAL MARINE PARK

JUST A SHORT DRIVE NORTH of Canada's most densely populated region, twin sanctuaries occupy much of the Bruce Peninsula and the islands and waters off its tip. The Bruce, a narrow finger of land that separates Lake Huron and Georgian Bay, has an elevational tilt. The low-slung Huron side on the southwest alternates rocky shoreline, beaches, and cedar swamps. Heading northeast, the peninsula rises to the parks' scenic highlight: the Niagara Escarpment, a phalanx of limestone cliffs standing up to 200 ft/60 m above the sparkling waters of Georgian Bay. Along these ramparts winds the Bruce Trail, Canada's most popular footpath.

Interior wetlands and forests of northern white-cedar and fir shelter more than 40 species of orchids, an unusually large number. The area around Dorcas Bay, on the peninsula's Huron side, is the richest site, with at least 25 kinds. For sheer numbers, the month of June triumphs, with yellow lady's-slippers flowering on the Bruce and on Fathom Five islands in weed-like intensity. For diversity, late June to early July is best.

Fathom Five, Canada's first national marine park, embraces 20 islands and the waters in between. (Fathom Five and Bruce Peninsula are separate parks administered jointly.) Wave action scooped out caves on Bears Rump Island and sculpted seastacks called "flowerpots" on Flowerpot Island. Reefs and shoals left a legacy of 20 known shipwrecks, the most concentrated assemblage in the Great Lakes. Each summer, thousands of scuba divers and snorkelers explore sunken schooners and steamers preserved in cold lake waters.

Composed of soft shale and limestone columns capped by hard dolostone, "flowerpots" in Fathom Five National Marine Park are pieces of eroded escarpment left stranded as the scarp receded westward over millions of years. The bases of some of these ancient forms have been cemented by man to prevent collapse.

Geology

The Bruce Peninsula is the most spectacular section of the Niagara Escarpment, a limestone ridge that arcs like a giant horseshoe from the Rochester area of upstate New York, through southern Ontario, across Lake Huron, and into Upper Michigan and Wisconsin. The story of the escarpment began about 400 million years ago, when the region was flooded by a shallow inland sea. Magnificent reefs formed in these tropical waters, which teemed with plant-like animals, crustaceans, and mollusks. (Rockcuts along Highway 6, which splits the Bruce, slice through reef remnants.)

For millions of years, the limy shells and skeletons of sea creatures settled on the floor of a bay of the sea, and accumulated into tremendously thick layers of limestone. Mud and sand later washed in and were transformed into shale and sandstone. The floor of the bay began to sink under the weight of these sediments, forming a vast, bowl-shaped depression known as the Michigan Basin. Then, little-known geologic forces within the mantle reversed the process. The basin rebounded, displacing the tropical sea in the process and thrusting up a ragged rim of rock along the northern perimeter of the bowl—today's Niagara Escarpment.

As the tropical seas dried, minerals dissolved in the brine became more and more concentrated. Magnesium in the water was absorbed into limestone, which then became a harder rock called dolomite. This compact mineral covered softer underlying shale and limestone, protecting it from erosion. Without this dolomite caprock, the escarpment would have eroded to dust eons ago.

Water is the subtle sculptor that carved—and is still carving—the Bruce. Rain falling through the air and then seeping through decaying vegetation picks up enough carbon dioxide to become a mild solution of carbonic acid. In time, this acidic water dissolves solid limestone and opens passageways along minute fractures in the rock. The Cyprus Lake area, just inland from Georgian Bay, has many examples of this erosion, including sinkholes, the St. Edmunds Cave System, and an underground stream that flows from Horse Lake to Marr Lake.

Wave action works in more obvious ways, chopping great grottoes, amphitheaters, and caves in the escarpment, and undercutting the dolomite cap, which eventually weakens and tumbles into the bay in great chunks. The famous "flowerpots" of Flowerpot Island—shoreline columns of dolomite and limestone—are bits of eroded escarpment left stranded as the scarp receded west over millions of years.

HISTORY

The first European reference to the *Saugeen*, as the Bruce was known in Algonquian, was by French explorer Samuel de Champlain, who probably heard of the peninsula during his trip to what is now southern Ontario in 1615–16. Around 1639, Jesuit missions were established in 10 Huron villages scattered around the Bruce; the most northerly was probably near Dyer Bay. Within 20 years, Iroquois raids had routed both the black-robed priests and the local Hurons.

Fear of the Iroquois kept the peninsula largely uninhabited until the founding of Southampton in 1848 at the western base of the Bruce. Then came waves of settlers who moved up the peninsula, farming the uncharitable soil, harvesting lake trout and lake whitefish from Huron's bountiful waters, and logging the vast tracts of pine and cedar.

Around 1850, Scottish pioneers founded a community at the tip of the peninsula and named it Tobermory, after a town on the island of Mull in the Hebrides. With two sheltered harbors, Little Tub and Big Tub, Tobermory became a welcoming port on the busy shipping lanes of the Great Lakes. Before the establishment of the Big Tub Lighthouse in 1885 and other navigational aids, vessels frequently foundered on treacherous rocks and shoals off the Fathom Five islands. The wrecks of at least 20 schooners and steamers litter the bottom, beckoning divers.

HABITATS

Logging in the nineteenth century eliminated the peninsula's mature stands of white pine. Today's second-growth forest consists of balsam fir mixed with northern white-cedar, paper birch, balsam poplar, and white spruce. Where pockets of deep, rich humus have accumulated on the generally thin-soiled Bruce, sugar maples grow in association with American beech and oak.

Some of Canada's oldest trees cling to exposed escarpment cliffs here. A gnarled redcedar rooted in the thin soil of a limestone crevice may be 700 years old. Creeping and common juniper and stunted birch also reach great ages in this habitat. Rare ferns—hart's-tongue fern, wall rue, and purple cliff-brake—feather the bluffs.

Acidic needles discourage growth beneath cedars, but elsewhere dogwoods, wild sarsaparilla, chokecherry, and other shrubs grow thickly beneath the canopy. In the Cyprus Lake area, the forest floor is made up of

Dramatically sculpted limestone cliffs face the sea near Wiarton, Ontario, on the Bruce Peninsula. Caves and grottoes, other products of erosions, can be seen throughout the park.

desktop-size limestone slabs. The soil-filled cracks in between are spongy with moss and brightened with wildflowers, especially Indian paintbrush, false Solomon's seal, starflowers, bunchflower, and bunchberry.

East of Cyprus Lake, at the headwaters of Crane River and Willow Creek, lies a poorly drained patchwork of lakes, brooks, and swamps fringed with white-cedar and balsam fir. This seldom visited corner of the mainland park is home to weasels, mink, and beaver.

Diverse vegetation communities thrive in a variety of habitats around Dorcas Bay, which can be explored easily on footpaths and boardwalks. Along Lake Huron, purple gerardia, harebell, and bird's-eye primula survive on the rocks. (The limestone shoreline here was fluted by Ice Age glaciers.) A fen bristling with sedges and rushes extends inland from Singing Sands Beach, a popular swimming area. Sundews, pitcher plants, and a number of orchids—rose pogonia, purple fringed orchid, and showy lady's-slipper—also grow in this damp domain.

To stimulate pollination, lady's-slippers invite bees into their pouched slipper through a slit whose incurved edges prevent the bee's exit. The bee is forced to fertilize the flower as it squeezes past sexual parts overhanging an escape hatch at the rear of the blossom. The insect's incentive in this work may be the soft hairs inside the slipper, perhaps sought as food or building material.

Farther inland from the beach, jack pine and juniper anchor sand dunes. Bearberry, twinflowers, and a number of orchids flourish here: the ram's-head, along with yellow and showy lady's-slipper, and the grass-like Alaska rein orchids, a species widespread in western Canada but found only at two other sites in eastern Canada (Manitoulin and Anticosti islands).

The Bruce is the last Ontario stronghold of the endangered massasauga rattlesnake, the province's only poisonous snake. The broad-headed massasauga slithers around jumbled rocks and wetland margins, feeding on frogs in spring and mice in summer. The rattler detects prey at distances of up to 3 ft/1 m by using a heat-sensing "pit" between its eyes and nostrils.

The common garter snake, most numerous of the Bruce's 10 kinds of serpents, can be seen almost anywhere. Equally ubiquitous is the northern water snake, at home along rocky shorelines or inland waters. Its favorite sunning spots are old beaver lodges and tree branches. Eastern ribbon snakes live in swamps, still-water wetlands, and drainage ditches. The population of the milk snake, a constrictor that feeds on mice and smaller snakes, has increased as its favored habitat of fields and meadows expands with the construction of cottages and other deforesting developments.

The heads of two red-sided garter snakes emerge from a resting group of about twenty snakes. The smaller head belongs to the male.

In Fathom Five's archipelago, larger islands such as Bears Rump, Flowerpot, and Cove are covered with the same fir-cedar forest as the mainland. The red squirrel, active in winter when ice connects the islands with the mainland, colonized Flowerpot Island; the eastern chipmunk, which remains dormant in winter, is not found there. For some reason, raccoons, striped skunks, and weasels, all of which prey on mainland snakes, haven't crossed the ice bridge to Flowerpot, which remains a predator-free haven for abundant garter snakes.

Great blue herons nest by the hundreds on Devil Island, still privately owned but within Fathom Five boundaries. Herring and ring-billed gulls, double-crested cormorants, and Caspian and common terns are seen frequently in the skies above Fathom Five and the Bruce.

OUTDOOR ACTIVITIES IN BRUCE PENINSULA

The park is open year-round, but the majority of visitors come from spring to autumn to enjoy woodland wildflowers, to camp at and swim in Cyprus Lake, and to hike the Bruce Trail and other park routes.

Scenic Drives

Some of the peninsula's best scenery is found east of the park boundary along the 5-mi/8-km *Cabot Head Drive* from the village of Dyer Bay north to the Cabot Head lighthouse. In places, the road tops the dramatic escarpment high above Georgian Bay.

Hiking

The most spectacular section of the *Bruce Trail*, which runs 457 mi/735 km along the entire Ontario section of the Niagara Escarpment, is in the park north of Cyprus Lake. The rugged stretch between Little Cove and Halfway Log Dump, where the Emmett Lake Road reaches the escarpment, follows the clifftops, then dips down to the shoreline, passing caves, overhanging rocks, terraced beaches, talus slopes, and bluffs covered with fossils 400 million years old.

Other favorite sections of the Bruce Trail south of the park include the route south of Dyer Bay to the Devil's Pulpit; the hike on the north shore of Hope Bay; and Jones Bluff and Sidney Bay Bluff within the Cape Croker Indian Reserve.

Four hiking routes start at the "Head of Trails" at the Cyprus Lake campground; they end up on the Georgian Bay shore. The *Horse Lake Trail* heads north along the marshy eastern shoreline of Horse Lake, where herons, caspian terns, and waterfowl congregate. The route then passes through cool cedar forest, descends steeply to a cobble beach, and intersects with the Bruce Trail.

The *Marr Lake* and *Georgian Bay trails* both head north together, then split soon after crossing Cyprus Lake's outlet creek. The Marr Lake Trail leads to Boulder Beach, which is covered with millions of cobblestones ranging in size from marbles to bowling balls. This is the best place in the park to find marine fossils.

The Georgian Bay Trail parallels the western shore of Horse Lake, along the way climbing rises that are the remains of ancient coral reefs, and passing over an underground river (unseen by hikers) that flows from Horse Lake to Marr Lake. A side trip on a boardwalk near the end of Horse Lake leads to a sinkhole. Emerging onto shoreline clifftops, the route joins the Bruce Trail and follows it west to a trio of natural attractions: Indian Head Cove, the Natural Arch, and The Grotto.

The level *Cyprus Lake Trail*, which circles around Cyprus Lake, passes through woodland that is prime habitat for orchids: lady's-slippers, coralroots, purple fringed orchids, rattlesnake-plantain, and ladies'-tresses are all found here. The bridge spanning the outlet stream is an excellent place to view birdlife—mallards, teal, wood ducks, red-winged blackbirds, American woodcocks, common snipe, and great horned owls.

Canoeing

The *Rankin River Canoe Route* is a leisurely, flat-water trip that starts at Sky Lake, about 50 mi/80 km southeast of the park. The route heads south through a chain of three lakes—Sky, Isaac, and Boat—and ends 11 mi/18 km later at Sauble Falls Provincial Park. The shallow lakes, partly covered with vegetation and edged with wetlands, are good places to view aquatic birds, especially loons, terns, and American bitterns.

Fishing

Cyprus and Emmett lakes yield smallmouth bass, chain pickerel, and yellow perch. Emmett also has northern pike. Rainbow and brook trout are caught in park streams.

Swimming

The best swimming is at Cyprus Lake, where there are sandy beaches supervised by lifeguards. Prevailing westerly winds push water away from the park's Georgian Bay shore, so that cold water from the depths wells up to replace it. Even in August, all but the hardiest find it too chilly for swimming. The best beach is Singing Sands at Dorcas Bay on the Huron side, where the shallow water just offshore warms up quickly in summer.

The spectacular shoreline of Lake Huron's immense Georgian Bay. The bay's deep, clean, and astonishingly clear waters offer scuba diving and snorkeling.

Cross-country Skiing

The season lasts from mid-December through March, with the best conditions just after the big year-end snowstorms. Skiers set out on the three trails in the Cyprus Lake area and glide through the campground.

OUTDOOR ACTIVITIES IN FATHOM FIVE

The marine park's biggest draws are boating, fishing, and scuba diving. Flowerpot Island is noted for its rare orchids and ferns and geological formations.

Hiking

The 1.6-mi/2.7-km *Flowerpot Trail* heads northeast on Flowerpot Island from the tour boat dock to two flowerpots. The taller seastack is 50 ft/15 m high; the smaller is 30 ft/9 m. On a popular side trip, steps lead to a platform for views of a "hanging cave," a wave-carved grotto stranded high on a

Awash with the brilliant waters of Georgian Bay, this cave is one of many ringing the base of Flowerpot Island.

bluff by water levels that have dropped drastically since the end of the Ice Age. The trail continues north to Castle Bluff and a lighthouse in operation since 1873, then swings southwest through the center of the island, skirting a meadow and a swamp before returning to the dock. The 5-mi/.8-km *Marl Trail* heads southwest from the dock, crossing an orchid-rich marl bed (marl is mucky soil formed from eroded limestone).

Fishing

Sport-fishing species in Georgian Bay and Lake Huron include largemouth bass, northern pike, Chinook salmon, splake, and lake trout.

Scuba Diving

Fathom Five is the world's most popular cold-water diving destination, with about 35,000 dives made each year from May to October. Twenty wrecks litter the bottom off the tip of the park, with something to suit every level of experience. To reduce possible damage to the wrecks, boats tie up to moorings adjacent to sites, rather than dropping anchor.

The most popular wreck is the schooner *Sweepstakes*, whose nearly intact remains lie in the shallow waters of Big Tub Harbor. Built in 1867 in Burlington, Ontario, the two-masted schooner sailed the lakes for nearly 20 years before meeting its end in 1885 while carrying a load of coal. The most photographed part of the wreck is the bow, where part of the starboard railing and wooden windlass draw camera-toting divers. Because of the sheltered location, visibility of the *Sweepstakes* is often superb, especially if there has been no recent rainfall.

The most spectacular wreck, the *Arabia*, sank in 1884 north of Tobermory while carrying a load of corn from Chicago to Midland, Ontario. The whereabouts of the vessel remained a mystery for 90 years, although local fishermen often referred to the "corn wreck" because fish caught in the area often had corn in their stomachs. In 1971, Capt. Albert Smith of Tobermory found the century-old barque, well-preserved in the cold waters. Its bow is nearly intact, with a north-jutting boom, wooden windlass still wrapped with chain, twin anchors, and bilge pump. For experienced divers only, the *Arabia* lies in 120 ft/36 m of cold water where visibility is often poor. Lines lead from mooring blocks to the wreck's stern and bow.

Erosional caves along the peninsula's Georgian Bay cliffs make for interesting and adventurous diving. The easiest access is by boat from Tobermory. Just west of Halfway Rock Point at Indian Head Cove, an underwater passage about 20 ft/6 m below the Georgian Bay waterline leads to a partially submerged grotto about 65 by 40 ft/20 by 12 m. East along the shoreline, a smaller cave at water level is actually a natural arch. The site, which is accessible by trail, is suitable for all levels of experience; a dive light is recommended.

EXPLORING BRUCE PENINSULA AND FATHOM FIVE

The parks are about 190 mi/300 km northwest of Toronto via Highway 401 and Highway 6. The parks' headquarters, along with visitors' and dive registration centers, are in the resort community of Tobermory at the tip of the Bruce. An extensive park interpretive program includes one- to three-hour guided walks to caves and sinkholes, orchid hunts at Dorcas Bay, and sunset hikes along Georgian Bay.

Tobermory has a full range of accommodations and travel services. Water taxis and boat rentals are available, along with registered dive charter boats. Three shops provide diving gear for sale or hire, compressed air, and dive charter arrangements: G & S Watersports (519-596-2200); Tobermory Divers Den (519-596-2363); and Big Tub Harbour Resort (519-596-2219). Pickup charters are available to individual divers who drop by the shops; groups may want to reserve in advance. Firm commitments usually are required by the end of March for summer weekend charters; at midweek in summer boats usually are available at short notice.

Three companies offer trips to Flowerpot Island and glass-bottom boat tours to wrecks lying in shallow water, including the *Sweepstakes:* Blue Heron (519-596-2020); True North II (519-596-2600); and Seaview III (519-596-2224). The Peninsula and St. Edmunds Township Museum on Highway 6, southeast of Tobermory, displays artifacts from area wrecks.

ACCOMMODATIONS: The Cyprus Lake campground (242 sites) provides the only mainland park accommodation. About 10 private campgrounds are scattered around the peninsula. In Fathom Five, camping is permitted only at the Beachy Cove campground (six sites) near the dock on Flowerpot Island.

ADDRESSES: For more information on the two parks, contact: The Superintendent, Bruce Peninsula and Fathom Five National Parks, Box 189, Tobermory, Ont. N0H 2R0; 519-596-2233. For details on the Rankin River Canoe Route and other places on the peninsula interesting for their natural history, contact the Sauble Valley Conservation Authority (519-376-3076) or the Ontario Ministry of Natural Resources office in Owen Sound (519-376-3860). For information on

private visitors' services, contact the Tobermory Chamber of Commerce, Box 250, Tobermory, Ont. N0H 2R0; 519-546-2452. The Bruce Trail Association (Box 857, Hamilton, Ont. L8N 3N9; 416-529-6821) provides details on hiking this superlative route.

BOOKS: Art Amos and Patrick Falkes, *A Diver's Guide to Georgian Bay.* Ontario Underwater Council. Published by the governing body for snorkeling and scuba diving in Ontario.

Bruce Trail Guide. Hamilton, Ontario: Bruce Trail Association, 1988. Now in its sixteenth edition, this indispensable guidebook leads thousands each year along the region's best walk.

Sherwood Fox, *The Bruce Beckons.* Toronto: Univ. of Toronto, 1988. Anecdotal history of the peninsula.

ALGONQUIN PROVINCIAL PARK

THE LANDSCAPE OF ONTARIO'S oldest and largest park embodies the essence of the north country—wind-whipped lakes cupped between rounded hills of ancient granite, softened only by twisted pines and blazing maples. The raw, elemental beauty of these images was expressed powerfully by Tom Thomson, a Toronto painter who created park scenes from 1913 until his drowning on Canoe Lake in 1917. The work Thomson accomplished in those five Algonquin summers eloquently expressed his love of the rugged Shield country and profoundly influenced other members of the Group of Seven, Canada's first major school of modern landscape painting.

For generations, Algonquin has furnished wilderness adventure just hours from populous southern Ontario. A watery maze of 1,500 lakes and rivers lures canoeists; hikers explore western highlands on two trail systems. Nature lovers seldom return home without encountering moose, loons, and other woodland creatures. Probably more people have had first-hand experience with wolves in Algonquin than anywhere else in the world—an experience of hearing, not seeing. On starry August nights, park naturalists lead visitors to places where their own howls are often met with spine-tingling responses that reverberate over hills and lakes—the true call of the wild.

GEOLOGY

Algonquin lies at the southern edge of the Canadian Shield, a vast formation of granite and gneiss that underlies most of central and northern Canada. Park rocks were formed from sediments deposited 1.5 billion years ago on the floor of a sea, where they compacted into sandstone and other types of sedimentary rocks. These rocks were buried by subsequent sedimentation and transformed by heat and pressure into granite and gneiss, which were uplifted during a time of mountain-building some 1.1 billion years ago.

Six hundred million years of erosion reduced these mountains to plains, which periodically were flooded by shallow seas. Then, for unknown rea-

Potters Creek, Algonquin Provincial Park. Although the southern part of the park is fairly developed, the other two thirds boast two major hiking trails and a thousand miles of canoe trails over calm lakes and rushing rivers.

sons, the western two-thirds of Algonquin was uplifted as much as 980 ft/ 300 m above the surrounding areas. This last uplift broke the bedrock into large, northwest-trending blocks bounded by faults. Erosion has deepened these crustal fractures to produce the park's valley-and-ridge topography. The most impressive fault is the Barron Canyon, a chasm along the Barron River that is 300 ft/100 m deep in places.

Four Pleistocene glaciations ground over Algonquin. The last ice sheet melted back just 11,000 years ago, leaving behind a veneer of glacial till in some places and barren bedrock in others. Raging meltwater rivers deposited sandy outwash plains in the park's eastern third, where Algonquin's magnificent white pine forests eventually would grow. The loveliest Ice Age legacies are clear lakes resting in glacially scoured upland hollows.

HISTORY

As early as 3,000 B.C. Paleo-Indians camped around such lakes as Rock, Opeongo, and Radiant, and along the Petawawa River and other waterways. Later, scattered Iroquoian bands inhabited the highlands, hunting, fishing, and gathering berries. Early French explorers, fur traders, and missionaries bypassed the region, however, heading into the interior of the continent via the Ottawa River to the east and the Mattawa to the west.

It wasn't until the 1830s that loggers from the Ottawa Valley came to "hurl down the pine," establishing sawmills and lumber camps throughout the Algonquin area. Ancient, arrow-straight eastern white pines, some 200 ft/60 m tall, were felled and squared in summer, and hauled in winter with horse teams to frozen lakes and rivers. At spring breakup, loggers assembled the timber into huge rafts that were floated down the Ottawa to the St. Lawrence River. At Quebec City, the lumber was loaded into sailing ships bound for Britain, where it was turned into furniture, planking, and masts for the Royal Navy.

Within 60 years, the big pine was gone and fires fueled by logging debris had ravaged huge tracts. In 1893, Ontario established Algonquin Park with multiple (and often conflicting) purposes: to maintain a logging preserve with sustainable yields; to serve as a wildlife sanctuary; to protect the headwaters of five major rivers; and to create a recreation area. Forestry, along with limited hunting and trapping, continues under certain guidelines. Logging is not permitted on lakeshores, islands, and portages, and lumber trucks operate in such a way that conflict with visitors is minimized. Recreationists often are unaware that logging occurs within park boundaries.

The six-hour Mizzy Lake Trail provides a good chance to see wildlife in Algonquin Provincial Park.

HABITATS

In the moist uplands of the western two-thirds of the park, hardwood forests of sugar maple, American beech, and yellow birch cover the rounded hillsides, with conifers—eastern hemlock, white spruce, balsam fir, and northern white-cedar—found in valleys and along lakeshores. The occasional giant white pine towers over the hardwoods from marginal locations—rocky lakeshores, islands, exposed clifftops, even bogs.

In the lower, drier, and sandier eastern third of Algonquin, the pines—white, red, and jack—dominate broad, level areas. Scrubby red oak covers ridgetops occasionally in association with white pine. Few giant white pines survived the intensive logging of the nineteenth century, although second-growth trees—for example, those behind the Achray campground on Grand Lake—are now a century old and about 80 ft/25 m high. Throughout the park, black spruce bogs occupy low-lying, poorly drained areas.

The broadleaf forests are habitats for southern birds and animals; the coniferous ones are home to creatures more often found in the north. Bird watchers find this meeting of habitats especially striking, with common loons, common ravens, gray jays, and spruce grouse mingling in the same sanctuary with such southern species as rose-breasted grosbeaks, brown thrashers, and scarlet tanagers. Moose, wolves, and fishers cohabit with raccoons and white-tailed deer from the south.

Probably no other tree in Algonquin surpasses the nutritious, widespread quaking aspen in importance to wildlife. Its buds are winter food for ruffed grouse; twigs of the young trees provide forage for moose and deer; the bark sustains mice, snowshoe hares, porcupines, and beavers. (A 1-acre/ 0.4-hectare aspen grove can support a colony of five beavers for up to three years.) Early summer leaves are the mainstay of the black bear's diet.

The leaves of the speckled alder, a widespread species around creeks, lakes, and beaver ponds, are four times richer in nitrogen than the leaves of other plants. When they fall into creeks and rivers in autumn, they contribute essential nitrogen felt throughout an aquatic food chain that culminates in Algonquin's prized brook trout.

Evening grosbeaks discard the fleshy fruit of chokecherries and pin cherries, prized by cedar waxwings and robins, and instead crack open the hard cherrystones with their massive, vise-like bills to find the big, nutritious seed within—a feat that requires 22 lb/10 kg of pressure. The white-winged crossbill, a colorful pink, black, and white finch, has a specialized bill (literally crossed at the tip) which it uses to pry open the cone scales of white spruce so it can pluck out the seeds with its tongue.

The seeds of the sugar maple, by far the most common west-side tree, are the principal food of the park's most common mammal, the deer mouse. Because seed production varies widely from year to year, so does the population of mice, along with the numbers of predators elsewhere on the food chain, including ermine, long-tailed weasels, red foxes, and great horned and barred owls.

Algonquin's once-plentiful deer have declined as openings left by logging and fire return to closed forest. In fact, deer probably owe their continued existence here to hemlock. Algonquin receives an average of 40 in/ 100 cm of snow each year, and deer have difficulty moving about in snow deeper than 20 in/50 cm. In winter, deer "yard up" under the hemlock's thick foliage, which intercepts most of the snow, making for easier movement to nearby feeding areas.

The deer's decline has been accompanied by a dramatic increase in the number of moose, which now number about 4,000. The earlier scarcity of moose was due partly to nematode worms, which infect deer and pass through them innocuously, taking up residence later in slugs and snails. When a browsing moose ingests these slugs, the nematode worms burrow into the moose's brain and spinal cord with devastating effects—blindness, loss of coordination, inability to stand, and death. Now, with fewer deer, fewer moose fall prey to deer parasites, and the population has rebounded.

The park's famous wolves, which number about 250 individuals, have had difficulty adjusting to the shift from deer to moose. On average, adult Algonquin wolves weigh less than 66 lb/30 kg, which means they have greater difficulty in preying on moose than do the larger, more northerly wolves. Packs, which consist of a mated pair and several offspring from previous years, gather throughout the summer at rendezvous sites, often old beaver meadows. Here, five or six pups are raised and trained until autumn, when they are big and strong enough to hunt with adults.

The pack travels ceaselessly over its vast range, often covering more than 9 mi/15 km in a single night. Wolves do not seem to employ any hunting strategy. They usually run down old or sick deer and moose. Healthy moose that stand their ground are seldom, if ever, successfully attacked. Even when they do flee, moose escape more than half the time.

A more reliable source of food for wolves in summer and fall are beaver, which are defenseless when surprised on land. Algonquin supports some 7,000 beaver colonies consisting of five or six individuals each. The park's interconnecting waterways are also an ideal habitat for the numerous and widespread river otter, a sleek, aquatic weasel that feeds on fish, frogs, crayfish, and the occasional muskrat or duck. The otter's only real competitor is the mink, another kind of weasel that limits itself to shorelines. Algonquin's well-represented weasel family also includes striped skunks, martens, ermine, and fishers.

OUTDOOR ACTIVITIES

Some wilderness-minded visitors may be discouraged by their first impression of the park: lots of people and, along Highway 60, cottage-lined lakes, campgrounds, lodges, and supply stores. Development, however, is limited to the highway corridor. The Algonquin of maple hills, pine-tufted ridges, and myriad lakes, rivers, and streams is just a short hike or paddle away.

May is a good time to visit the park. Trout fishing is at its best, and blackflies do not appear until late in the month. One main drawback for canoeists in spring is the frigid water, which makes capsizing life-threatening. Those who find blackflies a minor inconvenience have the park virtually to themselves in June. Blackflies subside by early July and mosquitoes taper off by the end of the month. Most of the 750,000 visitors come in July and August, many of them merely passing through on Highway 60. About 120,000 people use the Highway 60 campgrounds, and some 60,000 hikers and canoeists explore the park "interior," as the backcountry is known here.

Timberwolves, like the male above, are also known as gray wolves and live in packs. Although they seldom call when actually chasing prey, their howls encourage hunting and signal pack members to meet at an ambush point.

Quotas are used on some canoe routes and hiking trails in order to preserve the wilderness experience. September may be Algonquin's best month. Summer crowds are gone, hardwoods wear autumn colors, and the weather is still pleasant.

Hiking

There are 12 short nature trails along Highway 60 and secondary park roads. Detailed brochures and self-guiding signposts make these walks pleasurable lessons in park geology, fauna, flora, and human history. Among the more interesting outings are the *Brent Crater Trail*, which loops through the eroded crater of a meteorite that exploded some 450 million years ago at a spot just inside the northern park boundary; the *Barron Canyon Trail* along the rim of a spectacular gorge near the eastern boundary; and the *Lookout Trail*, which ascends a 400-ft/125-m ridge with panoramic views. The *Hardwood Lookout Trail* culminates in a fine view of Smoke Lake and the surrounding maple hills, a prime vantage from which to enjoy the park's spectacular fall foliage (usually the last week of September). For the best chance to see wildlife in the highway corridor (especially moose, beaver, and otter), follow the *Mizzy Lake Trail*, a 6.8-mi/11-km loop that requires six hours to hike.

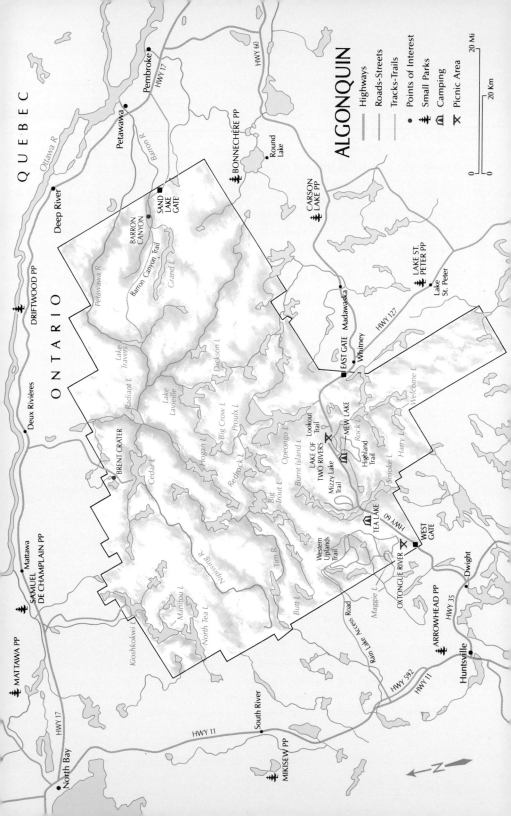

Two backpacking networks off Highway 60 lend themselves to trips ranging from a weekend to a week. The main trailhead for the *Western Uplands Trail*, which runs north of the highway, is at the Oxtongue River picnic ground, 1.8 mi/3 km inside the West Gate. The trail can also be reached from the Rain Lake access road. A three-day outing on the most southerly loop of the trail (20 mi/32 km) might include camping at Maggie Lake, a turquoise gem reminiscent of glacial lakes in the Rocky Mountains, and a second night at Ramona Lake. Long sections of the trail follow old logging roads through rolling hardwood hills south of Ramona.

Highlights of the second loop (34 mi/55 km) are the Pincher Lake campsites and a lookout with surpassing upland views at Susan Lake, a vista reached after climbing the steepest trail in Algonquin. The third loop (44 mi/71 km) goes farther north to Islet Lake, the most beautiful lake on the network. East-shore campsites take advantage of sunsets and bug-dispersing western breezes.

The trailhead for the *Highland Trail*, which consists of two loops south of the highway, is near the Mew Lake campground, 18.7 mi/30 km inside the West Gate. Hikers who seek solitude hurry through the busy first loop (11.8 mi/19 km) circling Provoking Lake. On the second loop (21.8 mi/35 km), moose often browse in the swamps between Mosquito Creek and Harness Lake. South of Fly Lake, hikers sometimes glimpse black bears feasting on raspberries ripening in July in an old beaver meadow. Harness and Head lakes at the southern end of the trail have attractive shoreline campsites sheltered in groves of hemlock, spruce, and white-cedar. Harness Lake has fine swimming and fishing (lake trout in early summer). Farther northeast, a gloriously situated campsite overlooks deep Faya Lake, where anglers take brook trout.

Boating

In general, lakes along the Highway 60 and those accessible from secondary roads are open to motorboats of unlimited horsepower. Some lakes, though, are restricted to boats with engines of ten and, in some cases, six horsepower during the height of the spring fishing seasons, and are closed to all motorboats in July and August.

Canoeing

A bewildering choice awaits canoe trippers: 29 access points to more than 1,000 mi/1,600 km of routes with 1,200 campsites. The term "routes" may be slightly misleading; park waters afford one huge interconnected network. Starting at a single access point, paddlers can link together multiple combinations of lakes and rivers. Virtually all routes involve portages that average 0.3 mi/0.5 km in length; trails are clearly marked and well maintained.

Algonquin rivers are generally not suitable for white-water canoeing, with the exception of the east-side Petawawa below Cedar Lake, which should be attempted only by experienced paddlers. Beautiful "paddle-and-portage" rivers in the western highlands include the *Tim*, the *Nipissing*, and the *Crow.*

Fishing

The park deserves its reputation for fine fishing, although Algonquin waters are not nearly as productive as those in southern Ontario. Lake trout and brook trout are widely distributed in deep, cold lakes throughout the park. Opeongo Lake is the largest and most heavily fished lake, with a catch of one lake trout for every seven hours' fishing. Fishing for lake trout is also good at the north end of Hardy Bay on Lavieille Lake.

Brook trout lakes include Dickson, Lavieille, Redrock, Proulx, Big Crow, Welcome, Harry, and Stringer. On Dickson Lake, one to two fish are landed per hour in May and June, the prime months.

Many lakes in or near the highway corridor support good populations of smallmouth bass, a species introduced here as early as 1899. Opeongo is the most productive lake, with one fish landed for every three hours' fishing. Provoking Lake is also good for bass fishing.

Among park rivers, the Nipissing is one of Ontario's best for brook trout, especially in May on the stretch of river above High Falls. The Crow River is also good for brook trout; the Petawawa below Squirrel Rapids is excellent for smallmouth bass.

Swimming

Water temperatures in July and August are very comfortable for swimming. Two sand beaches and changing houses are at the Lake of Two Rivers picnic grounds; swimming is unsupervised, as it is throughout the park. There are also beaches at the other campgrounds along Highway 60, with the exception of Tea Lake and Kearney. Sand beaches on Grand Lake are accessible to canoeists, as are the pools below High Falls on the Nipissing River—splendid for cooling dips.

Cross-country Skiing

Winter is the best season to see signs of wildlife because animals leave records in the snow. Skiers encounter the tracks of moose, deer, wolves, foxes, otters, and martens—and sometimes see the animals themselves.

Colorful wildflowers abound in the natural environmental park of Algonquin, one of the most varied recreational areas in the province. OPPOSITE: Unpredictable and dangerous, this bull moose in a beaver pond represents the world's largest deer.

Four trails off Highway 60 are designed and groomed specifically for skiing. The *Fen Lake Trail* just inside the West Gate has three loops ranging in difficulty from easy to advanced (total length: 9.3 mi/15 km). The route travels through hardwood forest where moose tracks are often seen.

Farther east, the *Minnesing Trail* stacks four loops north of the highway (length: 34 mi/55 km). The return leg follows part of the Minnesing Road, which ran from the Highland Inn on Cache Lake to Minnesing Lodge on Burnt Island Lake, a wilderness retreat torn down in the 1950s.

For most of its 5.2-mi/8.4-km length, the *Mew Lake Ski Trail* in the eastern half of the highway corridor follows the roadbed of the Ottawa–Arnprior–Parry Sound Railroad. This historic line was completed in 1896 by J. R. Booth, greatest of the Algonquin lumber barons.

The *Leaf Lake-David Thompson Trail* complex, just inside the East Gate, provides perhaps Algonquin's finest skiing, with eight interconnected loops winding through a variety of landscapes. Difficulty ranges from easy to advanced. Wildlife tracks encountered along the way include moose, otter, and ruffed grouse, as well as "bears' nests"—tangles of broken branches left in beech and oak trees by bears foraging in autumn for nuts and acorns. A centrally located rest area has a fireplace and firewood.

Snowshoeing

Those who like to bushwhack can go virtually anywhere in the park. Snowshoers who prefer designated routes follow the nature trails along the highway or set out on the park's two long backpacking routes.

EXPLORING THE PARK

The park's West Gate is 160 mi/257 km north of Toronto via Highway 400 to Barrie, Highway 11 to Huntsville, then Highway 60 to the western boundary. The section of Highway 60 that winds through the southwestern corner of the park is known as the Frank MacDougall Parkway, in honor of an Algonquin superintendent. The East Gate is 150 mi/240 km west of Ottawa via the Ottawa Valley Route of the Trans-Canada Highway (Highway 17) to Renfrew, then Highway 60. Six secondary roads lead to canoe access points in remote corners of the park from Highways 17 and 11. The main service centers are southwest of the park at the resort towns of Huntsville and Dwight.

The main gates and campgrounds operate from late April to mid-October. Highway 60 remains open year-round; the Mew Lake campground is maintained for winter campers.

Guidebooks, maps, brochures, and fishing licenses are available at visitors' centers near the West and East gates, at the park museum (705-633-5592), at the canoe centers on Canoe and Opeongo lakes, and from offices at the interior canoe access points. Canoes can be rented from numerous outfitters in and around the park; check the publication "Canoe Routes of Algonquin Provincial Park" for addresses.

The most popular events in the park's busy interpretive program are undoubtedly the wolf howls in August, with up to 1,000 people attending. The response rate is good: six sessions out of 10 elicit answering howls.

ACCOMMODATIONS: Eight campgrounds are situated along Highway 60. The most secluded are also the largest: Canisbay (248 sites) and Pog Lake (281 sites), both of which have good beaches. Canisbay also has 17 paddle-in shoreline campsites on Canisbay Lake. There are another 10 campsites on Crotch Lake accessible only by canoe. Sites at Mew Lake and some at Pog, Two Rivers, and Canisbay lakes may be reserved by writing or phoning the park office (705-633-5538 or 705-633-5725). Otherwise, camping is on a first-come, first-served basis, as is car camping at a few access points for canoe routes—Achray, Brent, Kiosk, and Rain Lake. Canoeists and hikers camping overnight in the interior must obtain a permit from park offices. Winter visitors stay at the Mew Lake campground or anywhere in the park out of sight or sound of the ski trails (no permit is required for camping in the interior).

Several private lodges are in the Highway 60 corridor. One of the best-known is Arowhon Pines Lodge (705-633-5661 or 416-483-4393), a resort with cottages scattered around wooded, lakeside grounds. The red-trimmed log cottages of Killarney Lodge (705-633-5551) cluster around the Lake of Two Rivers. Housekeeping cottages of Bartlett Lodge (705-633-5543) are on an island in Cache Lake. In the vicinity of the park, the most luxurious accommodation is probably The Deerhurst Inn and Country Club (705-789-5543), in Huntsville.

ADDRESSES: For more information, contact: Algonquin Provincial Park, Ministry of Natural Resources, Box 219, Whitney, Ont. K0J 2M0; 705-633-5572. The Friends of Algonquin Park (Box 248, Whitney, Ont. K0J 2M0; 705-633-5592) publish booklets on the park's natural and human history, as well as detailed hiking and canoeing maps. These publications are available from the Friends' bookstore in the park museum.

BOOKS: Ottelyn Addison, *Tom Thomson: The Algonquin Years.* Toronto: Ryerson Press, 1969.

Joanne Kates, *Exploring Algonquin Park.* Vancouver/Toronto: Douglas & McIntyre, 1985. A four-season guide to the park, along with human and natural history. Detailed descriptions of six recommended canoe trips.

Bill Mason, *Path of the Paddle: An Illustrated Guide to the Art of Canoeing.* Toronto: Van Nostrand Reinhold, 1980. Advice from Canada's foremost canoeing authority.

Ian Scott and Mavis Kerr, *Canoeing in Ontario.* Toronto: Greey de Pencier Publications, 1975. A guidebook to the province's routes, including those in the park.

ST. LAWRENCE ISLANDS NATIONAL PARK

FORGED FROM PINK GRANITE, limestone, and sandstone, quilled with pines and hardwoods, the Thousand Islands braid the upper St. Lawrence for 35 mi/56 km where the river exits Lake Ontario. The Algonquin called the region Manitouana, the "Garden of the Great Spirit." More prosaic French explorers named it Les Milles Iles. There are actually some 1,825 islands in this scenic archipelago, which has been a popular vacationland for more than a century.

Most islands have sprouted docks, boathouses, and cottages with wrap-around verandas. On some, improbable mansions and castles, moated by the St. Lawrence itself, rise among the pines. A summer armada of pleasure craft plies the river—low-slung runabouts, sleek yachts, boxy cabin cruisers. From time to time, a Great Lakes freighter, engines throbbing, slips by on the St. Lawrence Seaway, so out of scale as to seem unreal.

The 23 islands that comprise Canada's smallest national park are scattered between Kingston and Brockville. (A riverbank plot at Mallorytown Landing is home to park headquarters.) In the midst of such intense waterborne recreation and commerce, park islands offer quiet anchorages, woodland walks, secluded beaches, and private places for watching the summer sun silvering the mighty river. In these quiet pursuits, park visitors continue to cultivate the Garden of the Great Spirit.

GEOLOGY

Most of the Thousand Islands are actually the tops of granite hills that rise above a flooded landscape. The hills are the stubs of mountains that stood as high as the Rockies some 800 million years ago, then were relentlessly ground down by erosion. By about 500 million years ago, wind, rain, and frost had finished planing the peaks into rolling hills.

About that time, the earth's crust began to sag and shallow seas flooded the land. Eventually, the granite hills were covered with sediments that hardened into sandstone and limestone. Then the sagging stopped and the

The common resinous pitch pine can tolerate dry rocky soil. Formed largely by rockport granite, the St. Lawrence's Hill Island also hosts all nine species of local snakes and many of the region's frogs.

hills were gently uplifted atop an arch known as the Frontenac Axis, which runs northwest–southeast between the Canadian Shield of southeastern Ontario and the Adirondacks of New York.

Some 12,500 years ago, toward the end of the Ice Age, glacial meltwaters filled the basin of Lake Ontario and submerged these ancient hills. Within another thousand years, the ice had retreated to where Ottawa is now, but slower melting of the sheet near Quebec City formed an ice dam. The St. Lawrence backed up, creating the Champlain Sea, a body of fresh water that covered much of southern Quebec and southeastern Ontario.

Free of its icy burden, the land began to rebound, and Frontenac Axis hills rose above the waters to become the Thousand Islands. About 7,000 years ago, the ice dam broke, the Champlain Sea drained, and the St. Lawrence River began flowing around the archipelago at the start of its journey to the sea.

HISTORY

Archaeologists paint a portrait of prehistoric life in broad brushstrokes, based on artifacts unearthed at a campsite on Gordon Island, near Gananoque. The region was inhabited about 9,000 years ago by Paleo-Indians who hunted mammoths, mastodons, and other large Ice Age mammals. By 7,000 years ago, they were trading with distant tribes: copper from the western Great Lakes; flint from the Alleghenies; shells from the mid-Atlantic Coast. By A.D. 1000 agriculture had come to the area as early Amerindians began to cultivate corn, squash, and other crops to offset the uncertainty of the hunt.

Samuel de Champlain visited the region in 1615 in the company of Huron warriors on an expedition against the Onondaga, an Iroquois tribe living in what is now upstate New York. After Champlain came other explorers, along with fur traders, missionaries, and adventurers, all traveling the great river highway of the St. Lawrence to the inland seas and the heart of the continent.

Southeastern Ontario was settled by Loyalists fleeing the new American republic after the War of Independence. Known stateside as Tories, the Loyalists founded towns along the north shore of the St. Lawrence, cleared the land of towering oak and pine, and built gristmills, sawmills, brickyards, even a glassworks.

During the War of 1812, the St. Lawrence was a vital lifeline between Upper Canada (Ontario) and Lower Canada (Quebec). The British organized a flotilla of nine single-cannon gunboats to escort convoys through the area, where myriad channels were ideal for concealing raiding parties. (What is thought to be the gunboat *H.M.S. Radcliffe*, launched at Kingston just after the war, is at Mallorytown Landing.)

In the Thousand Islands, American hostilities were limited to harassment of British convoys and raids on Gananoque and Brockville. The British retaliated by attacking Ogdensburg. Under terms of the Treaty of Ghent, which concluded the War of 1812, commissioners establishing the U.S.–Canada boundary agreed that no island would be divided. Instead they set an irregular border, for the most part following the main channel of the St. Lawrence; islands north of the channel are Canadian.

In the late 1800s, the Thousand Islands became known as the Playground of Millionaires, rivaling Newport and Bar Harbor. The wealthy began flocking here, with tennis racquets, fishing rods, and evening dress packed in steamer trunks. While the rich built extravagant "cottages" on the islands, less affluent visitors stayed at riverside resorts.

George Boldt, a German-born hotel magnate and real estate operator, envisioned a 124-room Rhineland castle as a valentine for his wife, Louise. (The chef on Boldt's yacht invented Thousand Islands dressing, which soon garnished salads at Boldt's Waldorf-Astoria Hotel in New York.) In 1904, after Boldt had reshaped the island into a heart and spent $2 million on construction, Louise died. The millionaire halted work and never returned. Tour boats stop at Heart Island to see what love built and grief abandoned.

HABITATS

Despite its small size, the archipelago is rich in plant life. On park islands alone, an area of just 3 sq mi/8 sq km, more than 800 kinds of flowering plants have been identified. This tremendous variety occurs because the region straddles a Transition Zone, meaning a place where two floras—in this case the northern and southern—meet and mingle.

Although no two islands have exactly the same vegetation and each island has at least several species found nowhere else in the archipelago, most islands have open stands of pitch pine on the southwestern end, which gradually give way toward the northeast to eastern white pine, then eastern hemlock. Hardwoods dominate interior forests, with American basswood on lower slopes and red and white oak at higher elevations. Northern white-cedars grow on cliffs; swamps are dominated by silver maple. Eastern redcedar and shagbark hickory are widely scattered.

The scraggly, twisted pitch pine, the park symbol, reaches the northern limits of its range here. Large stands grow on Hill, Grenadier, and Endym-

Blue herons are a common sight on the Thousand Islands. Gangly and acrobatic, they are natural performers, but visitors strolling too close to their twilight perches will receive a raucous and scathing rebuke.

ion islands; some trees are more than 200 years old. Settlers used the pitch, or resin, in making charcoal, tar, and turpentine. The decay-resistant wood was turned into wharf pilings, waterwheels, and ship's pumps.

The region is also rich in amphibians and reptiles: six species of salamanders, five of turtles, eight of frogs and toads, and eight of snakes. Northern water snakes often sun on rocks off the west end of Mermaid Island. The harmless and fairly common eastern ribbon snake lives in deciduous woodlands and on wetland margins. The locally threatened black rat snake, Canada's largest, grows up to 8 ft/2.4 m in length. This nonpoisonous serpent slithers through open woodlands in search of rodents, lizards, birds, and bird's eggs. Rat snakes are superb climbers—an ability enhanced by their overlapping belly scales which flare outward as they move, thus providing traction.

The Thousand Islands, located between the Atlantic and Central flyways, attract large numbers of ducks during spring migrations, especially greater scaups and canvasbacks, along with mergansers and common goldeneyes. Birders pull off on the shoulder of the Thousand Islands Parkway just east of park headquarters to watch great rafts of scaups gather at staging areas. Ospreys can also be seen in summer from the parkway on either side of headquarters.

Common terns, ring-billed gulls, and herring gulls congregate on rocky shoals throughout the archipelago, especially in remote areas and off islands that have no cottages. Strollers along the usually deserted Grenadier Island township road (there are only a few cars on the island) see and hear such nesting songbirds as song sparrows, yellow warblers, rose-breasted grosbeaks, and northern orioles. In winter the Ivy Lea Bridge is a good place to sight bald eagles fishing for alewives in open water. Wild turkeys can be seen occasionally near the Canadian Customs office on Hill Island.

Few large mammals live in the park. Small rodents, including the meadow vole, the red squirrel, and the short-tailed shrew, inhabit the islands. White-tailed deer, coyotes, and red foxes have been observed in winter.

OUTDOOR ACTIVITIES

The park is a boater's paradise, with docks or moorings found throughout the archipelago. Wooded islands are threaded with footpaths, and the St. Lawrence is fine for swimming and fishing.

Scenic Drives

The *Thousand Islands Parkway* splits off from Highway 401, the busy divided thoroughfare between Montreal and Toronto, and follows the north shore of the St. Lawrence for some 22 mi/37 km between Butternut Bay and Gananoque. Trees sometimes screen the St. Lawrence, but numerous lookouts furnish motorists with excellent views of the waterway and its chain of forested islands.

For a bird's-eye view of the area, head south of the parkway to the *Thousand Islands International Bridge*, a five-span link between Ontario and New York. From atop the 400-ft/122-m *Thousand Islands Skydeck*, just off the bridge on Canada's Hill Island, views on clear days embrace a 40-mi/65-km sweep of both sides of the border. The elevator-equipped tower is open daily from May to October.

Hiking

The *Mainland Nature Trail*, an easy hour-long walk, starts at the Mallorytown Landing campground and winds through mixed woodlands. In early May, rare rue anemone borders the path, along with trillium, hepatica, and may-apple. Most of the islands also have woodland walks, some with interpretive signs.

OVERLEAF: *The Thousand Islands Bridge connects the United States and Canada and passes through the park's Georgina and Constance Islands.*

Bicycling

A bike path, paved between Gananoque and Butternut Bay, parallels the *Thousand Islands Parkway.* Washrooms, maps, and displays on the area's natural and human history are located at rest stops along the route. Westbound riders face generally uphill terrain, but that means easier cycling on the return trip, often assisted on sunny summer afternoons by strong southwest winds.

West of Butternut Bay, the path's eastern starting point, snacks and swimming are available at Brown's Bay Provincial Park, a day-use facility. Soon after, an alternate route follows the Old River Road through beautiful woodlands to Mallorytown Landing, a former steamboat dock and site of park headquarters. Beyond the Landing, cyclists pass La Rue Mills, a farmhouse built in the late 1700s by a Loyalist millwright who provided flour to the British during the War of 1812. Billa La Rue and his family are buried in the cemetery beside the bike path just west of the house.

Cyclists now enter a more developed tourist area. From Poole's Resort, about 0.6 mi/1 km west of La Rue Mills, riders can see Poole's Island with its large 1890s-vintage summer home and, in the distance, Grenadier Island. The picturesque Loyalist river town of Rockport, about halfway along the route, is a good place to stop; the Boathouse Tavern and Restaurant or the Rockport General Store serve lunch.

After Rockport, a succession of hills makes for tough cycling but good sightseeing, as hilltop lookouts offer glimpses of the river. West of the bridge interchange, one can make a side trip to the sleepy hamlet of Ivy Lea to see quaint Victorian architecture and boathouses perched over the river. Beyond Ivy Lea the bike path passes marinas and private campgrounds. Just beyond Landon's Bay, a good spot for picnicking and swimming off the rocks, is an exhibit on the geology of the Thousand Islands. Cooling dips can also be enjoyed at Gray's Beach near Gananoque, the path's western endpoint.

Mainland county and township roads are also suitable for bike touring. The lightly used *Rockport-to-Escott* road is especially scenic, with old farms, interesting rock cuts, and prime bird-watching woodlands.

Boating

The park's most popular activity is pursued from mid-May through October. There are docks or moorings on 21 of 23 park islands, and many also have picnic areas, campgrounds, and trails. *Cedar Island,* the westernmost park island, attracts day-trippers from nearby Kingston. Family outings are popular on *McDonald Island,* just off Gananoque, where ancient oaks and tall pines shade campsites. Small mammals abound in the forests of *Thwartway Island*, which has moorings instead of a dock; swimmers head for the west side of the island to a boulder-strewn bay with a sandy bottom. *Endymion* and *Camelot* have suitable anchorages for deep-draft boats. Rugged terrain, however, limits the number of campsites.

Gordon Island, comprised of low-lying limestone instead of the usual knobby granite, has three docks and a central open area that was cleared for camping early in the park's history. Thick forests on *Mulcaster Island* attract bird watchers in search of ruffed grouse and small raptors; the island's three sheltered docks fill early. A small beach and a large number of campsites are the attractions at *Grenadier South*. The easternmost park island, *Stovin*, offers good vantages for watching huge Great Lakes freighters as they navigate the St. Lawrence Seaway.

Fishing

More than 20 species of sport fish caught here include lake trout, northern pike, catfish, smallmouth and largemouth bass, yellow perch, and walleye. The premiere game fish is smallmouth bass, which is landed throughout the islands; Mulcaster Island is a top spot. Anglers fish the marshy shallows of Adelaide Island off Mallorytown Landing for largemouth bass, pike, and perch; the parkway bridge on Jones Creek in spring for brown bullheads; and Forty Acre Shoal south of Gananoque in autumn for muskellunge (the world-record "muskie," weighing 69.92 lb/31.72 kg, was caught there). Walleye are taken off Constance and Georgina islands and near the International Bridge. Ice-fishing enthusiasts catch pike and perch.

Swimming

The chilly, swiftly flowing water is usually described as "refreshing." There is a supervised beach at Mallorytown Landing. Unsupervised swimming is at Thwartway, Grenadier Central, and elsewhere.

Scuba Diving

Kingsdive (613-542-2892) of Kingston takes divers to about 10 sites west of the park, including the *George Marsh*, an intact schooner standing upright in 75 ft/23 m of water off Kingston harbor, and the paddle-wheeler *Comet*, which sank in 1865 after a collision in fog. St. Lawrence Dive Service (613-342-6553), based in Brockville, also guides divers to shipwrecks. A favorite destination is the schooner *Lily Parsons*, which sank in 1877 and rests upside down off Sparrow Island just upriver from Stovin. This outfitter also conducts drift diving through narrow cuts between islands to see glacially carved underwater formations.

EXPLORING THE PARK

Park headquarters at Mallorytown Landing is about 186 mi/300 km north-east of Toronto via Highway 401; 150 mi/240 km southwest of Montreal via Highways 40 and 401; and 40 mi/64 km north of Watertown, New York, via Interstate 81, which crosses the St. Lawrence River on the Thousand Islands International Bridge.

The main jumping-off points for various islands in the park are (from southwest to northeast): Kingston, the largest nearby city; Gananoque, a picturesque waterfront resort; Ivy Lea; Rockport, a favorite landfall of the boating crowd; Mallorytown Landing; and Brockville. All have launching ramps for small boats.

The interpretive program includes evening programs and films at park headquarters and guided cycling trips. Naturalists visit park islands in the Showboat, a floating interpretive center.

Most people travel to park islands in their own boats. Docking space is usually at a premium in July and early August; boaters may have to visit several islands before finding a berth. There is a small docking fee. Most towns also charge a small fee for use of public docks.

A monarch butterfly makes a brilliant contrast to asters in full bloom. Small distinct climate patterns caused by the rugged landscapes create an astonishingly wide range of animal and plant life in a relatively small geographic area.

Those without their own vessel arrange transportation to and from islands with privately operated water taxis out of Gananoque, Ivy Lea, and Rockport. Several marinas between Gananoque and Mallorytown Landing rent open aluminum boats and outboard motors. For longer stays, houseboat and sailing charters are available at river ports. Book early; this is a popular cruising area.

Private tour boats depart daily from May through October for cruises among the islands. The triple-decker replica of the paddle-wheeler *Island Queen* (613-549-5544) leaves daily from Kingston harbor. Gananoque Boat Lines (613-382-2144) operates one- and three-hour cruises, with stops at Boldt Castle. Ivy Lea 1000 Islands Boat Tours (613-659-2293 or 613-659-2295) takes small vessels through passages and channels inaccessible to larger boats; some outings stop at Boldt Castle. A double-decker boat of the Rockport Boat Lines (613-659-3402) cruises for two hours through narrow channels and shallow bays.

ACCOMMODATIONS: The Mallorytown Landing campground (64 sites) occupies a small field behind the administration building. The park's marina, boat-launching ramp, supervised beach, and interpretive center are on the other side of the Thousand Island parkway along the waterfront. Fifteen park islands have primitive campsites with wells. Reservations are not accepted for mainland or island campsites, except for the group campground at Grenadier South. There are private campgrounds, resorts, hotels, motels, and marinas in towns along this stretch of the St. Lawrence.

ADDRESSES: For more information, contact: The Superintendent, St. Lawrence Islands National Park, RR #3, Box 469, Mallorytown Landing, Ont. K0E 1R0; 613-923-5261. For general information on the Thousand Islands, contact the Eastern Ontario Travel Association, 209 Ontario St., Kingston, Ont. K7L 2Z1; 613-549-3682, or Tourism Ontario, which operates a toll-free number (800-668-2746) in Canada and the continental U.S. (except the Yukon, Northwest Territories, and Alaska). Tourism Ontario's number in the Toronto area is 416-965-4008.

BOOKS: Don Ross, *St. Lawrence Islands National Park*. Vancouver/Toronto: Douglas & McIntyre, 1983. Comprehensive guidebook available in local bookstores.

LA MAURICIE NATIONAL PARK

A PLATEAU OF ROUNDED HILLS, rivers, and more than 150 lakes characterize this horseshoe-shaped park in south-central Quebec. La Mauricie protects a representative example of the Laurentian Mountains, a landscape that embodies the lonely beauty of the Canadian wilderness in its Precambrian outcrops, latticework of water, and forests of hardwoods and conifers.

The park is bracketed on the north and east by the Mattawin–St. Maurice river system, on the west by Mastigouche Provincial Game Preserve, and on the south by the flat farmlands of the St. Lawrence Valley. Three water corridors beckon canoeists: Wapizagonke, Caribou, and Anticagamac lakes in the west; the central Edouard and Des Cinq chain of lakes; and, in the east, the Isaïe and A-la-Pêche lake system. A scenic parkway spans these riparian valleys. South of the road are campgrounds, beaches, and other recreational facilities. To the north lies wilderness.

GEOLOGY

The Laurentians are part of the Canadian Shield, the foundation of North America. Covered elsewhere by thick beds of sediment, the Shield is exposed in Canada in a broad arc that sweeps from Labrador to the Great Lakes and northwest to the Arctic coast. The oldest of this Precambrian rock has endured for three-quarters of the earth's existence.

The rocks of the Shield (named for its shape and long stability) are not uniform in composition or age. La Mauricie's gneisses date from the Shield's final phase of development, about 955 million years ago. They were formed deep in the earth's interior and brought to the surface by the uplifting that raised the Laurentians. This range, once as mighty as the Rockies, has been ground down to knobby hills by nearly a billion years of erosion.

The Ice Age, which peaked about 18,000 years ago, played a major role in creating the park's jumbled relief. Advancing glaciers flattened the topography, deepened major valleys, and scooped out depressions that are now filled with lakes and ponds. In the southwestern park, retreating glaciers left kettles (pothole lakes in glacial drift) and eskers (gravel ridges deposited by streams flowing beneath glaciers). At central Lake Du Fou, melting glaciers left precariously balanced shoreline erratics.

HISTORY

More than 30 prehistoric campsites dating back 5,000 years have been found along the Wapizagonke corridor, which formed a watery highway from the mighty St. Lawrence River to hunting grounds in the Quebec interior. The most striking legacy left by the Attikamek, an Algonquin tribe, are pictographs on a cliff along Lake Wapizagonke. These red-ocher rock paintings are among the oldest in eastern Canada, dating back some 2,000 years.

Trois-Rivières, Canada's second-oldest city (after Quebec City) was founded in 1634 at the confluence of the St. Maurice and the St. Lawrence, and soon became an important missionary and fur-trading center. Westbound traders and Attikamek traveled through La Mauricie by canoe to avoid the hostile Iroquois, who at the time controlled the upper St. Lawrence. The route lost much of its importance when Montreal was founded in 1642 about 125 mi/200 km upstream on the St. Lawrence.

Canada's first heavy industry was established in 1730 just north of Trois-Rivières. (The ironworks, which operated until about 1883, is now a National Historic Site called Les Forges du St. Mauricie.) Rights to La Mauricie timber were obtained by Quebec entrepreneurs starting in 1831, and soon winter forests rang with the axes of lumberjacks. At spring breakup, the Mattawin and St. Maurice bore log rafts down to Trois-Rivières for milling or export to Britain and the United States. La Mauricie forests were leased to paper companies right up to the establishment of the park in 1970.

HABITATS

The park straddles the Transition Zone between the mixed Great Lakes–St. Lawrence forest and the coniferous boreal forest. Twenty-five kinds of deciduous trees in the mixed forest are dominated by sugar maple and yellow birch, an association found nearly everywhere in southern La Mauricie on sunlit hillsides with deep, well-drained soil. Ten kinds of conifers, notably pine, fir, and spruce, grow on thin-soiled slopes and damp valley bottoms.

The most frequently observed birds in deciduous woods are Blackburnian warblers, red-eyed vireos, ovenbirds, and yellow-bellied sapsuckers. Coniferous patches of the mixed forest are home to ruffed grouse, blue jays, black-capped chickadees, and purple finches. In the central region, where hardwoods begin to yield to the conifers of the boreal forest, ruby-

La Mauricie's thick vegetation hides bedrock from the earth's first continental plate,

crowned kinglets, warblers (Tennessee, Nashville, and magnolia), hermit thrushes, evening grosbeaks, and dark-eyed juncos abound.

Mammals typical of the Laurentians range throughout the park. Perhaps the most representative are moose, which are seen often along the shores of Wapizagonke and Anticagamac lakes, black bear, coyote, red fox, beaver, and snowshoe hare. Gray wolves in two or three packs drift in and out of the park, feeding on moose, deer, and beaver and wintering northwest of Lake Anticagamac and Lake Du Fou.

Park ponds and lakes support abundant American black and ring-necked ducks, common goldeneyes, and common mergansers (marshes bordering Anticagamac Lake are especially good for sighting waterfowl). About 20 pairs of common loons nest on 18 lakes in La Mauricie; the best places to see these sleek and beautiful birds are in Des Onze Iles Bay on Lake Caribou and Lake Des Cinq. Among the park's 12 kinds of birds of prey, only the broad-winged hawk and osprey are sighted routinely.

La Mauricie's streams, rivers, and lakes are home to healthy populations of muskrat and mink and more than 160 beaver colonies. Beaver can be seen at dawn or dusk on nearly all park lakes, but especially on the south

more than 995 million years old.

side of Wapizagonke, on Etienne Creek near Lake Edouard, and all around Lake Bouchard.

The most playful aquatic creature here is the river otter, which toboggans down grassy banks and sports in the water. Otters often are sighted on Bouchard, Anticagamac, and Du Fou lakes and sometimes near the Shewenegan boat-launching ramp on Wapizagonke Lake.

OUTDOOR ACTIVITIES

This year-round park is used heavily from late June to late August by daytrippers who come to picnic and sightsee, and by car- and canoe-campers. Winter brings cross-country skiers.

Scenic Drive

A parkway open from May through October winds 38.5 mi/62 km through the southern part of La Mauricie, connecting the southeastern entrance (Saint-Jean-des-Piles) and the southwestern entrance (Saint-Mathieu). Westbound motorists first head northwest alongside the St. Maurice River past the A-la-Pêche River campground and recreation area, then angle west, skirting the southern tip of Lake Du Fou and the northern end of Lake Edouard, another major recreational area. West of Lake Alphonse is the most spectacular stretch of road. The parkway switchbacks up to a prominent lookout, Le Passage, which provides magnificent views of the main expanse of Lake Wapizagonke. (An interpretive exhibit explains the formation of the landscape.)

Proceeding downhill, the parkway crosses a bridge at the northern end of the lake, then heads south past a side road to the Wapizagonke campground. A short distance south, the Lake Gabet nature trail is an easy half-hour stroll through the loveliest and oldest maple forest in the park.

The route passes the eastern end of Lake Caribou, then rises again to the summit of a long ridge, where two lookouts—Le Vide-Bouteille ("Empty Bottle," named for a sandy point where fishermen traditionally stop for refreshments) and Ile aux Pins (Pine Island)—offer sweeping views of Wapizagonke and rolling woodlands. The road then zigzags past recreation areas before bridging the southern end of the lake and exiting the park at the Saint-Mathieu gate.

Hiking

A modest network of short and medium-length trails, many of which double as canoe portages, are clustered in three locations: the southeast, the northwest, and the southwest. Trailheads in the southeast sector are at A-la-Pêche River and Lake Edouard. The *Mékinac Trail* makes a pleasant, two-hour family hike north along the St. Maurice River. The first half is easy walking through a white spruce plantation established in 1932. The second half is a more strenuous climb to the Lake Rosoy lookout, with its panoramas of the river and the backcountry.

The 9.6-mi/15.5-km *A-la-Pêche Lake Trail,* the longest and most ambitious hike in the area, heads southwest along the western shores of Isaïe and A-la-Pêche lakes to Wabenaki and Andrew lodges. These rustic chalets were once owned by the Laurentian Club, a private hunting and fishing organization founded at the turn of the century, and are now open to visitors. The trail continues south to the warden station at the end of the lake.

Farther west along the parkway is the trailhead for the *Lake Edouard Trail,* which parallels Edouard's western shore, ending at a campsite.

Northwest sector hiking routes are essentially portage trails accessible only by canoe. The 5.6-mi/9-km *Waber–Anticagamac–Wapizagonke Triangle Trail* makes a diverting day-long outing. Paddle west 2.5 mi/4 km from the Wapizagonke picnic area to the end of the lake, then hike west on the portage trail to Waber Falls, which spills 100 ft/30 m (a good spot for a cooling dip in summer). The route goes northeast to the Anticagamac viewpoint, then southeast back to Wapizagonke for a return paddle to the picnic area.

Southwest sector hikes are short and suitable for all ages. A half-day loop (5 mi/8 km) with highlights from all area walks starts at the Shewene-gan picnic area as *Les Cascades Trail*, bridges a narrowing of Wapizagonke, and heads northwest to a series of waterfalls that tumble over a granite ledge. The route then becomes *Les Falaises Trail* as it climbs south to two scenic viewpoints overlooking Wapizagonke's western shoreline. The hike briefly follows Brodeur Brook, recrosses Wapizagonke on the parkway bridge, heads south as *L'Esker Trail*, and winds atop a glacially formed gravel ridge. The final leg is the *Vallerand Trail*, which goes north along the eastern shore of Wapizagonke back to the Shewenegan picnic area.

Bicycling

Southeast sector trails are all open to bikes. Cyclists can pedal to Wabenaki and Andrew lodges in about three leisurely hours.

Canoeing

This is the park's most popular summer activity. A tough 2.3-mi/3.7-km portage southwest from the Rivière-à-la-Pêche campground is required to reach the Isaïe and A-la-Pêche lakes and the twin backcountry lodges. Canoeists also have to portage 650 ft/200 m around an old logging dam at the southern end of Isaïe to reach Lake A-la-Pêche.

Farther west along the parkway, there is easier access for southerly and northerly trips. Along the southerly *Lake Edouard Route* are five secluded shoreline campsites. The northerly *Lake Des Cinq Route* heads deep into the heart of La Mauricie backcountry via a chain of five small lakes linked with portages (the longest is 0.6 mi/1 km). Six wilderness campsites rim Lake Des Cinq.

In the southwestern sector, the Wapizagonke picnic area is a convenient put-in for paddles south down the length of the lake; 11 campsites are scat-tered along the shoreline. La Mauricie's most dramatic scenery surrounds the lake, boxed in a narrow valley by high cliffs. Here and there are sandy beaches and coves veiled by waterfalls. (Lake trips can also start at the southern end from the Shewenegan day-use area.)

As discussed in the hiking section, canoeists paddle west from the picnic area to the end of the lake; from there, three portages lead to the backcoun-try. The *Des Onze Iles Bay Route* involves a fairly arduous southward sequence—portage to a small lake, then portage again—to reach Cobb Bay on Lake Caribou, with its loons and herons. The *Waber–Tessier–Maréchal Route* starts with a long portage (1.7 mi/2.8 km) west from the end of

The common loon calls in either a wild manaical laugh or a loud mournful wail. Expert divers, loons have been found in nets two hundred feet below the water's surface.

Wapizagonke. Waber, Tessier, and Maréchal lakes, connected by short portages, angle southward and link up with Lake Caribou. Returning to the head of Wapizagonke via Des Onze Iles Bay and paddling back to the original picnic area launch site usually is a four-day outing for canoe campers, but the route can be covered in a single day.

A third portage from the head of Wapizagonke angles northwest 1.5 mi/2.4 km to the *Anticagamac–Mattawin Route*. Canoeists paddle the length of Lake Anticagamac (no established campsites), head down a short creek, then enter the Mattawin River. A wilderness campsite is 1.2 mi/2 km downstream, but numerous sandy beaches also make good stopping places. After about 6 mi/10 km on the Mattawin, canoeists make a demanding 3.3-mi/5.4-km portage southeast and link up with the Lake Des Cinq Route, which eventually brings them back to Lake Edouard. The horseshoe-shaped trip takes three to five days.

Fishing

Brook trout represent 95 percent of the catch. Early in the season, which lasts from the last Saturday in May through Labor Day, it is routine to reach the daily limit of five trout, some weighing more than 1 lb/0.5 kg. Edouard, Anticagamac, Wapizagonke, Caribou, Ecarté, and Des Cinq lakes offer the best angling. Northern pike, walleye, and smallmouth bass also are taken from Lake Anticagamac and from the Mattawin.

HWY 55

Lake Des Cinq

St Maurice R.

Dauphinais Lake
Archange L.

Lake Houle   Petit Archange L.

Lake   Lake Dubon
Anticagamac   Lake Giron

Lake   Coeur L.   Lake
Avalon   Lake   Soumire   Lake Du Fou
                    Formont
WABER   Lake Ecarté   Lake
FALLS   LE PASSAGE   Rosay
            LOOKOUT   Lake   Lake Bouchard   A-LA-PÊCHE
Waber L.   Alphonse   HWY 55
Tessier L.   WAPIZAGONKE   Lake
Maréchal   Lake Edouard   Berubé
L.   Lake   St-Jean-
                                                Benoit   des-Piles
Cobb Bay   Lake Caribou   Lake Wapizagonke
                                                            Isaie L.   Grand-Mère
                LE VIDE-BOUTEILLE LOOKOUT

                PINE ISLAND LOOKOUT   Parker L.
                                                            A-la-Pêche L.
            SHEWENEGAN BEACH   WABENAKI AND
L'ESKER BEACH   ANDREW LODGES
                MISTAGANCE
            St-Mathieu   Warden Station

                                    HWY 351   Mattawin R.

LA MAURICIE

——— Highways
——— Roads-Streets
——— Tracks-Trails
   •   Points of Interest
   ⌂   Camping
   *   Scenic Lookout

0   5 Mi
0   5 Km

N

Shawinigan

Fishing rights are allocated by lottery daily at 7:00 A.M. at visitors' reception centers near both park entrances and in campgrounds. Unclaimed fishing spots are distributed to anglers on request during the day. All anglers must register and purchase a national parks license.

Swimming

There is supervised swimming at Lake Edouard, which has fine but busy beaches, and unsupervised swimming on Lake Wapizagonke at the Shewenegan, L'Esker, and Wapizagonke picnic grounds. Backcountry canoe-campers find good beaches on Lake Caribou and all along Wapizagonke.

Cross-country Skiing

Seven marked and groomed trails with a total length of about 50 mi/80 km are accessible from the A-la-Pêche River sector. The visitors' center has a waxing room, and there are warming huts with wood stoves every 3 mi/ 5 km along the trails, which are rated easy, difficult, and very difficult. The most interesting route follows the hiking trail southwest to Wabenaki and Andrew lodges.

Snowshoeing

The *Mékinac Trail* is used for snowshoeing, as is the parkway, which is closed to traffic in winter beyond the A-la-Pêche area.

EXPLORING THE PARK

One of the least-known but most accessible and beautiful of the national parks in southern Canada, La Mauricie is about 125 mi/200 km northwest of Montreal via Highway 40 and Highway 55. To reach the southwestern entrance (Saint-Mathieu), take Exit 217 off Highway 55 to Highway 351. To reach the southeastern entrance (Saint-Jean-des-Piles), take Exit 226 off Highway 55. Travel services are found in Saint-Mathieu, Saint-Gérard-des-Laurentides, Saint-Jean-des-Piles, as well as in Shawinigan, Grand-Mère, and Trois-Rivières.

The visitors' centers at Saint-Jean-des-Piles (819-538-3232) and Saint-Mathieu (819-532-2414) are open daily from mid-May through mid-October; the former contains interpretive displays and audiovisual material, and the latter is home to the local park cooperative association, Info-Nature Mauricie, which sells topographic maps of the park and nature books. During the off season, general information is available from the park administrative office (819-536-4575).

From the last week in June to the third week in August, there are as many as three interpretive activities daily. More limited weekend activities are held for about a month before and after those dates. These programs are mainly in French, but English summaries are given on request by the predominantly bilingual staff. Park road signs and interpretive displays are in French and English.

Visitors in car caravans travel the parkway for primers in La Mauricie geology. Naturalists lead two-hour beach walks and woodland strolls. The most popular activities are two-hour excursions in 12-person canoes. For the three weekday outings, obtain passes the evening before at the amphitheater interpretive program. Shorter Sunday afternoon trips are on a first-come, first-served basis. Those with their own canoes can paddle alongside. For more information, contact the park's interpretive service (819-532-2282).

Canoe rentals may be had from mid-June to Labor Day at the Shewenegan, Wapizagonke, and Lake Edouard day-use areas, and on weekends only from Labor Day to the third weekend in October at Shewenegan (paddle boats are rented there all summer). To reserve canoes, call 819-532-2237 or 819-535-3753. Ski equipment can be rented at Saint-Jean-des-Piles (819-538-2204).

ACCOMMODATIONS: Mistagance campground (90 sites) is near a boat concession and swimming beach at the southern end of Lake Wapizagonke. Farther north at Wapizagonke campground (219 sites) are beaches and a convenience store. A-la-Pêche River campground has 208 sites.

Wabenaki Lodge, accessible only by hiking, biking, and canoeing in summer and skiing in winter, has 53 beds, washrooms, a communal room with a fireplace, and a kitchen with a propane stove and cooking equipment. Adjacent Andrew Lodge has a total of eight beds in four rooms. There are canoes and mountain bikes for rent at both lodges. Reservations for Wabenaki and Andrew are made through Info-Nature Mauricie; in winter, reservations are accepted after the third Monday in November. A-la-Pêche campground is also open for winter camping, with washrooms, showers, hot water, cooking shelters, and wood stoves.

ADDRESSES: For more information, contact: The Superintendent, La Mauricie National Park, Box 758, 465 Fifth St., Shawinigan, Que. G9N 6V9; 819-536-2638. The local park cooperative association is Info-Nature Mauricie, Inc., Box 174, Shawinigan, Que. G9N 6T9; 819-537-4555. For more information on private accommodation and other activities in the area, contact: Association touristique du Centre-Mauricie, Box 274, Shawinigan, Que. G9N 6V9; 819-536-3777.

ATLANTIC CANADA

FORILLON
NATIONAL PARK   244

On a wildly beautiful peninsula at the tip of the Gaspé, fir-clad highlands plunge in steep limestone cliffs to cobble beaches and teeming tidal pools.

FUNDY
NATIONAL PARK   256

Washed by some of the world's highest tides, the sculptured cliffs of this park in eastern New Brunswick rise from the Bay of Fundy to the maple-clad hills of the Caledonia Highlands.

KEJIMKUJIK
NATIONAL PARK   268

In this riverine wilderness in south-central Nova Scotia, canoe routes date back to the days of the Micmac, and a coastal annex preserves untouched shoreline.

PRINCE EDWARD ISLAND NATIONAL PARK   282

On the north shore of an island province, sandstone cliffs back lovely beaches and sand dunes; inland lies the pastoral landscape that inspired *Anne of Green Gables.*

CAPE BRETON HIGHLANDS NATIONAL PARK   294

Rising high and wild above the Atlantic and the Gulf of St. Lawrence, this rugged tableland of bogs, barrens, and wind-gnarled spruce is encircled by one of Canada's finest scenic drives, the Cabot Trail.

GROS MORNE NATIONAL PARK   308

On Newfoundland's western shore, a coastal lowland rises to meet the Long Range Mountains, slashed with spectacular fjord-like lakes and capped with an alpine plateau, home to caribou and arctic hare.

FORILLON NATIONAL PARK

LOCATED AT THE TIP OF THE GASPÉ Peninsula, Forillon National Park appears as a massive, tilted block that juts seaward with the Bay of Gaspé on the southwest and the Gulf of St. Lawrence on the northeast. Descending in huge stairsteps from northwestern highlands, this rugged plateau declines southeastward, tapering into a narrow finger of land called Forillon Presqu'île ("peninsula" or "near-island" in French). Small coves scallop the bay shore, while an impressive phalanx of cliffs marches nearly the entire length of the gulf coast.

The Gaspé became the first part of Quebec to enter recorded history when Jacques Cartier anchored here in 1534, but the area wasn't settled for more than two centuries. Even then, the communities that grew up in coves around the peninsula remained isolated for another 150 years. Today, the Gaspé, whose name comes from a Micmac word meaning "land's end," still seems a place apart, dominated by the overwhelming presence of the sea.

GEOLOGY

Park bedrock was formed from marine sediments laid down in a vast basin 600 to 450 million years ago. Toward the end of this deposition, crustal movements crumpled basin rocks, producing the folding and tilting seen in the northern half of the park. A series of intense uplifts beginning at this time raised these limestones, sandstones, and shales into a high mountain chain that predated the Appalachians of the central Gaspé by about 75 million years.

Over the eons, erosion and faulting have produced a rumpled countryside characterized by elongated ridges with flattened tops and steep walls. This relief, visible from the Cap-Bon-Ami area, repeats to create a series of shelves and cliffs following one another in parallel rows, somewhat like a giant staircase marching down from the northwestern highlands to the Cap-des-Rosiers plain.

Freezing and thawing split limestone along vertical fracture planes to produce the park's spectacular coastal cliffs. At Cap-Bon-Ami visitors can enjoy the thrill of scrambling over these massive headlands tilted and jutting seaward, their sedimentary layers as clearly delineated as laminations in wood. Freezing water continues to drive icy wedges into the escarpment, splitting off great chunks of rock or subtly flaking off material that gathers at the base of cliffs in cone-shaped talus slopes, found especially along the northern shoreline of the Presqu'île.

Rockfalls provide material for Forillon's beaches. Waves polish and round the rock fragments, then spread them along the coast, where they collect in coves to form cobbled beaches. The beautiful limestone pebbles that make up these beaches are predominantly dark bluish gray and often are veined with white calcite. Erosion of the park's sandstone produced the sandy strands of Penouille on the bay side of the park.

Where waves break directly at the base of cliffs, sea caves may emerge, such as the one near Cap-Bon-Ami. In other places, pounding waves widen vertical fissures into marine potholes, some of which eventually consolidate into coves. There are more than 40 of these inlets along the southern shore of Presqu'île between Grande-Grave and Cap Gaspé.

HISTORY

Traces of early human habitation in the park date back 6,000 years—seasonal campsites on headlands close to beaches, on the Penouille sandspit, and in L'Anse-au-Griffon and Rivière-au-Renard valleys. For some reason, the Gaspé was uninhabited from the eighth century until the Micmac migrated to the peninsula early in the sixteenth century, just about the time fishermen from Brittany, Bristol, and elsewhere began working the waters of Atlantic Canada.

Jacques Cartier sailed into the Bay of Gaspé on July 14, 1534, where he encountered not Micmac but Iroquois on a fishing expedition from Stadacona, a village at the site of present-day Quebec City. Their chief, Donnacona, greeted the French with gifts and feasting, but he became uneasy when Cartier erected a tall cross bearing the arms of François I. In sign language, Cartier assured him it was simply a marker to guide future mariners. He took two of Donnacona's sons to France to be trained as interpreters; they guided Cartier to Stadacona the following spring.

During the late 1700s, after the fall of New France, merchants from Jersey and Guernsey established monopolistic cod-exporting companies that were to dominate the economic and social life of Gaspé for more than 150 years. Company stores supplied fishermen (on credit) with all the necessities of life. Fishermen paid in dried cod at prices set by the company, a system that amounted to economic slavery.

Gaspé's isolation ended in the 1920s with the coming of the railroad and the highway, but in some ways life did not change greatly until the 1960s, with the bankruptcy of the last company in the "Jersey system." In coastal villages, however, descendants of the first settlers until recently still split codfish which they salted and dried on wooden racks along the beach.

HABITATS

The forests that cloak Forillon's stepped upland are dominated by sweet-smelling balsam fir in association with paper and yellow birch. Pockets of deciduous trees grow in river valleys—sugar maple and yellow birch with scattered red oak and ash. This hardwood forest, with its spring carpet of bloodroot, may be a relic of southern woodlands that thrived during the warm climate of 5,000 to 7,000 years ago.

Abandoned fields along the coasts and in L'Anse-au-Griffon valley now support a rich variety of plant and animal life; in summer they seem to explode with colorful wildflowers: dandelions in June; oxeye daisies in July; fireweed and goldenrod in August. L'Anse-au-Griffon valley abounds with raptors, which rest here before or after crossing the St. Lawrence River. In spring and fall, rough-legged and American kestrels and, to a lesser extent, golden eagles and red-tailed hawks, swoop down after mice and other rodents populating these open areas. On summer nights, the valley echoes with the hooting of barred and great horned owls.

Some 30,000 seabirds colonize Forillon cliffs. The largest concentration is in Cap-des-Rosiers Cove, where black-legged kittiwakes nest by the thousands on narrow ledges. Double-crested cormorants build piles of sticks and branches on wider ledges higher up. Herring gulls nest both on cliffs and down below on rockfalls and the pebbly beach, the favored habitat of common eiders. Tilted bedrock provides convenient crevices for black guillemots to lay one or two eggs. These soot-colored birds with large white wing patches can sometimes be seen swimming underwater for small fish near L'Anse-aux-Sauvages dock.

In the salt marsh behind the Penouille sandspit, great blue herons spear small flounders and mummichogs; herring gulls congregate on grassy knolls in the middle of the marsh. The mouth of this wetland, where the tidal ebb and flow brings abundant food, is a favorite hunting territory for ospreys. Eelgrass and other marsh plants attract Canada geese, brant, American black ducks, and blue-winged teal during spring and fall migrations.

Much of Forillon's marine life resides on the rocky coast. The intertidal zone is divided into horizontal bands, or floors, like a high-rise building. In

In a land of unusual and varied rock formations, the cliffs of Cap Bon Ami are comprised of striated limestone; nearby, waves have cut into the rock to create dramatic overhangs. A variety of birds nest here.

the "penthouse," within reach of ocean spray but beyond the high-tide line, algae cover the rocks with a blackish smudge. A slippery, gelatinous covering protects this ancient life form from drying out. Periwinkles sometimes crawl up here from lower levels to graze on the algae, scraping them from rocks with an abrasive tongue-like radula that bristles with teeth. When the front end of the radula becomes dull, this fingertip-size snail simply pushes forward a new tooth-studded section.

The stretch of rock below is exposed to the air for several hours twice each day and pounded betweentimes by waves. Barnacles survive here by cementing their volcano-shaped shells to rocks with superstrong glue. Airtight plates at the top of the barnacle's shell clamp shut at low tide, preserving moisture inside, and open at high tide, letting feathery arms come out to net tiny bits of water-borne food.

The stationary barnacles are easy prey for the dog whelk, a sea snail that bores into barnacles with its radula and devours the animals inside. The color of the whelk's shell varies with its food. Those that feed mainly on barnacles are white; a diet of mussels may produce black, brown, or purplish shells. If a dog whelk alternates mussels and barnacles, its shell may develop stripes.

Whelks abound one zone down from the barnacles, where rockweed—a brown, rubbery seaweed—attaches itself securely to rocks by a mass of strong root-like structures. The receding tide leaves the plants draped over the rocks, its slippery fronds affording protection to mussels, periwinkles, limpets, and other small creatures.

At low tide, sea urchins, mussels, and crabs retreat to the lowest zone, which remains underwater nearly all the time. Here, starfish creep amid the long, leathery strands of kelp, another seaweed. Starfish have remarkable powers of regeneration: the loss of one arm—most species have five—results in the growth of a replacement arm.

Out beyond the rocky shore, humpback, minke, and fin whales cruise the frigid gulf. In August and September, long-finned pilot whales and white-sided dolphins migrate into Forillon waters. South of Cap-Bon-Ami, gray and harbor seals haul out on the boulder-strewn shore, where they lounge on surf-splashed rocks, fighting, barking, and mating.

OUTDOOR ACTIVITIES

Most visitors come in July and August for hiking, fishing, diving, and guided boat tours. Birders head to the cliffs at Cap-des-Rosiers. The winter season from January through March brings cross-country skiers and snowshoers.

Scenic Drives

Two-lane *Highway 132*, which circles the Gaspé, bears similarities to the Cabot Trail in Cape Breton, as it skirts the St. Lawrence River and the gulf, passes picturesque fishing settlements with wooden houses clinging to the rocky shore, climbs steep headlands, and descends to coves with sandy or pebbled beaches. A complete circuit of the Gaspé, a journey of about 550 mi/885 km, provides one of the most spectacular drives in eastern Canada.

Forillon contains many of the highway's highlights. At the village of Cap-des-Rosiers, a side road leads to the headland named by Champlain for the wild rose bushes that still thrive there. The lighthouse here, completed in 1858, is the tallest in Canada (112 ft/34 m) and the most important in a series of beacons built to guide ships along this stormy coast. Before the use of wireless radios in the early 1900s, incoming ships signaled their passing to the station by means of flags. The notice of arrival was then telegraphed to Quebec City.

The highway then winds across a coastal plain with mountains to the northwest and the Gulf of St. Lawrence to the east. At Cap-des-Rosiers the highway turns inland, cutting across the peninsula to the Bay of Gaspé. Before doing that, however, visitors should enter the northern part of the park, stop at the Visitor's Interpretation Centre, and visit the spectacular Cap-Bon-Ami area.

Backtracking to Highway 132, motorists drive southwest across the peninsula. At the Gaspé shore, they turn southeastward on a secondary road that passes the fine coastal scenery along Presqu'île, including dozens of tiny coves. At L'Anse-aux-Sauvages, the road ends and a trail continues on to the very tip of Forillon, Cap Gaspé.

About 70 mi/112 km south of the park on Highway 132 are two natural attractions near the town of Percé, once the largest fishing port in the Gaspé and now a tourist and resort town. Roche Percé stands just offshore, a huge block of limestone named by Champlain for its soaring natural arch. To the south is the larger Ile de Bonaventure, where tens of thousands of gannets nest on 330-ft/100-m cliffs from April to October. They constitute the largest colony of these seabirds in the world. In summer boats from Percé tour the two islands.

Hiking

Trails skirt the precipitous coastline, cross rocky shores, and wind through the hilly terrain of the central section of the park. In the Presqu'île area, the popular 5-mi/8-km *Mont-Saint-Alban Trail* starts at the Cap-Bon-Ami

Unlike seabirds which dive from the water's surface, gannets (above and opposite) perform like dive bombers, swooping down from 90 m.p.h. to conspicuously snatch their prey in a spraying splash. In spring and summer they nest by the tens of thousands on Bonaventure Island.

campground and ascends the park's highest summit, where views of gulf and bay await. On *Une Tournée dans les parages Trail* ("a tour of the neighborhood"), visitors gain an appreciation of the demanding life in an isolated Gaspé fishing community. This heritage walk winds among the re-created settlement of Grande-Grave, where the Hyman & Sons Store is stocked with fishing gear, barrels, and other antique dry goods. The trail heads east along the shore, passing abandoned fishing boats, hoists, and capstans, and ends at the Xavier Blanchette farm, with its reconstructed house and summer kitchen, tool shed, and "stage" (a wharf with a shed for drying cod). At both sites the interpretive staff wears 1920s-style clothing.

Hikers can continue 5 mi/8 km southeast on *Les Graves Trail* to Presqu'île's rugged and towering extremity, Cap Gaspé. (*Grave* is a French word that in this context refers to a pebble beach where cod are dried.) The route passes through the most beautiful walking area in the park—forests, fields, and clifftops with majestic ocean views. Wheeling gulls and gannets fill the sky; whales often show themselves offshore.

Farther inland along Highway 132 *La Chute Trail* is a 20-minute wood-land walk to a tiered cascade. Two trails start from a parking lot at the end of a side road off Highway 132 near the Penouille park office. The 4.2-mi/ 6.8-km *Le Portage Trail* is a former gravel road that cuts across the peninsula southeast–northwest in L'Anse-au-Griffon valley. It joins *La Vallée Trail*, which loops 5.5 mi/8.8 km through the northern part of the valley. Hikers and cyclists use one lane on these trails; horseback riders, the other. The challenging *Les Crêtes Trail* mainly follows ridgetops as it winds southeast 11 mi/18 km from the parking lot en route to Petit-Gaspé Beach. Two wilderness campsites are along the way.

Bicycling

Routes include *Le Portage Trail*, *La Vallée Trail*, *Les Graves Trail*, and the access road to the Penouille beaches.

Horseback Riding

La Ferme du Centaur (418-892-5525) organizes day rides on *Le Portage Trail* and *La Vallée Trail*, and along the southern boundary corridor from its stables in Cap-aux-Os southeast to L'Anse-au-Griffon.

Boating

Gaspé Tourist Agencies (418-892-5629) takes passengers on two-hour boat tours from the north area's modern, sheltered harbor out past Forillon's magnificent cliffs to Cap Gaspé. Highlights include colonies of seabirds, beaches where seals haul out, and occasional whale sightings.

Fishing

Visitors fish from the docks at L'Anse-aux-Sauvages, Grande-Grave, and Cap-des-Rosiers; the usual catch is Atlantic mackerel and flounder. Gaspé Tourist Agencies (418-892-5629) offers two-hour cod-fishing charters from Le Havre.

Swimming

The Penouille Peninsula has the finest bathing beaches and the warmest sea water in the park, a pleasant 70° F/21° C. A propane-powered minitram takes visitors to the sandy strand, which is supervised by lifeguards. Sometimes currents are warm enough to make swimming possible at Petit-Gaspé, Grande-Grave, L'Anse-aux-Sauvages, Cap-Bon-Ami, and Cap-des-Rosiers.

Scuba Diving

Deep water (90 ft/27 m) close to shore in the Bay of Gaspé makes this activity popular in Forillon off the beaches at Petit-Gaspé, Grande-Grave, and

L'Anse-aux-Sauvages. Divers can see marine life usually found in the Arctic by descending to depths of about 60 ft/18 m. Wet suits are necessary.

Cross-country Skiing

The average snowfall is 90 in/230 cm, and the ground usually is covered from mid-December through April. Almost everywhere along the park's 25 mi/40 km of groomed trails, skiers encounter the tracks of lynx, snowshoe hares, red foxes, and other animals active in winter. Parking lots are at the north and south ends of *La Vallée Trail*. A warming shelter is at the halfway point of this 4.3-mi/7-km round trip.

Four connected routes branch off La Vallée Trail and head southeast in the park's midsection. *La Cèdrière*, a moderately difficult trail that loops 6.8 mi/11 km through mountainous terrain, is named for its grove of 200-year-old cedars. Next comes *Le Ruisseau*, another moderately difficult 6-mi/9.6-km loop that follows the hiking trail of the same name. A shelter is along the way.

Access for the two most southeasterly skiing trails is from a parking lot off Highway 132. *Le Castor* and *Des Concessions* are connected loops (total length: 5.8 mi/9.4 km) that link up with Le Ruisseau. Le Castor passes through fairly flat terrain forested in one spot with a mature maple grove. A warming shelter is near the junction with Le Ruisseau. The short, easy Des Concessions Trail follows an old forest road before joining Le Castor.

EXPLORING THE PARK

Forillon is 435 mi/700 km northeast of Quebec City via Highway 132, which loops around the Gaspé Peninsula. Access from the south is via Highways 8 and 11 in New Brunswick. Reception centers, open from mid-June to early September, are off Highway 132 at Trait-Carré on the gulf coast (418-892-5040) and at Penouille on the bay side (418-892-5661). Park naturalists dispense essential information at the interpretive center in Le Havre (418-892-5572), south of Cap-des-Rosiers. Winter campers obtain permits from park headquarters in the town of Gaspé (418-368-5505) or from the operational center east of Penouille (418-892-5553). Scuba divers register at the Petit-Gaspé kiosk. For snow conditions, call 418-368-5221.

The park's interpretive programs, centered in the Petit-Gaspé and Cap-des-Rosiers campgrounds, include boat tours along the park's shoreline; examinations of tidal-pool life; and guided walks to Cap Gaspé. In the most popular activity, naturalist-divers bring up lobsters, giant scallops, and other marine specimens from the depths, present them for inspection and

Jutting dramatically into clouds and sea, the starkly vertical coastal escarpments at Forillon National Park have been created by water seeping into the open "veins" of

interpretive talks, then return the creatures to the sea. Evening talks in French are given at the Petit-Gaspé amphitheater; English-language programs are offered a few nights a week at the interpretive center.

Rental of scuba equipment and tank-filling service is available from an outfitter based in the Cap-aux-Os Esso station (418-368-7034). Mountain bikes are rented at the Auberge Cap-aux-Os (418-892-5153), a youth hostel adjacent to the park.

ACCOMMODATIONS: Petit-Gaspé (136 sites), situated in a wooded location on the south side of Presqu'île, is usually the first campground to fill in summer. Cap-Bon-Ami campground (32 sites) occupies the shelf of an escarpment that plunges more than 300 ft/ 100 m to the sea below. Above looms the sheer face of Mont Saint-Alban. Des-Rosiers campground (155 sites) is situated on a large, sloping meadow with the ridge of the peninsula as a backdrop and the ocean down below. Nearby are a beach and trails that lead to the shore. Winter campers ski or snowshoe in 1.5 mi/2.5 km to reach sites in Petit-

stratified limestone formations, along with the cracking of seasonal freeze and thaw cycles.

Gaspé; a warming shelter, stove, and firewood are provided, but no water.

The town of Gaspé and nearby villages offer a variety of services, including restaurants, hotels, motels, and private campgrounds.

ADDRESSES: For more information on the park, contact: The Superintendent, Forillon National Park, Box 1220, Gaspé, Que. G0C 1R0; 418-368-5505. For information, contact: Association touristique de la Gaspésie, 357 Route de la Mer, Sainte-Flavie, Que. G0J 2L0; 418-775-2223. For birders interested in obtaining more information about the region's bird-watching possibilities, contact: Club des Ornithologues de la Gaspésie, Box 245, Percé, Que. G0C 2L0. The club organizes whale-watching excursions (June to September) and operates a sales counter in the Penouille reception center, where field guides to birds, butterflies, and shells are available.

BOOKS: Maxime Saint-Amour, *Forillon National Park: The Harmony Between Man, the Land, and the Sea.* Vancouver/Toronto: Douglas & McIntyre, 1985. Longtime chief park naturalist's coverage of all aspects of Forillon. Available at the Penouille visitors' center and the interpretive center.

FUNDY NATIONAL PARK

THIS PARK IN SOUTHEASTERN New Brunswick is washed by some of the highest tides in the world. Past its deep, wide mouth, the Bay of Fundy—which separates New Brunswick and Nova Scotia—begins to narrow and grow shallow, compressing incoming water to tremendous heights. The greatest difference between high and low tide—as much as 53 ft/16 m—occurs in the shallow Minas Basin at the head of the bay on the Nova Scotia side. Tides in the park extend up to 40 ft/12 m. The length of the bay (170 mi/270 km) is such that the falling tide sweeps out to the Atlantic just as the rising tide begins to push back in. This creates "resonance," a pulse that gives Fundy waters the swaying rhythm that creates enormous tides.

Inland from the coves and cliffs of the Fundy shore, the forested Caledonia Highlands are incised with the valleys of rivers that lure anglers, especially the aptly named Upper Salmon. These rivers are tranquil near their headwaters high on the plateau, rapids-strewn where they cut through the central highlands, and shallow and rocky near the coast.

GEOLOGY

The ponderous geological forces that led to the formation of the Bay of Fundy began about 450 million years ago as continental plates bracketing the forerunner of the Atlantic Ocean began to drift together. When the plates collided, they thrust up a chain of high mountains, the eroded remnants of which are today's Appalachians. Then, some 350 million years ago, the plates shifted, and pressure that had been built up by the collision was released. A weakened section of the earth's crust slumped, forming the rift valley that eventually became the Bay of Fundy.

Great volumes of sediment washed down into the valley from the surrounding peaks. The erosion continued on through the Coal Age from about 345 to 280 million years ago, when lush forests of giant ferns and primitive conifers blanketed the valley's marshy lowlands. Plant fossils in coastal cliffs east of Herring Cove date from this period.

As the supercontinent Pangaea broke apart some 225 million years ago, movements of the continental plates caused volcanoes to erupt in what is now southwest Nova Scotia. Lava flowed into the valley, covering the sediments, which by then had hardened into shale and the reddish sandstone seen in the cliffs between Herring Cove and Point Wolfe. The rift sagged under the weight of this material, and formed a spoon-shaped trough, or syncline, that opened into what is now the Gulf of Maine.

The entire Bay of Fundy-Gulf of Maine area lay submerged about 20 million years ago as a shallow, seaward-sloping ramp resembling today's continental shelf. Lowered sea levels eventually exposed this area as dry land, and it remained so until after the Ice Age. It was only about 6,000 years ago that rising sea levels from melting glaciers flooded the ancient rift valley to form the Bay of Fundy.

HISTORY

When Samuel de Champlain founded settlements here in the early 1600s, the Micmac inhabited the upper Bay of Fundy, fishing for herring and Atlantic salmon, harvesting clams from mud flats, netting waterfowl on salt marshes, and hunting woodland caribou. This nation explained the bay's dramatic tides with a legend. The giant Glooscap was bathing in a river dammed by Beaver when Whale poked her head over the barricade and demanded to know why Glooscap had stopped the river from flowing into her domain. Not wanting to anger his friend, the giant stepped out of his bath. Whale smashed the dam with her tail, and sent salt water flooding into the river. As she turned and swam out to sea, the water sloshed back and forth, and the giant tides were born.

The park's land wasn't settled until the early nineteenth century, when Irish, English, and Scottish pioneers hacked farms from the forest (the park's golf course is on the site of an early homestead). Beginning in the 1820s, logging became the area's main industry. Lumber barons dammed the Goose, the Point Wolfe, and the Upper Salmon rivers near their estuaries, and built mills and wharves.

By the early years of this century, Fundy's forests were depleted. The region settled into a long decline as people moved away, settlements disappeared, and farmland returned to forest. Reminders of lumbermen and pioneers include abandoned fields near Matthews Head, the covered bridges on the Point Wolfe and Fortyfive rivers, and remnants of logging dams on all the larger streams.

HABITATS

The barren appearance of Fundy's glistening mud flats at low tide is misleading. The muck teems with burrowing worms, soft-shelled clams, and mud shrimp (up to 50,000 squeezed into an area the size of a card-table top).

Mud shrimp are the favorite food of semipalmated sandpipers, which gobble an estimated 14,000 of the tiny crustaceans during a single 12-hour tidal cycle. Other shorebirds commonly seen feeding on the flats include least sandpipers and semipalmated plovers.

Kelp, bladder wrack, and knotted wrack form slippery mats on rocky shores, which are encrusted with barnacles and periwinkles. A pair of edible red algae grow here: dulse, which is collected, dried, and eaten as a snack; and Irish moss, the source of carrageenan, used in ice cream, puddings, and soups as a thickening agent, as well as in cosmetics.

At Cannontown Beach, in the southeast corner of the park, tidal pools cupped in rocky clefts are home to tubeworms, green crabs, and sculpins. Sea anemones, the pools' most beautiful creatures, capture prey with poison-tipped stingers on feathery tentacles. Rock eels lie camouflaged on the sandy bottom.

Migrating waterfowl and shorebirds flock to salt marshes that fringe the broad estuaries of park rivers, where cordgrass, salt-marsh hay, and other salt-tolerant plants grow. Great blue herons stalk the shallows for threespine sticklebacks and eels. In spring, Canada geese, American black ducks, green-winged teal, greater yellowlegs, and other migrants feed in salt marshes. The most colorful marsh plant is samphire, known locally as "sandfire" for its bright red autumn hue.

The Caledonia Highlands are carpeted with Acadian forest, a transitional woodland that includes deciduous species from the Great Lakes–St. Lawrence forest to the southwest and conifers typical of the more northerly boreal forest. Atop the park's sandstone cliffs, frequent fogs nurture lush stands of red spruce and balsam fir. In forest clearings, shade-tolerant wild sarsaparilla, common wood-sorrel, clintonia, goldthread, creeping snowberry, and twinflower bloom sequentially throughout spring and early summer. Most prominent is bunchberry, the smallest member of the honeysuckle family. Its snow-white flowers bloom in June and its bright red bunches of berries attract grouse, robins, and mice in July and August.

Abandoned fields along the coast are bountiful larders for Fundy's 300 white-tailed deer. Mice and shrews race through grassy tunnels; snowshoe hares and woodchucks nibble on tender grasses. Coyotes, red foxes, and bobcats venture from the surrounding forest to hunt these small mammals, then slip back into the sheltering woods. Harmless snakes (common garter,

Verdant seaweed covers rocks near Herring Cove at low tide. Fundy's coastline is dotted with caves and two hundred foot cliffs, but exploration can be dangerous: those who lose track of time will find the tide comes in faster than they can climb to safety. Park headquarters can supply tide timetables.

smooth green, and red-bellied) sun themselves on rock piles made by pioneers as they cleared the fields. In winter raccoons den hereabouts, especially in the caves and fissures of the Devil's Half-Acre.

Song sparrows nest in dense stands of raspberry and hackberry, while American robins, cedar waxwings, and black-throated green warblers flit along the edges of fields. Red-tailed and broad-winged hawks soar on high. Peregrine falcons, reintroduced to the park beginning in 1982, nest on seaside cliffs. The swiftest birds of prey, peregrines plummet from high-altitude holding patterns at speeds of up to 275 mph/440 kph, plucking songbirds and shorebirds out of the air.

Inland from the coast, on the highlands' scarp, the main hardwood is yellow birch. Sugar maples predominate on well-drained, sunlit slopes, along with American beech. Paper birch and red maple are abundant along streambanks and lakeshores. Isolated stands of eastern white pine cling to ridgetops. In late spring, the sun-dappled forest floor is blanketed with flowers—dog's-tooth violets, Dutchman's-breeches, spring beauties, and purple trilliums. As the budding canopy begins to block the sunlight, these wildflowers seed and die. In a few weeks, the ephemeral palette vanishes.

In sheltered river valleys grow less common trees and shrubs—white ash, Canada yew, and striped and mountain maple. Roseroot, purple clematis, creeping juniper, and fir clubmoss cling to cliffs. Spray from the rivers' numerous small cascades produces mossy glades, such as the one along the Dickson Falls Trail west of park headquarters.

Starting in August, Atlantic salmon begin to swim up the Point Wolfe and Upper Salmon rivers, where they spawn in November. As many as 60 fish congregate at one time in the deepest pools, stacked four or five deep. The Black Hole Trail north of park headquarters leads to the most densely packed pool on the Upper Salmon River.

Another unusual migrating species in the park is the American eel. After hatching and spending a year in the Sargasso Sea south of Bermuda, the pencil-sized young fish, known as elvers, swim up Fundy's rivers. Undaunted by salmon-stopping falls, the eels wriggle upward, sometimes leaving the water completely to squirm through moss and rock rubble. They struggle to the headwaters of streams, where they live out most of their adult lives, feeding on small fish and insects. After nine or ten years, they return to the Sargasso Sea, lay their eggs, and die.

The rather flat northern part of the park's plateau is dotted with 10 small lakes and five ponds and is forested mainly with red spruce and balsam fir. These boreal woods are home to moose, black bears, porcupines, fishers, martens, red squirrels, spruce grouse, and gray jays. Roughly in the middle of the park, the Caribou Plain Trail winds through shady stands of spruce and fir, then emerges onto Fundy's only bog—an open expanse called Caribou Plain. (It is named for the woodland caribou, which was exterminated here at the turn of the century.) A boardwalk loops out across a spongy mat of sphagnum moss past carnivorous pitcher plants and round-leaved sundews and, on hummocks, Labrador-tea, leatherleaf, bog-laurel, and other shrubs.

Caribou Plain also has "flarks"—places where the sphagnum mat is torn and the underlying peat is exposed. This saturated organic material has taken the life of at least one moose heading to feeding grounds in the shallows of the bog's two small lakes. The animal stumbled into the flark, became trapped in the muck, and eventually succumbed to exhaustion.

A ghostly denizen of the highlands is the mountain lion, or cougar, the largest North American member of the cat family. These leopard-sized predators, which range over wide territories preying on deer, were considered extinct in New Brunswick in 1932. Each year, however, reliable reports of the big cat reach park wardens, most describing fleeting glimpses of a long-tailed tawny form that suddenly appears along a roadside, then seems to dissolve back into the forest.

OUTDOOR ACTIVITIES

Most visitors are car-based campers who swim and play golf and tennis. An increasing number of more active travelers take to the trails to explore coastal cliffs, river valleys, and highland forests.

Scenic Drives

The *Maple Grove–Hastings Road* forms a short one-way loop west of park headquarters. Maple Grove Road heads north up a hillside beneath mature hardwoods to Hastings Road, which returns south to the coast past old fields and ferny clearings where white-tailed deer often are sighted at dusk. Moose may be seen in the evening browsing in Laverty Lake at the midway point of *Laverty Road*, which winds 6 mi/10 km through the Caledonia Highlands. Both routes are dramatic during the fall foliage season, which peaks the first two weeks of October.

Hiking

Three popular day-use walks are near park headquarters. The *Devil's Half-Acre Trail* crosses a tortuous terrain of gaping crevasses, shattered rocks, and fallen trees, a particularly haunting landscape on foggy days. The *Kin-*

A white-tailed buck scent-marks a tree with his forehead glands. Once nearly extinct in some areas, these deer are now the most plentiful game animals in eastern North America. OPPOSITE: In autumn the hay-scented ferns in Fundy National Park turn golden.

nie Brook Trail northwest of headquarters descends a steep valley on wooden stairs to the brook, where the water disappears beneath the gravel streambed and reappears a short distance downstream. The *Dickson Falls Trail* follows a typical Fundy watercourse—a swift-flowing stream tumbling over rapids and mossy waterfalls as it cuts through the highlands. At the trailhead are tremendous views of the bay and Owls Head, a promontory often wreathed in fog.

The 31-mi/50-km *Fundy Circuit* links seven trails to provide a three- to five-day sampler of the park's major landscapes. Starting at park headquarters, the circuit angles southwest on the 6-mi/10-km *Coastal Trail*, which passes the mossy gullies of the Devil's Half-Acre, drops to the shore at Herring Cove, then rises to windswept sandstone cliffs. On clear days the coast of Nova Scotia can be seen across the bay. Closer to shore stands

Squaws Cap, a seastack created (according to Micmac legend) when angry Glooscap hurled his wife's feathered headdress into the bay. The trail turns inland at Mi 4.3/Km 7, then descends again through the coastal forest to the fjord-like mouth of the Point Wolfe River. One of the park's finest views is near the campground here, looking south down the conifer-clad estuary to the sparkling bay beyond.

At this point the circuit joins the 5-mi/8-km *Marven Lake Trail*, which heads northwest to Marven and Chambers lakes. Both wilderness lakes have primitive campsites. From a junction north of Chambers Lake, the *Bennett Brook Trail* descends into the Point Wolfe River valley. Here, Bennett Brook spills over a series of waterfalls before flowing into the river. Hikers ford the shallow Point Wolfe River, then ascend to the upper edge of the brook valley, heading north. For part of its 3-mi/5-km length, the trail is an old logging road where hikers can stroll side by side.

At Bennett Lake, the circuit picks up the 4.3-mi/7-km *Tracey Lake Trail*, which skirts the western shore of Bennett Lake, winds north to spruce-bound Tracey Lake and its two primitive campsites, then goes east across flat, soggy terrain—moose country—to Laverty Lake. Here hikers walk north a short distance on Laverty Road, then east on a spur road, where they rejoin the circuit. Along the 40-minute *Laverty Falls Trail*, Laverty Brook sweeps beneath a stand of white pines, then tumbles over a broad rock face in a 30-ft/9-m curtain waterfall.

The circuit now joins the *Upper Salmon River Trail*, which angles southeast in the valley of the Broad River past a primitive campsite, the remains of logging dams, spectacular potholes (ideal for brisk summer swims), and three waterfalls. This section contains the Upper Salmon's most impressive scenery, but hikers must ford the river twice and scramble over rocks in a difficult 1-mi/1.6-km section between the *Moosehorn* and *The Forks trails*—two westering side trips that intersect the main trail.

Another two fords await in a 2.5-mi/4.1-km section from The Forks south through the steep valley of the Upper Salmon River. A highlight of this stretch is the Black Hole, a deep pool at the circuit's junction with the *Black Hole Trail*. In autumn, Atlantic salmon congregate in the pool awaiting heavy rains that swell streams, enabling them to continue upstream to spawn. Another ford is in the 2.9-mi/4.7-km section between the Black Hole and park headquarters at the mouth of the river.

Boating

Canoes and rowboats can be rented at Bennett Lake in summer. Fundy's rivers are unsuitable for canoeing.

Fishing

Eastern brook trout are taken from Bennett and Wolfe lakes from mid-May to mid-September (limit of 10). The Atlantic salmon season on the Upper Salmon extends from mid-July to mid-October, with a daily limit of one grilse (a salmon spawning for the first time) and total limit of five grilse per year in all national parks in Atlantic Canada.

Swimming

Saltwater bathing in the bay is pleasant during a rising tide, when the water is a few degrees warmer than during an ebb tide. The best site is at Dennis Beach, 7.5 mi/12 km east of the park along Route 915 (constant updrafts also make this a great site for flying kites). Along the Broad River, secluded pools provide bracing dips. There are small beaches at Bennett and Wolfe lakes. A heated saltwater pool at Cannontown Beach near park headquarters is open from June to September.

Winter Activities

There is a 31-mi/50-km network of groomed loop trails for *cross-country skiing*. Most Fundy trails are open for *snowshoeing*.

Other Activities

Hazards on the nine-hole *golf* course at park headquarters, which is open from mid-May to mid-October, include white-tailed deer that graze at dusk most evenings on fairways. Players must also allow raccoons and porcupines waddling across the greens to "play through." Carts and clubs are rented at the clubhouse (506-887-2770). Three paved *tennis* courts are near park headquarters. The *lawn-bowling* green is open from mid-May to mid-October. Equipment can be rented at the golf pro shop.

EXPLORING THE PARK

Fundy is 120 mi/193 km northeast of Saint John, New Brunswick, and 60 mi/96 km southwest of Moncton, a convenient drive via the Trans-Canada Highway (Route 2) and Highway 114, which cuts diagonally northwest–southeast across the park. Airports are at Moncton and Saint John.

In summer, park interpreters organize daily 90-minute intertidal walks at Point Wolfe, Herring Cove, and Alma Beach. Hour-long nature programs are presented each evening at the outdoor theater at park headquarters. In August, the program features hikes to watch salmon spawning runs on the Upper Salmon River.

ACCOMMODATIONS: There are four campgrounds for car-based travelers. The campground at park headquarters has 132 serviced sites. The Coastal, Whitetail, and Devil's Half-Acre trails start nearby.

Chignecto campground (291 sites) is in a wooded location northwest of park headquarters on the upland plateau above the coastal fogs. This is the only campground at which campfires are permitted; firewood is sold by a concessionaire. Nearby are Kinnie Brook and Whitetail trails. Point Wolfe campground (181 sites) is a five-minute walk from the cobble beach at Point Wolfe Cove. Four trailheads are nearby: Marven Lake, Goose River, Coppermine, and Coastal. Wolfe Lake (32 sites) is an unserviced lakeside campground in the northwest corner of the park. Backcountry hikers camp in primitive sites at Goose River, Marven Lake, Chambers Lake, Rattail Brook, Broad River, and Tracey Lake.

Summer lodging in the park includes 64 housekeeping units at the Caledonia Highlands Inn (506-887-2930) and the Fundy Park Chalets (506-887-2808), both of which are near park headquarters.

Accommodations are also available in Alma, just down the hill and across the Upper Salmon River from park headquarters.

For winter campers, unserviced sites with nearby heated washrooms and enclosed picnic shelters with stoves and firewood are available in the headquarters campground. There are also enclosed picnic shelters at Chignecto. Bed-and-breakfast establishments in Alma remain open year-round.

ADDRESSES: For more information, contact: The Superintendent, Fundy National Park, Box 40, Alma, N.B. E0A 1B0 (506-887-2000). The Fundy Guild (Box 150, Alma, N.B. E0A 1B0), the local park cooperative association, sells booklets on Fundy at the information kiosks at the park entrances. Alma operates an information booth in summer at the village Activities Centre (506-887-2321).

BOOKS: Michael Burzynski, *A Guide to Fundy National Park.* Vancouver/Toronto: Douglas & McIntyre, 1984. This detailed guide is available from the park cooperative association.

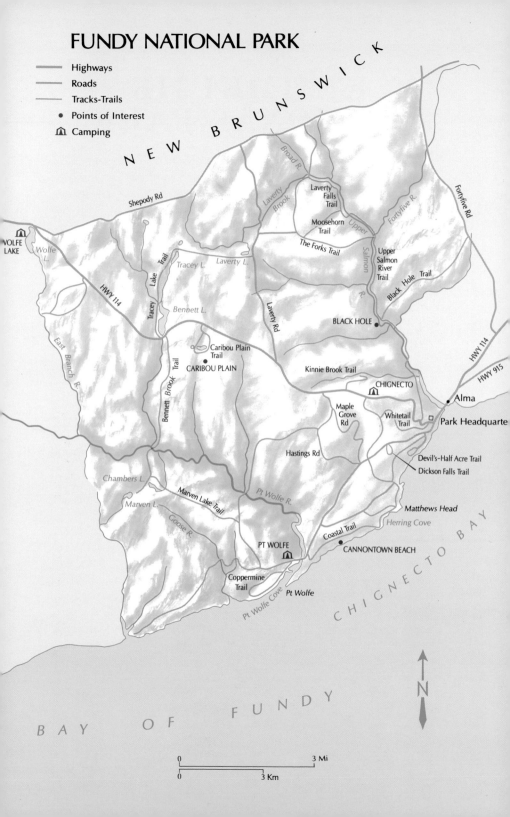

FUNDY NATIONAL PARK

Highways
Roads
Tracks-Trails
• Points of Interest
🏕 Camping

N E W   B R U N S W I C K

Broad R.

Shepody Rd

Laverty Falls Trail

Laverty Brook

Moosehorn Trail

The Forks Trail

Fortyfive R.

Fortyfive Rd

WOLFE LAKE

Wolfe L.

Tracey L.

Laverty L.

Tracey Lake Trail

Upper Salmon

Upper Salmon River Trail

Black Hole Trail

HWY 114

Bennett L.

Laverty Rd

Salmon R.

Caribou Plain Trail

CARIBOU PLAIN

BLACK HOLE

East Branch R.

Bennett Brook Trail

Kinnie Brook Trail

CHIGNECTO

HWY 114

HWY 915

Alma

Maple Grove Rd

Whitetail Trail

Park Headquarte

Hastings Rd

Devil's-Half Acre Trail

Dickson Falls Trail

Chambers L.

Marven Lake Trail

Pt Wolfe R.

Matthews Head

Herring Cove

Marven L.

Goose R.

Coastal Trail

PT WOLFE

CANNONTOWN BEACH

Coppermine Trail

Pt Wolfe Cove

Pt Wolfe

C H I G N E C T O   B A Y

N

B A Y   O F   F U N D Y

0   3 Mi

0   3 Km

KEJIMKUJIK NATIONAL PARK

IN SOUTHWESTERN NOVA SCOTIA, a wet and intricate wilderness embraces island-dotted lakes, stillwater streams, and mixed woodlands scored only by trail and portage. Kejimkujik (kedge-im-KOO-jik) was the ancestral territory of the Micmac and, later, the playground of sportsmen. Today, it beckons campers, canoeists, and hikers.

Recently, the tip of a wild and beautiful peninsula, the Seaside Adjunct, was added to Kejimkujik. This area, more than 50 mi/80 km southeast of the park entrance, protects one of the last undisturbed stretches of Atlantic shoreline along the Eastern Seaboard as well as the nesting grounds of the endangered piping plover. Even on a glorious summer afternoon, it is possible to wander this windswept realm of spruce forests, salt marshes, rocky headlands, and white sand beaches without encountering another person.

GEOLOGY

Three kinds of bedrock underlie the park. Some 550 to 500 million years ago, quartz-rich sandstones were eroded from high mountains in what is now northwestern Africa. This material was washed offshore into deep ocean waters, where it eventually hardened into the quartzites now found in the eastern third of Kejimkujik. During the next 50 million years or so, finer eroded material from the mountains was washed onto the continental margin. These marine muds became the slates that are found also in eastern Kejimkujik.

Some 375 million years ago, the African, European, and North American continental plates collided. The impact buckled and fractured the quartzites and slates. Superheated water and gases carried mineral-rich quartz to the crests of these folded sedimentary rocks. Crushed between the continental masses, rocks melted from the heat and pressure, then cooled to become the granites that underlie the western part of the park. Looking across Kejimkujik Lake from the eastern shore it is easy to see the huge rounded dome of granite on the western shore.

About 200 million years, Pangaea, the supercontinent formed by the collision of the plates, began to break up and the present Atlantic began to open. The fracturing occurred along a slightly different seam than had defined the earlier plates; bits of Africa were joined to Canada, including the Avalon Peninsula of Newfoundland and most of mainland Nova Scotia.

Pleistocene ice did its most drastic park landscaping between 100,000 and 80,000 years ago. Huge ice sheets advanced from the northwest, grinding over the soft slates and quartzites, breaking up the bedrock and scouring shallow basins now filled with lakes and ponds. Park granite proved more resistant, leaving that part of Kejimkujik with fewer bodies of water.

During a subsequent warming period, melting ice dropped huge granite boulders that had migrated here in the flow of glaciers from the northwest, hence their name, "erratics." The ice sheets also deposited clay and gravel in hills known as drumlins, and etched the bedrock grooves seen along many park shorelines. During the most recent warming period, about 11,000 years ago, streams flowing under the melting ice left gravelly ridges called eskers that can still be seen snaking across the countryside.

HISTORY

The earliest inhabitants of the park were people of the Maritime Archaic Tradition who migrated to Nova Scotia some 4,500 years ago. It is believed that groups consisting of one or two families harvested marine mammals and fish along the coast during spring and summer, then traveled up the Mersey River to the Kejimkujik area in autumn, setting up camps from which they foraged throughout the winter in the surrounding forests for mammals, fish, birds, and plants.

The cultural traditions of the Maritime Archaic continued until around 700 B.C., evolving gradually into the Woodland Tradition. The people of this culture occupied the same sites as their forerunners, with three main camps: at Merrymakedge Beach on Kejimkujik Lake and at the head and foot of the rapids on the Mersey River below George Lake. The aboriginals constructed stone fish weirs on the Mersey to harvest the fall run of eels from the lakes to the ocean. One weir was still in use up until the 1950s.

· The Micmac inhabited the region at the time of contact with Europeans, around 1500. A trading pattern soon was established with Basque and French fishermen: the Micmac gathered furs in the interior during winter and congregated in large groups along the coast in spring to barter the furs for weapons, clothing, and metal utensils. It is thought that the furs required for the trade were readily available near the coasts, since traditional campsites around Kejimkujik Lake became less frequently employed.

In 1605 Pierre de Monts and Samuel de Champlain established Port Royal north of Kejimkujik in the sheltered Annapolis Basin off the Bay of Fundy. It was the first white settlement north of Florida. A band of about a hundred Micmac led by a tall, bearded chief named Membertou greeted the French—the start of a generally cordial relationship.

Many brooks and streams snake their way through flat terrain in Kejimkujik, as do gravelly ridges called eskers, formed by under-ice streams thousands of years ago.

The first European to explore the park area was Jacques de Meulles, who had come to Annapolis from Quebec City to strengthen ties between France's colony on the St. Lawrence and its colony of Acadia, which included much of today's Canadian Maritimes and northern Maine. In 1686 Micmac guides led de Meulles southeast across the interior of Nova Scotia, through the Milford Lakes, then down the Mersey River, which flows into and out of Kejimkujik Lake and Rossignol Lake before emptying into the Atlantic. After six days, de Meulles reached the coast at what is now Liverpool. His journal makes no mention of Micmac in the interior.

During the 1700s, Micmac carvings began to appear on the low slate outcrops along the shores of Kejimkujik Lake. It is not known whether the tradition of carving petroglyphs dates back to the prehistoric era, since these fragile images are susceptible to erosion and it is likely that many have disappeared over the centuries. Common rock-art themes include moose and caribou, men fishing and hunting, women's headgear, and a four-legged bird surrounded by stars, thought to be the mythical bird "Kaloo."

By the time of white settlement in the Kejimkujik region in the 1820s, the Micmac had been decimated by European diseases. About 1840, officials

The park comprises 380 square kilometers of lakes and forests etched by little more than trails and waterways.

encouraged the Micmac to withdraw to reserves, including the Fairy Lake Reserve within today's park boundaries. Concurrent with white settlement of the region was the development of the timber industry. Hemlock and pine felled during winter were floated in spring down the Mersey River to feed some 60 mills.

After a minor gold rush from 1884 to 1905, which briefly turned nearby Caledonia into a boomtown, Kejimkujik began to gain a reputation among sportsmen as one of eastern North America's prime areas for moose hunting and trout fishing. A lodge and dozens of cabins sprang up along the shores of Kejimkujik Lake, welcoming well-heeled guests who followed Micmac guides. The park was established in 1965.

HABITATS

Three-quarters of park land is covered with a second-growth mixed forest of softwoods (eastern hemlock, red spruce, balsam fir, eastern white pine) and young hardwoods (sugar maple, American beech, yellow birch). In

April, the floor of this forest bursts into color with fragrant trailing arbutus, or mayflower (the floral symbol of both Nova Scotia and Massachusetts). Summer brings forth false lily of the valley, twinflower, partridgeberry, trillium, and star-flower.

These diversified woodlands provide food and shelter for abundant wildlife. White-tailed deer, grouse, and snowshoe hares browse on twigs, buds, and young leaves. Owls and warblers nest in big trees; woodpeckers and raccoons inhabit dead snags; salamanders seek out moist, rotting stumps. After a good rainfall in August and September, some of the more than 400 kinds of mushrooms appear on the forest floor, a bounteous larder for red squirrels.

Within this mixed forest are pockets of special plant communities. The crowns of the drumlins, with their deep, well-drained soils, are dominated by hardwoods, with a thick ground cover of bracken ferns, wood-ferns, wood-sorrel, beech-drops, and little forests of maple seedlings. These old hardwood stands are alive with small, insect-eating birds. American redstarts, the most abundant species, forage in the upper canopy together with northern parulas and red-eyed vireos, as well as in the lower stories, alongside least flycatchers.

Settlers cleared most drumlins of old-growth hardwoods to get at the region's best soil, but there are remnant stands along the Peter Point Trail and on nearby Peal Island in Kejimkujik Lake, as well as along the Big Hardwood Carry, a portage between Kejimkujik Lake and Mountain Lake. The giants of park forests are the eastern hemlocks that have survived fire and logging for 400 years. An impressive grove towers over the Hemlocks and Hardwoods Trail beside Big Dam Lake north of Kejimkujik Lake, the closest most people come to experiencing Nova Scotia's primeval forest.

Low-lying areas along rivers support red-maple floodplains, one of the park's richest communities. A fine example on the Mersey River is accessible via canoe or the Rogers Brook Trail. Tree swallows and yellow-bellied sapsuckers nest in the maples. American bitterns and common snipe feed in floodplain margins thick with sedges, bluejoint grass, and ferns, a habitat equally welcoming to beaver and painted turtles.

Only about 15 mi/25 km of roads wind through Kejimkujik, all of them confined to the east side, but these byways provide excellent opportunities for viewing wildlife. In spring, turtles often are seen nesting in gravelly

Flowing into Lake Kejimkujik and connecting Lakes Loon and George, the placid Mersey River, though clean, is stained brown by tannins in bogs and swamps. At Jake's Landing, the river is excellent for canoeing; at dusk, deer, beaver, and muskrat visit the water's edge.

shoulders. In the evenings porcupines and snowshoe hares nibble clover and grasses planted to stabilize embankments. White-tailed deer browse there morning and evening. Sweet-fern, which is actually a shrub with protein-rich buds and twigs, is a favorite winter food for deer.

Most park lakes and rivers are stained dark brown by tannins that feeder rivers pick up in bogs and swamps. Although this "Mersey tea," as the water is known locally, looks polluted, most of it is clean enough to drink. In stark contrast are the clear, spring-fed lakes in the southern part of the park. On a sunny day, plants and fish are clearly visible on the bottom of Beaverskin Lake, some 20 ft/6 m down. The most dramatic place to see this polarity is near the middle of Big Dam Lake, where the lake's clear southern water darkens to Mersey tea within a few strokes of the paddle.

Although water covers about a fifth of Kejimkujik, much of it drains from bogs and is acidic and therefore not conducive to life. Waterfowl and aquatic animals are not abundant, although terns, loons, and herons nest on some lakes. The most productive aquatic community is Kejimkujik's only marsh, which was formed by damming Grafton Lake, near the park's eastern boundary, in the 1930s. Cattails, bulrushes, bur-reed, and water-shield there sustain ducks, turtles, salamanders, and fish.

Kejimkujik has longer, hotter summers than elsewhere in Nova Scotia. Several of the park's reptiles and other creatures, including the southern flying squirrel, normally are found farther south: they may be descendants of life that flourished here in a warmer climate some 4,000 to 7,000 years ago. Five species of salamanders, eight kinds of frogs and toads, five snake species, and three varieties of turtles live in the park. The eastern ribbon snake and Blanding's turtle are found nowhere else in Atlantic Canada.

The Seaside Adjunct of Kejimkujik, a separate block of land in the Port Mouton area about 50 mi/80 km southeast of the rest of the park, presents an entirely different landscape: a ruggedly beautiful and often deserted peninsula accessible only by two hiking trails. From April through November, harbor seals haul up on the rocks, especially Harbour Rocks and Black Point. Between the headlands curve two spectacular white sand beaches, the nesting grounds of eight to ten pairs of endangered piping plovers.

In back of these barrier beaches are tidal flats, brackish lagoons, and salt marshes where migrating shorebirds rest and feed from late July through October. Hikers spot about 10 species on a typical outing, including semipalmated sandpipers, semipalmated plovers, and short-billed dowitchers. Migrating waterfowl start coming through in October. In winter, grebes and a few harlequin ducks bob in the frigid surf off Port Joli Point.

OUTDOOR ACTIVITIES

Kejimkujik is known primarily as Atlantic Canada's finest canoeing park, with routes that date from the days of the Micmac. About 9,000 people visit the backcountry each year, but carefully positioned campsites and a reservation system that limits the number of canoeists ensure a memorable wilderness experience. September is the best time for hiking, when spring insects and humid summer weather are gone and forests burst into brilliant color. Winter visitors cross-country ski on a network of groomed trails.

Hiking

The 60 mi/100 km of trails include more than a dozen nature walks and day hikes in the eastern part of the park off the Main Park Road and the Peskowesk Road, as well as backcountry trails that lead through a variety of park landscapes.

The 90-minute *Peter Point Trail* passes through three habitats as it travels the length of a peninsula on Kejimkujik Lake: a red-maple glade, a hemlock grove, and a mature hardwood stand atop a drumlin. The route is excellent for bird-watching.

The *Grafton Lake Trail* is an hour's walk through hardwood forest and past a marsh filled with birds, frogs, and turtles. Highlight of a half-day outing on the *Hemlocks and Hardwoods Trail* is a grove of huge hemlocks, where thick mosses and delicate orchids carpet the floor of a cool, shady forest that has survived 400 years.

The 16-mi/26-km *Channel Lake Trail*, which basically follows the first half of the canoe route by the same name, is an easy overnight loop through slate country, passing eskers, hemlock groves, and mixed woods that are particularly lovely in autumn. The park's longest backcountry route is the four-day *Liberty Lake Trail*, a 40-mi/65-km horseshoe-shaped route from the Big Dam parking lot in the north to the Peskowesk Road parking lot in the south. It starts as the Channel Lake Trail, then continues southwest, following the park boundary as it angles south to Peskawa and Peskowesk lakes, then northeast to end at Peskowesk Road. The campsite at Liberty Lake, in the far western corner of the park, is the most remote in Kejimkujik. Several spur trails penetrate the park interior (*West River, Luxton Lake,* and *Fire Tower Road*).

Two trails lead into the Seaside Adjunct. A side road off Highway 103 heads south to South West Port Mouton. From there, hikers angle 3 mi/ 5 km southwest on an old gravel road to Little Port Joli Beach. Farther

This quartzite dates back 500 to 600 million years to the Cambrian Age of the Paleozoic Era. OPPOSITE: Near Big Dam Lake in the park's northern section, a grove of three- to four-hundred-year-old hemlocks towers above the trail.

west on Highway 103, a side road goes south along Port Joli Bay to the community of St. Catherines River. From there, hikers walk 1.2 mi/2 km on an old cart track to the Harbour Rocks of St. Catherines River Bay and St. Catherines River Beach. Portions of both beaches are closed during piping plover nesting season from late April to late July.

Boating

Motorboats are allowed only on Kejimkujik Lake. There is a launch at Jakes Landing.

Canoeing

Most canoeing is on flat water, with early morning and late evening the best times for paddling. In summer, west winds kick up by late morning. Portages are clearly marked by square orange signs, numbered, and keyed to park maps.

The *Maitland Bridge–Jakes Landing Route* is a lovely half-day paddle on the reed-fringed Mersey River from the bridge on Highway 8 south to where the Mersey empties into Kejimkujik Lake. There are two portages (Mill Falls and the Oak Ledges, both near the Visitor Centre at the start of the trip), as well as two sets of ledges to run. The best time to paddle the

route is before mid-June when water levels are still high. Deer, beaver, muskrats, turtles, and water birds are seen along the way.

Kejimkujik Lake, the watery heart of the park, is big, shallow, usually windy and wave-lashed, with a rocky western shore. For a day trip, canoeists set out in the early morning, lay over with a picnic lunch if the afternoon proves windy, then return in the early evening. One itinerary is a paddle northwest from the main campground into sheltered Jeremys Bay. The beach and picnic area in the lee of Indian Point is usually deserted, as is the gravel beach on Luxie Cove at the head of the peninsula that creates the bay. Another appealing option is to overnight at one of six island campsites; several have beaches.

The 16-mi/26-km *Big Dam–Frozen Ocean Route,* a two- or three-day circuit in the northwestern corner of the park, garners most accolades as the park's finest backcountry trip. The put-in is at the end of a portage from the access road to Big Dam Lake; most people end the trip at Jakes Landing on Kejimkujik Lake. Six portages and 10 wilderness campsites are along the way. Highlights include the centuries-old hemlock grove on Frozen Ocean; wildlife sighted along Still Brook, which connects Big Dam and Frozen Ocean; and the red-maple floodplain at Inness Brook where it enters Frozen Ocean.

Fishing

Brook trout is the most abundant cold-water species. Warm-water species, including white and yellow perch and brown bullhead, are taken in summer. From April to June there is good trout and perch fishing all along the Mersey River, especially at the Eel Weir Bridge and, for canoeing anglers, at the Hemlock Run, where the Mersey enters Loon Lake in the southeast, and below Loon Lake Falls. Canoeists on the *Big Dam–Frozen Ocean Route* find good fishing in spring at the mouths of three brooks flowing into Frozen Ocean.

Swimming

Shallow park lakes warm up to 70° F/21° C by early summer. There are change houses and lifeguards at Merrymakedge Beach on Kejimkujik Lake, which is sheltered by a grove of pines and hardwoods, and unsupervised swimming farther north at Meadow, Jim Charles Point, and Slapfoot beaches. Backcountry travelers have to wade or paddle far from shore to find water deep enough for swimming. Canoeists have been known to pull their craft up on the rocks that dot some park waters and take a refreshing dip in the Mersey tea out in the middle of a lake.

Cross-country Skiing

One of the most popular ski outings is the *Big Dam Lake Trail*, which follows the Big Dam Lake Road (closed to traffic in winter). An enclosed shelter with a wood stove in the *Merrymakedge* area serves as a hub for a network of ski trails on the eastern side of Kejimkujik Lake. Farther south, off the Peskowesk Lake Road, the *Peter Point* and *McGinty Lake* trails are also highly rated for skiing. The McGinty route has the biggest hills in the park. Experienced skiers head 16.8 mi/27 km into the backcountry, first along the southern part of the *Peskowesk Lake Road*, then on the southern leg of the *Liberty Lake Trail*, for a wilderness weekend at Masons Cabin on Peskawa Lake near the southern park boundary.

EXPLORING THE PARK

Kejimkujik is 100 mi/160 km southwest of Halifax via Highways 103, 325, and 8. The park is 118 mi/190 km northeast of the ferry terminal in Yarmouth via Highways 101 and 8 South, and 56 mi/90 km south of Digby via Highways 101 and 8. The Seaside Adjunct is 15.5 mi/25 km southwest of Liverpool via Highway 103.

Most people drive to Nova Scotia from New Brunswick on the Trans-Canada Highway (Highway 2 in New Brunswick and Highway 104 in Nova Scotia). Others take Marine Atlantic ferries (800-563-7701 in Newfoundland and Labrador; 800-565-9470 in the Maritimes; 800-565-9411 in Quebec and Ontario from area code 705 east; 902-794-7203 elsewhere in Canada; 800-432-7344 in Maine; and 800-341-7981 elsewhere in the continental U.S.). It takes about 10 hours to reach Yarmouth, Nova Scotia, by ferry from Portland, Maine, and about six hours from Bar Harbor. The crossing from Saint John, New Brunswick, to Digby is 2.5 hours. Reservations are recommended in summer.

The Visitor Centre (902-682-2772) at the park entrance is open year round to dispense interpretive information, a free guide to front-country nature trails, and the *Backcountry Guide,* a topographical map that shows hiking trails, canoeing routes, portages, and campsites. A slide show in the center's theater provides an excellent introduction to the park. More elaborate productions are staged on summer evenings at the outdoor theater in the main campground. Perennially popular interpretive programs include guided canoeing trips and the "Micmac Memories Walk," which passes a 5,000-year-old campsite and a shoreline gallery of petroglyphs.

Pabek Recreation, a concession at Jakes Landing (902-682-2817), rents canoes and rowboats. Loon Lake Outfitters (902-682-2220) supplies independent canoeists and hikers with equipment, and also organizes backcountry canoe trips in the park and elsewhere. The Snow Country Ski Shop (902-682-2409), 3 mi/4.8 km southeast of the park entrance on Highway 8, rents cross-country equipment.

Other visitor services are adjacent to the park, in Caledonia, and a few hours' drive southeast and northwest in Liverpool, Bridgewater, and Annapolis Royal. Grocery stores near the eastern park boundary and in Caledonia sell camping supplies.

ACCOMMODATIONS: The Jeremys Bay campground (329 sites), open year-round, has a wooded shoreline setting on Kejimkujik Lake. Backcountry travelers register at the Visitor Centre for the 46 primitive campsites along trails and canoe routes. At three sites, maximum group size is 10; most sites take only four to six people. Reservations are accepted from early May. Campsites usually are filled on holidays, spring weekends, and during August.

Winter visitors camp at Jeremys Bay. There are enclosed day-use shelters for skiers and snowshoers at Merrymakedge Beach, at the group campground above Jim Charles Point, at Mill Falls near the Visitor Centre, at wilderness campsites, and at Masons Cabin on Peskowesk Lake, which has a wood stove and two bedrooms that sleep a total of eight.

ADDRESSES: For more information, contact: The Superintendent, Kejimkujik National Park, Box 36, Maitland Bridge, N.S. B0T 1N0; 902-682-2772; or Area Manager (Park Warden), Kejimkujik Seaside Adjunct, 19 Fort Point Rd., Liverpool, N.S. B0T 1K0; 902-354-2880. For ferry schedules and other information, contact: Maritime Atlantic Reservations Bureau, Box 250, North Sydney, N.S. B2A 3M3; 902-794-7203. The Nova Scotia Department of Tourism and Culture offers a free information and reservation system called Check In: 800-565-0000 in Canada; 800-492-0643 in Maine; and 800-341-6096 elsewhere in the continental U.S.

The trail to Grafton Lake leads through a rich hardwood forest and a marsh teeming with frogs, birds, and turtles. Visitors may swim anywhere in this "sportsman's paradise"; anglers will need a National Park Fishing License.

PRINCE EDWARD ISLAND NATIONAL PARK

WASHED BY THE WARM WATERS of the Gulf of St. Lawrence, this shoreline park has the finest sandy beaches in an island province famed for them. Dunes and red sandstone cliffs back the long, wide strands (some white, others pinkish). In places, sandspits nearly seal off bays, giving rise to brackish wetlands that abound with waterfowl. Farther inland, scattered stands of coniferous forest slowly reclaim what was once rich farmland.

The park is small—only about 25 mi/40 km long and, in many places, only a few sand dunes wide. It's also one of the most popular of Canada's national parks. Each year, more than 1.5 million people come here to soak up sun, splash in gulf waters, and visit the tidy farmhouse where the novel *Anne of Green Gables* was set.

GEOLOGY

The island is underlaid with sandstone 250 million years old. This bedrock, which weathers into rich, red soil, is generally covered with a thick layer of glacial till left by Pleistocene glaciers, but at a few places in the park the island's bones protrude, most notably in the ocher-colored cliffs between Orby Head and North Rustico Harbour.

Rivers have cut shallow valleys into the till, giving the countryside its rolling appearance. Rising sea levels since the end of the Ice Age have flooded the mouths of these gulf-bound waterways. Five such estuaries back the park's dunes and beaches. These saltwater bays are nearly enclosed by long sandspits breached by narrow channels.

This slender, changeable shoreline endlessly shifts and reshapes itself. Currents and waves create the beaches, scouring and dredging the sea bottom, which is sandy for 20 mi/32 km offshore, carrying the grains landward. Winds pile dry sand above the tideline into dunes, particularly impressive at Brackley Beach in the park's midsection and at east-end Blooming Point, where dunes reach a height of some 65 ft/20 m.

HISTORY

About 10,000 years ago, Amerindians reached Prince Edward Island from the mainland via a now-submerged land bridge. Camping along shorelines, they had access to abundant food supplies from the sea—fish, shellfish, waterfowl, and sea mammals, especially seals.

The Micmac, who arrived at the end of the first century A.D., called the island Abegweit, "cradled upon the waves." One Micmac site has been found within park boundaries: a seasonal camp on Rustico Island in the middle of the park.

Acadian settlers arrived in 1717 but were deported some 40 years later by British troops. Eventually many of these exiles returned from the United States and elsewhere to farm and to fish the rich waters off their beloved island. British tenant farmers came around 1770 to work the land, then struggled for a century to gain clear titles from absentee landlords. In the late 1800s, affluent families from the United States and central Canada discovered the pleasures of Prince Edward Island's North Shore and built grand summer homes, including Dalvay-by-the-Sea, now operated as a hotel in the park.

The island's brightest literary light, Lucy Maud Montgomery, was born in 1874 in New London, southwest of Cavendish. (The house is now a museum.) In 1911, she married Ewan Macdonald at nearby Park Corner in a house that is now a homey museum furnished much as it was 75 years ago. In Cavendish, Green Gables House draws hundreds of thousands of visitors each year. The house was once the property of Lucy Montgomery's cousins, David and Margaret MacNeill, and provided the author with inspiration for the setting of her novel, *Anne of Green Gables.* Preserved within the park, the house is furnished to portray the 1890 period described in the book. The grave of the world-famous author, who died in Toronto in 1942, is in the nearby Cavendish Community Cemetery.

HABITATS

Hardy marram grass is the first to take root on the shifting sand of new dunes. Known scientifically as *Ammophila breviligulata,* or "sand-loving," these plants anchor the dune landscape with stringy roots that proliferate as deep as 10 ft/3 m below the surface. When covered with blowing sand, marram grass quickly grows upward, and it is impervious to salt spray.

By anchoring the sand and adding organic material, the grass enables northern bayberry to establish itself in the more sheltered hollows of dunes, along with wrinkled rose, beach pea, seaside goldenrod, hudsonia, and starry false Solomon's-seal. In damp areas between the dunes, cranberries thrive. In some places, a short distance inland, white spruce struggle to survive in the unstable sand. Stunted by salt spray, shorn by the wind, these weirdly contorted trees are often older than they look; trees 50 years old may be only hip high.

Farther inland, where high dunes block winds and spray, white spruce grow straight and tall, marking the start of the coastal forest. These woodlands also contain some red spruce, red maple, paper birch, quaking aspen, and balsam fir. Ferns and mosses carpet the forest floor, brightened with the colorful berries and flowers of bunchberry, twinflower, and wild sarsaparilla. Even in these woods, surf is heard pounding nearby shores.

Migrating waterfowl stop over in park estuaries and barachois ponds scattered the length of the park behind the dunes. (*Barachois* is an Acadian word for "barricade" and refers to an inlet that has been cut off from the sea and gradually filled with fresh water. An example is Long Pond in the Dalvay area, which was open to the sea less than 200 years ago.) Canada geese gather at Brackley Marsh to feed on rushes, sea-lavender, and cordgrass. Mallards, teals, ring-necked ducks, American black ducks, and mergansers dabble throughout the park's wetlands.

Vast numbers of migrating seabirds and shorebirds also pass through the area in spring and autumn. Whimbrels, plovers, phalaropes, sandpipers, yellowlegs, godwits, and dozens of other species congregate in the thousands on beaches and salt marshes throughout the park. Common tern colonies are found at the tip of Cavendish Sandspit, at Covehead, and on Rustico Island. The endangered piping plover also nests on several park beaches, including Cavendish Sandspit and Blooming Point. Pigeon-sized black guillemots colonize seaside cliffs near Orby Head. Perhaps the best single spot for sighting the greatest variety of birds is Brackley Marsh on the west side of Covehead Bridge.

The great blue heron is the largest of the park's 255 kinds of birds, which include 92 nesting species. Twenty or more of the tall, stately herons may be sighted foraging together at low tide in Brackley, Rustico, and New London bays, as well as in most ponds in the area.

Constant winds and churning waters continually erode the sandstone cliffs of Prince Edward Island National Park. Renowned beaches, deep-sea fishing, and a timeless way of life lure visitors to this picturesque island.

Park woodlands resound with song sparrows, dark-eyed juncos, red-eyed vireos, Swainson's thrushes, and a host of warblers. Good places for sighting perching birds include the woods around the Rustico Island campground, the Bubbling Springs/Farmland trails, the Balsam Hollow Trail, and the Haunted Wood Trail.

Raccoons and striped skunks, introduced to the island in the early 1900s, have adapted well to wooded areas near streams and marshes. Beavers and muskrats are found in some park ponds. Red foxes, the park's largest mammal, feed on meadow voles in the dense thickets where dunes and forest meet (the area surrounding the Rustico campground is a favorite haunt); farther inland they hunt snowshoe hares.

OUTDOOR ACTIVITIES

Most visitors to the park come to enjoy the renowned beaches, the famous Green Gables farmhouse, and the picturesque drive along the Gulf of St. Lawrence shoreline. Anglers charter boats from nearby ports for deep-sea fishing excursions.

Scenic Drive

The *Gulf Shore Parkway* extends most of the length of the park, providing magnificent views of the gulf and linking beaches, campgrounds, and points of interest. Those with literary interests drive 7 mi/11.2 km southwest of Cavendish on Highway 6 to the New London birthplace of Lucy Maud Montgomery. The white cottage trimmed in green is now a museum open from mid-June to early September. In Park Corner, about 5 mi/8 km northwest of New London on Highway 20, is the Anne of Green Gables Museum, in the house where the author's wedding took place and where she often visited her relatives. The museum is open from mid-May through October.

The parkway proper branches off Highway 6 at the park entrance in Cavendish. Shortly after Maud's birth, her mother died, and Maud went to live with her grandparents in Cavendish. Not far away was Green Gables, the home of Maud's elderly cousins, David and Margaret MacNeill. Maud spent many happy hours roaming the farm and its woodlands, and based her characterizations of Matthew and Marilla Cuthbert on her beloved relatives. Green Gables House, furnished to reflect a typical 1880s island farmhouse, is open daily from May through October.

From Green Gables House, the Gulf Shore Parkway angles north to the pinkish sands of Cavendish Main Beach. Heading east, the route skirts an impressive stretch of red sandstone cliffs up to 100 ft/30 m high backing the beach between Orby Head and North Rustico Harbour. No bridge spans the harbor entrance, so motorists loop around Rustico Bay on Highway 6, then drive north on Highway 15 to pick up the parkway again.

At the intersection of Highway 15 and the parkway, drivers backtrack west to reach Rustico Island. Construction of the road's causeway in the 1950s turned the island into a sandspit extending across the mouth of Rustico Bay. East of the highway intersection the parkway leads to the extensive sand dunes of Brackley Beach. This is the best spot in the park to see dune succession: bare sand colonized by marram grass yields to older dune ridges stabilized by bayberry, wrinkled rose, and scrub white spruce. Wooden walkways wind between the dunes and lead to the beautiful beach.

At Covehead Harbour, common terns have established a colony beneath the bridge that connects Brackley and Stanhope Beach. The eastbound road skirts a salt marsh and numerous barachois ponds, favorite stopovers for migrating waterfowl. Past Dalvay Beach the parkway heads south to rejoin Highway 6. Beyond the narrow opening to Tracadie Bay lies Blooming Point Beach. (A telescope at Dalvay Beach affords long-distance views of Blooming Point's extensive dune system.) In this remote eastern end of the park, dunes migrating inland centuries ago buried a shoreline forest. Now the bleached bones of spruce and fir are gradually being disinterred by ceaseless gulf winds.

This area is accessible by looping around the southern end of Tracadie Bay on Highways 6, 219, and 218. From Highway 218, on the east side of the bay, a dirt road leads to a parking lot near the park boundary. From there, visitors walk about 1 mi/1.6 km through the dunes to the beach. The area is closed from May to mid-August during the nesting season of the endangered piping plover.

Hiking

The park's six short nature trails are suitable for all ages, and most of them are marked with interpretive signs for self-guiding walks. In the Cavendish area, the *Balsam Hollow Trail* leads through one of L. M. Montgomery's favorite woodland haunts. The path starts at Green Gables House and wanders along a spring-fed brook beneath a shady arch of mature sugar maples, yellow birches, balsam firs, and white spruce—one of the few remaining stands of the park's original forest.

The *Haunted Wood Trail*, which begins at the bottom of the hill in front of Green Gables House, explores a spruce woodland that inspired part of the setting for the "Anne" novels. Interpretive signs explain the connection between the author's life in Cavendish and her fiction. A side trip leads to the Cavendish Community Cemetery and the graves of L. M. Montgomery, her husband Ewan Macdonald, and other relatives. The twin loops of the

Rosy-hued from the sun, a fresh-water stream flows into the St. Lawrence. Much of Prince Edward Island's soil is red in its own right, oxidized iron in a fine clay soil bringing forth an excellent potato crop.

Homestead Trail wind through woods and former farmland and lead to fine coastal views along New London Bay. Starting west of the entrance to Cavendish campground, the inner loop is 3.4 mi/5.5 km; the outer loop is 5 mi/8 km long.

In the Dalvay end of the park, the *Bubbling Springs Trail* and the *Farmlands Trail* share the same trail head off the Gulf Shore Parkway between Stanhope and Dalvay. Before splitting off on separate loops, the twin routes wind through spruce woods and past the Old Stanhope Cemetery. The Farmlands loop passes through old fields and apple orchards returning to forest, and offers opportunities to view such wildflowers as bunchberry, clintonia, star-flower, and pink lady's-slipper, as well as birds and small mammals. Bubbling Springs wanders through spruce woods along the shore of Long Pond, where a viewing platform enables bird watchers to observe waterfowl. At the halfway point of this short walk, water wells up through the sandy forest floor in the "bubbling springs" for which this route is named.

Maram grass, also known as American Beach Grass, is the most common dune plant along the Atlantic Coast. Its elaborate root system and ability to withstand burial make it an important dune stabilizer.

The *Reeds and Rushes Trail* crosses Dalvay Pond on a boardwalk. Wetland creatures to be sighted include muskrats and waterfowl. A short side trip leads to an elevated viewing platform ideal for bird watchers.

Bicycling

This increasingly popular activity is enjoyed from late April through October. Wide cycling paths paralleled the 18.6-mi/30-km *Gulf Shore Parkway.* Cyclists are allowed also on the *Homestead Trail,* two concentric loops 3.4 mi/5.5 km and 5 mi/8 km long suitable only for mountain bikes. Roads through rolling farmland outside the park attract many riders. Bikes can be rented in the park area from Stanhope-by-the-Sea in Stanhope (902-672-2047) and Sunset Campground Bike Rentals (902-963-2440) in Cavendish.

Boating

Rowboats and canoes are allowed on Dalvay Lake and Long Pond in back of east-end Dalvay Beach. Motorboats are not permitted on ponds and lakes.

Fishing

Sport fishermen from around the world come to Prince Edward Island to charter boats out to the rich waters of the Gulf of St. Lawrence. No license is required for deep-sea fishing. Deep-sea charters generally last four hours. Bluefin tuna charters last eight or more hours; most depart at 9 A.M. In the park region boats depart from New London, North Rustico Harbour, and Covehead and Tracadie bays.

Fishing in park streams and ponds is poor to moderately good. The best fishing for brook trout is in Rollings Pond near North Rustico Beach, and Long and Campbells ponds near Dalvay Beach.

Swimming

Water temperatures here average a balmy (for Canada) 70° F/21° C during July and August. Seven supervised swimming beaches are spaced along the length of the park. Lifeguards are on duty from late June to early September. Facilities include change rooms, showers, and food stands. The busiest beaches are Cavendish Main, Stanhope, and Brackley; for a relatively uncrowded beach, try Dalvay, Ross Lane, and North Rustico. For even more seclusion, beachgoers can stroll east or west of supervised areas.

Windsurfing

New London, Rustico, Brackley, and Stanhope bays provide some of Canada's best windsurfing; rentals are available at Stanhope-by-the-Sea (902-672-2047) and at other establishments in the area.

Winter Activities

Snow often lasts through April, making for moderately good *cross-country skiing* conditions. The *Cavendish Trail* loops 12.5 mi/20 km over the park golf course. The 3.7-mi/6-km *Dalvay Trail* also is groomed. Skating is popular on park ponds.

Other Activities

Two *golf* courses beckon. The Babbling Brook, Haunted Wood, and other places familiar to readers of *Anne of Green Gables* are on or near the 18-hole Green Gables Golf Course (902-963-2488), built in 1939. Just outside the park south of Stanhope Beach, the Stanhope Golf and Country Club (902-672-2842) sets one of the island's longest and most challenging courses alongside lovely Covehead Bay. *Tennis* is available at Cavendish and Dalvay (two courts each) and at Brackley (one court). There is a *lawn bowling* green at Dalvay; bowls and mats are available for a small fee.

EXPLORING THE PARK

This island province is cradled between New Brunswick and Nova Scotia. Two ferry services carry autos and passengers across the Northumberland Strait to Prince Edward Island. Northumberland Ferries (800-565-0201 in Prince Edward Island, New Brunswick, and Nova Scotia; 902-566-3838 elsewhere) operates from May to December between Caribou, Nova Scotia, to the Wood Islands ferry terminal, a 75-minute crossing. Marine Atlantic (800-565-9470) sails year-round from Cape Tormentine, New Brunswick, to the Borden ferry terminal, a 45-minute crossing. A half-dozen roads fan north from Charlottetown, the provincial capital, to various corners of the park; Highway 6, the main route, parallels the park.

Park headquarters is at Dalvay; the visitors' center is at Cavendish. The summer interpretive program includes beach walks, pond walks, bird-watching outings, campfire programs, and other presentations at the park's two outdoor theaters, and guided walks to places familiar to readers of the "Anne" novels, including the Haunted Wood and the Babbling Brook.

ACCOMMODATIONS: The park's three campgrounds, open from June through early October, operate consistently at full capacity in July and August. Cavendish campground (304 sites) occupies a lightly wooded west-end site near the park's most popular beach. The Rustico Island campground, with 148 wooded and meadow sites facing Rustico Bay, is the quietest of the three park campgrounds and the last to fill up. The Stanhope campground (118 sites) is in woods across the road from two supervised beaches.

Hotels, motels, cottages, tourist homes, and some 1,500 private campsites are within a short drive of the park. Cavendish offers the most extensive facilities for travelers in the park vicinity. The most elegant private accommodation is green-roofed Dalvay-by-the-Sea (Box 8, York, P.E.I. C0A 1P0; 902-672-2048 in summer, 902-672-2546 in winter), a rambling Victorian structure built in 1895 as a summer home for Cincinnati oil tycoon Alexander Macdonald. The 26-room hotel, open from mid-June to mid-September, has bicycles and canoes available. There are also two housekeeping cottages.

Shaw's Hotel and Cottages (Brackley Beach, P.E.I. C0A 2H0; 902-672-2022), established in 1860 in the village of Brackley Beach, is the island's oldest family-owned summer resort. Stanhope-by-the-Sea (Box 2109, Charlottetown, P.E.I. C1A 7N7; 902-672-2047 in summer, 416-529-2807 in winter), has been a country inn since 1817. There are 35 rooms in the original building, 24 rooms in a new annex, and a three-bedroom housekeeping cottage.

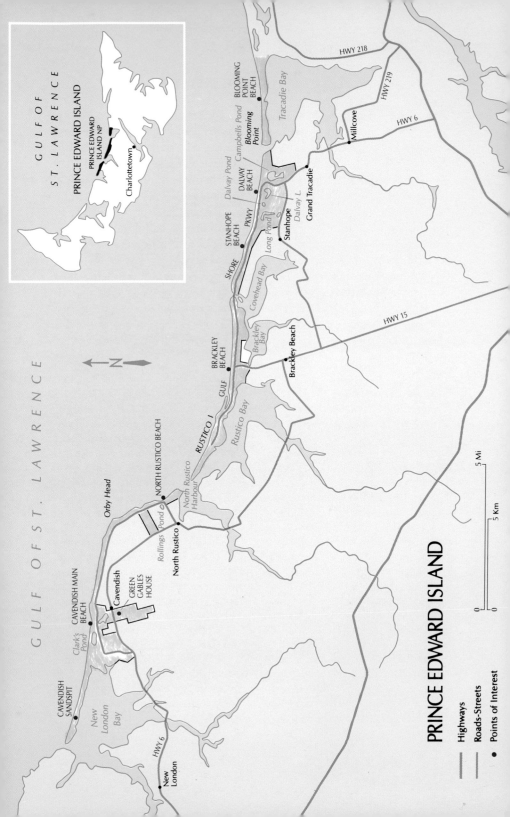

PRINCE EDWARD ISLAND

Highways
Roads-Streets
• **Points of Interest**

GULF OF ST. LAWRENCE

GULF OF
ST. LAWRENCE

PRINCE EDWARD ISLAND

PRINCE EDWARD
ISLAND NP

Charlottetown

HWY 218

HWY 219

HWY 6

Millcove

BLOOMING
POINT
BEACH

Tracadie Bay

Blooming
Point

Campbells Pond

Dalvay Pond

DALVAY
BEACH

PKWY

Dalvay L.

Grand Tracadie

STANHOPE
BEACH

Long Pond

Stanhope

SHORE

Covehead Bay

HWY 15

BRACKLEY
BEACH

Brackley
Bay

Brackley Beach

GULF

Rustico Bay

RUSTICO 1

NORTH RUSTICO BEACH

North Rustico
Harbour

Orby Head

Rollings Pond

North Rustico

CAVENDISH MAIN
BEACH

Cavendish

GREEN
GABLES
HOUSE

Clark's
Pond

CAVENDISH
SANDSPIT

New London
Bay

HWY 6

New
London

N

5 Mi
5 Km

0
0

ADDRESSES: For more information on the park, contact: The Superintendent, Prince Edward Island National Park, Box 487, Charlottetown, P.E.I. C1A 7L1; 902-672-2211. Additional park information is available from the local cooperative organization, Parks and People Association, which operates a sales shop in summer in the Cavendish Visitor Centre (Box 1506, Charlottetown, P.E.I. C1A 7N3; 902-894-4246), and at Green Gables House during the off-season. For general information, contact Prince Edward Island Tourism, Visitors Services, Box 940E, Charlottetown, P.E.I. C1A 7M5; 902-368-4444. For travelers in Nova Scotia or New Brunswick, a toll-free reservations number (800-565-7421) can be used from mid-May through October to reserve accommodations.

BOOKS: L. M. Montgomery, *Anne of Green Gables.* This Canadian classic is beloved by readers around the world. Available at the Parks and People Association sales shop in Cavendish and at most island bookstores.

A familiar American shorebird, the semipalmated plover calls with a plaintive two-note whistle or a soft chuckle.

CAPE BRETON HIGHLANDS NATIONAL PARK

THE RUGGED, BROODING BEAUTY of Cape Breton Island, Nova Scotia, stamps an indelible imprint on the memory of all who visit. The national park spreads like a band across Cape Breton's northern tip, protecting the island's finest scenery, from the cove-scalloped Atlantic shore on the east to the sentinel headlands and cliffs above the Gulf of St. Lawrence on the west. In between is the largest wilderness in Nova Scotia, a highland plateau of forests, lakes, bogs, barrens, ancient river gorges, and canyons up to 1,000 ft/300 m deep. Skirting the eastern, northern, and western park boundaries is the Cabot Trail, one of Canada's most scenic highways.

GEOLOGY

The same forces of mountain-building that raised the Appalachian chain between 395 and 345 million years ago lifted Cape Breton high above sea level. Subsequent faulting and erosion left steep cliffs and headlands on the gulf coast of what is now the national park, a central upland plateau where rounded hills rise 1,600 ft/500 m, and a fairly level eastern plateau that tilts seaward and slips into the Atlantic along a coastline of beaches separated by low headlands.

Over millions of years, rushing rivers carved deep canyons in the highlands, especially along their precipitous western edge. Several rivers, however, flow through steep-walled faults, gorges formed not by water erosion but by the shifting of Cape Breton bedrock. The north-central Aspy Fault, the park's most prominent fracture, directs the flow of the North Aspy River northeast into the Atlantic. Similarly, the Chéticamp River in the southwest corner of the park and the Clyburn Brook in the southeast also flow along fault lines.

The west-central highlands escaped most of the bulldozing effects of the Ice Age. During the late Wisconsin, when Pleistocene ice was at its thickest and most extensive (and, therefore, most destructive), continental ice from the northwest rode up and over Cape Breton's gulf-coast cliffs, then slid across the western highlands on a thin sheet of local ice left over from earlier glaciations. This frozen covering protected underlying surface features.

Except for wind and rain erosion, the topography of the west-central park has remained essentially unchanged for 65 million years—an ancient landscape by Canadian standards.

As the continental ice flowed toward the Atlantic, it scoured the unprotected eastern upland, gouging shallow basins now filled with wetlands and interconnected lakes. When the ice melted about 11,000 years ago, it left bedrock striations, a blanket of debris 20 ft/6 m deep in the lowlands, and erratics—boulders transported great distances by glaciers and dropped in unlikely places. The Clyburn Valley Trail passes several car-sized erratics.

HISTORY

Northern Cape Breton has been inhabited for some 8,000 years. In the southeastern part of the park, prehistoric camps on the north shore of Warren Lake and on Ingonish Island, northeast of Middle Head, are evidence of two prehistoric cultures. The Micmac, who are part of the island's population today, emerged about A.D. 1000. They fished for Atlantic salmon, hunted moose and caribou, and trapped river otter, beaver, and muskrat.

Leif Ericsson may have sailed past Cape Breton during an epic voyage down the North American coast in 1001. John Cabot came ashore just north of today's park on June 24, 1497, and claimed the island—and the entire North American continent—for Britain. By the early 1500s, French and Portuguese fishermen were catching and curing fish along the coast. The Portuguese built a village at Niganis (later Inganiche, then Ingonish) in 1521—nearly a century before the Pilgrims stepped onto Plymouth Rock— but abandoned the site after only one winter.

Cape Breton's earliest farmers came from the French fortress of Louisbourg, southeast of today's park, and settled around Ingonish in the early 1700s. Their community was destroyed about 1760 by the British during the struggle between France and England for supremacy in North America. The British deported the settlers in the 1750s and 1760s, primarily to other parts of Cape Breton and the isolated Magdalen Islands in the Gulf of St. Lawrence. Some exiles eventually returned to settle around Chéticamp.

Scottish immigrants began arriving in 1791, when lairds back home found more profit in grazing sheep and cattle than in renting their lands to tenant farmers ("crofters"). By 1828 about 25,000 Gaelic-speaking farmers

OVERLEAF: *Cape Breton's Presqu'ile Point illustrates a dramatic meeting between grassy slope, craggy headland, and sea. Bordering both the Gulf of St. Lawrence and the Atlantic Coast, the park offers innumerable and spectacular coastline vistas.*

had settled in Cape Breton, where the misty mountains, heathlands, and lakes reminded the newcomers of the highlands, moors, and lochs they had left behind across the sea.

HABITATS

Raucous colonies of seabirds—black guillemots, common and arctic terns, great and double-crested cormorants, herring and great black-backed gulls—summer on the park's coastal cliffs, rock pillars, and ledges. Offshore, pods of pilot whales pursue herring and mackerel, mainstays of their diet. Finback and minke whales feed singly or in pairs. Harbor porpoises and seals are also on the roll call of marine mammals.

On the park's coastal fringes and in river valleys grow the mixed deciduous and coniferous trees of the Acadian forest. Sugar maples and American beeches dominate mature forests and combine with birches, spruces, and pines in younger woodlands. Almost pure hardwood forests carpet several rich river-valley bottoms, including the Grande Anse Valley in the northwest, which shelters one of the finest undisturbed stands of sugar maple in the Maritimes.

These old-growth forests shade understory plants usually found farther south: rose-twisted stalk, sweet cicely, maidenhair fern, Braun's holly fern, silvery spleenwort, bellwort, and toothwort. In spring, before leaves emerge to block the sunlight, the forest floor blooms with Dutchman's-breeches, spring beauty, starflower, and Canada mayflower. (The wildflower show is particularly dazzling along the Lone Shieling Trail in the northwest.) The American redstart, the most common bird here, shares the forest with the red-eyed vireo, ovenbird, Swainson's thrush, rose-breasted grosbeak, and 18 kinds of warblers.

Higher on the slopes of river valleys and on the highland plateau above 1,000 ft/330 m, boreal forest characterized by balsam fir, paper birch, and black spruce replaces the rich Acadian forest. Where the forest cover is dense, shading prevents extensive shrub layers and the ground cover is dominated by mosses. Trees are smaller than those in the valleys and generally live no more than a century.

Scattered highland ponds and lakes are home to green-winged teal, American black and ring-necked ducks, common and red-breasted mergansers, and common goldeneyes. Moose, which were reintroduced to the park in 1947, are found here, along with black bears. Both animals also range upper river valleys. Lynx prowl dense evergreen thickets, preying on spruce grouse and snowshoe hares (the park is one of the last strongholds of the lynx in the Maritimes).

Elevations above 1,300 ft/400 m show another side of the highland plateau, a barren, cloud-hung landscape of extremes, where snow sometimes falls in June and gales gust up to 155 mph/250 kph. Plants hug the ground, keeping out of the wind; trees are grotesquely pruned and stunted. Hip-high balsam fir and black spruce may be 150 years old. Large areas, especially in the central and western highlands, are covered with tundra-like wet barrens—blanket bogs and ponds where the plants are sphagnum mosses, sedges, grasses, insectivorous pitcher plants and sundews, and heath plants such as Labrador-tea, bog-laurel, cranberry, and leatherleaf.

In the stark dry barrens, good drainage prevents the formation of bogs and ponds. On the sheltered lower hillsides, dense tangles of black spruce and balsam fir, known as "tuckamore," grow 9 to 12 ft/3 to 4 m high. Dwarf birches, alpine whortleberry, pink crowberry, and other subarctic plants also survive here, along with rhodora, sheep-laurel, and crowberry. Open, flat expanses are often hummocked with mounds of lichens, mosses, and heath plants up to 3 ft/1 m high.

OUTDOOR ACTIVITIES

More than a half-million people visit the highlands each year. Most come in summer to drive the Cabot Trail, although brilliant fall foliage also attracts motorists in late September and early October. Day-hikers wander along valley trails, up mountains, and onto headlands for spectacular views; relatively few backpackers venture into the highland plateau. In winter, moist air rising off the Gulf of St. Lawrence dumps 160 to 200 in/400 to 500 cm of snow on the northern highlands, creating good skiing conditions.

Scenic Drive

Starting and ending at Baddeck, the *Cabot Trail* loops 185 mi/296 km through northern Cape Breton. About 62 mi/100 km of the paved two-lane highway weave along the east, north, and west boundaries of the park. Seldom far from the sea, the drive concentrates much scenic variety in a short distance—rounded mountains, lush glens threaded by salmon streams, sandy beaches, and sheer headlands towering over surf-pounded coves. Many consider the highway North America's most spectacular day-drive, but itineraries of two days or more are possible, with stops for nature walks, picnics, swimming, and sightseeing.

Driving the Cabot Trail counterclockwise means that the best scenery (the western coastline) comes at the end, creating a natural crescendo. The highway enters the southeast corner of the park at Ingonish Beach. The first highlight is a side trip onto Middle Head, a forested promontory jut-

A young hardwood forest along the Cabot Trail, often called North America's most scenic drive, where Acadian forests give way to the tempestuous coastline.

ting into South Ingonish Bay. The view south embraces massive Cape Smokey, a 1,200-ft/365-m headland often wreathed in mist. Just north of Ingonish Beach, at the Broad Cove campground, a second side trip leads 4 mi/6.5 km north to Mary Ann Falls on Mary Ann Brook.

The highway hugs the Atlantic shore as it heads north, passing the Lakies Head lookout, with its telescopes for spotting whales and other marine life, and skirting coves with sand and cobble beaches. On the road's northwest angle along the park boundary, a short side trip on the Paquette Lake road provides great views of the highland barrens. Shortly after, the road leaves the park briefly, then heads southwest along the North Aspy River valley back into the park.

At about the halfway point of the drive, a side road branches off at the town of Cape North and heads north through scenery that rivals the park's dramatic landscapes. The 15-mi/24-km digression ends at the fishing community of Meat Cove on St. Lawrence Bay. Back on the main trail, the drive southwest is punctuated by another short side trip, this time south to lacy Beulach Ban Falls, one of many cataracts on brooks and rivers tumbling down from the highlands. About 15 mi/24 km west, a level trail just off the

highway meanders through sugar maples some 300 years old to the "Lone Shieling," a replica of an eighteenth-century cottage used by crofters in the Scottish Highlands.

The Cabot Trail then dips into the valley of the Grande Anse River and follows it to Pleasant Bay on the park's western shore. Now the drive unfolds vista after vista of the gulf coast, with its steep headlands, 1,000-ft/300-m cliffs, and wave-lashed coves. It heads inland to climb MacKenzie and French mountains, descends Jumping Brook valley to the sea again, clings to the shore, then turns inland through a narrow valley, and leaves the park at the Chéticamp River.

Hiking

Twenty-eight trails include nature walks just off the Cabot Trail suitable for the whole family, short but steep climbs to mountain and coastal lookouts, and extended backcountry hikes that explore the interior plateau and lead down to the western coastline.

In the southeast corner of the park, the level 2.5-mi/4-km *Middle Head Trail* wanders through woods busy in summer with warblers and evening grosbeaks, and ends at the tip of the promontory with views of North and South Ingonish bays, Cape Smokey, and Tern Rock, an offshore seastack where common and arctic terns nest in June and July. Pilot whales are sighted occasionally from mid-June through August.

In the southwestern corner of the park, wildlife usually is seen along the 45-minute *Le Buttereau Trail*, an interpretive walk that makes a pleasant family outing. Starting near the Grande Falaise picnic area, the route crosses the former hayfields and pastures of Acadian farmers, now the woodland haunts of bobcats, snowshoe hares, red squirrels, magnolia and yellow warblers, and boreal chickadees. Foundations of pioneer houses can still be seen along the trail, where blue flag, prickly wild roses, white Canadian burnet, and other wildflowers bloom throughout the summer. To the north on the Cabot Trail near MacKenzie Mountain, a 15-minute stroll along the *Bog Trail* boardwalk explores wetland barrens of the highland plateau.

For superlative Atlantic-coast views, climbers ascend for two heart-pounding hours up 1,404-ft/428-m Franey Mountain on the *Franey Trail*, just west of Ingonish Centre. From the summit are panoramas of the Atlantic, Middle Head, and Cape Smokey to the east, Money Point to the north, the sheer face of Franey Mountain to the south, and, far below, the Clyburn Valley. Most hikers return via a fire-tower road. North of Ingonish, the equally steep 2-mi/3.2-km *Broad Cove Mountain Trail* switchbacks 590 ft/180 m to a summit overlooking the Atlantic Ocean and Warren Lake.

Gulf-coast views abound on the 4.4-mi/7-km *Skyline Trail*, a nearly level loop which begins at a parking lot on a Cabot Trail side road near the summit of French Mountain. Followed clockwise, the trail passes through an evergreen forest ravaged by spruce budworm, then through open stands of stunted hardwoods, to arrive at the lip of a windswept cliff on Jumping Brook Mountain. Pilot whales frequently are seen offshore. The trail returns to the parking lot via the evergreen forest. The 6-mi/9.6-km *L'Acadien Trail* at Chéticamp also offers fine gulf views, as well as a succession of life zones as it climbs 1,200 ft/366 m from deciduous river-valley forest to hill-top boreal forest.

The park's finest shoreline walk, the 7-mi/11-km *Coastal Trail* on the Atlantic side, usually is traversed south to north beginning at Black Brook Beach just off the Cabot Trail north of Ingonish. The route passes through a mixed forest to Squeaker's Hole, a tiny cove noted for the rich marine life of its tidal pools; it then skirts bays and cobble beaches littered with drift-wood, climbs a forested headland, and drops down to a sandy cove where Halfway Brook flows into the sea. Here, hikers retrace their steps or take a shortcut (2.5 mi/4.1 km) back to the starting point via the Cabot Trail.

Backpackers who want to camp overnight in the wilderness interior have two options. At 8 mi/12.8 km, the *Lake of Islands Trail* is the park's longest hiking route. Starting at the end of a branch road off the Mary Ann Falls road on the eastern side of the park north of Ingonish, this former fire road heads due west past bogs and across barrens to end at a primitive campsite deep in the highland plateau. It is a difficult route that subjects backpackers to harsh, changeable weather, an altitude gain of about 1,150 ft/350 m, and generally wet trail conditions. Two emergency shelters are situated along the way.

On the western side of the park, the 5-mi/8-km *Fishing Cove Trail* begins off the Cabot Trail 15 mi/24 km north of Chéticamp, winds down the steep valley of the Fishing Cove River, and ends at Fishing Cove, which offers the park's only coastal wilderness camping. The cove, with its cob-bled beach, was the site of a village founded in 1830 and abandoned in 1912. Among this route's attractions are swimming in the river and in the cove, shoreline explorations, and fine fishing for brook trout.

Bicycling

Cyclists in excellent physical condition ride the *Cabot Trail* clockwise to take advantage of prevailing westerly winds and the eastward tilt of the plateau.

Creating classic highland landscapes, the Fishing Cove River descends to a surfside campsite. Cape Breton's waterways feature excellent fishing, especially for salmon and trout.

Fishing

According to local legend, Atlantic salmon once ran so thickly on the Chéticamp River that Acadian farmers fished with pitchforks. Threatened elsewhere with pollution, overfishing, and dams, salmon are still abundant in the Chéticamp. The Trous de Saumon Trail from the Chéticamp campground leads to three salmon pools. The North Aspy River contains some of Nova Scotia's largest speckled sea trout. Several hiking trails, including Benjies Lake, John Dee Lake, Jigging Cove Lake, and Lake of Islands, lead to wilderness lakes where brook trout are plentiful.

Whale-Watching

Chéticamp Boat Tours (902-224-3376 or 902-224-2412) conducts popular three-hour excursions up the gulf coast as far north as Fishing Cove once a day from mid-May to July 1, then three times daily until mid-September. Pleasant Bay Boat Tours (902-224-2547), north of Chéticamp, scans the

Framed by a range of flat-topped blue hills, this highland plateau is an expanse of native wildflowers and grasses. Some plateaus are subject to extreme winds and early snowfalls.

same stretch of coastline in search of whales twice daily from June through September. Whale Works Enterprises (902-383-2981), based in Bay St. Lawrence at the northern tip of Cape Breton Island, offers cruises on a former lobster boat three times daily from June to September. The whale checklist includes pilots, fins, and minke. Dolphins and porpoises may be sighted too, as well as bald eagles patrolling the cliffs of the spectacular gulf coast.

Swimming

Ingonish Beach is one of the few places in Canada where freshwater and saltwater swimming can be enjoyed by merely crossing a barachois, a natural breakwater of rock and sand. On one side of the magnificent sand beach that stretches south from Middle Head to Ingonish harbor, swimmers splash in the Atlantic, and on the other side, in Freshwater Lake. The beach north of Middle Head, at the North Bay day-use area, is usually less crowded. There is also swimming at nearby Warren Lake, and farther north along the coast at Broad Cove and Black Brook Cove. On the gulf coast, swimming occurs at Corney Brook, Fishing Cove, and La Bloque Beach north of the Chéticamp park entrance.

Downhill Skiing

A ski resort (902-285-2778) on Cape Smokey, just outside the park south of Ingonish, includes a chairlift, a tow lift, and four runs with a maximum vertical drop of 1,000 ft/330 m.

Cross-country Skiing

Near Ingonish, 33 mi/53 km of groomed trails wind along the Highland Links golf course and up the Clyburn Valley. Groomed trails are maintained also on the former Cabot Trail roadbed east of French Mountain, in the Chéticamp campground, and on the *Trous de Saumon Trail*, which passes beneath steep valley walls and through mature stands of American beech, birch, and maple.

Golfing

An 18-hole *golf* course, Highland Links (902-285-2600), is open from mid-May to mid-October. The course extends from the seacoast on Middle Head up the picturesque Clyburn Valley. Three paved *tennis* courts at the Ingonish Beach day-use area are open from late April to October. Equipment may be rented at the golf pro shop.

EXPLORING THE PARK

This preserve is near the northern tip of Cape Breton Island, Nova Scotia, about 290 mi/465 km northeast of Halifax, and 80 mi/130 km north of Sydney.

Most people reach the park by car, following the numerous highways from the Nova Scotia–New Brunswick border, and from the Nova Scotia ferry terminals at Digby, Yarmouth, and North Sydney. A causeway over the Strait of Canso connects Cape Breton Island with the mainland.

Visitor services are in Ingonish Beach, site of park headquarters, and in Chéticamp. Information centers in both communities (Ingonish, 902-285-2535; Chéticamp, 902-224-2306) operate daily from late spring to fall, dispensing permits for fishing and backcountry camping, as well as schedules of park activities, including shows at outdoor theaters in Broad Cove and Chéticamp campgrounds. At other times of the year, information is available on weekdays from the park office at Ingonish (902-285-2691).

ACCOMMODATIONS: Six serviced campgrounds are scattered around the perimeter of the park on the Cabot Trail. Ingonish (90 sites), Broad Cove (261 sites), and Chéticamp (162 sites) are the most developed. Ingonish, a five-minute walk to Ingonish Beach, fills early each evening in summer. Chéticamp, which is seldom crowded, is near some of the park's best hiking and fishing. Big Intervale, MacIntosh Brook, and Corney Brook are small campgrounds with more limited facilities. Backcountry camping is on the Fishing Cove and Lake of Islands trails. Chéticamp and Ingonish campgrounds are open year-round, with reduced services in winter. Most of the other campgrounds are open mid-May to early October.

The park's principal commercial accommodation is Keltic Lodge (Box 70, Ingonish Beach, N.S. B0C 1L0; 902-285-2880), a resort hotel on Middle Head with 32 rooms in the main lodge, 40 rooms in a modern inn, and 26 rooms in two- and four-bed cottages scattered about the grounds. Cape Breton Highland Bungalows (Box 151, Ingonish Beach, N.S. B0C 1L0; 902-285-2000), adjacent to Freshwater Lake in Ingonish Beach, has 25 cottages. Many privately operated motels, hotels, and inns are located in communities adjacent to the park.

ADDRESSES: For more information, contact Cape Breton Highlands National Park, Ingonish Beach, N.S. B0C 1L0; 902-285-2691. For information on accommodations and activities, call the provincial tourism bureau's toll-free service, Check-Inn Nova Scotia (800-341-6096). The Cape Breton Tourist Association (20 Keltic Drive, Sydney River, N.S. B1S 1P5; 902-539-9876) operates six bureaus around the island from mid-May to mid-September. Additional information, including books, hiking guides, and topographical maps, can be purchased from Les Amis du Plein Air (Box 472, Chéticamp, N.S. B0E 1H0; 902-224-3814), a nonprofit organization that promotes the park.

BOOKS: Pat and Jim Lotz, *Cape Breton Island*. West Vancouver, B.C.: 1974. General history and descriptions of Cape Breton.

The Rev. Anselme Chiasson, *History and Acadian Traditions of Chéticamp*. St. John's, Nfld.: Breakwater Books, 1986. An entertaining history of the settlement, economy, and social life of the Chéticamp area.

Ron Caplan, ed., *Down North: The Book of Cape Breton's Magazine*. Wreck Cove, N.S.: Cape Breton Magazine, 1980. History and folklore of this storied island.

GROS MORNE NATIONAL PARK

EARTH SCIENTISTS CALL THIS PARK on the west coast of Newfoundland the "Galápagos of geology" for its rare rock formations that support the theory of plate tectonics. This hypothesis, which holds that continents drift ponderously over the earth's surface like enormous ice floes, accounts for the presence in Gros Morne of igneous rock normally found deep within the earth's mantle, volcanic pillow lavas formed on the floor of a now-extinct ocean, and a mountain chain uplifted by colliding continents.

Gros Morne (pronounced in English GROSS MORN), is best known, however, for having some of the most spectacular scenery in eastern Canada. The Long Range Mountains run the length of the park. Atop this ancient tableland is a starkly beautiful alpine barren often wreathed in swirling mists and battered by winds and storms. In fact, the French name of the park's eponymous mountain, a brooding, desolate massif, literally means "Big Gloomy."

The escarpment that forms the seaward edge of the range is deeply incised by four landlocked fjords—or "fjord ponds" as they are called in Newfoundland—that lie in glacially carved canyons where waterfalls tumble from towering cliffs. Below the escarpment, a coastal lowland extends to the Gulf of St. Lawrence shoreline, which alternates great cliffs, fjords, and shallow coves fringed with sandy or cobble beaches.

GEOLOGY

Preserved in park rocks is a remarkable record of plate tectonics, or continental drift. When plates bearing ancient North America and Eurafrica drifted apart some 600 million years ago, an ocean called the Iapetus formed between them. About 100 million years later, the plates began to move together and the Iapetus Ocean slowly closed. The plates crunched against each other, raising the Appalachian Mountain Belt, including Newfoundland's Long Range Mountains.

When plates collide, denser oceanic sheets usually slide beneath lighter continental plates in a process called subduction. In Newfoundland, the

Gros Morne offers strikingly diverse physical features, including mountains, bogs, and sand dunes.

opposite occurred. As the Iapetus closed, bits of ocean floor and mantle trapped between the colliding plates were thrust up on top of the continental margin. Evidence of this rare reversal, known as obduction, is found south of Bonne Bay. Along Green Gardens Trail, hikers pass cliffs of pillow lavas formed from magma that oozed out of fissures on the floor of the Iapetus Ocean and cooled into distinctive, bulging formations.

Even more impressive is the nearby Tablelands, a high plateau littered with ocher-colored boulders. This massif formed from molten magma deep under the ocean floor. Uplifted millions of years ago, the Tablelands offer a rare glimpse of mantle rock, or peridotite, usually found 10 mi/16 km beneath the earth's surface. High concentrations of heavy metals in the rock thwart most plant life in the Tablelands.

Pleistocene glaciers molded Gros Morne as well, descending from the Long Range Plateau down old river valleys to carve four fjords that later became landlocked by the rising of a coastal lowland unburdened from the weight of the ice. Western Brook Pond, which 10,000 years ago opened into the gulf, is now 1.5 mi/2.4 km inland and 100 ft/30 m above sea level.

HISTORY

Migratory aboriginal people of the Maritime Archaic culture arrived in the park region about 4,500 years ago to hunt seals, walrus, and seabirds along the coast and caribou inland on the plateau. These "red paint people," so called for their use of ocher in burial rites, died out around 1000 B.C.

For unknown reasons, the area remained uninhabited for a thousand years—or at least archaeologists have yet to find campsites from this period. Then the so-called Dorset people arrived from the north, settling along the coastline to hunt sea and land mammals. These ancestors of today's Inuit (Eskimos) lasted until about A.D. 600. (The Broom Point Trail south of St. Paul's Bay leads to the site of a Dorset hunting camp.) Around 900, the Beothuk came to Newfoundland, establishing seasonal camps primarily around Red Indian Lake southeast of the park and along the southern coast. The large stature and light complexion of the Beothuk led to theories that they had intermingled with Vikings, who settled north of Gros Morne about a century after the arrival of the Beothuk.

The Beothuk also adorned themselves with red ocher, and descriptions of them led to the use of the term "Red Indian." The tribe came into conflict with Europeans starting in 1613, when a fishing vessel fired on natives awaiting a trading party. In retaliation, the Beothuk began pilfering fishing gear. Fishermen and trappers started killing these "nuisance" Indians, eventually considering it a sport. Exposure to European diseases proved even more deadly than bullets. The tragic extinction of a people was completed in 1829 with the passing of the last Beothuk, a young woman named Shanawdithit, who died of tuberculosis.

The Treaty of Paris in 1783 gave fishing rights on Newfoundland's west coast to France. In the agreement, Britain stipulated that no permanent settlements be established. Settlement did in fact occur, and by the 1870s a number of outports dotted the "French Coast." As late as 1900 a British man-of-war shelled some of these "illegal" villages north of today's park. The French officially did not relinquish their claim until 1904, and only then did settlements along the west coast begin to grow to their present size.

HABITATS

Marine mammals ply the cold gulf waters. Whale sightings are not common, but on average pilot whales are seen weekly during July and August in Bonne Bay and off Lobster Cove Head. There are less frequent sightings in Bonne Bay of fin whales, minkes, and Atlantic white-sided dolphins. Harp seals whelp offshore in March and April, and harbor seals are seen throughout the warm part of the year basking on sandbars near the mouth of St. Paul's Inlet.

Salt marshes on the inlet's north shore attract a multitude of shorebirds. Common and arctic terns begin nesting here in June. By late July, least sandpipers outnumber other species, mainly semipalmated plovers, common snipe, and ruddy turnstones.

North along the coast, common eiders, scoters, oldsquaws, and other migratory sea ducks flock to Cow Head and Shallow Bay. At nearby Belldowns Point, ring-billed gulls feed in a frenzy during the late-June runs of capelin, a smelt-like fish. Prevailing winds from the Gulf of St. Lawrence have driven sandbanks at the mouth of Western Brook up to 1 mi/0.6 km inland, burying coastal forest. Bleached branches of fir and spruce protrude like ghostly fingers above dunes up to 100 ft/30 m high.

Brooks meander across the park's poorly drained coastal lowland, which is blanketed with raised bogs separated by limestone ridges supporting spruce and fir. Cloudberries, a low-growing cousin of the raspberry, but larger and juicier, grow widely in these wetlands and elsewhere in the park. From late July to mid-August, local people harvest the wild fruit, known in Newfoundland as bakeapples.

Yellow, pink, green, and white orchids, pink bog-laurels, and the red goblets of pitcher plants (Newfoundland's provincial flower) fleck the wet-

Gros Morne Mountain, on the left, is the second highest peak in Newfoundland. Beginning at park headquarters, the trail to it passes through swimming, fishing, and rustic camping areas. The park also offers longer hikes.

lands with color. Insects are attracted by the scent of the pitchers' leaves and often by the odor of decay within the plant. Once inside the pitcher, which is a modified leafstalk that collects rainwater, the insects drown. Bacteria begin to decompose the insect bodies, which provide nitrogen and other nutrients needed by the pitcher plant. The larvae of a specialized mosquito species swim unharmed in the small pool of water at the base of the pitcher, and feed on the bacterial broth that develops there.

Drier lowland slopes and valleys have been extensively logged and in many places there is a dense second growth of balsam fir and paper birch. Scattered red maples reach their northern limits in these sheltered woodlands, inhabited by moose, black bears, red foxes, and lynx. Moose are not among the 14 land mammals native to the island; they were introduced as a source of meat in two lots—a bull and a cow from Nova Scotia in 1878 and two bulls and two cows from New Brunswick in 1904. An estimated 120,000 moose now roam Newfoundland, including more than 2,000 in Gros Morne. Also imported to the island were ruffed grouse, red squirrel, and snowshoe hare, which became an important wild game species.

Exposed ridges and mountain slopes support shrub-like heath vegetation, stunted black spruce, and green alder. On coastal cliffs and on the exposed flanks of the Long Range scarp, there is a zone of low, nearly impenetrable balsam fir and black spruce, similar to the krummholz of the

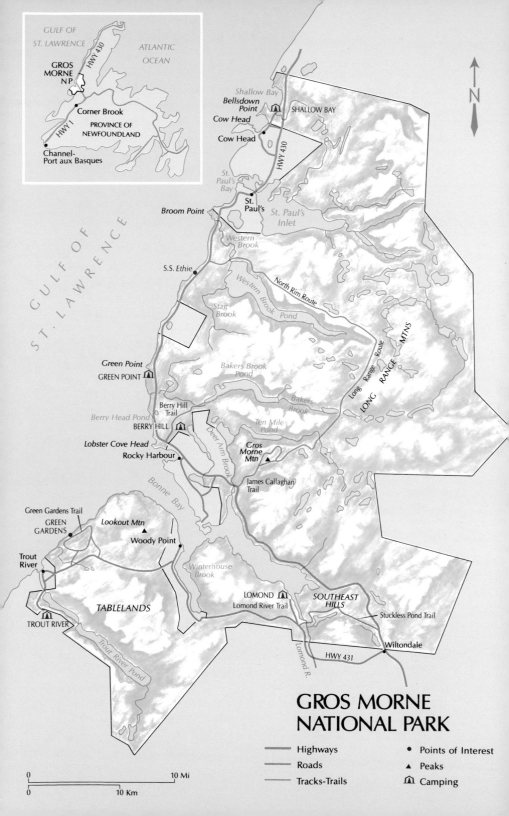

GULF OF
ST. LAWRENCE

ATLANTIC
OCEAN

HWY 430

GROS
MORNE
N P

Corner Brook

PROVINCE OF
NEWFOUNDLAND

HWY 1

Channel-
Port aux Basques

N

Shallow Bay
Bellsdown
Point
Cow Head
SHALLOW BAY
Cow Head

HWY 430

St.
Paul's
Bay

Broom Point
St.
Paul's
St. Paul's
Inlet

Western
Brook

S.S. Ethie
North Rim Route
Western Brook Pond

Stag
Brook

LONG RANGE MTNS

Long Range Route

Green Point
GREEN POINT
Bakers Brook Pond

Berry Hill
Trail
Bakers
Brook
Berry Head Pond
BERRY HILL
Ten Mile Pond
Lobster Cove Head
Gros Morne Mtn
Rocky Harbour
Deer Arm Brook
James Callaghan Trail

Bonne Bay

Green Gardens Trail
GREEN GARDENS
Lookout Mtn
Woody Point
Trout River
Winterhouse Brook
LOMOND
Lomond River Trail
SOUTHEAST HILLS
Stuckless Pond Trail

TABLELANDS
TROUT RIVER
Trout River Pond
Wiltondale
Lomond R.
HWY 431

GROS MORNE
NATIONAL PARK

Highways   • Points of Interest
Roads   ▲ Peaks
Tracks-Trails   ⛺ Camping

0   10 Mi
0   10 Km

Alps and known locally as "tuckamore." Pruned by wind and frost, tuckamore is hellish for hikers but home to a chorus of warblers and thrushes.

The upper tier of the park, some 2,000 ft/610 m above sea level, is a vast, tundra-like alpine plateau covered with tuckamore, subarctic heath, and wetlands. Rock barrens here form the year-round haunt of rock ptarmigan and the park's sizable population of arctic hares. The hares, North America's largest, graze singly and in pairs, and in winter move down to the treeline to feed on shrubs and tree branches.

The treeless barrens provide summer grazing for moose (especially south of the head of Western Brook Pond) and year-round pasture for several hundred woodland caribou, handsome animals with beautiful racks of antlers by late summer. The caribous' primary calving grounds hereabouts are on the plateau south of Western Brook Pond and on the Gregory Plateau south of Bonne Bay, just outside the park. A single, well-developed calf is born in spring snowbeds and is able to run within hours of birth.

South of Bonne Bay, the Tablelands are nearly devoid of vegetation. Tablelands rock, peridotite, contains toxic amounts of heavy metals and almost no nitrogen or potassium, which most plants require for growth. Pitcher plants, sundews, butterworts, and bladderworts, which derive nutrients from insect prey, manage to grow in moist conditions at the base of the plateau and on its flanks. Balsam ragwort survives due to its high tolerance for the heavy metals found in peridotite.

OUTDOOR ACTIVITIES

Most visitors come here in July and August to hike, fish, cruise the waters of Bonne Bay, Western Brook Pond, and St. Paul's Inlet, and drive through some of Atlantic Canada's finest scenery.

Scenic Drive

Winding nearly the length of the park along the coastal lowland, *Highway 430* enters the southeast corner of the park, where three lookouts provide views of the rolling, heavily forested Southeast Hills. A 10-minute hike on Southeast Brook Falls Trail leads to a lovely cascade in a woodland setting.

Along the East Arm of Bonne Bay a series of road cuts reveal steeply dipping layers of shale, limestone, and quartzite that originated as sediments from the shores of the Iapetus Ocean. To the north lies Gros Morne, Newfoundland's second-highest peak (2,644 ft/806 m). The road passes the park's visitors' reception center and Rocky Harbour, the area's largest community. Just north of Rocky Harbour is Berry Head Pond Trail, a 40-minute boardwalk loop around a pond near a bog and a flower-filled forest.

The highway continues along the coast with the Long Range escarpment as a constant companion to the east. At a viewpoint just north of the village of Sally's Cove, the ship's boiler from the sunken S.S. *Ethie* can be seen on the rocks below. When this coastal steamer ran aground on a stormy night in December 1919, local people rigged up a breeches buoy and brought ashore all 92 passengers and crew members, including a baby who was hauled to safety in a mail bag. At Broom Point, three picturesque spits of tilted sedimentary rock are riddled with sea caves. The route passes through the community of St. Paul's, then leaves the park north of Shallow Bay, with its extensive sand dunes and beaches.

In the southern part of the park, a car ferry links the north and south shores of Bonne Bay. From the ferry dock at Woody Point, *Highway 431* heads through a deep gully that separates the green forested hills and the barren yellow rock of the Tablelands plateau. Visible from the Tablelands viewpoint is the U-shaped valley of Winterhouse Brook. The road leads to the fishing community of Trout River and the day-use area and campground near Trout River Pond, one of the park's four "fjord ponds."

Hiking

Trails lead to representative areas of the park's diverse terrain—coast-line, coastal plain, forests, and the alpine tundra atop the Long Range Mountains.

Walking the entire 11-mi/18-km *Green Gardens Trail* south of Bonne Bay makes a varied and scenic day trip. Hikers start at the Long Pond (western) trailhead off Highway 431. The trail starts about 5 mi/8 km northwest of the parking lot for the Tablelands exhibit, climbs a barren hill to a rock cairn with views of glacially carved Trout River Gulch to the east. Take the left fork and descend stairs through stunted spruces, firs, and tamaracks that gradually reach normal height approaching the coast.

The route breaks out of the forest into a field that marks the beginning of the Green Gardens. For generations, the people of Trout River pastured their livestock in this series of clifftop coastal meadows. Past the campsite, stairs descend to the beach. To the north is a headland of lavas that formed in a tropical sea 480 million years ago. At low tide, clamber northeast around the headland and cross a tidal terrace to see a large sea cave. Southwest of the headland are seastacks and gray and reddish cliffs of lava. Past one seastack a stream tumbles onto the cobble beach in a waterfall.

At this point, day-trippers retrace their steps to the parking lot, making a four-hour outing. Hikers who want to camp overnight press on, enjoying terrific coastal scenery and alternating forest and meadow environments. Beyond a second campsite in the largest "Green Garden" the trail climbs a

The trees along this sand dune have been stunted by wind. The park's coastline offers

steep ridge, then descends to a sheltered campsite at the mouth of Wallace Brook. The last leg heads south up the forested ravine carved by the brook and back to Highway 431. Footbridges along this section have deteriorated, but at low water Wallace Brook can be forded easily on steppingstones. Check with park officials for trail conditions.

Two trails start near the junction of Highway 431 and the road to the Lomond campground. The *Stuckless Pond Trail* loops 4.6 mi/7.5 km east of the Lomond River up through thick forest to a quiet inland lake. One branch of the *Lomond River Trail* leads fishermen to upstream salmon pools; the other goes 2.8 mi/4.5 km downstream through one of the park's rare hardwood stands, past Lomond River estuary viewpoints and an old sawmill operation, and ends near the Lomond campground.

The 5-mi/8-km *James Callaghan Trail*, the park's best-known hike, ascends Gros Morne. The trailhead is on Highway 430, 1.8 mi/3 km southeast of the park's visitors' center near Rocky Harbour. The gradual hour-long ascent to the base of the mountain is suitable for all ages. The steep scramble to the summit is far more demanding.

Soon after leaving the highway the trail crosses Crow Gulch Brook, then climbs up the side of the valley through stands of speckled alder and moun-

periwinkles, sea urchins, volcanic sea-stacks, and caves.

tain maple. The trail heads northeast up Ferry Gulch; a short side trip here leads to several active beaver ponds. The main trail crosses Ferry Gulch Brook, then forks at the base of a scree slope. The left branch crosses the scree and ascends the gully.

Glorious views await on the plateau atop Gros Morne. The trail, marked with stone borders and cairns, angles northeast across the windy, exposed plateau. Quartzite rock shattered by frost forms an extensive felsenmeer (German for "sea of rock"). Species to watch for include arctic hare, American pipit, horned lark, and—in the gullies—rock ptarmigan. Caribou sightings on the plateau and in Ferry Gulch have increased in recent years, especially in May and June.

At the northern rim of the plateau, the land drops away sharply into the gorge containing Ten Mile Pond. Waterfalls veil some of the valleys "hanging" high on granite cliffs. The trail descends the eastern flank of Gros Morne, then heads southwest down Ferry Gulch back to the highway. The walk takes about eight hours.

Several short trails are clustered around the Berry Hill campground. Hour-long *Berry Hill Trail* spirals around "The Hummock" for views of the coastal lowland and the Long Range. *Berry Hill Pond Trail* connects different sections of the campground as it circles a beaver pond; a beaver dam parallels the footbridge on the west side of the pond. *Bakers Brook Falls Trail* crosses wildflower-covered wetlands, leads through woods (the haunt of moose and beavers), and winds along Bakers Brook to a series of impressive waterfalls, the largest in the park by volume. This makes a fine morning outing with lunch at the falls.

The hour-long *Western Brook Pond Trail,* which heads east from Highway 430 to the tour-boat dock, is the best way to explore the coastal lowland (boardwalks span boggy sections). Bakeapples, pitcher plants, and beautiful orchids grow in these wetlands, and it's a good area for spotting moose and beavers. At the boat dock, a spur trail parallels the shoreline south to a fine sandy beach. A second spur trail leads north to a bridge over Western Brook, then continues 3.1 mi/5 km east along the north shore of Western Brook Pond. The trail ends at Snug Harbour, where a primitive campsite is located at the base of the cliffs rimming the pond.

For experienced backpackers, unmarked plateau routes are Gros Morne's ultimate hiking challenge. The *North Rim Route* climbs east from Snug Harbour 2,130 ft/650 m up onto plateau cliffs north of Western Brook Pond (one campsite is along the way). Some backpackers take the tour boat to the campsite at the end of the pond, scramble up out of the gorge onto the plateau, then hike south on the *Long Range Route* to Gros Morne, where they pick up the James Callaghan Trail heading down to Highway 430. This traverse requires four or five days.

Other popular routes include a challenging one-day climb from the town of Woody Point up *Lookout Mountain* (1,968 ft/600 m), with its views north to the lighthouse at Lobster Cove Head, south to the Tablelands, and southwest to the Green Gardens escarpment rising sheer from the sea.

Boating

Powerboats are permitted on Trout River Pond, the only fjord lake accessible by car (Highway 431); a boat ramp is located in the day-use area. Boaters on Bonne Bay use launches at Winterhouse Brook, south of Woody Point, and at Lomond. Gros Morne's most popular attraction is the 2.5-hour boat tour of Western Brook Pond, offered three times daily from mid-June to mid-September.

The scenery rivals that of Jasper's Maligne Lake. Waterfalls leap from 2,000-ft/610-m cliffs and turn to mist before reaching shoreline rocks; winds funneled by the stark cliff faces whip up whitecaps. An eerie, otherworldly feeling arises during the cruise down the sinuous gorge into the wilderness heart of the park.

Fishing

Bonne Bay yields such saltwater species as cod, haddock, flounder, and Atlantic mackerel, along with Atlantic salmon and sea-going brook trout. Deer Arm Brook and the Lomond River provide the park's best river fishing for salmon and brook trout. Salmon quotas vary from year to year on the Lomond River. Fishing for brook trout is moderately good in Mitchell's, Bakers, and Wallace brooks.

Swimming

The warmest water in the park (57° F/14° C) is in the north at Shallow Bay, where a magnificent beach arcs between Belldowns Point and Lower Head. There's also relatively warm water and a small beach at the Lomond day-use area on Bonne Bay. Both locations have change houses; Lomond has outdoor showers. Elsewhere, the ocean generally is not safe for swimming. For freshwater try Trout River Pond and the indoor pool at the Gros Morne Recreation Complex near park headquarters in Rocky Harbour.

Cross-country Skiing

The best conditions are in the Southeast Hills, where the season extends well into April. From Highway 430, just north of Wiltondale, the *Wigwam Pond–Stuckless Pond Trail* is a half-day outing. The route heads 7.8 mi/ 12.5 km west in the East Lomond River valley to Island House Pond, where moose often winter. It continues on to Stuckless Pond, angles southwest, spans the Lomond River on an old bridge, crosses a bog, and ends up at Highway 431. From there, skiers join the *Lomond River Trail* and glide 2.5 mi/4 km through deep and silent woods down to the warming shelter at Lomond campground.

Burridges Gulch, where moose winter, provides access to unmarked ski-touring routes atop the *Tablelands* plateau. The open, windswept base of the Tablelands is also a popular off-trail touring area, although avalanches pose an occasional hazard. Near the coast, there are easy trails at the *visitors' center, Berry Hill,* and *Shallow Bay.* The *Western Brook Pond Trail* also is open to skiers.

EXPLORING THE PARK

Gros Morne is 75 mi/120 km north of Corner Brook, the province's second-largest city, via the Trans-Canada Highway (Highway 1) and Highway 430. Car and passenger ferries from North Sydney, Nova Scotia, dock at Chan-

nel-Port aux Basques, about a six-hour drive south of the park. Air Nova, Air Canada's regional affiliate (800-776-3000) has six flights a week to Deer Lake, 19 mi/30 km from the park entrance. Woody Point, Rocky Harbour, and Cow Head, all adjacent to the park, have motels, guest houses, private campgrounds, stores, and other services for travelers. Facilities are more limited in other communities.

The visitors' center at Rocky Harbour is open year-round (709-458-2066). The summer interpretive program includes one- to three-hour guided walks to the Tablelands, Green Point, Lobster Cove Head, and along the Western Brook Pond Trail. An exhibit in the Lobster Cove Head Lighthouse interprets the 4,500-year history of the west coast with text, photos, and artifacts. At Broom Point, ex-fishermen tell the story of the inshore fishery, leading visitors through a typical fisherman's summer house and a restored equipment warehouse, known on the island as a "fish store."

The source for reservations, prices, and departure times for cruises on Western Brook Pond is Bontours (709-458-2730). This outfitter also cruises Bonne Bay. Two other outfits operate on a more or less regular basis in summer. Norm Martin organizes charters on Bonne Bay (709-453-2361). Seal Island Boat Tours (709-243-2376) circles St. Paul's Inlet. Mitours (709-783-2455), based in Corner Brook, makes bookings with local guides in Norris Point for sea kayak trips on St. Paul's Inlet, Trout River Pond, and Bonne Bay, where there is the possibility of paddling alongside whales during capelin runs in early summer.

ACCOMMODATIONS: Berry Hill campground (156 sites), on a wooded hillside north of Rocky Harbour, includes five secluded walk-in sites. Lomond campground (29 sites), which occupies a grassy field sloping down to the East Arm of Bonne Bay, attracts boaters and fishermen. Trout River campground (30 sites) makes a good base for boating and fishing on the pond and for exploring the nearby Tablelands. Green Point (18 sites), north of Rocky Harbour, is pocketed by forest and faces the sea. Shallow Bay (51 sites) is beside a long, curving beach backed by dunes and grassy meadows.

ADDRESSES: For more information, contact: The Superintendent, Gros Morne National Park, Box 130, Rocky Harbour, Nfld. A0K 4N0; 709-458-2417.

BOOKS: Keith Nicol, *Best Hiking Trails in Western Newfoundland.* St. John's, Nfld.: Breakwater Books, 1987. Includes maps and trail descriptions of some 20 hikes, including four in Gros Morne.

Rangifer caribou, part of the wildlife found at Gros Morne National Park.

THE NORTH

KLUANE NATIONAL PARK RESERVE 324

Canada's highest mountains, vast icefields, and hundreds of glaciers fill this southwestern corner of the Yukon, sanctuary for Dall's sheep and the country's greatest concentration of grizzlies.

NAHANNI NATIONAL PARK RESERVE 338

The South Nahanni River twists through forbidding canyons and thunders over Virginia Falls in this roadless preserve in the Northwest Territories.

AUYUITTUQ NATIONAL PARK RESERVE 352

Jagged peaks, broad U-shaped valleys, fjords, and a massive ice cap make this back-of-beyond wilderness park straddling the Arctic Circle on the east coast of Baffin Island one of Canada's most spectacular.

NORTHERN WILDLANDS 366

NORTHERN YUKON NATIONAL PARK: Mountains, spruce forests, broad valleys, tundra, and Arctic seacoast form a rich habitat for vast herds of migratory caribou, grizzlies, polar bears, Dall's sheep, and wolves. **BANKS ISLAND BIRD SANCTUARIES:** On the westernmost of the Arctic islands, these twin sanctuaries shelter thousands of snow geese, eiders, and old-squaws, as well as muskoxen, caribou, and wolves. **WOOD BUFFALO NATIONAL PARK:** Canada's largest park, a wilderness of boreal plains, muskeg, forest, and broad rivers, protects more than a million migratory birds, the world's largest bison herd, and the only nesting site of the endangered whooping crane. **BATHURST INLET:** Surrounding this drowned rift valley on Coronation Gulf are stark uplands where peregrines and other migratory birds nest, and rolling tundra that is home to caribou, muskoxen, and wolves. **THELON GAME SANCTUARY:** Canoeists exploring the raging rivers in this wild, uninhabited portion of the Barren Grounds encounter muskoxen, grizzlies, caribou, moose, and wolves. **POLAR**

BEAR PASS NATIONAL WILDLIFE AREA: One of the largest concentrations of mammals and birds in the high Arctic congregates here on Bathurst Island, including 53 species of birds, muskoxen, arctic fox, and polar bears that migrate through in spring and fall. **ELLESMERE ISLAND NATIONAL PARK RESERVE:** At the tip of Canada's northernmost island lies a fierce wilderness realm of fjords, tundra, mountains buried under a perpetual shroud of ice, and an oasis of plant and animal life encircling the largest lake north of the Arctic Circle. **BYLOT ISLAND BIRD SANCTUARY:** Thousands of murres and kittiwakes nest on vertical shoreline cliffs and polar bears patrol frigid seas surrounding this desolate realm of glacier-mantled peaks and sprawling icefields off the tip of Baffin Island.

KLUANE NATIONAL PARK RESERVE

THIS VAST WILDERNESS PARK—at 8,500 sq mi/22,000 sq km more than half the size of Switzerland—is tucked into the southwest corner of the Yukon. In the northeastern third of Kluane (Kloo-AH-nee), the Kluane Ranges sweep upward 8,000 ft/2,400 m from the broad Shakwak Valley. These imposing ramparts hold the greatest array of large mammals in North America. Moose, caribou, grizzlies, black bears, Dall's sheep and mountain goats thrive amid spruce forests, braided rivers, mountain-walled lakes, and high-country meadows.

In the southwestern two-thirds of the park, just 40 mi/65 km from the Pacific Ocean, soar the Icefield Ranges, North America's highest chain (surpassed only by the single massif of Alaska's Mt. McKinley). Ten peaks exceed 15,000 ft/4,500 m, and the highest, Mt. Logan, is 19,524 ft/5,951 m. Mantling these summits is the world's largest nonpolar icefield, from which radiate more than 2,000 glaciers. From the air the region looks like a sea of snow-covered ice punctuated by jagged islands of rock.

GEOLOGY

Two ranges of the St. Elias Mountains running northwest–southeast dominate the landscape: the Kluane Ranges on the park's eastern boundary and the interior Icefield Ranges, which are twice as high. The mountains are underlaid by five crustal blocks, or plates, bounded by faults that extend from the Alaska Panhandle to eastern Alaska. Shifting blocks give the southwest Yukon more earthquakes than any other part of Canada except the Queen Charlotte Islands off the coast of British Columbia.

Sixty million to 20 million years ago, these blocks were above sea level, except near the coast of Alaska. Rivers flowed in broad valleys through a gently rolling landscape. Lush vegetation thrived in a warm, perhaps subtropical climate. Then, about 10 million years ago, the St. Elias peaks began to rise. As the landscape of today's park took shape, the climate cooled with the onset of Pleistocene glaciations.

Much of Kluane's present topography was carved during the most recent glaciation, which began about 25,000 years ago. Valley glaciers in the Kluane Ranges flowed into the Shakwak Valley, partially filling it before shrinking to their present size by about 9,800 years ago. The Icefield

Ranges, however, survive in the current interglacial period. The park's largest glacier is 40-mi-/65-km-long Lowell Glacier.

HISTORY

The oldest archaeological site in the park is an obsidian quarry near the Kaskawulsh River Valley, where crude weapons and implements were made some 5,000 years ago. During this period of postglacial warmth, extensive grasslands supported large-horned bison and other grazers. Forerunners of today's Southern Tutchone moved camps frequently, following game.

Within a millennium the climate cooled. Spruce forests expanded at the expense of grasslands, restricting the range of grazers. About 3,000 years ago, habitat loss and hunting pressure had exterminated large-horned bison and other Ice Age megafauna. By A.D. 1000 the forest had expanded to its present extent.

Vitus Bering recorded the first European visit to this area in 1741, naming what he thought was the highest peak in the coastal mountains Mt. St. Elias. In 1890 guide Jack Dalton and journalist E. J. Glave explored what is now the park. Dalton returned in 1896 and blazed the Chilkat Trail between Haines, Alaska, and the Yukon River. Haines Road now follows much of Dalton's route.

The Kluane Gold Rush began in 1898 at Shorty Creek near Dalton's Post. Soon prospectors were staking claims on creeks farther north around Kluane Lake, including Bullion and Sheep creeks within what is now the park. For all the frenzy, Kluane creeks yielded only about $70,000 in gold.

During World War II, fears of a Japanese invasion spurred construction of the Alaska Highway to transport military supplies between Dawson Creek, British Columbia, and Fairbanks, Alaska. This awesome engineering feat normally would have taken five years. Work began in March 1942 and was completed just nine months later. The isolated Yukon of the sourdough and trapper finally was linked to the outside world by road.

HABITATS

The Kluane Ranges harbor perhaps the greatest variety of plants and animals in the Canadian North. White spruce dominates the montane forest of valley bottoms and lower mountain slopes, with stands of quaking aspen and balsam poplar. Dwarf birch and crowberry grow in damp areas. Wild sweet pea and soapberry, favorite late-summer bear food, thrive in river gravels and other coarse, well-drained soils. Bluegrass, wheat-grass, and prairie sagewort form patchwork prairie in some valley bottoms.

Lords of the backcountry, Kluane's 250 grizzlies range from valley bottoms to alpine tundra, especially in the Slims River Valley and around Kathleen and Mush lakes. About a hundred black bears remain in montane forests year-round, yielding ground in encounters with the larger grizzlies.

The world's largest subspecies of moose, which weighs up to 1,800 lb/815 kg, frequents the shores of Dezadeash, Kathleen, and Sockeye lakes in the southern part of the park. Most of Kluane's 500 moose migrate vertically, spending the summer feeding on subalpine willows, dwarf birch, and alder, then wintering in valleys.

Moose provide about half the food intake of Kluane's 50-odd gray wolves. These predators round out their diet with arctic ground squirrels, snowshoe hares, and the occasional Dall's sheep and mountain goat. The largest wolf pack in the park roams the forests around Dezadeash and Kathleen lakes. Populations of snowshoe hares, which are the main prey of the lynx, rise and fall in synchronous 10-year cycles over the animal's entire range, from North America to Siberia to northern Europe.

In lower elevations of the subalpine zone, which extends between 3,300 to 5,000 ft/1,000 to 1,500 m, are scattered stands of white spruce and tall shrubs, mainly willow, dwarf birch, and alder. In June and July wildflowers in these regions—columbine, monkshood, and larkspur—are spectacular, especially in meadows around St. Elias Lake.

Above the subalpine zone, extending to the permanent snow line, is alpine tundra, where tiny mosses, lichens, and herbs hug the ground, sheltered in places by ankle-high evergreens. In shaded basins where snow lingers all summer, hardy rushes, buttercups, mountain sorrel, and purple mountain saxifrage survive despite the brief growing season. Meltwater from these snow basins nurtures rich growths of sedges and colorful swatches of valerian and spring beauty.

Few birds live year-round in the North, but three kinds of ptarmigans—white-tailed, rock, and willow—winter over in Kluane's high country. American pipits, the most abundant species here, lesser golden-plovers, yellowlegs, and wandering tattlers nest in wet areas. Tattlers, named for their noisy protests when intruders approach a nest, winter on Pacific islands, then return to the same patch of streamside dwarf willow that they left eight months earlier.

On rocky pinnacles above the tundra nest rare peregrine falcons and gyrfalcons. Golden eagles, the park's most abundant raptor, may be seen most summer days above the Alsek and Slims valleys. These birds engage in spirited dogfights—diving, rolling, and climbing without collision.

Dall's sheep, Kluane's most abundant mammal, graze peacefully near Slims River. Bands of these snow-white animals can be seen year-round.

Kluane contains the Yukon's greatest concentration of Dall's sheep, with a population of 4,400. A herd of about 200 animals grazes primarily on sage at Sheep Mountain, northwest of Haines Junction on the Alaska Highway. This is one of the few places in Canada where Dall's sheep are regularly visible from a road.

Mountain goats replace Dall's sheep in southern park habitats. Unlike sheep, which migrate seasonally between elevations, goats usually remain at high altitudes year-round.

OUTDOOR ACTIVITIES

Except for 150 mi/240 km of trails and old mining roads that lead into and beyond the Kluane Ranges, little backcountry development exists. Wilderness on such a grand scale is found in few North American parks.

Hiking

There are three kinds of trails in the unglaciated eastern third of the park: short nature trails just off Haines Road and the Alaska Highway; longer posted day-use trails; and unmarked backcountry "routes" that require topographical maps, a compass, and considerable hiking experience. A park brochure outlines the general direction of these overland routes, which typically follow such natural highways as streambeds and valleys. Check with park personnel for specific directions.

The *St. Elias Lake Trail*, 36 mi/58 km southwest of Haines Junction on Haines Road, offers a pleasant three-hour round-trip to a small lake set in an amphitheater. Common loons nest here; mountain goats haunt surrounding cliffs. A primitive campsite is on the lakeshore.

North of the St. Elias Lake Trail is the 53-mi/85-km *Cottonwood Trail*, a popular horseshoe-shaped backcountry hike that circles the Dalton Range. Most people make this a four-night, five-day outing starting at the Kathleen Lake campground and hiking counterclockwise. The trail heads southwest along the southern shore of Kathleen Lake on the old Jehobo Mine road. The thick montane forest here is excellent grizzly habitat, as revealed by copious trailside scat.

The route then curves south and ascends the backside of the Dalton Range in the pleasant, open valley of Cottonwood Creek. En route to Dalton Pass the trail crosses alpine tundra abloom with wildflowers in June and July. Willow ptarmigan hereabouts often remain motionless and unseen in subalpine shrubs until hikers are close by, then explode into the air with a heart-stopping racket.

While descending from the pass, hikers enjoy superb views of the wide mountain valley that cradles Mush and Bates lakes. The trail then goes east on an old mining road in the Alder Creek Valley, a favorite moose habitat. A rigorous side trip heads north up Shorty Creek, climbing 2,000 ft/610 m in about 4 mi/6.5 km. Views down the valley to Mush Lake are superb and hikers pass abandoned gold-mining equipment along the way. The trail ends at Haines Road, 15 mi/25 km south of the Kathleen Lake campground.

The *Auriol Trail*, 4.5 mi/7 km south of Haines Junction, climbs steadily but gently 9 mi/15 km through the montane, subalpine, and alpine zones. Upslope from the primitive campground at the trail's highest point looms one of the park's many rock glaciers, which consist of icy lobes covered with an insulating layer of frost-shattered rock. At several points on this five-hour trip are superb views of the Shakwak Valley.

Starting in Haines Junction, the *Dezadeash River Trail* winds 2.5 mi/4 km along the park's only nonglacial river. Moose, muskrats, mallards, teal, and belted kingfishers can be seen in a marshy section.

The *Alsek Trail*, 8 mi/13 km north of Haines Junction, is a relatively easy 18-mi/29-km hike on an old mining road over grassland, across creeks, gravel washes, and alluvial fans, and through stands of spruce and poplar, eventually emerging onto the wide valley bottom. The trail follows the west bank of the Dezadeash River, curls around the southern flank of Mt. Archibald, and ends at Sugden Creek. There are often sightings of moose, black bears, Dall's sheep, mountain goats, trumpeter swans, and eagles. Gravel ridges visible on lower mountain slopes are ancient beaches of lakes created when Lowell Glacier, about 25 mi/40 km south, surged to the foot of Goatherd Mountain and dammed the Alsek River. The Lowell has surged across the valley at least five times in the past; the last surge was in 1725. About 60 Kluane glaciers experience such spectacular movement for a few months every 50 to 100 years.

Two routes in the Slims River valley lead to the terminus of Kaskawulsh Glacier, the park's most accessible glacier. The *Slims River East Route* begins 41 mi/66 km northwest of Haines Junction and heads 13 mi/21 km south to the glacier. Most people make this a three-day outing, camping in the first 8 mi/13 km, then making a day trip to the toe of Kaskawulsh.

The more popular *Slims River West Route* follows the other riverbank to the same destination. The trail head is at the warden's cabin and parking

OVERLEAF: *Measuring 6,050 meters at its summit, Mt. Logan is Canada's highest peak. Much of Kluane is covered by mile-deep icefields, and the park offers many challenges for skilled mountaineers, whose carefully planned expeditions must be approved by the park superintendent.*

area 1.5 mi/2.5 km west of the highway on an abandoned section of the Alaska Highway. Hikers must ford Sheep Creek, Bullion Creek, and Canada Creek, where there is a primitive campsite north of the glacier terminus.

About five minutes into the Slims River West, a signpost for *Sheep Creek Road* directs hikers on an interesting side trip. A moderately difficult 4-mi/6.4-km ascent through montane forest leads to a meadow from which Dall's sheep usually are seen on nearby Sheep Mountain.

A second side trip, the *Sheep–Bullion Plateau Trail*, starts just after the trail crosses Sheep Creek. There, a signpost directs hikers northwest along the west bank of the creek. After a steep two-hour climb, the trail emerges above the tree line and levels off on the Sheep–Bullion Plateau, affording views of Slims Valley, Kaskawulsh Glacier to the south, and Vulcan Mountain's alpine glaciers across the valley. Some hikers make this a day trip and return the same way. Others camp on the plateau, then return to the valley via Bullion Creek to the southwest.

A backcountry route takes hikers northwest from the plateau, over the pass at the head of Sheep Creek, and down Congdon Creek to the Alaska Highway. This wedge-shaped route ends up about 10 mi/16 km northwest of Sheep Mountain. An even more demanding unmarked route continues northwest from the Sheep–Bullion Plateau, down Dickson Creek, and north in the Duke River valley to the highway. This week-long hike ends up about 40 mi/64 km northwest of Sheep Mountain.

Mountain Biking

Trails include the *Mush–Bates Lake* section of the Cottonwood Trail, the *Alsek Trail*, and the *Slims River Trail (East and West)*.

Climbing

Kluane is one of the few parks in North America where climbers mount high-altitude expeditions. The most popular summits are Mt. Logan (19,850 ft/6,050 m) and, to its north, Mt. Steele (16,644 ft/5,073 m). Climbs occasionally are made in the mounts Kennedy–Alverstone–Hubbard area southeast of Logan. Expeditions generally take 10 to 20 days. Walks into Mt. Logan can include 65 mi/105 km of glacier travel.

The more accessible Kluane Ranges provide alpinists with 6,000 ft/1,800 m of climbable relief in a series of peaks with good potential for ridge walking. The preferred routes are to the Auriol Range via the Auriol Trail; Mt. Archibald, a twin-peaked summit northwest of Haines Junction; and Vulcan Mountain overlooking the Slims Valley.

Horseback Riding

Two outfitters operate Kluane trail rides. Mabel's Yukon Trail Rides (403-634-2386) offers outings in the southern half of Kluane twice daily, usually along the Mush–Bates Lake, Quill Creek, and Alsek trails. Ruby Range Adventure (403-667-7790) conducts rides in the northern park, including trips on the Slims River East Trail to Kaskawulsh Glacier, and in the Duke and Donjek valleys.

Boating

It is prohibited except on Kathleen Lake, where there is a launch. Boating waters near the park include Kluane, Dezadeash, and Rainbow lakes.

Canoeing

Canoeists on Yukon lakes must always stay close to shore. Winds are frequently high and even in midsummer a dunking in the frigid water may result in hypothermia. Paddlers with four-wheel-drive vehicles transport canoes on the old Mush–Bates Lake mining road to a primitive campsite at the east end of *Mush Lake*. They canoe down the lake, skirt a small waterfall on a five-minute portage, and continue south on *Bates Lake*. This makes a pleasant week-long backcountry outing.

The put-in for the canoe route on the *Kathleen River* is outside the park just north of the Kathleen Lake campground at Upper Rainbow Lake. The river broadens into Lower Rainbow Lake, then flows north to its confluence with the Dezadeash River west of Haines Junction. This 10-hour trip, which is for experienced canoeists only, includes several Class III and Class IV rapids and two half-hour portages. The put-in for the longer *Dezadeash River* route is 17 mi/28 km farther south at the northern end of Dezadeash Lake. This four-day paddle swings northeast, then heads west alongside the Alaska Highway to Haines Junction. The river has long stretches of Class I and Class II currents and numerous blind channels that end in piles of driftwood.

Rafting

Several outfitters offer trips down the *Tatshenshini* and the *Alsek*, which some people consider to be Canada's premiere wilderness rafting rivers. The Alsek flows 56 mi/90 km south through Kluane, then continues another 100 mi/160 km across northwestern British Columbia and the Alaska panhandle before emptying into the Pacific at Dry Bay, Alaska. Most outfitters put in at Haines Junction and float down the Dezadeash to its confluence with the Alsek, then head south through the park to just above Turnback

Tinged pink by the sun, Kluane National Park Reserve hosts some of North America's finest wildlife populations, as well as the greatest diversity of birds north of the 60th parallel, and a wide variety of plants.

Canyon in northern British Columbia. There, helicopters portage river runners and gear below the canyon's virtually impassable rapids so rafters can continue down to Dry Bay. Rafting outfitters also put in at Dalton Post and float down the Tatshenshini River to its confluence with the Alsek south of Turnback Canyon, thereby avoiding the nearly unnavigable gorge.

Fishing

There is excellent fishing in and near the park. Separate licenses for Kluane and Territorial waters can be purchased at the Reception Centre, the Sheep Mountain information kiosk, and at local businesses.

Lake trout is the most widely distributed game fish, occurring in all major lakes. Kathleen Lake also contains arctic grayling and sockeye, or kokanee, salmon. Sockeye salmon also are taken from the Tatshenshini River. Dezadeash Lake yields arctic grayling, whitefish, lake trout, and northern pike. Rainbow trout are found in the Kathleen River and Rainbow Lakes.

Winter Activities

The best conditions for *cross-country skiing* are in March and early April. Trails include *Dezadeash, Auriol, Quill Creek, Cottonwood,* and *St. Elias.*

Most trails are packed or track-set. *Mountain ski touring* attracts about two dozen adventurers each year. They fly to the Mt. Logan area and to the south arm of the Kaskawulsh Glacier for seven- to 10-day mountain ski tours. The best weather for this activity is in May and June. *Snowmobiling* is permitted only on the frozen surface of Kathleen Lake from December to April.

EXPLORING THE PARK

Kluane is 100 mi/160 km northwest of Whitehorse, capital of the Yukon Territory. Most visitors come via the Alaska Highway (Highway 1). Park headquarters are in Haines Junction. Visitors from Haines, Alaska, take Haines Road (Highway 7 in Alaska; Highway 3 in the Yukon) 165 mi/265 km north to Haines Junction. In summer North West Stage Lines (Box 4932, Whitehorse, Yukon Y1A 4S2; 403-668-7240) offers bus service to Haines Junction from Whitehorse.

Nonhikers who want to see the interior of the park charter planes at Burwash Landing northwest of Haines Junction on the Alaska Highway. Glacier Air Tours (Box 4146 GTB, Whitehorse, Yukon Y1A 3S6; 403-668-7323 in Whitehorse or 403-841-5171 in Burwash Landing) flies to Mt. Logan and other peaks in the Icefield Ranges.

Boat fishing on Kathleen Lake may yield lake trout, arctic grayling, rainbow trout, kokanee, and other fish, for Kluane is an Indian word meaning "place of many fish." More remote fishing spots include Mush, Bates, and Onion lakes; rivers also provide excellent catches.

The park offers free guided interpretive hikes in summer to Sheep Mountain, the Dezadeash River, the Auriol Ranges, Kathleen Lake, and other destinations. The hikes range in length from one to seven hours.

Hikers staying overnight in the park must register at the Haines Junction Reception Centre or at the Sheep Mountain information center. Bear canisters for storing food are mandatory for hikes in the Slims River valley and are recommended elsewhere. The hard plastic cylinders, which weigh about 2 lb/1 kg and fit inside most packs, are loaned at no charge at the Reception Centre and at Sheep Mountain.

Mountain climbers must register at least three months in advance, detailing the experience and physical fitness of expedition members, along with arrangements for air and radio support. The minimum group size is four. Icefield Ranges Expeditions (59 13th St., Whitehorse, Yukon Y1A 4K6; 403-841-4561 in summer and 403-633-2018 in winter) flies in supplies and climbers on fixed-wing aircraft from Haines Junction. Trans-North Air (Box 5311, Haines Junction, Yukon Y0B 1L0; 403-634-2242; in Whitehorse, 403-668-2177) offers the same services by helicopter.

ACCOMMODATIONS: The park's only campground is at Kathleen Lake (41 sites). Eight Territorial campgrounds are scattered along Haines Road and the Alaska Highway. Accommodations, restaurants, private campgrounds, and other facilities are adjacent to the park in Haines Junction, Destruction Bay, and Burwash Landing, as well as at lodges alongside the highways.

ADDRESSES: For more information, write or phone: The Superintendent, Kluane National Park Reserve, Haines Junction, Yukon Y0B 1L0; 403-634-2251, or Tourism Yukon, Box 2703, Whitehorse, Yukon Y1A 2C6; 403-667-5340.

BOOKS: John Theberge, *Kluane: Pinnacle of the Yukon.* Toronto: Doubleday, 1980. Now out of print; check libraries.

Walter A. Wood, *A History of Mountaineering in the St. Elias Mountains.* Banff: Alpine Club of Canada, 1967. For mountaineers. Now out of print; the Alpine Club of Canada (Box 1026, Banff, Alta. T0L 0C0; 403-762-4481) produces photocopies for a small fee.

Omnivorous grizzly bears feed on plants, roots, fungi, berries, insects, mammals, and carrion, and can catch fish with a swift snap of their huge jaws. When salmon spawn, bears establish dominance among themselves through size and threats, the more aggressive individuals taking the choicest fishing spots.

NAHANNI NATIONAL PARK RESERVE

LOCATED IN THE MOUNTAINOUS southwest corner of the Northwest Territories, this wilderness park protects the lower two-thirds of the South Nahanni River and the lower half of its principal tributary, the Flat River. The South Nahanni has long inspired legends as wild and mysterious as the river itself. At one time, tales abounded of the area's gigantic "mountain men," murdered prospectors, lost gold mines, and tropical valleys.

Those who paddle the remote and powerful river find myths dispelled by an even more remarkable reality: hot springs; a limestone plateau riddled with caves and sinkholes; cliff faces shattered by frost into clusters of isolated pinnacles; and the deepest canyons in all Canada.

The centerpiece is Virginia Falls, at the halfway point of the South Nahanni's journey through the park. In a thundering prelude to the waterfall, the river boils between eroded limestone cliffs in a steep stretch of white water called the Sluice Box. After rounding a tight bend, the South Nahanni slams into a pillar of rock, sending up billowing clouds of mist where a rainbow hangs suspended above the churning foam. The south side of the river, launched over a limestone ridge, flares out in a broad sheet and plunges 294 ft/89 m. The narrower north channel curls around the pillar, then tumbles 170 ft/52 m down a steep staircase of ledges. Nearly twice the height of Niagara, Virginia Falls is a scenic wonder of the Canadian North.

GEOLOGY

Erosion produced the park's most impressive geological features. The South Nahanni River originates in the glaciers and icefields of the Ragged Range of the Selwyn Mountains, close to the Yukon Territory, then angles southeastward, flowing some 240 mi/385 km through the park. En route to its confluence with the Liard River, the South Nahanni severs the spines of successive north–south ranges in the Mackenzie Mountains—the Caribou, the Funeral, and the Headless—carving deep canyons along the way.

The riverine breach in these ranges results from a geological phenomenon called antecedence: that is, the river is older than the mountains through which it flows. As the Selwyn and Mackenzie chains were thrust up some 65 million years ago, the South Nahanni maintained its ancient course by cutting through the soft uplifted sedimentary rock.

The result is a string of gorges in the southeastern half of the park, each one deeper than the last. Named by explorers lining and poling their boats upriver, the canyons seem to be in reverse order to paddlers heading downstream. The first is called Five-Mile Canyon, also known as Painted Canyon for its walls ribboned with brilliant orange and yellow hues caused by oxidation of iron in the rocks. The gorge was excavated by the upriver migration of Virginia Falls, a process that will eventually reduce the mighty cataract to a series of rapids.

Some 25 mi/40 km downriver, the South Nahanni flows between the 1,400-ft/425-m shale ramparts of the Third Canyon, at the center of which stands Pulpit Rock. This isolated pinnacle guards The Gate, a hairpin turn that is—surprisingly—unruffled by rapids. Second Canyon is a 2,500-ft/760-m cross-section of the layered-limestone Headless Range.

The river flows through a wide oval depression called Deadmen Valley, then gathers speed as it approaches First Canyon, the most awesome chasm along the South Nahanni. Riverside cliffs rise straight up 3,000 ft/915 m: layer upon layer of dolomite, topped by limestone that soars even higher, ending in a craggy crest.

Scattered along the length of the park are other geologic wonders. The intrusion of magma that formed the Ragged Range still fires park hot springs. The thermal waters of Rabbitkettle Hotsprings are rich in dissolved minerals, chiefly calcium carbonate. As springwater seeps outward, minerals precipitate and harden into tufa, a porous rock that forms coral-colored circular terraces. The larger of Rabbitkettle's two tufa mounds is a stepped tower almost 90 ft/27 m high and 230 ft/70 m across. A pool of clear, warm water is neatly centered on the topmost terrace.

Glaciers in the early Pleistocene era stripped the shale mantle off the Nahanni Plateau north of First Canyon, exposing the softer underlying limestone. The region escaped subsequent glaciation—a rare occurrence this far north—so that the plateau has been exposed to 300,000 years of water falling onto and percolating through and dissolving the porous limestone. The result is a karstland populated by caves, sinkholes, arches, rock towers, and labyrinths of deep corridors formed along fault lines and fissures.

Tucked away on a forested mountain slope in the southwestern corner of the park is another geological oddity, a tiny desertscape that the Slavey named *Nintzi Enda*—"live wind." Rain and wind have sculpted soft sandstone into arches, pedestals, and pillars in shades of ivory, pink, amber, and mauve. Settlers dubbed it the Devil's Kitchen; today's maps label it the Sand Blowouts. Wind-rounded sandstone orbs scattered over the Blowouts' floor of fine white sand range in size from marbles to baseballs.

Monumental and austere, a mountain of shale in the Nahanni Valley shoulders its way into the mist. Sandstone, shale, and limestone dominate the park's naturally dissected mountains. OPPOSITE: Virginia Falls, the most spectacular undeveloped waterfall in North America, shows a face of almost two vertical hectares of water.

HISTORY

Three native groups lived in the region before the arrival of the Europeans. The Slavey lived in the Mackenzie Lowlands east of what is now the park. The Mackenzie and Selwyn chains were shared by the Mountain, or Goat, Indians and a less populous group called the Kaska, known to the Slavey as the *Nah'aa*—"the people over there far away."

Although related culturally and linguistically, the groups had infrequent contact. The nomadic Slavey traveled extensively over well-defined areas in small family groups, fishing, trapping beaver and snowshoe hare, and hunting moose and caribou. The two alpine tribes lived in a similar fashion, moving from valley to valley, seldom venturing into the lowlands. Dall's sheep and woodland caribou were staples.

The first fur-trading post in the region was built in 1800. The Slavey who traded at the post, which stood near today's Fort Simpson, authored the first legends about the inaccessible country to the west. They regarded the mountain groups with fear and superstition, and told of giants and evil spirits, legends later embellished by trappers and prospectors.

In 1823 Alexander McLeod, chief trader at Fort Simpson, traveled up the Liard and its tributaries, including the South Nahanni, and successfully

persuaded the mountain groups to bring their furs to the fort, instead of trading with Russians on the coast of Alaska. In this enterprise, McLeod became the first European to explore what is now the park.

In the 1890s prospectors panning their way north to the Klondike gold-fields ventured into the watershed of the South Nahanni River. None found gold; most found their grave. One unfortunate sourdough lost in the somber labyrinth of the Mackenzie and Richardson mountains scribbled a farewell and tacked it to a tree: "Hell can't be worse than this trail. I'll chance it." And with that he shot himself.

Gold fever waned until a Slavey named Little Nahanni brought gold-bearing quartz into Fort Liard around 1900. From then on, persistent rumors of placer gold up in the Nahanni country lured prospectors, many of them woefully unprepared. Their misfortunes live on in a rich legacy of legend and melodramatic place-names: Funeral Range, Headless Range, Broken Skull River, Murder Valley, Death Lake.

Macabre incidents in the early 1900s deepened the mystery of Nahanni country. Two McLeod brothers went prospecting and were found by a third brother three years later as headless skeletons in what became known as Deadmen Valley. The skeleton of Martin Jorgensen was discovered in his burned-out cabin on the Flat River—headless. John O'Brien froze to death atop The Twisted Mountain and was found, solid as a rock, still kneeling by the remains of his fire. Angus Hall, impatient with his companions, marched on ahead over a ridge and was never seen again. . . .

No one ever found the motherlode, or much gold at all. The region's inaccessibility, its lack of commercial ore bodies, and its harsh climate all helped to ensure that Nahanni country remained unspoiled and untamed.

HABITATS

Mixed valley-bottom forests dominated by white spruce, balsam poplar, and quaking aspen shelter Nahanni's great diversity of wildlife. Moose, black bears, gray wolves, and woodland caribou, relatives of mass-migrating barren ground caribou, slip through these dark stands, where forest floors of peat are patterned with lacy horsetails and silver pillows of lichen known as reindeer moss.

Extensive wetlands occur along broad valley bottoms, primarily upstream of the canyonlands and in the lowlands at the southeastern end of the park. These soggy landscapes are home to moose, muskrat, mink, and beaver. Shallow valley lakes are major bird-nesting sites for mallards, common goldeneyes, and other waterfowl. Common and red-throated loons nest on marshy shores and floating sedge mats. Phalaropes, common snipe, and dowitchers stalk grasses, rushes, and sedges, probing the mud for food. Semipalmated plovers, perhaps North America's most common shorebird, gather in large flocks on these summer breeding grounds.

Bald eagles share islands in Yohin Lake, near the park's southeastern boundary, with a pair of trumpeter swans, North America's largest wild waterfowl species, with a wingspan of 10 ft/3 m. By the early 1920s, these birds were nearly extinct, with the count down to an estimated 450 individuals (an Alaskan population of several thousand was only discovered in 1954). The swans had great commercial value: their quills made excellent pens, their down was used for powder puffs, their snow-white feathers served as adornment; even their skins were used. Today, however, the trumpeters are protected and the population seems secure.

White-tailed and mule deer browse in meadows that dot aspen, birch, and spruce forests surrounding Yohin. Downriver at The Splits, where the South Nahanni braids into wide channels en route to its meeting with the Liard, biologists have reestablished the indigenous wood bison, a larger and darker cousin of the plains bison.

Above the valleys, some mountainsides are barren, littered with broad scree slopes. Others are forested with mixed stands of white and Engelmann spruce, lodgepole pine, and quaking aspen. Dwarf birch, a tenacious shrub known to some hikers as "shin tangle," forms an understory that enflames mountainsides with scarlet in autumn. The blue-black berries of common juniper, another widespread shrub, feed a variety of animals and birds, including spruce grouse and rock ptarmigan. In summer, wide swaths of some Nahanni mountainsides are blanketed with powder-puff balls of cotton-grass, making it look as though a freak snowstorm had just swept through. The tiny flowers of cotton-grass, which actually is a sedge, hide within the downy heads.

The tundra-like plateaus high above the canyonlands in the southeastern half of the park are treeless realms of lichens, ground-hugging arctic willow, and purple mountain saxifrage, moss campion, and other tiny, tough alpine flowers. This is the favored habitat of Dall's sheep, which are especially abundant on the Tlogotsho Plateau south of Deadmen Valley. In summer the sheep descend from their windswept heights to visit valley salt licks along Prairie Creek.

Nahanni is also noted for flora found far north of their usual range. *Buella elegans*, for example, is a lichen that usually grows 2,000 mi/3,200 km southeast, on the American Great Plains. Other unusual plants flourish in microclimates generated by some of the park's geologic attractions. Mists thrown up by Virginia Falls sustain delicate orchids: heartleaf tway-

The fur of the arctic fox changes to blend with the landscape, from white or light gray in winter to brown or blue-gray in summer.

blade and yellow and white lady's-slippers. Along the upper Flat River, the moderating influence of Wildmint and Old Pots hot springs nurtures delphiniums and a recently discovered species of aster named for the park, *Aster nahaniensis.*

Kraus Hotsprings, upstream on the South Nahanni from Yohin Lake, sustains an eerie 18-acre/8-hectare patch of lush, steaming vegetation that was probably the source of the legends of a tropical valley. The park's largest poplars grow here amid luxuriant fields of cow-parsnip. Dense stands of chokecherry bushes attract numerous warblers. The beaver that inhabit the springs enjoy the year-round comfort afforded by thermally heated pools and lodges.

OUTDOOR ACTIVITIES

Of the thousand people who visit the park each year, a third fly in for the day to see Virginia Falls. The rest run Canada's most spectacular wilderness river. Most canoeists spend part of their trip hiking out of the river corridors, especially around Deadmen Valley. Alpinists from all over the world come to climb the Ragged Range at Nahanni's northwest boundary.

Hiking

There are no developed trails, but unmarked routes up tributary valleys lead to spectacular alpine scenery and tundra plateaus. A very challenging 12-mi/19-km route south of Rabbitkettle Lake along the Rabbitkettle River ends at *Hole-in-the-Wall Lake,* a turquoise tarn at the foot of the Thunderdome. All around are the cirques, hanging valleys, and Matterhorn-like peaks of the Ragged Range.

At Virginia Falls, canoeists paddle across the South Nahanni from the campground to climb *Sunblood Mountain* (5,250 ft/1,600 m), which looms over Virginia Falls. The moderately difficult hike, the most popular in the park, takes about four hours return. About 3 mi/5 km downstream from the falls, a demanding 6-mi/9.6-km bushwhack trail up *Marengo Creek* leads to a quadruple cataract.

Deadmen Valley makes a superb base for hiking. An excursion up *Prairie Creek* leads to *Caribou Flats,* part of the Nahanni Plateau. Dall's sheep often come to a mineral lick along the way, but despite the name, woodland caribou are not present here. A 3.5-mi/5.6-km hike north of the valley up *Dry Canyon Creek* also leads to the Nahanni Plateau. In places the walls of this extraordinary defile soar 3,200 ft/1,000 m above a floor less than 325 ft/100 m wide. Hiking up the canyon means scrambling over and around jumbled, house-sized boulders. By midsummer the creek is reduced to isolated pools.

In summer dense tufts of white cotton-grass, eriophorum, sometimes cover entire hillsides. The park's wildflowers include goldenrod, yellow moneyflower, asters, and wild orchids.

On the south side of the valley a rigorous eight-hour hike up *Sheaf Creek* ascends to the Tlogotsho Plateau with its spectacular views of the canyonlands below. Hikers usually camp overnight before returning to Deadmen. (They carry water with them and are prepared for rapidly changing weather.) The only way to reach the bizarrely eroded karstlands above First Canyon on foot is to hike 15 mi/24 km up the streambed of *Lafferty Creek*, a demanding day-long outing.

Climbing

The Ragged Range just west of the park is well known to the international mountaineering community. It offers icefields, glaciers, deep valleys, and sharp peaks of quartz monzonite, a highly resistant kind of granite. One popular destination is the Cirque of the Unclimbables, an ice-carved mountain amphitheater with sheer, 3,000-ft/915-m cliffs. Others are Lotus Flower Tower and Parrot's Beak. Outfitters fly climbers to a campsite on Glacier Lake. From there, the climbers hike about 4 mi/6.4 km to the cirque.

Canoeing and Kayaking

Outfitters drop off river runners at four places. Paddlers with white-water expertise land at *Moose Ponds*, northwest of the park on the wild upper reaches of the South Nahanni. There the river drops an average of 30 ft/9 m every mile, ripping through dozens of boulder-choked Class II and Class III rapids known as the *Rock Gardens*. This five-day roller-coaster ride down to Rabbitkettle Lake offers some of Canada's finest white-water canoeing and kayaking.

Others start at *Rabbitkettle Lake*, where there is an idyllic, sheltered campground. Paddlers lug boats and gear to the *South Nahanni* over a moderately difficult 1,900-ft/600-m portage. The 130-mi/210-km trip down the South Nahanni to Nahanni Butte just outside the southeastern park boundary takes about 12 days.

Between Rabbitkettle and Virginia Falls, the river is broad, moderately swift, and free of rapids; paddlers have time to scan the riverbanks for moose and black bears. Charters drop off some river runners above *Virginia Falls*. A 0.7-mi/1.2-km portage bypasses the cataract; about half the distance is boardwalk. It takes most of a day to haul gear, with time for hikes that lead to scenic overlooks above the powerful cascade.

Exciting water lies below the falls, where the river slips swiftly through the canyonlands. A portage bypasses the Class IV Figure-Eight Rapids, the best-known white water in the park, although experts usually run the maelstrom in July and August when water levels are lower.

It is worthwhile to spend a few days enjoying the beautiful Deadmen Valley, hiking or fishing. Other features in a trip filled with excitement include Pulpit Rock and The Gate; George's Riffle, the understated name for a hydraulic riot at the entrance to First Canyon (to add to the excitement there's no portage); White Spray Spring, where ice-cold water gushes from the base of a cliff after percolating down from the karstlands above First Canyon; Lafferty's Riffle at the exit of First Canyon; and Kraus Hotsprings just below the canyonlands, where weary paddlers soak in sulphurous but soothing 95° F/35° C waters. There is also a riverbank seep pool; the frigid South Nahanni flows by a canoe-length away.

The Slavey Indians called the Flat River *Too Nakadeh*, or "white-water river," a much more accurate description than the English name for a waterway strewn with rapids that range from Class II to Class VI. Highlights include the Cascade-of-the-Thirteen-Steps, a wild series of ledges and chutes that must be portaged; limestone hoodoos that cover a long stretch of shoreline with wing-like vanes and pillars where the Caribou joins the Flat; and the high bluffs just downstream from the Caribou.

Each year charters drop off a handful of paddlers on *Seaplane Lake* just outside the park boundary near the headwaters of the Flat. A 1,490-ft/ 455-m portage leads to the launch site. The 80-mi/130-km trip to the Flat's meeting with the South Nahanni can be covered in three days. From that confluence to Nahanni Butte takes about eight days.

Rafting

Four outfitters take wilderness travelers down the South Nahanni. The usual launch site is upstream of Rabbitkettle Lake and the take-out is at Nahanni Butte.

Fishing

The silty South Nahanni makes for poor fishing, except near White Spray Spring in First Canyon and at the mouths of tributary creeks, where arctic grayling are landed. Dolly varden and lake trout are taken from Prairie Creek in Deadmen Valley.

EXPLORING THE PARK

Nahanni is in the southwest corner of the Northwest Territories, 650 mi/ 1,045 km northwest of Edmonton, Alberta. No road leads to the park. The Liard Highway (Highway 7) comes closest, passing near the hamlet of

OVERLEAF: *The rugged and pristine Nahanni Valley provides many opportunities for scenic views. No roads enter this park, which is accessible only by river and air.*

Nahanni Butte downstream from Nahanni's southeast boundary. Both hamlet and park, however, lie west of the Liard River, the highway hugs the east bank, and there is no bridge or ferry.

Air access is the only practical way to reach the park. Major fly-in and supply points in the Northwest Territories are Fort Simpson, east of the park on the Liard Highway, and Fort Liard, to the southeast along the same road. Other points are Watson Lake, Yukon Territory, southwest on the Campbell Highway (Highway 4), and Fort Nelson, British Columbia, to the south at the southern terminus of the Alaska Highway. All centers except Fort Liard are served by scheduled flights. Charter aircraft, canoes, and other rental equipment are available at all centers. Aircraft are allowed to land in the park only at Rabbitkettle Lake and Virginia Falls.

For those unwilling or unable to meet the wilderness challenge of Nahanni, outfitters in Fort Liard, Fort Simpson, Yellowknife, Watson Lake, and Fort Nelson fly day-trippers to Virginia Falls. On clear days, these excursions offer spectacular overviews of Nahanni country.

The park is open year-round. The best time to visit is July and August, when the weather is more predictable and there's little chance of snow. Water levels generally peak in late June or early July; they drop considerably during August and September.

Visitors register on arrival and deregister after their trip. They can do this at park headquarters in Fort Simpson or at the warden stations at Nahanni Butte and Rabbitkettle Lake. The park's interpretive program is limited to displays and films at the Fort Simpson office and guided hikes from the Rabbitkettle Lake campground to Rabbitkettle Hotsprings, a fascinating half-day outing.

ACCOMMODATIONS: There are only three developed campsites along the South Nahanni. Rabbitkettle Lake campground, a short distance from the river, has a fine site overlooking a shallow, placid lake in the shadow of the Ragged Range. (The breezy gravel bar across the river from the put-in makes a good alternative, though undesignated, campsite when Rabbitkettle is buggy.) Virginia Falls campground has a wooded setting on a high bank above the river and just upstream from the famous cascade, with boardwalks linking camping areas. At the Kraus Hotsprings campground near the southeastern end of the park, the former log cabin of prospector Gus Kraus affords shelter for cooking during rainstorms.

There is also camping just downriver from the park at the hamlet of Nahanni Butte, where a park office is located, and at Blackstone Territorial Park, a five-hour paddle down the South Nahanni and Liard rivers from Nahanni Butte. From there, paddlers arrange road transportation to Fort Simpson or Fort Liard.

Hotel accommodation is found in Fort Simpson, Watson Lake, and Fort Liard. These communities have grocery stores, but supplies are limited. Travelers should arrive as completely equipped as possible.

ADDRESSES: For information on Nahanni, as well as lists of charter operators, guides, and outfitters licensed to operate in the park, contact: Nahanni National Park, Box 300, Fort Simpson, N.W.T. X0E 0N0; 403-369-3151. For general information on the Northwest Territories, contact TravelArctic, Government of the Northwest Territories, Yellowknife, N.W.T. X1A 2L9; 403-873-7200.

BOOKS: Pat and Rosemarie Keough, *The Nahanni Portfolio*. Don Mills, Ont.: Stoddart, 1988. This lavishly illustrated volume relates the human and natural history of the Nahanni.

Raymond M. Patterson, *Dangerous River*. Post Mills, Vt.: Chelsea Green, 1990. Reissue of classic 1923 Nahanni chronicle.

Dick Turner, *Nahanni*. Surrey, B.C.: Hancock House, 1989. Anecdotal account by an old northern hand and bush pilot.

AUYUITTUQ NATIONAL PARK RESERVE

THE FIRST PARK established above the Arctic Circle, Auyuittuq embraces a formidable wilderness on the Cumberland Peninsula of Baffin Island: jagged peaks, U-shaped valleys, fjords, and a vast icefield. It is, in the words of Canadian poet Al Purdy, the land "north of summer."

Auyuittuq (ah-you-EE-took) means "the land that never melts" in the language of the Inuit, as Canadian Eskimos prefer to be called; it is an apt description for the birthplace of the last Ice Age. The park protects the most spectacular stretch of the eastern Arctic coast and Davis Strait Highlands, a mountain range that extends between northern Labrador and Ellesmere Island. The northern and eastern coasts of the park are deeply incised with fjords and bays. Above the eastern fjords soar cliffs 3,000 ft/ 900 m high.

In Auyuittuq's frozen center sprawls the Penny Ice Cap, a forbidding upland that spawns more than a dozen massive outlet glaciers. The longest, Coronation Glacier, tumbles 20 mi/32 km before ending in an ice cliff at the head of a fjord. In the southeast corner of the park Pangnirtung Pass winds between mountains carved into fantastical spurs and massive faces. The dramatic defile is one of the wildest, most beautiful valleys on earth.

GEOLOGY

About 60 million years ago, Greenland and Baffin Island were joined, or separated, by only a narrow strait. The two land masses began to split apart, accompanied by extensive volcanic activity and a massive uplift of the entire eastern margin of Canada. This uplift formed the park's mountains.

About 2 million years ago, the Arctic climate cooled for reasons that are still not clearly understood. Baffin Island became the birthing ground for the Laurentide ice sheet, the largest of three ice sheets that mantled much of North America during the Late Wisconsin glaciation. Snowfields on Baffin plateaus, developed over an extended period of abundant snowfall and reduced summer melting, thickened and metamorphosed into ice, eventual-

Soaring 1,500 meters, Mt. Thor was named after the Norse god of thunder. Its uninterrupted cliff face—about one kilometer—is the longest in the world.

Mt. Asgard stands immediately recognizable amid a scene from a Norse legend. The flat top of its cylindrical tower attracts experienced climbers from all over the world;

ly pushing southeast and southwest to merge with younger ice from Labrador and the central Northwest Territories. The ice, 13,000 ft/4,000 m thick in places, slowly ground west, to the shadow of the Rockies, and south, through New England and into the midwestern United States. At its greatest extent, the Laurentide blanketed 6 million sq mi/15.5 million sq km.

The Cumberland Peninsula was probably never completely ice-covered. Much of the flow of the Penny Ice Cap was channeled into outlet glaciers that deepened and straightened existing valleys until, after successive glaciations, they formed the fjord and valley systems of today. Small local glaciers added flourishes to Auyuittuq's spectacular architecture. These alpine, or cirque, glaciers chiseled the park's summits into razor-edged ridges, columns, horns, and incisors—one of the most strikingly rugged landscapes on earth.

When the climate started to warm again, 15,000 years ago, the ice began a long retreat. On Baffin the ice caps were tenacious, and two still remain: the Barnes Ice Cap midpoint on the island, and, to the southeast, the Penny Ice Cap. Inevitably, travelers on the Penny's frozen expanse ponder when the great, groaning juggernaut of ice will once again descend from the Baffin highlands and rumble across the land.

the ideal climbing months are June and July, when there is no darkness. Other spectacular peaks nearby include Mt. Odin and Tête Blanche.

HISTORY

The first signs of human activity in the park date back 3,500 years; these are hunting camps of the Pre-Dorsets, a nomadic people who wandered east from Beringia, the land bridge connecting Alaska and Siberia during the Ice Age. Their descendants, known as the Dorsets, lived in camps of rectangular skin-covered tents and produced highly artistic carvings and geometric designs. For reasons still not known, they failed to prosper and were quickly displaced or assimilated when another people from the western Arctic, known as the Thules, reached the Cumberland Peninsula about A.D. 1200.

The Thules were superb hunters on tundra and sea and lived in houses made of sod, stone, and the ribs and skin of whales, often occupying the same seasonal sites for generations. This highly mobile people developed the dogsled, kayak, and umiak (circular multiperson boat). Their descendants became today's Inuit.

In the late tenth century, at least 200 years before the Thules arrived, the rectangular sails of the Vikings appeared off Baffin's rocky shores. Eric the Red is generally believed to be the first European to visit the island, which in the Norse sagas is called Helluland. Five centuries later came

European whalers, followed by explorers searching for a seaway to the Orient—the fabled Northwest Passage. English mariner Martin Frobisher reached the southern tip of Baffin in 1576 and collected "blacke stone" that turned out to contain not gold, but worthless pyrite.

In 1585, another Englishman, John Davis, made the first recorded entry into Cumberland Sound, encountering no inhabitants. Three decades later, pilot William Baffin, one of the great Arctic explorers, circumnavigated Baffin Bay in a vessel skippered by William Bylot. On the southward journey he discovered Lancaster Sound, which later proved to be the entrance to the Northwest Passage.

By the late 1850s, whalers had established winter stations around Cumberland Sound, including one, Kivitoo, on Auyuittuq's northern coast. A small graveyard spiked with weathered crosses testifies to the hardships of a long winter's confinement and the devastation visited on the Inuit by European diseases. Iron vats used for boiling down blubber still stand on the beach. The whalers hired the Inuit as hunters during the spring and fall, dispensing rations of biscuits, coffee, molasses, and tobacco each Saturday. In exchange, the Inuit relinquished a way of life that dated back thousands of years.

HABITATS

Despite its forbidding nature, Auyuittuq is a storehouse of life. During the Arctic's brief summer, 24 hours of daylight offer warmth and sustenance to tough plants and versatile animals that during the rest of the year must endure snow, ice, and darkness. In summer, when temperatures can reach the mid-60s F/high teens C, swarms of insects appear, flowering plants burst forth, and hundreds of thousands of birds migrate here to nest. Of the 35 species of birds found in Auyuittuq, only four are year-round residents.

Frigid waters surrounding the park abound with marine mammals. The most common species is the ringed seal, while harp and bearded seals occasionally are seen. Narwhal, killer whales, and walrus sometimes are sighted off the park's northern coast, along with bowhead and humpback whales, and the white whale, or beluga. White whales are still quite common in Cumberland Sound, although most sightings are in Clearwater Fjord southwest of the park; their hides were once shipped to England to be made into high-quality bootlaces.

The remote northern fjords of the park are important denning and feeding grounds for the polar bear, the largest and the only potentially dangerous animal hereabouts. These solitary maritime carnivores live primarily on ringed seals, although lone bears looking for carrion and berries sometimes wander in spring and autumn into the northern half of Pangnirtung Pass, known as the Owl River valley.

The park's coastline is a prime habitat for seabirds. An estimated 100,000 northern fulmars nest in a colony at Cape Searle; these gull-like birds, with a stocky body and short neck, are sighted near the mouths of northern fjords. Thick-billed murres patrol the park's coastal waters, where they feed on small fish and crustaceans. Black guillemots sport in southern fjords, along with common and king eiders.

Washed by 30-ft/9-m tides, Pangnirtung Fjord is fringed with extensive tidal flats, the haunts of ringed and semipalmated plovers and sandpipers (purple, white-rumped, and Baird's). Small, sandpiper-like red and red-necked phalaropes often swim in tight circles, spinning like tops as they dab for food. Salt-tolerant plants here include sandwort and scurvygrass, which are extensive only where bird manuring is heavy. Scurvygrass is rich in vitamin C, hence its name.

Due to frequent flooding and persistent icing, vegetation on gravel flats farther inland is restricted to such hardy colonizers as arctic poppies and sandwort. Rock deserts here contain crustaceous and foliose lichens (rock tripe) growing on the rocks, and between them other lichens, mosses, and cushion plants such as moss campion and saxifrage (its name means "rock breaker" in Latin).

The most diverse and colorful community is found scattered along the upper Weasel River valley of Pangnirtung Pass and the Owl River valley. Dwarf willows, dwarf birch, and berry-bearing members of the heath family form what is called dwarf shrub-heath tundra in association with mosses and reindeer moss lichens (*Cladonia*). Caribou and arctic hares browse on willow twigs and buds; rock ptarmigan, the arctic representative of the grouse family, eat crowberries and bilberries.

On damper, rawer soils, and on alluvial flats of former rivers and lakes, is the grassland tundra, where grasses and sedges predominate, with broad swaths of sphagnum moss and cotton grass in the wetter parts. Broad areas of the Owl Valley and isolated sections of the Weasel Valley are covered by tussocky terrain, known as *thurfur* in Iceland. Each tussock, which can be 12 in/30 cm or more in height, has a core of heaved mineral soil and a whitish tuft of dead rhizomes and leaves on its top and sides.

Owl Valley thurfur is prime habitat for the Lapland longspur and the American pipit, two of the most common small birds of the park interior. Phalaropes nest in thurfur depressions near ponds. This valley is also the haunt of the snowy owl, a raptor greatly dependent on the population fluctuations of its main prey, lemmings. (Owl Valley got its name because scientists saw so many snowy owls there during 1953, a populous lemming year.)

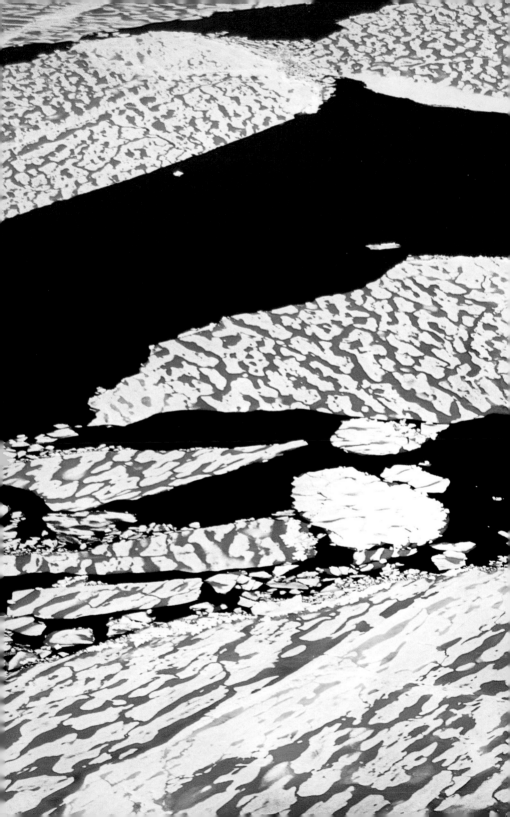

The polar bear, or Nanuk, lives mainly on pack ice at sea or in coastal areas. An uncommon sight in the park, these bears are dangerous and should never be approached. OPPOSITE: Ice break-up occurs each year for about two weeks from mid-June to mid-July. Travel to Auyuittuq by boat or snowmobile is then impossible, though one can hike the thirty-kilometer trail from Pangnirtung.

The tundra blooms with a surprisingly rich array of flowers in July and early August. Many species are dwarf versions of southern counterparts; the permafrost, harsh climate, and short growing season repress growth. As if in compensation, flowers bloom with an intensity of color rarely seen in more temperate areas. Pink-flowered, broad-leaved willow-herb, an arctic cousin of fireweed and perhaps the showiest of the park's flora, grows in profusion along riverbanks and other floodable soils.

Cinquefoils brighten park tundra with bright yellow flowers. Also abundant are mountain avens, the floral symbol of the Northwest Territories. Avens have an eight-petaled parabolic flower that swivels to follow the sun, thus concentrating heat at its center. This trait, called heliotropism, is shared by the arctic poppy, which stores heat in its open bowl. Insects bask there, sheltered from cool air, and, as though to return a favor, they pollinate as they move from flower to flower.

At one time, tundra in the Weasel and Owl valleys supported large populations of barren ground caribou, as evidenced by antlers bleaching on the ground. Today, these migratory ruminants are confined to the northwest corner of the park. Another herd of about one hundred animals periodically migrates through the southwest angle. Gray wolves trail the caribou, though, like all land predators here, they feed primarily on lemmings.

Two lemming species occur in the park. The brown lemming favors damp tundra meadows and the edges of watercourses and lakes, living mainly on shoots of grasses and sedges. The more abundant Greenland collared lemming feeds primarily on willow leaves and forbs on drier heath slopes. In cycles of three to four years, lemming populations boom and bust. In boom years, Pangnirtung Pass crawls with lemmings; a year later, there may be very few. When populations peak, lemmings may exhaust their food sources, removing 95 percent of the vegetation cover.

Arctic hares range throughout the park. At 6 to 12 lb/3 to 6 kg, this species outweighs not only its southern relatives, but also one of its predators, the arctic fox. The fox's winter coat provides such good insulation that the animal needs to increase its internal heat production only when temperatures drop to $-40°$ F/$-40°$ C. (Some tropical animals need a three-fold metabolic increase just to maintain essential warmth in a temperature drop of only $18°$ F/$10°$ C.)

The snow bunting, perhaps the most common small bird of the interior, nests in the crannies and crevices of tundra rock piles. The male breeding plumage is a striking pure white with sharply contrasting black back, bill, and legs. Overhead, these sturdy finches look almost entirely white, like a flurry of snowflakes. The arrival of buntings heralds spring; when they depart, the last migrants to leave, the short, hectic summer is over.

OUTDOOR ACTIVITIES

Most of the 400 people who visit the park each year spend 10 days to three weeks in and around Pangnirtung Pass between mid-July and mid-August. Seven emergency shelters about a day's hike apart in the pass contain first-aid kits and radio telephones. Mountain climbers and hikers heading off the main trail must be prepared for any emergency; park staff cannot perform alpine rescues. Glacier travelers should be equipped and experienced in crevasse rescue.

Windproof and rainproof gear and a rainproof backpack cover are essentials. So are good boots, a walking stick (particularly useful for crossing streams), gloves, and a toque. The weather varies dramatically from year to year and locally within the park. The warmest month is July, when the daily mean temperature in low-lying regions is $42°$ F/$6°$ C. Visitors are likely to encounter at least one or two days of heavy rain or snow over the course of a two-week stay.

Unpredictable weather also means that Arctic-bound travelers must build sufficient time into their schedules to allow for delays. Following the old adage, "Plan for the worst and hope for the best," reduces frustration and anxiety when driving rain keeps hikers tent-bound and summer storms ground airplanes.

Hiking

The park's only designated trail parallels both banks of the Weasel River, with a loop around Summit and Glacier lakes at the midpoint of the pass. It is clearly marked by inukshuks, small stone cairns built in human form that once guided Inuit on their travels. Hikers usually cover no more than 1.8 mi/3 km an hour.

Most trekkers start at the Overlord campground and head north along the east side of the river. They trudge over flats on the valley floor, ford glacial meltwater streams, cross a raging tributary on a footbridge, scramble up and over moraine barriers, and battle winds that deposit sand in dunes—a most unexpected high-Arctic landscape. Some rise to 100 ft/30 m.

Just north of Crater Lake, on the west side of the pass, Schwartzenbach Falls leaps 300 ft/90 m from a cliff at approximately the latitude of the Arctic Circle; a trailside cairn marks the specific location as 66°33'. No other place in the world offers such a spectacular entry into the Arctic realm. (Hikers on the secondary trail along the west bank of the Weasel make the falls a day-long side trip.)

About 2.5 mi/4 km north of the falls, on the west side of the valley, rises Mt. Odin, at 7,044 ft/2,147 m the highest summit between the Carolinas and Ellesmere Island. The tilted granite wall of 5,495-ft/1,675-m Thor Peak leans out over the valley from the east. This is the highest uninterrupted rock face in the world—about 3,200 ft/1 km.

Beyond, Fork Beard Glacier hangs on the lip of an east-side rock wall, with boulders as big as boxcars embedded in its ice. Every few minutes, with a crack like a rifle shot, the glacier spits out debris, sending it clattering down to the valley floor trailing rooster tails of dust.

At the halfway point of the pass, some 25 mi/40 km north of Overlord, Summit Lake nestles in the mountains. Most years its surface glitters with ice, even in midsummer. Where the Weasel River pours out of the lake, Parks Canada has constructed a cable-car crossing, enabling hikers to switch between west-side and east-side branches of the trail. Distant ice caps can funnel gales of 50, even 100 mph/80 to 160 kph, down to the Summit Lake area. Wardens often find that poorly anchored tents have been blown into the middle of the lake.

The moraine of Turner Glacier separates Summit Lake from Glacier Lake, which feeds the Owl River. The easily accessible rounded summit of

In the park, these rock forms were generally built to guide hikers, though the Inuit formerly built them for food caches, landmarks, and to frighten caribou toward easy hunting grounds. They are called inukshuk, Inuit for "that which has the likeness of man."

Mt. Battle east of Glacier Lake gives magnificent views up and down the pass, west to Mts. Asgard and Loki, and north up the huge Highway Glacier to the thin white line of the Penny Ice Cap on the distant horizon.

Summit Lake makes a good base for day trips. The *King's Parade Route*, a popular 15-mi/25-km U-shaped glacier trek, heads north up the snout of Caribou Glacier, takes a right turn on adjoining Parade Glacier, then takes another right on Turner Glacier to head back down to Summit Lake. This makes a splendid day-long outing. *Tupermit Glacier* on the east side of Summit Lake is another interesting day trip via the cable crossing from the campground, as is *Highway Glacier* northeast of Glacier Lake.

The Owl Valley, north of Summit Lake, is unblazed wilderness with its own hiking pluses and minuses: gentler terrain and no moraines, but more streams to ford and difficult walking on tussocky terrain. Side trips include unmarked trails up valleys flanking Mt. Fleming and east into the June River Valley.

Climbing

Those who venture out of the valley and up surrounding glaciers and mountains experience Auyuittuq's full range of beauty. The magnificent peaks and sheer walls attract climbers from around the world. Continuous daylight make June and July ideal for this activity. The rock is rough granite and the ice is steep and solid, although by July wet snow and slush pools on glaciers make movement tedious without snowshoes or skis. Favorite summits, which rise 5,000 to 6,500 ft/1,500 to 2,000 m from valley floors, include Mt. Odin, Thor Peak, Mt. Northumbria, Tyr Peak, Tête Blanche, Mt. Asgard, and Sigmund Peak.

Fishing

Park rivers and lakes contain few fish; arctic char are landed at Pangnirtung hamlet.

Winter Activities

In April, May, and early June the park draws only a few visitors. During these months temperatures rise but the snow retains its hard surface. This is the best time to *snowmobile* and *cross-country ski* the length of the pass. Almost completely glaciated, Auyuittuq offers some of the world's finest *mountain ski touring* throughout much of the year. Day trips include a 12.5-mi/20-km circuit around Mt. Battle, a 3-mi/5-km ascent of the central glacier on Tyr Peak southwest of Summit Lake, and the King's Parade Route. Among numerous two- and three-day trips near Summit Lake are Rundle Glacier and the Caribou–Norman glacier loop. A park brochure describes and maps out routes.

Ice caves are one of the more fantastic and unusual features of Auyuittuq, "the land that never melts." The park's Penny Highlands are largely covered by the thousand-foot-thick Penny Ice Cap, a true remnant of the last ice age's continental glaciers.

EXPLORING THE PARK

Auyuittuq is 1,500 mi/2,400 km northwest of Montreal. First Air (Carp Airport, Carp, Ont. K0A 1L0; 613-839-3340 or 819-979-5810), an Air Canada affiliate, has flights from Montreal, Ottawa, and Yellowknife to Iqaluit, with connecting flights to Pangnirtung.

Visiting Auyuittuq is expensive and requires considerable planning. This park, which has few facilities, is recommended only for experienced wilderness enthusiasts who are in good physical condition; novice and intermediate hikers should attempt the journey only if accompanied by a guide or an expert backpacker.

The interpretive program at park headquarters in Pangnirtung is limited. Park officials brief visitors on possible hazards: high winds, sudden blizzards, hypothermia, waist-high glacier-stream crossings, rockslides, snowslides, quicksand, ankle-twisting morainal rubble, and polar bears.

In Pangnirtung the Angmarlik Centre (819-473-8737), a first-rate museum and visitors' center, arranges for local outfitters to make the two-and-a-half-hour ride in an open freighter canoe 19 mi/30 km up the fjord to the park entrance at the Overlord campground. The trip can only be made within two hours on either side of high tide. Those with abundant time and energy hike two or three days to Overlord along the fjord's rugged shoreline. During the two-week breakup of ice, which can occur anytime from mid-June to mid-July, and the freeze-up period from mid-October to mid-November, this hike is the only way to get to the park, though flooded streams in spring make the journey arduous.

About 20 people each year reach the park through the "back door" of Broughton Island in order to hike the pass from north to south. First Air flies from Iqaluit to Broughton Island, where there is a park warden station (819-927-8834). If seas and fjords are clear of ice, outfitters boat hikers to the park's northern entrance, an expensive and potentially hazardous four-and-a-half-hour trip that crosses open water. Hikers then proceed south through the pass and call park headquarters from an emergency shelter at least a day before they reach Overlord. Park personnel then contact the Angmarlik staff, who arrange for the boat trip on to Pangnirtung. The northern fjord is usually icebound until the end of July and some years remains frozen all summer. If the trip is made before breakup, guides take hikers about 60 mi/90 km south by snowmobile to the park entrance at the head of North Pangnirtung Fjord. During breakup and freeze-up, outfitters drop off hikers at a Canadian Parks Service cabin at the head of the fjord to make the 35-mi/56-km trip on foot. Ice conditions, however, may prevent any travel from Broughton.

From freeze-up in November until May, it is possible to walk, ski, or snowmobile into the park from north and south.

ACCOMMODATIONS: There are primitive campgrounds at Overlord and Summit Lake, as well as wilderness camping sites all along the trail. The only accommodation in Pangnirtung is the Auyuittuq Lodge (Pangnirtung, N.W.T. X0A 0R0; 819-473-8955). A Territorial campground is on the edge of town (tent platforms, wind shelters, washrooms; no charge). Hikers can also seek shelter at the parish hall during weather too foul for camping. The only place to stay on Broughton Island is the Tulugak Co-Op Hotel (Broughton Island, N.W.T. X0A 0B0; 819-927-8833 or 819-927-8932). Naphtha fuel and dried food may be purchased in Pangnirtung and Broughton Island; other fuels and freeze-dried food are not available locally.

ADDRESSES: For more information, write or phone: The Superintendent, Auyuittuq National Park, Pangnirtung, N.W.T. X0A 0R0 (819-473-8962); TravelArctic (the Northwest Territories travel bureau), Box 506, Yellowknife, N.W.T. X1A 2N4 (403-873-7200); and Baffin Tourism Association, Box 820, Iqaluit, N.W.T. X0A 0H0 (819-979-6551).

BOOKS: Roger Wilson, ed., *The Land That Never Melts.* Toronto: Peter Martin Associates, 1976. Out of print but the best guide to the geology, climate, history, and ecology of the park; check libraries.

NORTHERN
WILDLANDS

THE CANADIAN NORTH offers outdoor travelers a wilderness of staggering size and beauty, of profound solitude. The land "north of 60"—that is, north of the 60th parallel, which marks the southern boundary of the Yukon and much of the Northwest Territories—covers a third of Canada, an area larger than India with a population that could fit easily into Yankee Stadium. A flight north from Toronto to Resolute Bay on Cornwallis Island (the end of the line, as it were, for scheduled jet service) covers the same distance as flying south from Toronto to Venezuela. Yet four hours of flying remain from Resolute before one reaches Ellesmere Island National Park, less than 500 mi/800 km from the North Pole.

This is a land of desolate beauty, of mountains and coastal plains, tundra, rock deserts, wetlands, and the immense Arctic Archipelago sprawling in a vast triangle north of the mainland, the ice-bound tip of the continent. This austere realm is locked in snow and ice for three-quarters of the year. The blackness of a winter night can stretch for more than two months. During the Arctic's brief summer season of life, plants and animals hurry to feed, reproduce, and prepare for the coming cold.

The wildlands featured in this chapter, selected for their national and international significance, are accessible only by charter airplane or boat, with the exception of Wood Buffalo National Park, which can be reached by car. Travel here is expensive and requires time, adaptability, and self-reliance. In this unforgiving place, a simple miscalculation—an unexpected fall or soaking—can be fatal. The returns, though—for independent adventurers as well as for those traveling with outfitters—can be enormous. Magnificent mountains, glaciers, and fjords; masses of migrating caribou that rival in number the great herds of the Serengeti; rookeries with hundreds of thousands of birds; whales, seals, polar bears, grizzlies, and those exotic Ice Age survivors, muskoxen—all are part of the unsurpassed spectacle of the northern wildlands.

Dotted with snow, this icy landscape on Ellesmere Island National Park Reserve powerfully suggests the spectacular beauty and solitude of Canada's northernmost park. Above the Arctic Circle, marked by mountains, fjords, glaciers, and icefields, Ellesmere is a place of long harsh winters, short cool summers, cold dry winds, and very light snowfalls.

NORTHERN YUKON NATIONAL PARK

This sanctuary in the northwestern corner of the Yukon was established in 1984 to protect a representative section of the Arctic coastal plain. In the southern half of the reserve the British Mountains rise 5,500 ft/1,700 m near the Alaska border. On the smooth slopes of these bald, rounded summits lives Canada's northernmost population of Dall's sheep. North of the range the treeless coastal plain slopes down to the Beaufort Sea, a broad highway for the Porcupine caribou herd, 180,000 strong. The plain and coastal lagoons are critical staging and molting areas for tremendous numbers of waterfowl. White whales, ringed and bearded seals, bowhead whales, and the occasional walrus cruise along the coast.

The Firth River rises just across the border in Alaska, winds through the British Mountains in a wide valley, threads a rapid-flecked 25-mi/40-km canyon with sheer 150-ft/45-m walls, then descends to the plain where it braids into a massive delta fan. The river's sheltered valley contains Canada's most northerly forest, which extends within 8 mi/13 km of the Beaufort Sea. The British Mountains and the coastal plain west of the Firth River are the only extensive landscapes not glaciated during the last Ice Age.

Exploring the Park

Northern Yukon is 310 mi/500 km north of Dawson and 125 mi/200 km northwest of Inuvik. Both communities are accessible by road and provide aircraft charters. Mandatory park-use permits are available from the park office in Inuvik. For more information, write or phone: The Chief Park Warden, Northern Yukon National Park, Box 1840, Inuvik, N.W.T. X0E 0T0; 403-979-3248.

BANKS ISLAND BIRD SANCTUARIES

Two sanctuaries on the westernmost island in the Canadian Arctic protect the summer grounds of the snow goose. Sanctuary Number One embraces 7,700 sq mi/19,943 sq km of low, rolling plain in the southwest corner of the island. Some 200,000 snow geese—about 95 percent of the western Arctic population—nest and breed at the junction of the Egg and Big rivers. The

Excellent swimmers, walrus are fond of sunbathing, spending more time out of water than other aquatic carnivores. Their tusks, primarily for defense, are also used as grappling hooks to help haul themselves onto ice.

site is 5 mi/8 km inland, unusually far from water for this species. In addition, some 3,000 brant geese nest in deltas, small lakes, and ponds.

In early spring, a polynya (a recurring area of open water) appears in the ice a short distance offshore from the island's west coast, providing a staging habitat for about 100,000 king eiders and several thousand migrating oldsquaws. Many of these birds remain through the summer, nesting on river deltas, coastal islands, and barrier beaches, and feeding offshore and in coastal lagoons. Other bird species include tundra swan, sandhill crane, ruddy turnstone, and red phalarope.

The area in and around the sanctuary is noted also for its large muskox and arctic fox populations. Other mammals include polar bears, arctic hares, and lemmings. Marine mammals such as beluga and bowhead whales and ringed and bearded seals occur offshore.

Sanctuary Number Two, situated in the north-central part of the island, protects a molting habitat for the snow goose and the brant, which are flightless from early July to early August. The geese are attracted to ponds, lakes, and extensive swards of grasses and sedges in the lower Thomsen River Valley, an environment that is relatively free of predators. The Thomsen delta and Castel Bay are also feeding and nesting grounds in summer for gulls, jaegers, terns, sandpipers, and plovers.

The lower Thomsen River Valley is also home to several thousand muskoxen. The Banks Island herd, which once faced extermination, now numbers about 25,000 individuals—a quarter of the Canadian population. The Thomsen, which is the most northerly canoeable river in Canada, and nearby badlands, canyons, and rugged coastline form the core of a proposed national park.

EXPLORING THE SANCTUARIES

Sachs Harbour, the island's only community (pop. 160), is accessible by scheduled air service from Inuvik, 310 mi/496 km southwest on the mainland. Food and lodging are available.

The island's abundant wildlife attracts an increasing number of hikers and photographers. There is fishing for arctic char and lake trout in the Thomsen River and large lakes. Canoeists on the Thomsen are virtually assured of spotting several hundred muskoxen during a week-long paddle down the shallow, gentle river. Although birds are protected within the sanctuaries, Banks Island native peoples are permitted to hunt, trap, and fish there and to guide nonnative hunters on strictly controlled expeditions for polar bears and muskoxen.

Entry permits can be obtained from the Canadian Wildlife Service, Box 637, Yellowknife, N.W.T. X1A 2N5; 403-920-8530. Two package-tour operators offer trips to Banks Island: Arctic Tour Company (Box 2021, Inuvik, N.W.T. X0E 0T0; 403-979-4100) organizes two- and three-day wildlife safaris, with fishing and accommodation with an Inuit family if desired; Nature Travel Service (127A Princess St., Kingston, Ont. K7L 1A8; 613-546-3065) has naturalist treks in July.

For details regarding hunting in the territory, write or phone: The Director, Conservation Education/Resource Development, Department of Renewable Resources, Government of the Northwest Territories, Box 1320, Yellowknife, N.W.T. X1A 2L9; 403-920-8716. For accommodation in Sachs Harbour, write or phone: Icicle Inn, General Delivery, Sachs Harbour, N.W.T. X0E 0Z0; 403-690-4444.

WOOD BUFFALO NATIONAL PARK

Designated a UNESCO World Heritage Site, this huge wilderness park straddles the border of northern Alberta and the southwestern Northwest Territories, just south of Great Slave Lake. At 17,300 sq mi/44,800 sq km (roughly the size of Switzerland), Wood Buffalo is the largest park in Canada and among the largest in the world. Its terrain is a mixture of bogs, slow-running streams, wide rivers, and shallow lakes interspersed with meadowland and forests of spruce, pine, and aspen. Spruce oases dot vast salt plains in the southeastern corner of the park, a landscape unique in Canada. Throughout the park is the most extensive gypsum karstland in the world. Subsurface runoff has dissolved underlying soft rock, causing the collapse of the surface terrain into huge sinkholes, underground rivers, caves, and sunken valleys.

The park was established in 1922 to protect Canada's last remaining herd of wood bison, a larger and darker relative of the plains bison. Then, from 1925 to 1928, the government transferred nearly 7,000 plains bison to the park to prevent these protected animals from overgrazing their range in southern Alberta. The unintended result was an interbreeding with the 1,500 wood bison already in the park.

For years, interbreeding was thought to have extinguished the pure strain of wood bison. But an aerial survey in 1957 detected a small, isolated herd of wood bison, which officials relocated to Elk Island National Park west of Edmonton, Alberta, and to a preserve at the eastern end of Great Slave Lake. The current park herd—all thought to be hybrids—numbers 4,500 individuals, the largest free-roaming bison herd in the world. Between

Grazing on large expanses of green grass, herds of bison are sometimes preyed upon by wolves. Free-ranging bison occur only in Wood Buffalo National Park, the Northwest Territories, and in Yellowstone National Park, Wyoming.

five to 50 percent of the animals, however, carry brucellosis and tuberculosis, diseases that some biologists think threaten cattle raised south and west of the park. A federal environmental review panel has recommended eradicating infected bison and rebuilding the Wood Buffalo herd with healthy stock from Elk Island and the Great Slave Lake sanctuary. No final decision has been made, though, and public debate on the fate of the park's bison continues.

In 1954, a pilot investigating a forest fire spotted the only natural nesting site of the endangered whooping crane among the spruces and tamaracks in a bog. Each spring about 160 whoopers return to the northeast corner of the park after wintering in the Aransas National Wildlife Refuge on the coast of Texas.

In the southeast corner of the park is the Peace–Athabasca delta, one of the world's largest inland deltas. It forms where the Peace, Athabasca, and Birch rivers deposit their sediments at the outlet of Lake Athabasca. In spring and fall, the food-rich wetlands abound with more than a million migrating geese, swans, and ducks from four North American flyways.

EXPLORING THE PARK

Wood Buffalo is 435 mi/696 km north of Edmonton, a long two-day drive via the Mackenzie Highway (Highway 35) and Highway 5. The nearest towns are Fort Smith, N.W.T., 12 mi/19 km northwest of the park on Highway 5 and site of park headquarters, and Fort Chipewyan, Alberta, outside the southeast corner of the park. There are flights from Edmonton to both communities, which have visitors' facilities.

Despite its superlative wilderness, the park remains relatively unknown. Facilities are limited to a campground (36 sites), interpretive theater, warden's station, and boat launch on Pine Lake, 40 mi/64 km south of Fort Smith. Naturalists conduct evening nature shows and such field activities as "bison creeps" and "salt-plains walks."

Outfitters in Fort Smith and "Fort Chip" lead backcountry trips to the park: boating, canoeing, and hiking in summer (the hiking routes are usually unmarked bison trails); skiing and dogsledding in winter. One of the North's most respected outfitters, Jacques van Pelt of Subarctic Wilderness Adventures (Box 685, Fort Smith, N.W.T. X0E 0P0; 403-872-2467), has been organizing backpacking, canoeing, and dogsledding trips to Wood Buffalo for more than 15 years. The best times to visit are May to June and Sep-

CLOCKWISE FROM TOP LEFT: A ruddy turnstone, typical arctic shorebird, on its nest; a sandhill crane on Banks Island; the king eider duck, world-renowned for its warm feathers; a male oldsquaw duck, mottled denizen of northern sanctuaries.

tember to early October when mosquitoes and other insects are less voracious. The park is also open in winter.

For more information on the park and other outfitters in Fort Smith and "Fort Chip," write or phone: Superintendent, Wood Buffalo National Park, Box 750, Fort Smith, N.W.T. X0E 0P0; 403-872-2349.

BATHURST INLET

This arm of Coronation Gulf in the central Northwest Territories is surrounded by a striking combination of level tundra, rolling hills, and stark uplands that rise abruptly from steely arctic waters. Some islands rear up 1,000 ft/300 m straight out of the sea. These landscapes and the rocks they contain provide dramatic proof that the inlet is a submerged rift valley.

The relatively mild climate at the southern end of the inlet supports diverse and luxuriant vegetation, which in turn provides prime habitat for animals, including barren-grounds grizzly, gray wolf, arctic fox, wolverine, arctic hare, and especially muskox. The most impressive display of wildlife is in early May, when the Bathurst caribou herd migrates through the area en route to calving grounds northeast of the inlet. This herd numbers nearly 500,000, perhaps the largest free-ranging herd of mammals in the world. There are few sights more memorable than the spectacle of thousands of caribou sweeping over hillsides and fording swift rivers in a vast living stream.

Among 125 bird species is a large, healthy population of peregrine falcons, with more than 150 active nest sites on the inlet's steep cliffs. Gyrfalcons and rough-legged hawks also nest on these glacier-carved cliffs, which provide impressive backdrops for golden eagles spiraling lazily in the summer air. Red-throated loons nest on small tundra lakes, while Pacific and yellow-billed loons often are seen winging across the inlet. The most abundant inlet waterfowl are common eiders, white-winged scoters, surf scoters, and oldsquaws. Shorebirds are common, especially Baird's sandpipers, least sandpipers, golden plovers, and semipalmated plovers. Glaucous, herring, and Thayer's gulls nest on a small island in the inlet, safe from hunting foxes.

Archaeologists have found sites more than 2,000 years old near Fishing Lake, a small arm of the inlet. The Hudson's Bay Company established a trading post in 1930 at the mouth of the Burnside River. Before it opened, no permanent settlement existed. Until 1964, when the post was shut down, some 40 Inuit families gathered round the post at trading time and built their snowhouses there. Now about two dozen Inuit live year-round at Bathurst Inlet, hunting, fishing, trapping, and guiding.

Exploring the Inlet

Bathurst Inlet is 447 mi/715 km northeast of Yellowknife by charter aircraft. The only accommodation is at Bathurst Inlet Lodge, which occupies the former trading-post buildings and Roman Catholic missionary chapel. Guests are invited to visit the homes of nearby Inuit families. Guides take visitors by barge to sites around the inlet where they can hike the tundra, view wildflowers, muskoxen, or birds, or fish for arctic char and lake trout.

The lodge owns two small aircraft which may be chartered for fly-in fishing, viewing the Bathurst caribou herd in migration, and flight-seeing tours of the Hood River and Wilberforce Falls, at 160 ft/49 m the highest cataract north of the Arctic Circle. The lodge also organizes guided wildlife trips and supplies canoes and other equipment for white-water trips on the Burnside, Hood, and Mara rivers. The lodge is open from mid-June to mid-August. Book well in advance: Box 820, Yellowknife, N.W.T. X1A 2N6; 403-873-2595.

Black Feather Wilderness Adventures (1341 Wellington St. West, Ottawa, Ont. K1Y 3B8; 613-722-9717) and Wilderness Bound (43 Broderick St., Hamilton, Ont. L85 3E3; 416-528-0059) conduct escorted canoe trips on the Burnside, Mara, and Hood rivers.

THELON GAME SANCTUARY

The rolling, treeless tundra of the Barren Grounds sweeps across nearly 500,000 sq mi/1.3 million sq km of the Northwest Territories, from Hudson Bay northwest to the Mackenzie River delta, and from the tree line north to the Arctic Ocean. In 1927 the Canadian government set aside 21,500 sq mi/ 55,700 sq km of the Barren Grounds as the Thelon Game Sanctuary to protect the muskox, which had been hunted since the 1880s as a source of sleigh robes. As late as 1936, only a few thousand animals remained in Canada. The species has made a spectacular comeback and now numbers more than 85,000 individuals on the mainland and in the Arctic islands.

The sanctuary encompasses the lower waters of the Clarke and the rapid-choked Hanbury, all of the Finnie and the Tammarvi rivers, as well as much of the Thelon itself, a designated Heritage River that flows generally east across the tundra and into Baker Lake. The sheltered valleys of the Thelon and its tributaries, though far beyond the tree line, nurture sizable spruce and willow, along with shrubs, sedges, and mosses. The vegetation turns the river valleys into verdant strips winding across a northern desert

Arctic hares are known for their large populations on Ellesmere Island, where they gather in hundreds to feed on bright arctic wildflowers and other available plants. OPPOSITE: Once hunted down to make sleigh-robes, muskoxen have returned from near extinction.

of gray rocks and lichens. This meeting of boreal forest and tundra accounts for the sanctuary's rich diversity of plant and animal life.

Sandy eskers, deposits left by ancient rivers that flowed under Pleistocene ice sheets, snake across the countryside like railroad embankments. Comprised of loosely compacted sand, gravel, and river boulders, the eskers are favored denning grounds for gray wolves, foxes, and grizzlies. The wooded country of the Thelon attracts increasing numbers of moose, roaming far north of their usual habitat.

The Beverly herd of barren-ground caribou, which numbers between 200,000 and 400,000 individuals, winters near the tree line along Saskatchewan's northern border, then migrates through the sanctuary in early spring to calving grounds north of the Thelon. (The animals sometimes use the flat-topped eskers as highways.) In late July and August, the herd heads back again toward the boreal forest.

The sanctuary also shelters wolverines, peregrine falcons, gyrfalcons, tundra swans, huge numbers of Canada geese, snow geese, oldsquaws, jaegers, arctic terns, bald and golden eagles, and a multitude of smaller birds. Beverly and Aberdeen lakes, which straddle the sanctuary's eastern

boundary, are the summer molting grounds for more than 10,000 nonbreeding Richardson's geese, the highest concentration of this subspecies of Canada goose in the North.

EXPLORING THE SANCTUARY

Access to the game sanctuary and the Thelon River is usually by charter aircraft from Baker Lake, 75 mi/120 km southeast, or from Yellowknife, about 260 mi/420 km southwest of Sifton Lake and 300 mi/480 km southwest of the Thelon River.

It wasn't until the 1960s that recreational canoeists discovered the Barren Grounds. Now the Thelon is considered one of the North's premier wilderness canoeing rivers. Although several expeditions head downstream each summer, one can spend a month without encountering another party.

Some canoeists fly in to Sifton Lake and canoe 75 mi/120 km down the Hanbury River, which flows through tundra and over several spectacular waterfalls before joining the Thelon River near the southwestern boundary of the sanctuary. Nearly 7 mi/11 km of portages are along the way. Others prefer the southern approach on the Upper Thelon, starting at Lynx Lake. From the junction of the Hanbury and Thelon, the next 200 mi/320 km to Beverly Lake are portage-free and offer abundant opportunities for viewing moose, caribou, muskoxen, grizzlies, wolves, and other wildlife.

Three successive lakes—Beverly, Aberdeen, and Schultz—are subject to sudden squalls and must be crossed with caution. The final stretch of the Thelon down to Baker Lake is filled with exciting Class II and Class III rapids with no portages. The total length of the Sifton–Baker Lake trip is 478 mi/765 km; Lynx–Baker Lake, 603 mi/965 km. The trips take five to six weeks.

An excursion down the Dubawnt, the least traveled of the major Barren Grounds rivers, begins at Wholdaia Lake, southeast of Lynx Lake. The river flows northeast through the sanctuary and joins the Thelon at Beverly Lake. The trip to Baker Lake is about 750 mi/1,200 km, requires about two months, and should be attempted only by experienced wilderness canoeists.

For more information on the sanctuary, contact: TravelArctic, Government of the Northwest Territories, Yellowknife, N.W.T. X1A 2L9; 403-873-7200. Two outfitters operate in the sanctuary. Canoe Arctic Inc. has 19-day trips through the sanctuary led by a wildlife biologist: Box 130, Fort Smith, N.W.T. X0E 0P0; 403-872-2308. East Wind Arctic Expeditions, which offers seven- to fourteen-day outings in the sanctuary, specializes in wildlife photography, hiking, and guided canoe trips on the Thelon system: Box 2728, Yellowknife, N.W.T. X1A 2R1; 403-873-2170.

POLAR BEAR PASS NATIONAL WILDLIFE AREA

This ecological reserve straddles the midsection of Bathurst Island between Bracebridge Inlet on the west and Goodsir Inlet on the east. It is a "polar oasis" sheltering an impressive array of wildlife, including 54 species of birds (snowy owls, rock ptarmigans, king eiders, brant, and snow geese) and 11 kinds of mammals. The pass is on the migration route of the island's small herd of Peary caribou, and it forms an important rutting area for muskoxen. Polar bears, usually seen in August and September, find the pass a convenient route between Bracebridge and Goodsir inlets.

On the north side of the pass are rock outcrops that date back 365 million years, when shallow seas covered the area. The receding seas left behind reefs, which later eroded into these tall rock stacks, arranged in lines and often in unusual shapes. The weathered and fractured rock provides nesting sites for rough-legged hawks and snow buntings and dens for arctic foxes.

Exploring the Wildlife Area

The nearest community is Resolute Bay on Cornwallis Island, 93 mi/149 km southeast. Only recently have wilderness travelers begun visiting Polar Bear Pass. Nonnatives require a visitation permit. Hunting and fishing are not allowed. For information on permits, write or phone: The Manager, Northern Operations, Canadian Wildlife Service, Box 637, Yellowknife, N.W.T. X1A 2N5; 403-920-8530.

High Arctic International Explorer Services Ltd., the only outfitter operating in the pass, organizes 11-day camping, hiking, and nature photography outings: Box 200, Resolute Bay, N.W.T. X0A 0V0; 819-252-3875.

ELLESMERE ISLAND NATIONAL PARK RESERVE

At 15,250 sq mi/39,500 sq km this park at the tip of Ellesmere Island, northernmost point of North America, is the second largest preserve in Canada (after Wood Buffalo). The northwestern two-thirds of the park is dominated by the Grant Land Mountains, mantled with icefields more than

OVERLEAF: *Majestic and starkly beautiful, icebergs are large floating ice masses which have been detached from glaciers and carried out to sea.*

0.5 mi/0.3 km thick and 100,000 years old. The fields spawn hundreds of glaciers, some 25 mi/40 km long, which extend into fjords along the northern coast. Mt. Barbeau (8,543 ft/2,604 m), the highest mountain in eastern North America, projects dramatically above its icy shroud.

Southwest of the mountains lies the Hazen Plateau, a river-dissected upland that ends in 3,280-ft/1,000-m cliffs on Lady Franklin Bay on the park's southeastern flank. In the midst of this generally barren landscape lies Lake Hazen, centerpiece of Canada's most northerly "polar oasis," an area of abundant and diverse life.

Here, south-facing mountain slopes act as giant solar receivers while the lake, ice-covered well into the summer, reflects the sun, elevating local temperatures. Lush meadows of grasses, sedges, forbs, mosses, lichens, and arctic willows support a small but stable population of muskoxen. Feeding at higher elevations is a widely scattered population of Peary caribou, the smallest of all caribou (males weigh only about 400 lb/180 kg). Arctic hares often gather in tundra meadows by the hundreds, and there are sizable populations of Greenland collared lemmings. Polar bears, gray wolves, arctic foxes, and ermines are the primary predators.

King eider ducks and red-throated loons nest on the lakeshore and nearby ponds. Ptarmigans and long-tailed jaegers nest on the tundra. After breeding here in summer, arctic terns set out in the fall on a journey that carries them to Greenland, down the coasts of Europe and West Africa, and ultimately, for some, to the tip of South America—a total round-trip distance of some 22,000 mi/35,400 km. Common marine species include snow goose, oldsquaw, and ruddy turnstone (named for its habit of using its bill to flip over stones, shells, and seaweed as it searches for food).

This polar desert was once a primeval swamp. Dawn redwoods *(Metasequoia)*, sycamores, and elms with enormous leaves nearly 19 in/0.5 m wide have been found at fossil forests on Axel Heiberg Island southwest of the park. The redwoods, believed to date from between 40 million and 65 million years ago, grew to a height of about 160 ft/50 m. *Metasequoia* is now found only in an isolated area of China. Lizards, snakes, tortoises, alligators, tapirs, and flying lemurs once thrived in these forests. The presence of such plants and animals, as well as the radical change in the climate, have yet to be fully explained.

A rich archaeological record shows that ancestors of today's Inuit inhabited Ellesmere 4,000 years ago when the climate was warmer. The Norse visited the island as early as the twelfth century, as evidenced by chain mail, boat rivets, and knife blades unearthed at Bache Peninsula, south of the park. The next Europeans came 700 years later searching for the third expedition of Sir John Franklin, lost in 1845 on its quest for the Northwest

Passage. Fort Conger, established in 1875, on the coast 55 mi/88 km east of Lake Hazen, was used as a base by various scientists and explorers, including Robert E. Peary on his 1909 dash to the Pole. Preserved nearly intact by the cold, dry climate, the fort can be visited by groups accompanied by park staff.

EXPLORING THE PARK

The preserve is 1,550 mi/2,480 km northeast of Yellowknife, and just 12 mi/ 20 km from Greenland. Only about 400 people a year visit the park, most on guided expeditions. The jumping-off point is Resolute Bay, on Cornwallis Island, 583 mi/933 km southwest of Lake Hazen. It is the most northerly community in Canada served by scheduled jet flights, usually two a week from Montreal and two from Edmonton. Charter aircraft make the four-hour flight from Resolute into the park, landing at Lake Hazen and nearby Tanquary Fjord, where a park office is located in one of the Arctic's most spectacular settings.

Activities in the park include hiking on unmarked trails in the Tanquary Fjord–Lake Hazen corridor and up surrounding mountain valleys; ski touring and glacier travel in spring and on the ice cap in summer; and fishing for arctic char in Lake Hazen. For more information about Ellesmere and the charter companies and outfitters operating in the park, write or phone: The Superintendent, Auyuittuq/Ellesmere Island National Parks, Canadian Parks Service, Pangnirtung, N.W.T. X0A 0R0; 819-473-8828.

BYLOT ISLAND BIRD SANCTUARY

The sanctuary embraces all of this desolate island off northeastern Baffin Island. From the mountainous interior, massive glaciers sweep north to Cape Hay and Maud Bight, where they calve tanker-size icebergs. Vertical cliffs on the eastern and northern sides of the island provide a haven for some 300,000 thick-billed murres and 46,000 black-legged kittiwakes. About 45,000 snow geese breed on the flatlands on the southwest shore, along with long-tailed jaegers, common ravens, glaucous gulls, red-throated loons, and lesser golden-plovers. In all, 52 kinds of birds have been recorded on Bylot, including ringed plovers and northern wheatears, which winter in Europe.

In addition to its birds, the sanctuary and its waters are home to 21 species of mammals. Polar bears den on the north and east coasts; offshore are hooded, ringed, and bearded seals as well as white whales that drift through the inky blue waters.

Exploring the Sanctuary

Pond Inlet (pop. 796), on Baffin Island across a narrow strait from Bylot, has scheduled air service from Iqaluit and Resolute Bay. Local outfitters take visitors into the sanctuary for mountain climbing, ski touring on the glaciers, and hiking and camping along the southern coast. Hunting for terrestrial and marine mammals is allowed within the sanctuary. A portion of the annual community polar bear quota may be assigned to nonnative hunters at the discretion of the Pond Inlet Hunters' and Trappers' Association.

For more information, write or phone: Canadian Wildlife Service, Box 637, Yellowknife, N.W.T. X1A 2N5; 403-920-8530, or TravelArctic, Government of the Northwest Territories, Yellowknife, N.W.T. X1A 2L9; 403-873-7200.

Greenland Cruises, a New York–based outfitter, offers guided eight-day snowmobile circumnavigations of the island on sea and ice in May: 10 Park Ave., New York, NY 10016; in New York State, 212-683-1145, or from elsewhere in the U.S., 800-648-2544.

Bylot Island Bird Sanctuary protects nesting grounds and large populations of black-legged kittewakes, greater snow geese, and thick-billed murres, which are related to puffins. OPPOSITE: Bright dwarf fire-weed grows on Ellesmere Island, a polar desert growing enough meadows of sedge, grasses, and arctic willows to support musk-oxen, caribou, and arctic hares.

INDEX

Numbers in *italics* indicate illustrations; numbers in **boldface** indicate maps.

Agoseris *(Agoseris)*, 33
alder *(Alnus)*, 47, 48, 70, 134, 327
alder, green *(Alnus crispa)*, 312
alder, speckled *(Alnus rugosa)*, 210, 316
Algonquin Provincial Park, **10–11**, *206*, 207–12, *209*, **213**, 214–16, 218–19
anemone *(Anemone)*, 33
anemone, prairie *(Anemone occidentalis)*, 78
anemone, rue *(Anemonella thalictroides)*, 225
anemone, western *(Anemone occidentalis)*, 78, 79
arbutus, trailing *(Epigaea repens)*, 272, 298
arnica *(Arnica cordifolia)*, 33, 48, 56, 103, 126
arrowhead *(Sagittaria)*, 178
ash *(Fraxinus)*, 246
ash, black *(Fraxinus nigra)*, 178
ash, blue *(Fraxinus quadrangulata)*, 187
ash, green *(Fraxinus pennsylvanica)*, 156, 163, 166, 190
ash, mountain *(Sorbus)*, 33, 178
ash, white *(Fraxinus americana)*, 260
aspen *(Populus)*, 93, 178, 371
aspen, quaking *(Populus tremuloides)*, 71, 118, 122, 134, 137, 138, 140, 143, 145, 146, 147, 149, 161, 164, 166, 176, 210, 284, 325, 342, 343
Assiniboine Indians, 144, 155, 162
aster *(Aster)*, 33, 53, 56, 103, 155, 177
aster *(Aster nahaniensis)*, 344
aster, golden *(Chrysopsis villosa)*, 91, 120
aster, many-flowered *(Aster multiflorus)*, 118

aster, smooth *(Aster laevis)*, 164
Attikamek Indians, 233
auklet, Cassin's *(Ptychoramphus aleuticus)*, 20
auklet, rhinoceros *(Cerorhinca monocerata)*, 20
Auyuittuq National Park Reserve, **10–11**, *352*, 353–57, *354–55*, *358*, 359–65, *362*, *363*
avens *(Geum)*, 155
avens, mountain *(Dryas hookeriana)*, 74, 359
avens, three-flowered *(Geum triflorum)*, 164

Badger *(Taxidea taxus)*, 144, 158, 164
bakeapple. *See* cloudberry
Banff National Park, **10–11**, *62*, 63–64, 66–68, 70–71, 74–75, *76*, 77–83, *77*, *80*, *81*, **84**, 85–87, *88*
Banks Island Bird Sanctuary, **10–11**, 368, 370–71
barnacle *(Balanus)*, 248, 259
barnacle, acorn *(Balanus)*, 20
bass, largemouth *(Micropterus salmoides)*, 181, 191, 203, 229
bass, smallmouth *(Micropterus dolomieui)*, 181, 201, 215, 229, 238
bass, white *(Morone chrysops)*, 191
basswood, American *(Tilia americana)*, 187, 189, 223
bat, 57, 188
Bathurst Inlet, **10–11**, 374–75
bayberry, northern *(Myrica pennsylvanica)*, 284, 287
bean, golden *(Thermopsis rhombifolia)*, 155
bear, black *(Ursus americanus)*, 21, 33, 39, 48, 71, 82, 91, 122, 146, 163, 165, 178, 210, 214, 216, 234, 260, 298, 312, 324, 327, 329, 342, 346
bear, grizzly *(Ursus arctos)*, 48, 53, 71, 91, *93*, 123,

125, 324, 327, 328, 336, *337*, 367, 374, 376, 378
bear, polar *(Ursus maritimus)*, 356, *359*, 367, 370, 379, 382, 383, 385
bearberry *(Gaultheria procumbens)*, 164, 199
beardtongue *(Penstemon)*, 154
beargrass *(Xerophyllum tenax)*, 123, 125, 126
beaver *(Castor canadensis)*, 48, 57, 71, 82, 90, 122, 135, 138, 145, 146, 147, 149, *153*, 164, 165, 178, 198, 210, 211, 212, 234, 272, 278, 286, 317, 318, 342, 344
bedstraw, northern *(Galium boreale)*, 150
beech, American *(Fagus grandifolia)*, 197, 209, 216, 260, 271, 298, 306
beech-drops *(Epifagus virginianus)*, 272
bellwort *(Uvularia)*, 298
beluga. *See* whale, white
Beothuk Indians, 310–11
bicycling: Banff NP, 80; Cape Breton Highlands NP, 303; Forillon NP, 252; Garibaldi PP, 36–37; La Mauricie NP, 237; Point Pelee NP, 191; Prince Albert NP, 150; Prince Edward Island NP, 289; Riding Mountain NP, 168; St. Lawrence Islands NP, 228
bilberry, 357
birch *(Betula)*, 70, 178, 298, 306
birch, bog, 147
birch, dwarf *(Betula glandulosa)*, 299, 325, 327, 343, 357
birch, paper *(Betula papyrifera)*, 138, 176, 197, 246, 260, 284, 298, 312
birch, yellow *(Betula alleghaniensis)*, 209, 233, 246, 260, 271, 287
bison, plains *(Bison bison)*, 122, 125, 132, 137, 145, *163*
bison, wood *(Bison bison)*,

78, 132, 137, 138, 343,
371–72, *372*
bittern, American *(Botaurus lentiginosus)*, 156,
201, 272
blackberry, Pacific *(Rubus ursinus)*, 33
blackbird, red-winged *(Agelaius phoeniceus)*, 70,
165, 201
blackfly *(Simulium)*, 177,
211
Blackfoot Indians, 133
bladderwort *(Utricularia)*,
70–71, 122, 314
bloodroot *(Sanguinaria canadensis)*, 246
bluebell *(Mertensia)*, 71, 78,
122
blueberry *(Vaccinium)*, 33
bluebird, mountain *(Sialia currucoides)*, 71
bluegrass *(Poa)*, 325
boating: Algonquin PP, 214;
Banff NP, 82; Elk Island
NP, 140; Forillon NP, 252;
Fundy NP, 264; Garibaldi
PP, 37; Gros Morne NP,
318; Jasper NP, 95;
Kejimkujik NP, 276;
Kluane NPR, 333; Northern Wildlands, 373; Prince
Albert NP, 150; Prince
Edward Island NP, 289;
Riding Mountain NP, 168;
St. Lawrence Islands NP,
228–29; Waterton Lakes
NP, 127. See also canoeing; kayaking; rafting
bobcat *(Felis rufus)*, 158,
259, 302
boxelder *(Acer negundo)*,
156, 163
brant *(Branta bernicla)*,
246, 370, 379
Bruce Peninsula National
Park, **10–11**, 195–202,
198, 202, 204–05
buckbean *(Menyanthes trifoliata)*, 146
budworm, spruce *(Choristoneura fumiferana)*,
303
buffalo. See bison
buffaloberry, Canada *(Shepherdia canadensis)*, 135,
156
buffaloberry, silver *(Shepherdia argentea)*, 122
bullhead, brown *(Ictalurus nebulosus)*, 229, 278

bulrush *(Scirpus)*, 122, 156,
187, 274
bunchberry *(Cornus canadensis)*, 21, *39*, 163, 177,
198, 259, 284, 288
bunchflower *(Melanthium virginicum)*, 198
bunchgrass *(Andropogon)*,
122
bunting, snow *(Plectrophenax nivalis)*, 360, 379
Burgess Shale Beds, 64, *65*,
115
burnet, Canadian *(Sanguisorba canadensis)*, 302
bur-reed *(Sparganium)*,
178, 274
buttercup *(Ranunculus)*,
33, 79, 123, 327
buttercup, prairie *(Ranunculus rhomboideus)*, 164
butterwort *(Pinguicula)*,
70, 314
Bylot Island Bird Sanctuary,
10–11, 383, *385*

Cactus, pincushion, *156*
caddisfly, 122
calla, wild *(Calla palustris)*,
178
camping: Algonquin PP, 214,
218–19; Auyuittuq NPR,
365; Banff NP, 86–87;
Bruce Peninsula NP, 195;
Cape Breton Highlands
NP, 307; Elk Island NP,
141; Fathom Five NP, 195;
Forillon NP, 253, 254–55;
Fundy NP, 266; Garibaldi
PP, 41–42; Glacier NP, 53,
55, 60–61; Grasslands
NP, 159; Gros Morne NP,
321; Jasper NP, 99, 101;
Kejimkujik NP, 280;
Kluane NPR, 336; Kootenay NP, 104, 107; La
Mauricie NP, 241; Mt.
Revelstoke NP, 60–61;
Nahanni NPR, 351;
Northern Wildlands, 373,
379, 385; Pacific Rim NP,
29; Point Pelee NP, 193;
Prince Albert NP, 153;
Prince Edward Island NP,
29; Quetico PP, 183; Riding Mountain NP, 169; St.
Lawrence Islands NP,
231; Waterton Lakes NP,
129; Yoho NP, 114–15
campion, moss *(Silene acaulis)*, 74, 123, 343, 357

canary, wild. *See* goldfinch,
American
canoeing: Algonquin PP,
214–15; Banff NP, 82;
Bruce Peninsula NP, 201;
Garibaldi PP, 37; Kejimkujik NP, 276, 278; Kluane
NPR, 333; Kootenay NP,
104, 106; La Mauricie NP,
237–38; Nahanni NPR,
346–47; Northern Wildlands, 370, 373, 375, 378;
Pacific Rim NP, 24–25;
Point Pelee NP, 191;
Prince Albert NP, 150–
51; Quetico PP, 179, 181
canvasback *(Aythya valisineria)*, 224
Cape Breton Highlands
National Park, **10–11**,
294–95, *296–97*, 298–
300, *300*, **301**, 302–07,
304, 305
capelin *(Mallotus villosus)*,
311, 321
cardinal, northern *(Cardinalis cardinalis)*, 187,
190
caribou *(Rangifer tarandus)*, 48, 74, 91, 98, 147,
314, 317, *320*, 324, 342,
345, 357, 359, 367, 368,
374, 375, 376, 378, 379,
382
carp *(Cyprinus carpio)*, 187
carrion-flower *(Smilax herbacea)*, 178
catfish, 229
cattail *(Typha)*, 122, 133,
156, 187, 190, 274
cedar, 47, 188, 200, 201,
253
cedar, northern white-
(Thuja occidentalis), 176,
195, 197, 198, 209, 214,
223
char, arctic *(Salvelinus alpinus)*, 38, 55, 83, 106,
347, 363, 370, 375, 383
cherry, pin *(Prunus pensylvanica)*, 135, 163, 210
chickadee, black-capped
(Parus atricapillus), 71,
122, 233
chickadee, boreal *(Parus hudsonicus)*, 47, 74, 146,
302
chickadee, chestnut-backed
(Parus rufescens), 34, 47
chickadee, mountain *(Parus gambeli)*, 79

PHOTOGRAPHY CREDITS

Principal photography by First Light Associated Photographers. All photographs © 1991 photographers listed below.

Cover: © Bill Ross. Back cover: © Thomas Kitchin. 2: © Brian Townsend. 6, top: © A. D. Dickson; middle: © Brian Milne; bottom: © Donald Standfield. 7, top: © Thomas Kitchin; bottom: © Malak. 14, top: © Thomas Kitchin; middle: © John Bartosik; bottom: © Steve Short. 15, top and bottom: © Thomas Kitchin. 18–19: © Stan Czolowski. 22: © Thomas Kitchin. 23, all: © Thomas Kitchin. 26: © Wayne Wegner. 30: © Chris Speedie. 34: © Gail Ross. 35: © Thomas Kitchin. 38: © Chris Speedie. 39, left: © Ted Bringloe; right: © Frank Mayrs. 42: © Gail Ross. 43: © Chris Speedie. 46: © Roger Laurilla. 50–51: Dave Watters. 54: © Thomas Kitchin. 55: © Ken Straiton. 58: © Thomas Kitchin. 62: © Malak. 65: © Thomas Kitchin. 68: © Scott Rowed. 69: © Thomas Kitchin. 72–73: © A. D. Dickson. 76: © Patrick Morrow. 77: © Dawn Goss. 80: © Thomas Kitchin. 81: © Thomas Kitchin. 88: © Jim Brandenburg. 92: © Thomas Kitchin. 93: © Thomas Kitchin. 96–97: © Jake Tapo-schaner. 104: © Thomas Kitchin. 108: © Patrick Morrow. 109, left: © Brian Milne; right: © Thomas Kitchin. 112–113: © Scott Rowed. 117: © Steve Short. 120: © Brian Milne. 121: © Thomas Kitchin. 124–125: © Scott Rowed. 130, top: © Robert Semeniuk; bottom: © Todd Korol. 131, top: © Brian Milne; bottom: © Grant Black. 134–135: © Robert Seme-niuk. 138: © Parks Canada. 139: © K. Jack Clark. 142: © Todd Korol. 145: © Robert Lankinen. 152: © Todd Korol. 153, left: Brian Milne; right: © Wayne Wegner. 156, top left: © Brian Milne; top right: © Brian Milne; bottom right: © Brian Milne; bottom left: © Mary Ellen McQuay. 157: © Brian Milne. 160: © Parks Canada. 162: © Grant Black. 163, left: © Parks Canada; right: © Thomas Kitchin. 166: © Parks Canada. 170, top: © Thomas Kitchin; middle: © Grant Black; bottom: © Devries/Mikkelsen. 171, top: © Thomas Kitchin; middle: © Thomas Kitchin; bottom: © Jacques Pleau. 175: © Donald Standfield. 177: © Donald Standfield. 180: © Natural Resources Ontario. 181: © Thomas Kitchin. 184: © Wayne Wegner. 188: © Grant Black. 189: © Grant Black. 192: © Robert Lankinen. 194: © Wayne Wegner. 198: © Malak. 199: © Brian Milne. 202: © Devries/Mikkelsen. 203: © Wayne Wegner. 206: © Donald Standfield. 209: © Donald Standfield. 212: © Peter McLeod. 216: © Donald Stand-field. 217: © Wayne Wegner. 220: © Thomas Kitchin. 224: © Robert Lankinen. 226–227: © Thomas Kitchin. 230: © Thomas Kitchin. 234–235: © Jacques Pleau. 238: © Robert Lankinen. 242, top: © Thomas Kitchin; mid-dle: © Brian Townsend; bottom: © Thomas Kitchin. 243, top: © John Sylvester; middle: © Thomas Kitchin; bottom: © Dawn Goss. 247: © Thomas Kitchin. 250: © Thomas Kitchin. 251: © Thomas Kitchin. 254–255: © Thomas Kitchin. 258: © Brian Townsend. 262: © Brian Townsend. 263: © Wayne Weg-ner. 270–271: © Thomas Kitchin. 273: © Brian Townsend. 276: © Thomas Kitchin. 277: © Thomas Kitchin. 281: © Thomas Kitchin. 285: © John Sylvester. 288: © John Sylvester. 289: © John Sylvester. 293: © John Sylvester. 296–297: © Brian Townsend. 300: © Stephen Homer. 304: © Thomas Kitchin. 305: © Thomas Kitchin. 308: © Mike Beedell. 312: © Lorraine C. Parow. 316–317: © Alan Kemp. 320: © Brian Milne. 322, top: © Brian Milne; middle: © Robert Semeniuk; bottom: © Mike Beedell. 323: © Patrick Morrow. 326: © Patrick Morrow. 330–331: © Patrick Mor-row. 334: © Mike Beedell. 335: © Wayne Wegner. 337: © Brian Milne. 340: © Robert Semeniuk. 341: © Mike Beedell. 344: © Albert Kuhnigk. 345: © Albert Kuhnigk. 348–349: © Robert Semeniuk. 352: © Mike Beedell. 354–355: © Roy Hamaguchi. 358: © Mike Beedell. 359: © Paul von Baich. 362: © Malak. 363: © Mike Beedell. 366: © Mike Beedell. 369: © Brian Milne. 372: © Brian Milne. 373, top left: © Brian Milne; top right: © Peter McLeod; bottom left: © Brian Milne; bottom right: © Brian Milne. 376: © Mike Beedell. 377: © Brian Milne. 380–381: © Mike Beedell. 384: © Brian Milne. 385: © Brian Milne. 400: © Brian Milne.

The type in this book was set in Century Expanded 701 a and b,
input on the Macintosh IIx in QuarkXpress 3.0,
and output on the Mergenthaler Linotron 202
at Graphic Arts Composition, Inc., Philadelphia, Pennsylvania, USA.

The book was printed and bound by
Dai Nippon Printing Company, Ltd., Tokyo, Japan.